T0268960

# The New York Times

## TRULY TOUGH CROSSWORD PUZZLES
### VOLUME 2

First published in the United States by St. Martin's Griffin,
an imprint of St. Martin's Publishing Group

THE NEW YORK TIMES TRULY TOUGH CROSSWORD PUZZLES, VOLUME 2.
Copyright © 2022 by The New York Times Company. All rights reserved.
Printed in the United States of America. For information, address
St. Martin's Publishing Group, 120 Broadway, New York, NY 10271.

www.stmartins.com

All of the puzzles that appear in this work were originally published in
*The New York Times* from September 12, 2008, to November 7, 2008; from June 10, 2011,
to July 2, 2011; from February 1, 2013, to June 1, 2013; from July 1, 2016, to October 29, 2016;
from January 6, 2017, to April 15, 2017; from June 8, 2018, to July 28, 2018;
from February 7, 2020, to March 28, 2020; or from January 1, 2021, to July 17, 2021.
Copyright © 2008, 2011, 2013, 2016, 2017, 2018, 2020, 2021 by The New York Times Company.
All rights reserved. Reprinted by permission.

ISBN 978-1-250-83171-2

Our books may be purchased in bulk for promotional, educational,
or business use. Please contact your local bookseller or the Macmillan Corporate
and Premium Sales Department at 1-800-221-7945, extension 5442,
or by email at MacmillanSpecialMarkets@macmillan.com.

First Edition: 2022

10  9  8  7  6  5  4  3  2

# The New York Times

## TRULY TOUGH CROSSWORD PUZZLES, VOLUME 2
### 200 Challenging Puzzles

## Edited by Will Shortz

ST. MARTIN'S GRIFFIN
NEW YORK

# Looking for more Hard Crosswords?

## The New York Times

### The #1 Name in Crosswords

Available at your local bookstore or online at
us.macmillan.com/author/thenewyorktimes

 ST. MARTIN'S GRIFFIN

## ACROSS

1. ___ 500
6. Building manager, informally
10. Mimics Nicki Minaj
14. Role for Nichelle Nichols and Zoë Saldana
15. Sue at Chicago's Field Museum, e.g.
16. Glow
17. Seminal William S. Burroughs novel, 1959
19. Proof of purchase
20. Tar
21. Galaxy competitor
23. Adolph Coors or Frederick Pabst
26. Crown ___
29. "Te ___" (Spanish words of affection)
30. Big name in cosmetics
31. Corporate bigs
32. Actress ___ Dawn Chong
35. Start of a citation
36. Samurai swords
38. Car company that sponsors the World Cup
39. Before, in odes
40. Sty occupants
41. Some marsh flora
43. Spinning
45. Help to cover
46. "The fault lies here"
49. Comics title character who says "Getting an inch of snow is like winning 10 cents in the lottery"
50. Folds
53. Instead
54. Pittsburgh is its most populous city
58. Manipulative sort
59. Ring bearers
60. Special ops force
61. Super Bowl LIII winners, informally
62. Course obstacle
63. Defaults?

## DOWN

1. Tanning agent
2. "Eureka!" moments
3. Quickly heat up
4. Fantasized
5. Emmy-nominated host of "Top Chef"
6. ___ double
7. Spigot site
8. Something a bodybuilder might flex, informally
9. Case opener
10. Breakfast quantity
11. Bodybuilder?
12. Trim
13. Fencing piece
18. Miss
22. Certain P.R., in two different senses
24. In an even manner
25. Remains
26. Say mockingly
27. "Do I ___!"
28. "Good to go!"
31. Rant and rave
33. Fictional Ethiopian princess
34. "Careful now"
37. Put off
42. Erased
44. Equivocates
45. Farmer's place, in song
46. Freeze
47. Lightweight wood
48. Sudden movement
51. Muay ___ (martial art)
52. It may be fine in a stream
55. Plague
56. ___-brained
57. Intensifying suffix, in modern slang

by Mary Lou Guizzo and Erik Agard

# 2

## ACROSS

1 Modest qualifier, online
5 Sling
9 Where it's at
13 Easy kill in Fortnite, say
14 ___ days
16 Nabe
17 Problems with pay or paper
18 Information in a shopping guide
20 End of some business names
22 Media pro
23 Rides into battle
25 Grease
26 Bratty kid
27 Bomb
28 U.N. agcy. headquartered in Geneva
31 Many a staffer for a late-night show
34 "Keen!"
35 Musical alter ego of Donald Glover
37 Minute
38 Relatives of water skis
39 Go soft, in a way
40 Rocker Joan
41 Lights or darks, e.g.
42 One way to take stock?
43 Gardeners' tools
46 Beer with an astronomical name
49 What Brits call a "saloon"
50 Cookout option for a vegetarian
53 Last option on a survey
54 Corvine : crows :: strigine : ___

55 Word said with a handshake
56 Lip, in slang
57 When doubled, "I heard you the first time"
58 Cartoonish wail
59 Hullabaloo

## DOWN

1 Worshipers of the rain god Illapa
2 Knight's need
3 Office-sharing system, in modern lingo
4 To an excessive degree
5 One-sixth of a fl. oz.
6 One might make a splash

7 Possible insight for a psychologist
8 Irreverence
9 Exactly
10 Sci-fi beam makeup
11 Packed with plasticware, perhaps
12 The plot of Genesis?
15 Deserving of condemnation
19 Extend, as an employment contract
21 "Bridesmaids" co-star Chris
24 Tries and fails
28 Getting a strange vibe
29 Helper
30 Plains people
31 Hwy. crossings
32 North/South divide, with "the"

33 Feels no remorse
34 They get big bucks from big Bucks
36 Climates
40 Part of a frame job?
42 Pet peeve?
44 Businesswoman Zuckerberg, sister of Mark
45 Not look so good?
46 Break-dancer, in slang
47 Home-improvement chain eponym
48 Where Kareem Abdul-Jabbar played college ball
51 Prefix with system
52 Counterpart of FF

by Hemant Mehta

## ACROSS

1 Rock and Roll Hall of Fame band led by Iggy Pop
11 Intermediate gait
15 Do thumb traveling?
16 Someone who's well-off
17 "Well, then . . ."
18 Balanced
19 See 20-Across
20 19-Across pitcher
21 "No you ___!"
22 Tankerful
25 Successor language to Common Brittonic
27 0 on the Beaufort scale
31 Billionaire philanthropist ___ Broad
32 Some road trip entertainment
34 Basement feature
38 Former Supreme Court justice William
39 (x, y), in math
41 Low, low price, in an expression
42 Subuniverses
44 Lessen
46 Losing money
47 Superimposed
51 Message in smoke signals, maybe
52 Chummy
53 "___ So Fine," 1963 #1 hit for the Chiffons
55 Deal with it
59 ___ Douglas-Home, 1960s British P.M.
60 Corellia, to Han Solo
63 Roman counterpart of the Greek goddess Selene
64 "Flash Gordon" genre
65 Trousers part
66 Driving distractions

## DOWN

1 No, not that!
2 Very small amount
3 ___ Candy, friend of Wonder Woman
4 Thought experiment in quantum physics
5 Fourth letter in Arabic
6 Kind of grass
7 Apex predator of the sea
8 Composer Puccini
9 Automotive sponsor of "Wagon Train" in the 1950s
10 Date
11 "You're doomed!"
12 Get tangled up
13 Things with timers
14 Constitutional amendment regarding states' rights
21 Rebus symbol for "everything"
23 Much-admired person
24 1987 #1 hit with Spanish lyrics
26 Kim Jong-un and others
27 Uses a tissue, maybe
28 Capital of Latvia
29 Mideast's Gulf of ___
30 Actress Anderson of old TV
33 Grammy-winning metal band with a tasty-sounding name
35 Georgia was once a part of it
36 Social media phenomenon
37 V.A. concern
40 Second coming?
43 Premium channel since 1980
45 Nellie who circumnavigated the world
47 Precious collection of Queen Victoria
48 Prize
49 Author Ferrante of the "Neapolitan Novels"
50 "Fingers crossed!"
54 η, in a legal footnote: Abbr.
56 Remarkable person
57 Cheeky
58 H H H
60 Presidential monogram
61 Word with sweet or snow
62 Not just a "heh"

by Daniel Larsen

# 4

## ACROSS
1 Drink every last drop from
8 Give a sop to, maybe
15 Was naturally a part of something
16 Street protester or Tibetan monk
17 Duds
18 Largest of the British Virgin Islands
19 Bad vibrations
20 Things picked up on beaches
21 Pipe filler
23 Epoch when modern mammals arose
24 "See you then"
25 Soft leathers
26 Like bodybuilders' arms
27 Fruity and fragrant compounds
29 Ending with many fruit names
30 Competitor of Century 21
31 Marijuana, in older slang
34 Be in charge of
36 Subjects of baseless charges?
38 Food that's cured
41 Dangers for swimmers
43 Benchmark test for British students
44 1960s catchphrase
45 Young hares
47 Takes stock?
48 21st-century health menace
49 Millinery items
50 Source of running water
51 Chanel fragrance with a French name
52 S.R.O.
53 Units in a horse race

## DOWN
1 Mourn, in a way
2 Cold
3 Hynde of the Pretenders
4 Bob of old children's TV
5 Theater portmanteau
6 It had a major part in the Bible
7 N.F.L. stat: Abbr.
8 Official proceedings
9 Call on a hot line?
10 British sitting room
11 Draws in
12 Made up (for)
13 Sister of Helios
14 Gets the lead out
20 What are depicted in some blue prints?
22 Knight mare?
28 Jungle herbivore
30 Chewed out
31 Personal agenda
32 Desperate hour
33 Judges
34 "Here, try this"
35 Title for a retired professor
36 Had plateful after plateful
37 Animal hunted in "Lord of the Flies"
38 Site of a western gunfight
39 Third-largest city of the later Ottoman Empire, surpassed only by Constantinople and Cairo
40 Duties
42 Fur
46 Cough syrup amts.
49 Daughter of Loki, in Norse myth

by Randolph Ross

## ACROSS

1 Caseload?
8 Not the main action
15 Like someone who answers a question with a question
16 Time for warm-up shots, in more ways than one
17 Land that abuts four oceans
18 Obsolescent office desk item
19 Common Hawaiian shirt design
21 Celebrity with a namesake cereal in the '80s
22 Gets down
23 Hidden valleys
24 Old Italian V.I.P.
25 Mount Sinai people: Abbr.
26 Make by hand
27 Got in line
28 Thomas who wrote "Liberty Tree"
29 Attempts to befriend, with "up"
30 It's a rush, appropriately enough
32 Prayers
33 The America's Cup and others
34 Monk in "The Da Vinci Code"
35 Sam with clubs
36 Chap
39 "___ pass"
40 Egyptian Nobelman?
41 Some camel riders of note
42 Helpful word in solving cryptograms
43 A mare might be found in one
45 Bit of road trip entertainment

47 Not serious
48 Big source of political talk
49 Part of a book deal
50 G.R.E. sitters, e.g.
51 Sportscast staples

## DOWN

1 Quarreled (with)
2 Egglike
3 Decks revealing the cards you've been dealt
4 They range from terrible to great
5 Daughter of Steve Jobs, after whom an early Apple computer was named
6 Dastardly looks
7 It doesn't have to land on land

8 Dash
9 Smooths
10 Neighbor of a pec
11 Nwodim of "S.N.L."
12 Trash
13 Comes out of one's shell
14 Like emojis
20 Parts of some ballots
24 Party poopers
26 Lean on them
27 Bronze
28 Almost ready to be a butterfly
29 Secret for video gamers
30 Noted feature of Spanish pronunciation
31 Recipient of a lot of #@&! money

32 Tug at one's heartstrings, say
34 Not take any action
35 Brazilian soccer team that Pelé played for
36 Alexandria Ocasio-Cortez, e.g.
37 Word with federal or insurance
38 Some somber music
40 "Calvin and Hobbes" girl
41 Palace, in Hindi
43 Fill the hold, say
44 "Let me know if you're coming"
46 Object of veneration in ancient Egypt

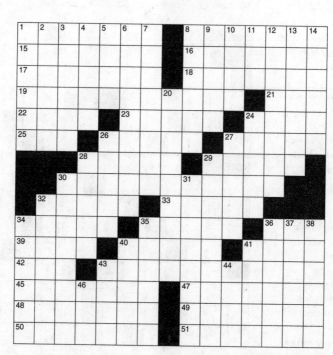

by Erik Agard and Anne Flinchbaugh

# 6

## ACROSS

1 Senator who wrote "Faith of My Fathers"
7 Bound for
12 Expression of one at sea, perhaps
14 What two fingers on each hand can represent
15 Part of a hot plate
16 "Uncle Tom's Cabin" girl
17 Energizer choice
18 Some radio antennas
22 Something instructors explain
24 Member of the starling family
26 Going by
27 Sweets
28 "Lido Shuffle" singer Boz
30 Itinerant sort
31 Emulate a 30-Across, say
34 Negotiation talks
36 Imagist poet Doolittle
37 "Little help here"
39 Getaway locale
40 Energize
41 Tesla, e.g.
45 Jamaican genre
46 To the nth degree
48 Extinct bird that grew as tall as 12 feet
49 Takes the high way?
51 Creature with eyespots on its wings
53 Summer cocktail that sometimes has a strawberry garnish

57 Place characterized by ill repute
58 Marsh flora
59 "___ Lupin Versus Herlock Sholmes" (1910 story collection)

## DOWN

1 Unstable subatomic particle
2 Made an example of
3 Bygone sovereigns
4 The F.D.A. approved it in 1987
5 First Super Bowl to be called "Super Bowl"
6 Base fig.
7 "Stand and Deliver" star, 1987
8 Tent feature
9 "Bad, bad, bad!"
10 Yokohama is on it
11 Clears
12 What a hafiz has memorized
13 Put up
14 Landing spot
15 Sound made by a slug
19 Hairstyle associated with Prince Valiant
20 Texter's exclamation
21 Only inductee into both the Rock and Roll Hall of Fame and the National Inventors Hall of Fame
23 Binds
25 Digression
27 Weevils' targets
29 No. brain?
30 New Deal org.
31 "Get ___!"
32 100% guaranteed
33 Lacking support
35 Quilting technique with patches
38 UV index monitor
40 Egypt's Mubarak
42 Virginia's ___ & Henry College
43 Indian flatbread
44 "Poppycock!"
46 Perils for mariners
47 Dealer's quick query
50 Men's sportswear brand
52 Tiny amount
53 Prez who said "Repetition does not transform a lie into the truth"
54 ___ test
55 Put on
56 Certain test subjects

by Trenton Charlson

## ACROSS

**1** See the seasons pass quickly?
**11** Celle-là, across the Pyrenees
**14** Something that requires thinking inside the box?
**15** What mustache-twirling might suggest
**16** Dangerous places
**17** Dress style
**18** They're often high, but never dry
**19** Zippo
**20** Something Winnie-the-Pooh lacks
**21** Equal ___
**22** Fire a second time
**24** "I'm blushing!"
**28** Sows and cows
**29** Edited, as a film
**30** ___ boom
**31** Common middle name
**33** Momentous
**36** Labor of love?
**37** Stones that diffract light
**38** ___ nova
**39** Those who practice energy medicine
**41** Like many Egyptian pyramids
**42** Upper part of a cruise ship
**43** Help wanted sign
**44** Pays (up)
**45** About .4% of the weight of the human body
**47** Z4 and i3
**51** Lone Star State sch.
**52** Give out cash freely
**54** Store one inside another
**55** "You can't make me!"
**56** Exhibits at an exhibition
**57** Bottling up

## DOWN

**1** Twins, e.g.
**2** "Gotcha"
**3** Org. that holds many conferences
**4** Prohibition-era guns
**5** N.T. book after Galatians
**6** Amenity in many a picnic box
**7** Assemblage
**8** Its scientific name is Bufo bufo
**9** Separated couple with kids, say
**10** Royal Navy letters
**11** Proselytizer
**12** Intuition
**13** Group of stars
**15** Field added to the I.R.S.'s Form 1040 in 2019
**20** Controls, of a sort
**21** Driving hazards
**23** Discharge
**24** It may get a good licking
**25** Recruiter
**26** Audition
**27** When repeated, a reproof
**28** Some farm births
**30** 2013 disaster film with a cult following
**32** "Holy moly!"
**34** On ___ (without a firm commitment)
**35** Kanga's kid
**40** Crackerjack
**41** 1955 novel with the line "It was love at first sight, at last sight, at ever and ever sight"
**42** Part of a bathhouse
**43** Pine, for one
**46** One-named singer with the 2006 hit "Smack That"
**47** Bread enricher
**48** Spa job, informally
**49** "Because of ___-Dixie" (2000 award-winning children's book)
**50** Slight problem
**52** Karaoke need
**53** Lead-in to light

by Aimee Lucido

# 8

## ACROSS

1 Base for many a chef's rose garnish
7 Big name in Irish whiskey
14 Self-titled 1961 debut album
15 Barbecue variety featuring vinegar-based sauces
16 Attend by oneself
17 Approximate proportion of the world's population that lives on an island
18 Spots
19 Main issues?
21 Easter activities
23 Some "Grey's Anatomy" settings, for short
27 Game
28 Bugs used to be seen on it
29 Trounce
30 Reduce in intensity
31 Market built around short-term engagements
33 Cranial : skull :: brachial : ___
34 Early arrival
35 "___ Death" (2006–10 Fox sitcom)
36 Frank type
38 It may rise in anger
39 Feeling akin to the German "Weltschmerz"
40 Long
41 "Critique of Pure Reason" philosopher
42 Leave agape
43 Skort circuit?
45 Former home of the Seattle SuperSonics
47 Follower of Marx?
50 Information on a game box
53 Title pig of children's literature
55 Chef in a grocery store
56 They have chairs at the circus
57 Siberian stretches
58 Lively wit

## DOWN

1 Accompaniment at an Indian restaurant
2 Major-league All-Star turned TV analyst, informally
3 List of frozen assets?
4 Member of the Addams Family
5 Long, thick and unkempt
6 Titular comic strip character from the A.D. 800s
7 Grammy-nominated singer who made her on-screen film debut in "Moonlight"
8 Spheres
9 Title whose name comes from the Greek for "alone"
10 Something Cap'n Crunch has
11 ___ tax
12 It's on the St. Lawrence: Abbr.
13 Casual turndown
15 Job requirement, often
20 Bygone parts of newspapers with local gossip
22 "Wowzers!"
24 Tributary of the Hudson
25 Site in Philadelphia, Denver and San Francisco, for short
26 Barber
27 One raising an issue
29 Down state?
30 Nursery contents
31 Miracle-___
32 Part of a pack, in slang
34 Symbol for the golden ratio
37 Bass-heavy hybrid music genre
38 Two before 34-Down
41 Tree huggers Down Under
43 Paul of the old "Hollywood Squares"
44 Bond backed by the govt.
46 Big name in Old West justice
48 Tech assistant
49 A boom might come out of it
50 Core part, informally
51 Pulled a fast one on
52 Rebus symbol for a pronoun
54 Small annoyance

by Andrew J. Ries

## ACROSS

1 Artificially inflates
5 Sub (for)
9 "The Emancipation of ___" (6x platinum Mariah Carey album)
13 Oath locale
14 Men's grooming aid
16 Oath locale
17 404 Not Found, e.g.
18 Shower amenity
19 Tight
20 Turner on a record
22 Subject of a scandal, maybe
23 "Heavens to Betsy!"
27 Points
31 ___ suit
32 Smoking or procrastination, e.g.
34 Alfred who pioneered in I.Q. testing
35 "Make it snappy!"
38 Set out on the highway?
39 Big cast?
40 Barely
41 Lose sleep (over)
42 Dirty look
44 Literary character played by Gregory Peck, Patrick Stewart and Orson Welles
48 You can bet on them
49 Help to set the scene
53 Old knockout?
57 Counter sign?
58 Per diem
59 Wretch
60 Casual phone greeting
61 Make (out)
62 Matches
63 Co-author of the 1957 memoir "The Untouchables"

## DOWN

1 Standard part of preppy attire
2 An exhausted person might be on it
3 Like a hospital gown, maybe
4 They're in good hands
5 Place "rocked" in a 1982 top 10 hit
6 Noble sort
7 "The Spanish Playing Cards" and "Nude With Mirror"
8 Novel filler
9 Faux alcoholic drink
10 A part of
11 French for "noon"
12 Grammy winner whose name sounds like a beverage
13 Low-___
15 Threat bearing small arms?
21 One famous for seeing double?
23 Cuts out
24 "I've ___!"
25 Poet Marianne who won a 1952 Pulitzer
26 Sources of buzz
28 Opposite of mainstream
29 Like a bad apple, maybe
30 Punk, e.g.
33 Hand dryers
34 Wasn't conspicuous
36 Crystal collectors, maybe
37 Like big fans
43 Big 12 school, familiarly
45 Do a cowboy's job
46 Pines
47 Two whole notes, essentially
49 Soaks (up)
50 Drop ___
51 Dustups
52 City on a lake of the same name
54 Cat sound
55 Eugene O'Neill's "Desire Under the ___"
56 Kvass ingredient

by Caitlin Reid

## ACROSS

1 Gray with the 3x platinum album "On How Life Is"
5 Sandwich shop purchases
10 Out to lunch
14 Fit for a sweater
15 Well-ventilated
16 Golfer Aoki
17 "Hey, can I talk to you briefly?"
19 Pass up
20 Overprotective type
21 Mark of a swordsman?
22 Shakespearean production
23 Appreciates
24 Fast learner
26 One of four on Pluto
27 Small cardinal
28 Himalayan native
29 Declaration upon walking in the door
33 It might go over some students' heads
34 Like many a password
35 Individual, for one: Abbr.
36 Source of Roquefort cheese
37 Legal, after "of"
38 Highest point
40 Blowout
42 Chemical suffix
45 Back
46 Seafood in shells
48 End notes
49 Ones set for a wild party?
50 Tech-focused website
51 Support structure
52 Nobelist Wiesel
53 Lots and lots (of)
54 Gem
55 Vixen

## DOWN

1 Source of igneous rock
2 Do ___ deed
3 Direction in a film script
4 "Right on!"
5 Query following an interruption
6 Company that makes Valium
7 Some decorative plants
8 Brown alternative
9 Cartoonist Hoff
10 What the Copacabana becomes at the end of "Copacabana"
11 "Everybody says so"
12 OK to target
13 One-up
18 Bit on a bun
21 Calls attention to
24 Like some flotsam
25 Squeeze (out)
26 One of seven in 14th-century Avignon
27 Actress Polo
29 Is lost
30 Sound
31 Neighbor of Ill.
32 Give birth to
33 Obsolescent means of communication
34 Civil War inits.
39 Summer annoyances
40 Character who steals from the dragon Smaug
41 Literary lion
42 Recurrent health scare
43 Passé, say
44 New Jersey county whose seat is Newark
46 Typical stocking stuffers
47 "Hello . . . I'm right here"
48 Hospital amts.
49 What Joe Biden and Al Gore are: Abbr.

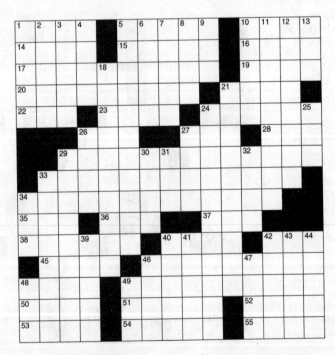

by Robyn Weintraub

## ACROSS

**1** Opera style using everyday events rather than myth
**8** Less than required
**10** Something drawn for sport
**12** Pro
**13** Home to sedges and reeds
**14** Those: Sp.
**16** Rawboned
**17** National ___ Day (March 16 observance, appropriate to this puzzle)
**18** It has a lot of competition on TV
**20** Ctrl-Shift-___ (shortcut for a force-quit)
**21** Common recipient of an erroneous apostrophe
**22** Fly
**23** "Yikes!"
**24** Product whose package has a splash of milk
**26** Good name for a financial adviser
**27** Title setting for a Hemingway novel, with "the"
**28** Basketball Hall-of-Famer nicknamed "The Answer"
**30** Little drink
**31** When many workdays begin
**33** Wish one could
**35** League standings format
**36** Situated away from the point of origin
**37** Possibly not even that

**39** 1909 Physics Nobelist for radio communications
**40** Research complex in Bethesda, Md.
**41** Aromatic flower from China
**43** Annual hoops event, for short
**44** Put on
**46** Strain to recall?
**47** Princess in L. Frank Baum books
**48** Not pro
**49** Collection at the entrance to a mosque
**50** Rivers of New York City
**51** Some census info
**52** G, in the key of C

## DOWN

**1** Wedding words
**2** H
**3** Jousting venue, informally
**4** Tab key, e.g.
**5** Dastards
**6** Wall: Fr.
**7** "Puss in Boots" villain
**8** You name it
**9** Bad place for a long run
**10** Like 17-Across
**11** Home for some famous 17-Acrosses, informally
**12** People who do not eat meat but do eat fish
**15** Representation of one's personality in the natural world

**16** Tony-winning actress for "Miss Saigon"
**19** Kind of ice cream
**24** Manages
**25** Opposite of returnable
**28** Like xenon
**29** Like la nuit
**32** Wedding words
**34** Foreign policy advisory grp.
**38** Per
**39** Noted Marilyn Monroe feature
**42** Pal of Piglet
**45** Put the kibosh on
**47** Brunch beverages, informally

by Alex Eaton-Salners

# 12

## ACROSS

1 Openness
7 Launch
13 State capital whose name is pronounced as one syllable (not two, as many think)
14 Pamper
15 What a good tip can lead to
16 Unnamed women
17 Activity for kids out for kicks?
19 Dental hygienist's order
20 ___ justice
21 Tastes, say
23 Chain named phonetically after its founders
25 Refuse to go there!
26 Green org.
30 So-called "good cholesterol"
31 "Ah, all right"
33 Participant in a 1990s civil war
34 Thai neighbor
35 Final part of a track race
37 It comes three after pi
38 Member of an old Western empire
40 Popular photo-sharing site
41 Waiting room features
42 Calls on
43 Tea company owned by Unilever
44 George W. Bush or George H. W. Bush
46 Handout at check-in
49 Rewards for good behavior, maybe
50 Lumberjack

53 Guy who's easily dismissed
55 It's office-bound
57 "Amscray!"
59 "Sounds 'bout right"
60 N.L. Central player
61 Bouncer's confiscation
62 Costing a great deal, informally

## DOWN

1 Reconciler, for short
2 Prized footwear introduced in 1984
3 Chronic pain remedy
4 Formal
5 Around there
6 Heave
7 Force onto the black market, say
8 "S.N.L." castmate of Shannon and Gasteyer
9 Complex figure?
10 Classic film with a game theme
11 Neighbors of the Navajo
12 Present
14 Carnival bagful
16 Informal name for a reptile that can seemingly run on water
18 1990 Robin Williams title role
20 Mexico's national flower
22 Make a delivery
24 Blubber

27 "Quit horsing around!"
28 Not needing a pump
29 Causes for censuring, maybe
32 Glad competitor
36 Wrench with power
39 With disapproval or distrust
45 Roughly 251,655 miles, for Earth's moon
47 Ramen topping
48 "Independents Day" author Lou
50 "That's rich!"
51 Bonus, in ad lingo
52 Compliant
54 Pat on the back
56 Peeved
58 Get burned

by Peter Wentz

## ACROSS

1 Needs to recharge, maybe
11 One whose coat of arms displays a unicorn
15 Sporty/casual fashion trend
16 Derisive interjections
17 Acted cheekily (in two senses?)
18 Cry of frustration
19 Drag
20 Advance
21 They touch people's funny bones
23 Icon of the small screen?
25 & 27 What you might do "to pay Paul"
28 Required wear in some Hindu temples
30 Google search results
32 ___ flour
33 Sponsor of the Poetry Out Loud program, for short
34 Discounted
36 They're kept at Area 51, supposedly
37 Host's responsibility
39 Complete . . . or completely destroy
41 "Errare humanum ___"
43 Marvel
45 Scolding word
47 Go on and on
48 Visibly forbidding
49 Hastily applied, as makeup
52 El ___
54 Surround, with "in"
56 Botanical opening
57 Dance craze mentioned in the Beatles' "Revolution 9"
59 Pants part
61 Go "Vroom vroom!"
62 Kind of horn pitched in E♭
63 Online commentariat
66 Appear
67 Sticker in a restaurant window
68 Beau ideal
69 Pen name of Ruth Crowley and Eppie Lederer

## DOWN

1 Wallops
2 Place for dogs to rest
3 Tabloid question next to two people in the same outfit
4 Wing
5 Land, at sea
6 "Gotta run!"
7 "The Tin Drum" narrator
8 Cataclysmic
9 Shrinks, e.g., briefly
10 Group hangout time, slangily
11 "Tsk, tsk!"
12 "Can you say more about that?"
13 "Just what I needed," sarcastically
14 They might be shot from a basketball court
22 Shaken
24 ___ Watson, role for Lucy Liu on "Elementary"
26 Actor Benjamin of "Law & Order"
29 Fat: Sp.
31 Man's name that's an anagram of DOLLY
35 "Uh, yeah!"
38 Chores
40 Be up against
41 It lends a golden color to baked goods
42 Big name in baked goods
44 Chess concession
46 Mother of Persephone
50 Toward the rear
51 ___ Bridal, wedding dress chain
53 Family name in New York politics
55 Lead, e.g.
58 Chichén ___ (Mayan city)
60 Start of an encouragement
64 Colorless
65 "Sweet!"

by Wyna Liu and Paolo Pasco

## ACROSS

1 Slangy part of a conversation recap
11 "We deliver for you" sloganeer, for short
15 They come with strings attached
16 Sports org. headquartered in Indianapolis
17 Fakes
18 It's the truth
19 Woman with a 32-Down
20 Two-time Emmy nominee for playing Suzanne Sugarbaker
22 Peach or plum
24 Mobile dwelling on a steppe
25 Commanding the situation
31 Move clandestinely
34 Civil rights activist buried in Arlington National Cemetery
36 Wrong
37 Something to shoot for
38 Special
39 Go with
40 Inits. in 1970s–'80s rock
41 Satay dip
44 Little theorem within a bigger theorem
46 "You betcha!"
47 Arrange, in a way, as hair
49 Common address ender
50 Classic rock hit that asks "Is it tomorrow or just the end of time?"
55 Big Apple?
59 Doing the job
60 Race car, e.g.
62 Way to watch shows beginning in 1999
63 Tricky swap
64 Algorithm part
65 Ones trying to cover all the bases

## DOWN

1 Pound sign?
2 Hanauma Bay locale
3 Where the biblical Esther and Daniel are purported to be buried
4 Tusked savanna dweller
5 ___ tear
6 Ash, e.g.
7 Instrument with a bent neck
8 Proofreader's abbr.
9 R. J. Reynolds brand
10 Attempt
11 Roll out
12 Sign of healing
13 Get ready, in a way
14 Not just meet the needs of
21 Bit of osculation
23 "Por ___ Cabeza" (tango classic)
25 Encourage
26 Zora ___ Hurston, writer of the Harlem Renaissance
27 Much-used technology in the 1990s that's largely outmoded today
28 Event that's not for singles
29 Like a lamb
30 "___ remember . . ."
32 Girl with a 19-Across
33 Dealt a low blow
35 Reserve
41 Cathedral eponym
42 Cone head?
43 Like idols
45 Beatlesque hairstyle
48 Pop label
50 Some ironware
51 Something that's often named after a scientist
52 "Death Becomes Her" co-star, 1992
53 Arabic leader
54 Big tubes
56 Seconds
57 Spanish sweetheart
58 Biz bigs
61 "We move the world" sloganeer

by Damon Gulczynski

## ACROSS

1 Saucy ones
6 Brand with Prime Cuts
10 "Deck the Halls" octet
13 Seller of Halloween costumes, perhaps
15 Highland body
16 "Fingers and toes crossed . . ."
17 Need to play, say
18 Show tiredness
19 Cave ___ (beware the dog)
20 Texas A&M athlete
21 Kind of wave
22 Supersmall, futuristic medical device
24 Series of tweets
27 Series of tweets
28 Humanitarian Wallenberg
29 Skilled at dodging
30 Afflict
31 Like zero
32 Lines on a park map
33 Abbreviated title without the second, third, fourth and sixth letters
34 Conducted
35 Oscar-nominated director of "Network" and "Dog Day Afternoon"
36 Statues of mermaids, typically
37 Didn't use the can?
39 Great shakes
40 "Grant them ___ rest" (requiem opening)
41 Barely
42 Some R.S.V.P.'s
43 Favorite bar, say
45 Big retailer in outdoor gear
48 Daft
49 Device found between gutters
51 Applies
52 Record kept for travel reimbursement
53 Code for Australia's busiest airport
54 Call it a day
55 Honkers

## DOWN

1 Take a turn
2 Home of N.Y.C.'s Colonnade Row
3 Album holder
4 Little pointer
5 Off-menu offering
6 When "S.N.L." ends on the East Coast
7 Seating request
8 Senior moment?
9 Ref. work in which the verb "set" has a 60,000-word entry
10 Four-wheeled transports that developed out of surf culture
11 One of the top things on a to-do list
12 What a pane!
14 Word after "take a" or "take the"
15 Africa's largest city that's not a national capital
20 Guitarist Summers of the Police
21 Alone, to Alain
23 Trojan War participant
24 Transportation option in Philadelphia and Seattle
25 Not experience the same difficulties as others
26 Like cars at Consumer Reports
27 Held in suspense
29 Expensive coat material
32 Aqua ___
33 Befit
35 It helps you focus
36 Little something put away for later
38 Lock
39 Jazz great who took his name from Egyptian mythology
41 Cocktail with bourbon and sugar over crushed ice
44 "It was ___ dream"
45 Be awesome
46 Freudian concept
47 Writer nicknamed the "Playwright of the Midwest"
49 "The Ultimate Driving Machine" sloganeer
50 Aid in driving

by Kyle Dolan

## ACROSS

1 Eschew the bus or subway, say
8 Lead-in to -tainment
11 Org. overseeing the Epidemic Intelligence Service
14 Words said while pointing
15 Person on horseback?
17 Something David Copperfield has that Penn and Teller don't
18 Salon, fancily
19 Some choice words
21 Timeline swath
22 With 51-Down, part of a golf club
24 Fish that may be served meunière
25 Like a lamb
26 Flavor of some bottle-shaped gummies
28 Section often symbolized by a speech bubble
31 They don't give you much to stand on
35 1980s disco hit that became a gay anthem
37 Native name for the Iroquois Confederacy
39 Rider on a carousel?
41 Germany, France, the U.K., Italy, Spain and Poland, collectively
42 Endnote abbr.
43 Rock formation
47 Kind of shot that's the opposite of a 38-Down in a screenplay
48 Actor with the 2007 memoir "Things I Overheard While Talking to Myself"
49 Trial run

52 Number in a pharmacy, informally
54 Opposite of "Yay!"
57 Kind of wind across the Aegean
58 Massachusetts home of Phillips Academy
59 Mystery title: Abbr.
60 Alias
61 Plain lodging

## DOWN

1 Cleveland ___ : Abbr.
2 "Well, looky there!"
3 Vegetables, fruits, nuts, roots and meat, classically
4 "Merci ___ aussi"
5 Chesterfield and others
6 Chili variety
7 Nut variety

8 Unwanted effect on a recording
9 Treasured
10 Sports getup, for short
11 Like email addresses, practically
12 Kevlar developer
13 Parts of many an urban skyline
16 Drink container that doesn't easily spill
20 Catch up
22 Acer offerings
23 Indian flatbread
25 Rolex competitor
27 People of NE France
29 Lima locale
30 Shoe size specification
32 Burp, more formally
33 "I did it!"
34 Draws
36 Refusal overseas

38 Kind of shot that's the opposite of a 47-Across in a screenplay
39 Got sudsy
40 Watching TV after midnight, say
44 Capital on the Atlantic
45 Apologize with actions
46 Rock formation
49 Proboscis
50 Poet ___ St. Vincent Millay
51 See 22-Across
53 Unaccounted-for, briefly
55 "Wasn't I right?"
56 Many promgoers: Abbr.

by Erik Agard

## ACROSS

1 Pirates
8 Part of N.A.A.C.P.: Abbr.
12 "___ rico!" ("Delicious!": Sp.)
15 Start of a haughty declaration
16 Do a vet's job on
17 German conjunction
18 Like some mushrooms
20 Prefix with graph
21 You might get a kick out of this at a restaurant
22 Parts of the body that are slightly larger in the evening than morning
23 Résumé asset, in brief
26 Animal known to "juggle" rocks
27 Chokes, say
28 Did a hook spin or knee swing
32 "It's true!"
33 Backdrop for the Compromise of 1850
34 "I don't care either way"
36 Test with a Social Studies sect.
37 A fifth
39 Fast-fashion retailer
43 Outdoor apparel chain
44 Title heroine of a James Joyce story
45 Modern marketplace
50 Party hearty
51 Passé
53 Opposite of petit
54 Work on software
55 Need for protein synthesis
56 Things shortened at bitly.com
57 Some instant breakfast packets
61 Complete a lap?
62 Star student's goal
66 Emotive verse
67 Isn't oblivious
68 Isn't oblivious
69 Patriarch Stark of "Game of Thrones"
70 ___ Park Corner (London tube station)
71 Basic dance move

## DOWN

1 In
2 Cases to consider
3 Delight
4 Principal
5 Small Pacific salmon
6 Metaphor for a tricky problem
7 TV sets?
8 Hard to fool
9 Enlivened
10 Screen ___
11 12/31
12 Onetime Bravo series or its Netflix reboot
13 Term for a censored dissident in "1984"
14 Censors, say
19 Inescapable bind
22 Unrestrained violence
23 Dashboard abbr.
24 Appropriately named ghost in Nintendo games
25 More than most
29 Without borders
30 Movie villain with a signature pinky gesture
31 Pulitzer-winning poet W. H. ___
32 Still
35 Cops' targets
38 First graduates of the new millennium, informally
39 Missouri setting of 2014 civil rights protests
40 Countermand
41 Refused to accept the status quo, say
42 Made more waterproof, maybe
46 Crowning event?
47 Poetic contraction
48 Took off
49 Timeline division
52 Thickheaded
54 Only one of the Seven Dwarfs without a beard
58 Say frankly
59 Best Supporting Actor winner for "Dallas Buyers Club"
60 Honorifics that can be repeated to indicate higher status
62 Traditional source of fertilizer
63 Do one's part?
64 "Hadn't thought of it like that"
65 Special gift, for short

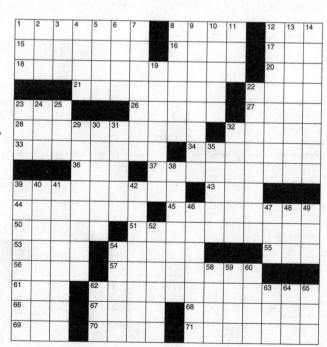

by Milo Beckman

## ACROSS

1 Delicacy also known as sablefish
9 Band for an awards ceremony, maybe
13 It has wheels and flies
15 Work one's way through, as a maze
17 Some "M*A*S*H" characters
18 Speed up
19 Mauna ___
20 "That wasn't just talk on my part"
22 Canceled
23 Show one's humanity, perhaps
24 Where the flash drive was invented: Abbr.
25 ___ Sword (night sky sight)
27 Vessels for vintners
29 The lion's share
31 Merck work, for short
34 Aren't wrong?
35 Actress/YouTube star Koshy
36 Noted relationship in physics
39 Bond
40 Pirate's activity
41 Word sometimes followed, mysteriously, by an ellipsis
42 Artificial object in orbit?
44 Sci-fi leader of the Resistance
45 So-called "People of the Sun"
46 Shade from the sun
47 Philharmonic sect.
50 Euro forerunner
51 Milk, slangily
54 "He hath but a little ___ face": Shak.
55 Child's one-piece outer garment
57 Caribbean locale across the water from Morro Castle

59 Become incapable of parting?
60 Like much Halloween candy
61 "You're ___!" (reproof)
62 Shanghai or Mumbai

## DOWN

1 Slow down
2 Paper, vis-à-vis scissors
3 Promising area
4 Browns, in brief
5 Actress Russell of "The Americans"
6 Rap sheet, so to speak
7 Dwell (on)
8 Capital on the Cape Verde peninsula
9 "That's enough out of you!"
10 Musica, for one, in ancient Rome

11 Like some exotic drinks at tiki bars
12 Fits in between?
14 "Family Feud" airer
15 Drink that you could really use
16 "Hi" follower
21 Arthur and Garfield, for two
26 "Très chic!"
27 Level best?
28 Actress Thurman
29 "___ Up" (N.F.L. feature with in-game dialogue)
30 Smidges
31 Simon of the "Mission: Impossible" movies
32 Do-o-ope
33 Dance-based class in a pool
34 German : Freundin :: French : ___
37 Go-ahead

38 Sea urchin in sushi
43 Mortal mother of Dionysus
44 Stopped a ship using the wind, in nautical lingo
46 Fluorescent bulb, maybe
47 Language of southern Africa
48 2020 Christopher Nolan sci-fi thriller
49 Primed
50 Bit of work
52 Bit of work
53 Three o'clock, so to speak
56 Back stroke?
58 Trader ___

by Joe Deeney

# 19

## ACROSS

1 Longtime soft drink slogan
9 Cosmetics brand owned by Revlon
14 Simply not done
16 Make one's hair stand on end?
17 Welcome abroad
18 Rage
19 Tours can be found on it
20 Like una montaña
22 Drop a line, say
23 Brook no refusal
25 Locale in a children's song title
27 Lead-in to brain or body
28 "The Gray Lady": Abbr.
29 Curry on TV
31 Fabric choice for a gown
33 Signal
36 Award-winning architect Zaha __
37 "See, someone understands what I'm saying!"
40 Blackens
41 A real head-scratcher?
42 Void, in a way
44 Team __
45 Pro in Ohio, in brief
48 Saharan menace
49 Whom Grogu resembles on "The Mandalorian"
51 Actress Kidman
54 "__ that?"
56 Weighs (down)
58 Cozy spots
59 Algerian currency
61 Token reprimand
63 Whiff, say
64 Resolve
65 Loser to Roosevelt in 1944
66 Rechargeable city transport

## DOWN

1 Home to the so-called "Silicon Docks," a European equivalent to Silicon Valley
2 Like the taste of a bialy
3 Muslim or Christian, e.g.
4 Milliner Bendel with a bygone chain of women's accessories stores
5 Rain gutter locales
6 Dr. __
7 Chef Lewis who wrote "The Taste of Country Cooking"
8 "Right?"
9 This can help you find your balance
10 Part of some tables
11 Digital filing service?
12 Lead-in to an opinion
13 "Your point being . . . ?"
15 Bash
21 Ice Bucket Challenge cause, for short
24 Sharp quality
26 "Chicago Hope" actress Christine
30 Friend or foe
32 Stun, in a way
33 Pressing
34 Assignment that sounds like its third and fourth letters
35 Headaches for talent agents
37 Setting with hobbit-holes
38 "See what you've started?"
39 Pulitzer-winning author Jennifer
40 Cajun cuisine catch
43 Really easy question
45 Order to stop
46 Certain hydrocarbon
47 Evening prayer
50 Columnist Maureen
52 First class
53 Pink drink, for short
55 Uniform
57 Doesn't go anywhere
60 Good name for a marine biologist?
62 Jiffy

by Evan Kalish

# 20

## ACROSS

1 Coltrane's rendition of "My Favorite Things," for one
10 ___ friends
15 A nonzero amount
16 Word with car or talk
17 Marked by stately beauty
18 Roman leader?
19 Accessory that might have a netsuke attached
20 Move fast, as clouds
21 Like some letters and lines
22 Modicum
23 Very unfortunate
25 C-worthy
26 North Carolina county near the Tennessee border
28 Dined with a menu, say
30 Quandary
31 Beams
33 In heaven
35 ___ Crawford, the N.B.A.'s all-time leader in four-point plays
38 Senior member
39 But not that exactly
42 V.I.P. of industry
44 Travelers from a faraway place, for short
45 Crow's home
47 Release
51 Biblical character who lived to be 912 years old
53 Gets down
55 Singer on the album "Live Peace in Toronto 1969"
56 Hoarse
58 Crib cry
59 Result of a clutch hit, maybe, for short
60 Sea serpent in the night sky
61 Sazerac garnish
63 In a swing state?
64 How Prince Harry met Meghan Markle
65 Modicum
66 Zip

## DOWN

1 Southwestern shrub that yields a cosmetic oil
2 Wolf-headed god of Egyptian myth
3 Summit
4 State of madness
5 Obtain by force
6 "Hit the bricks!"
7 Plumlike fruits
8 Proceed wearily
9 This is the end
10 Ship that survived the Clashing Rocks, in legend
11 Selling points
12 Anthem of the European Union
13 Sarcastic response to backpedaling
14 Finding a four-leaf clover, they say
21 Certain bra spec
24 Acknowledgment of a debt
27 Things sometimes named for kings
29 Finish line?
32 Scores
34 Put to sleep
35 Everyman
36 "Go ahead"
37 Ice age beast
40 Hinge (on)
41 Something shot from a cannon nowadays
42 Kind of tile
43 Master of meditation
46 ___ Hayden, actress who voices Milhouse on "The Simpsons"
48 Doctor in an H. G. Wells novel
49 Still being tested, say
50 Can
52 Head of cabbage?
54 Does some shop class work
57 Danny who played Walter Mitty
61 Great Society monogram
62 "Stat!"

by Trenton Charlson

# 21

## ACROSS

1 Ballpark figure
7 Sentimentality
15 Wallet holder since 2015
16 Hit Netflix reboot starring the Fab Five
17 Matured
18 There's often a lot of them for sale
19 Some office desk clutter
20 Writers Roald and Sophie
21 Bottom of an interrobang
22 Safari's compass, e.g.
23 Feel for
24 Nested layers?
25 Mass
26 Breakneck . . . or something to break
27 Sticky snack made with a stick
29 Eclipsed everyone else
32 One getting fired up for competition?
35 Shower heads, perhaps
37 "The Wolf in Sheep's Clothing," for one
39 Mindless
40 Iowa college
41 Game that can be played on bicycles or elephants
42 Change for some sawbucks, maybe
43 Symbols of strength
44 Fantasy monster
45 Catches
47 XXXL
48 Complete loss of self-identity
50 Hot streak?
51 Where one might hear a call for action
52 Metaphorical incentive
53 Members of some blended families
54 Goes quietly, perhaps

## DOWN

1 Honchos
2 Fruits that are the basis of Marillenschnaps
3 Dance with jerky movements
4 Actress Julie of "Modern Family"
5 Cross to bear
6 Casual agreement
7 Topic in property law, colloquially
8 Like a good job, maybe
9 Prominent part of a pump
10 Rx pickups
11 Story ___
12 Honcho
13 County in Northern Ireland
14 Peels off?
20 Spilled the tea, so to speak
23 Model Boyd who inspired the songs "Layla" and "Wonderful Tonight"
24 Kind of manual
26 Wild
27 Uses a manual, say
28 Israel's Dayan
30 Ferrari alternative, slangily
31 Percussion in some folk music that may be improvised
33 Captured, in a way
34 Fashion designer's portfolio
36 Employs as a backup plan, with "to"
37 Blanked on
38 Recess
41 Frost accumulation
42 Written in the stars
43 Really weird
45 Number shown in brackets?
46 "Hidden Figures" org.
47 ___ jacket
49 Baba ghanouj, e.g.
50 Hosts

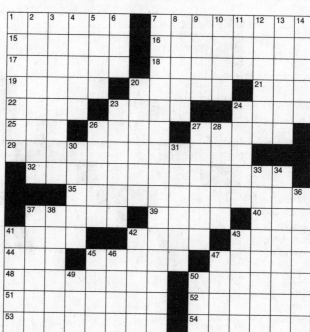

by Josh Knapp

## ACROSS

1 Be in charge . . . as a doctor?
13 Remains to be seen, say
14 "Sheesh, just move on!"
15 One of the knights of the Round Table
16 Con ___ (musical direction)
17 Lead-in to some water-dwelling "folk"
18 Car loan nos.
19 How Superman often poses
21 Galoot
22 Small hybrid instrument with six strings
24 Layperson?
26 Where you may be waited on hand and foot?
27 Make tracks
28 "Where are your manners!"
29 Player of Julia in "Julie & Julia"
31 Walk all over the place
34 2008 horror film sequel
36 What frozen foods may do in paper grocery bags
37 "Arthur" airer
40 Visibly dizzy, quaintly
42 One might have a photographic memory
44 Strengthening crosspiece
45 Disassociate, as with a Bluetooth device
47 Bears: Lat.
48 D.O.J. V.I.P.s
49 Bass organ
50 Pennsylvania city where the Delaware and Lehigh Rivers meet

52 World Series opener
55 Command to stop saluting
56 Savory snack in England

## DOWN

1 Something absolutely adorable, with "the"
2 "___ happens . . ."
3 Bad way to be poisoned
4 Galoot
5 So-called "America's Network"
6 "Get what I'm saying?"
7 Like a deaccessioned book, for short
8 Slangy psychedelic
9 Make tracks, quaintly
10 One with a "Yes we can" attitude

11 It was once a challenge to eat
12 Compound found in latex
13 Company at which business always comes before pleasure?
14 Drink from a bowl, maybe
15 Jokes
20 It's below belowdecks
23 What one of the Olympic rings represents: Abbr.
25 Word before or after strong
30 Predate?
31 Polo of TV's "The Fosters"
32 Cans
33 Twitch or Yelp

34 River that begins in the Adirondacks
35 Comment that prompts the reply "Doitashi-mashite"
36 Bouillabaisse tidbit
38 Chest
39 It's got you covered
41 Actor profiled in the biography "The Immortal Count"
42 Sensational coverage
43 Historic town NW of London where some of the Harry Potter series was filmed
46 Wild cards in "baseball" poker
51 Working hard
53 Man's name that's also a suffix
54 ___ vapeur (steamed)

by Sam Ezersky

## ACROSS

1 Some internet humor
8 It shares a key with a "3"
15 Apple product launched in 2015
16 Vital hosp. worker
17 Beheader of Medusa, in Greek myth
18 One engaged in a struggle
19 Need for translation, in biology
20 Coined word in the title of 2008's Best Picture
22 Congresswoman Demings ___
23 Many mainframes
25 Brewery stock
26 Western city where copper-riveted jeans were invented
27 Water nymph
29 Big Ten football powerhouse, for short
30 Big name in apple juice
31 Dangerous thing to catch
33 Two swings and a slide, maybe
35 Do or ___ (punny hair salon name)
36 The Depression, for one
37 Rally feature
41 Team player who's not really a team player
45 Wears
46 Burning sensation
48 Came to
49 African antelope
50 Group with the 2000 hit "This I Promise You"
52 Website with the headings "Craft Supplies" and "Jewelry & Accessories"
53 Cable channel owned by Discovery
54 Convenient place to work out
56 T.S.A. overseer
57 "De-e-eluxe!"
59 Elvis Presley sings it in "Blue Hawaii"
61 Corpulence
62 Tracking device
63 Sells
64 Some printers

## DOWN

1 Facial piercing
2 Place for free spirits
3 Where the University of Wyoming is
4 Contents of some towers, in brief
5 Some sign language users
6 In fact
7 "Tough luck . . . I don't care what you think"
8 "Watch it!"
9 Cant
10 Make out in England
11 ___ army, villainous force in Disney's "Mulan"
12 Pot supporters
13 Actor Armand ___
14 "Beat it!"
21 Attachment to Christ?
24 Place to build a castle
26 Fancy "I"
28 Israeli leader with an eye patch
30 Actress Gibbs of "The Jeffersons"
32 Cubs' hangout
34 Pastoral setting
37 When a poser might be presented?
38 Place for a stud
39 Eager, informally
40 Causes consternation
41 Language of the Literature Nobelist Rabindranath Tagore
42 Test in chemistry?
43 "Yeah, I'm listening"
44 Yellowstone attractions
47 Bourbon relative
50 Murphy's co-star in 1982's "48 Hrs."
51 Robotic adversary in "Battlestar Galactica"
54 Bad fall?
55 Not serious
58 Cause of a trip
60 Once-in-a-lifetime trip

by Daniel Larsen

## ACROSS

**1** Bands popular in the '70s
**10** Uses a letter opener on
**15** Later on, when appropriate
**16** "The Pirates of Penzance" ingénue
**17** Is resolute
**18** Grammy winner with the surname Adkins
**19** National ___ Hall of Fame, in Rochester, N.Y.
**20** Flip, say
**21** Esther of TV's "Good Times"
**22** "Breaking Bad" protagonist
**23** Offer sheet?
**25** Refresh, in a way
**28** "Quit your bickering!"
**29** Left on deck
**30** Reached the point of no return?
**33** Like many Ariz. residents
**34** Fraught with risk
**35** Gubernatorial option
**36** Snow-capped peak of song
**38** Yellowstone traffic halters
**39** One going paperless in April, say
**40** Gags
**41** Once-common mall fixtures
**43** Nut chewed as a stimulant
**44** Harshly colorful
**45** Certain computer key
**47** Face-covering dance move
**50** Star N.F.L. receiver ___ Beckham Jr.
**51** "Stoned Soul Picnic" songwriter
**53** Counterpart of butch

**54** Language in which "Hello, how are you?" is "Saluton, kiel vi fartas?"
**55** Its penultimate line is "Poems are made by fools like me"
**56** Franchise with the "Dominating the Deep" DVD set

## DOWN

**1** Sight in a produce aisle
**2** "I'm ___ you!"
**3** Danny ___, ventriloquist dummy for Jimmy Nelson
**4** Pressure over a debt
**5** Second or third version
**6** "Life ___" (2014 Roger Ebert documentary)
**7** Pester playfully
**8** Finance co. rebranded as Ally Financial
**9** Branch of mathematics that uses ∪ and ∩ operations
**10** Brain
**11** Classic film that gave us the term "paparazzi"
**12** "Pretty sure"
**13** Restless movements, maybe
**14** Unwelcome forecast
**22** "I . . . I can't even"
**24** Like presses
**25** Certain paddy crop
**26** Car with a lightning bolt logo
**27** French dessert of soft custard
**28** Patch growth

**30** Things that generate a lot of cookie dough?
**31** Early educator of George Orwell
**32** Dijon denials
**34** Course division
**37** Some airplane seats
**38** Fortification
**40** Traditional wedding vow word
**41** Up
**42** Showing less refinement
**43** Gene who's considered "the founding father of the modern drum set"
**46** Far from deliberate
**47** 10 micronewtons
**48** Museo contents
**49** Enter into a calendar
**52** "Thanks anyway, pardner"

*by Doug Peterson and Brad Wilber*

## ACROSS

1 Article of attire akin to a tarboosh
4 Facetious response to "How'd you know that?"
7 One might be forever
12 Union deserters
14 Choice for those eager to retire and travel?
16 ___ Plus (brand with a "Lubrastrip")
17 Brownish-orange shade
18 Big brass
20 Reliable
21 Baglike structure
22 Spacewalk, e.g., in NASA shorthand
23 Insect repellent ingredient
24 Twitter : retweet :: Facebook : ___
26 Email notification, maybe
27 Go (for)
30 Hot dogs do this
31 Bar exam?
33 Early trans-Atlantic voyager
34 Creature in Liberty Mutual ads
35 Build
36 Small bit of floor décor
38 Material harvested for its hydrophobic properties
39 Basic cleaner
40 Actor who voiced the title character in 2018's "Sherlock Gnomes"
41 Like some toothpastes
42 Choice for a cinematographer
43 Swab
44 Exec with a noted mansion
46 "The weapon of the powerless against the powerful," according to Molly Ivins

49 "100% happening!"
51 State in which you might get a tax deduction
53 One with briefs, briefly
54 Defcon 1 mentality
55 Lisa with the 1994 hit "Stay"
56 Fuji, e.g.
57 ___ Lovett of "Sweeney Todd"
58 Snoop

## DOWN

1 Achievements
2 Really, really hot
3 "100% not happening!"
4 First name on the Supreme Court
5 Desertlike
6 /, maybe
7 Something you can't get in a restaurant
8 Food for a grizzly bear
9 Doesn't hesitate
10 Apt name for a yoga instructor?
11 Talk up?
13 Uncle ___
14 Hot spot
15 George Washington signed America's first one in 1790
19 TV roommates for 50+ years
23 Fix, as in beta
25 Penny-___
26 Recapitulate
27 Excessive
28 Unlikely member of the "clean-plate club"
29 Bit of ink

31 Some guest roles on cop shows
32 Pressing need
33 Bud
37 Convictions
41 Le ___ (newspaper)
42 Von Trapp daughter who sings "Sixteen Going on Seventeen"
43 Indicative and subjunctive, e.g.
45 Spacecraft activity
46 Org. concerned with lab safety?
47 50+ group
48 Word with round or road
49 Symbol of opportunity
50 Indian lentil dish
52 What you might say after reading a tricky crossword clue

by Robyn Weintraub

## ACROSS

1 Hero of Philadelphia
7 IG-11 on "The Mandalorian," e.g.
12 Stereotypically arcane subject
14 Wry comment on a sorry situation
15 Decline
16 One temporarily donning a cap
17 Spent
18 Decked out
19 "Between the World and Me" author, 2015
21 Frequently flooded land
22 Team that infamously blew a 28–3 Super Bowl lead they had late in the third quarter: Abbr.
23 Doctor's office, maybe
24 Piece of the pie?
26 Standard of comparison
28 Lock holder?
29 Sharp feeling
30 Smear
31 Shell, maybe
34 Little ball of fur
38 ___ change
39 Makes clean . . . or less clean
40 Rigmarole
41 Buck, boomer, jack, flyer or jill, informally
42 One might carry a torch
44 Like some brows and berets
45 Longtime Sacha Baron Cohen persona
47 Was on
48 Turns over
49 Bit of encouragement for someone's success

52 "Decision time!"
53 Spike in activity on a sports field?
54 Absolutely trounced

## DOWN

1 Dog . . . or a type of dog
2 Dos y dos y dos y dos
3 America's first historically Black sorority, in brief
4 Set the wheels in motion
5 Continuously improve, in tech-speak
6 Subject of a family feud, maybe
7 Lead-in to belief
8 Certain mouthpiece attachment
9 Not with "them"
10 Frosty air?
11 De-frosting?
12 Queens, e.g.
13 Lines in an application?
14 Setting of a 1945 conference
15 Natural cover
19 Holding up the line for?
20 Workers with talent
23 Angles
25 Color that comes from the Latin for "red"
27 Earth-shattering
28 Glossy alternative
30 Makes out
31 Material that artists get all fired up about?
32 Amphibian that Ogden Nash once rhymed with "bottle"

33 "Little Women" actress Ronan
34 Milan ___, author of 1984's "The Unbearable Lightness of Being"
35 Openness
36 Parting word
37 Little 'uns
39 Singing style with African-American roots
43 Say "Ta-da!," say
44 Excited, with "up"
46 Actress Rowlands
48 Natural recess
50 Many a 31-Down piece
51 Banh ___ (sticky rice cake)

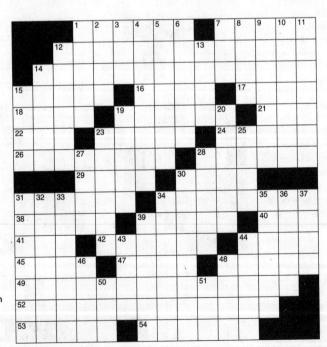

*by Nam Jin Yoon*

## ACROSS

1 Them's fightin' words
6 Deems suitable
13 Pop up a lot, perhaps?
15 Try
16 "Rock-a-bye" locale
18 Raised
19 Reconstruction, e.g.
20 Bit of ancient writing
22 ___ Dove, former U.S. poet laureate
23 Snitch (on), informally
25 Concern in geomorphology
26 Send off
27 Spicy sandwich spread
29 What you're in when you're in the zone
32 Umbilicus, familiarly
34 "Deuce and a quarter" automaker
35 Subject of H.R. 40, introduced in every Congress since 1989
38 Product from Bevel or Oui the People
39 Train stations
41 "Tell me now"
45 Beat in the news business
47 Seconds, say
48 Hip-hop's ___ Soul
50 Be wildly successful, as at a comedy club
51 ___ Louis, capital of Mauritius
52 Finally
54 Jazz great Mary ___ Williams
55 Not much
57 Pair of rings?
59 Provisos
60 Run through
61 Online magazine co-founded by Henry Louis Gates Jr.
62 Observes one of the Five Pillars of Islam

## DOWN

1 Plan
2 Concern in geomorphology
3 A fine way to discourage foul language?
4 Homage of a sort
5 2019 M.L.B. champs
6 Pay, as big bucks
7 Actor James ___ Jones
8 One-named rapper who became a co-host of CBS's "The Talk"
9 Underground rap?
10 Revered woman in Islam
11 "Totally makes sense"
12 Yet
14 Many nonfiction films, for short
17 Spelman figure, informally
21 Unit officially defined as 42 gallons
24 Résumé go-with
28 Home of many a Sherpa
30 Devices sold with motion sensors
31 Language in which you might be greeted "Hullo, hoo are ye?"
33 Do nothing
36 Subject of a Car and Driver report
37 Features of some film reviews
40 Beyoncé became one in 2003
41 Influence
42 Dough
43 Achieve stardom, so to speak
44 Wood strip
46 Distinctive features of Marcus Garvey's helmet
49 Inits. one might hear at the office
52 Spanish opposite of bajo
53 Inits. one might hear at the office
56 "___ Te Ching"
58 Major export of Kenya

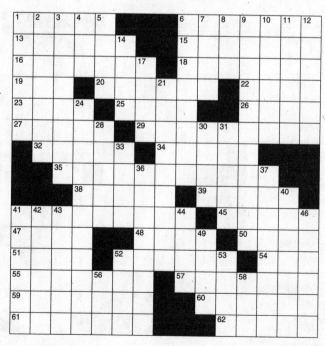

by Erik Agard

## ACROSS

1 First name in Russian literature
4 Big jackpot, for short
7 "What do you think you're doing?!"
10 Requiring
13 Give an edge
14 Princess of Monaco
16 ___ Hufflepuff, one of the co-founders of Hogwarts
17 Nice pair of boxers?
18 Chronicles from a feminist perspective
20 Long-proposed constitutional inits.
21 Once-popular resort area in the Catskills, informally
22 Sad song
24 A real cinematic tour de force?
25 Fault-finds to a fault
27 Share, as a plot?
28 Informal address at school
30 Kind of tone
32 Charles ___, how Angelo Siciliano is better known
34 Marketing ploy
36 Stuffed
39 Onetime Apple Store stock
41 Government program?
43 ___ process
44 Just-the-facts-please
45 Young amphibians
46 Plain as day
47 Not hold back on criticism
49 Hardwood option
50 Music genre that includes "geeksta rap"
51 Many characters in "Kill Bill"
52 Twain
53 "Inside the N.B.A." airer

## DOWN

1 Did a Daffy Duck impression, say
2 Intestine-related
3 Like many engagement stones
4 [Shrug]
5 Home of the Nez Perce Indian Reservation
6 Ones practicing social distancing
7 More venerated . . . or ventilated?
8 Author of 1884's "The Origin of the Family, Private Property and the State"
9 You might get a rise out of this
11 Some records, for short
12 Some records
13 Traditional 19-Down soother
15 Get out
16 Getting started the wrong way?
19 See 13-Down
21 "Give it time"
23 "Nice job!"
26 Mercedes-Benz sedan type
29 High-___ (looked down on)
31 What a mule kicks with
33 Like jacket lining, typically
35 Intersection sign
36 Big scoop
37 Hero of Virgil
38 Attacked, in a way
40 Octave's follower in a Petrarchan sonnet
41 Certain govt. security
42 World leader with a role in 1961's annexation of Goa
45 Abbr. sometimes written three times in a row
48 Affirmation of commitment

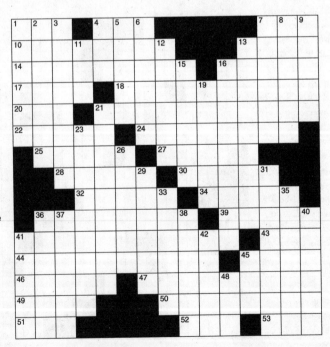

by Kameron Austin Collins

## ACROSS

1 Star Bucks, say?
8 Trap
15 Gal Gadot, by birth
16 Major retail outlets
17 A famous one is often connected with a school
18 True celeb
19 It's always up to something
21 Let someone know if you can go
24 "___ be in England . . ."
25 Sister channel of HGTV
28 Carrier for many a 15-Across
29 Influenced
31 Follower of boo or woo
32 Company whose most famous product once claimed it "does what Nintendon't"
33 Fail miserably
34 Melon seeds?
36 One of the few gemstones that naturally occur in a single color (olive green)
38 Goes past
40 Russian prince nicknamed "Moneybag"
41 It may be added to the mix
43 Trick
44 Sum of the first three prime numbers
45 Beast vanquished by Oedipus
47 Bath occupant, say
48 Record finish?
49 Cope, with "it"
50 Semisynthetic fabrics
52 "You can figure it out"
54 Dangerous compound to mix with bleach

57 Postdelivery announcement, maybe
61 Italian dessert topped with crumbled macaroons
62 It flows with the wind
63 One who's out of action?
64 Player of Warren Buffett in "Too Big to Fail"

## DOWN

1 Chilly quality
2 Eagles' org.
3 Cable news host Melber
4 Unnecessarily spell out, in a way
5 Sporty Chevy
6 Accepts, as a lesser charge

7 Noted speaker of more than 20 languages
8 Swell
9 Cry heard by Alice in "Alice in Wonderland"
10 Released in segments
11 Trick, in slang
12 Scrap of food
13 "No ___!"
14 Musical acuity
20 Speckled, say
21 Letup
22 Arms repositories?
23 Drifter
25 It's usually around 9/10 of a pound
26 Adds, as a disk to a disk drive
27 Mollycoddles
30 Accessory that might hang out of a waistcoat

35 Bowlers
37 Dreaded fate for a samurai
39 Adult and then some
42 Sharp increase
46 Coating produced by oxidation
51 Lost
52 Heap love (on)
53 One of 3,365 in U.S. Route 20
54 4×4, for one
55 Rapper Kool ___ Dee
56 TV/film star who became a pro wrestler
58 Storage option
59 "___ to a Superhero," Weird Al's parody of "Piano Man"
60 "___ out!"

by Grant Thackray

## ACROSS

1 Like the emo genre
7 Chocolate or caramel
10 Contretemps
14 Wait here!
16 See 4-Down
17 Holiday production?
18 Really feeling
19 Item on a toothpick
20 Insects that may lack mouths
22 Subject of many a conspiracy theory
23 Hajj, e.g.
24 "And . . . we're ___!"
25 Overplay
27 Word with red or reason
28 The Atlantic, but not the Pacific, for short
29 Devour, with "up"
30 Metaphorical setting in which everything is inverted from the norm
32 Be peevish with
34 Sometime
35 Many are under the influence of this at college parties
37 Covered with fat
38 "Sure, I'm game"
39 Breathing exercises, in brief?
42 Vehemence
43 Bottom lines
44 Mind
45 Sorting label for a Twitter search
46 Jazzman who was a pioneer of Afrofuturism
48 Thoroughly examined, in a way
49 Couple's word
51 Upbraids
53 Texted lead-in to an alternative
54 "Thanks, Captain Obvious!"
55 Literary member of the League of Extraordinary Gentlemen
56 "Why, every fault's condemn'd ___ it be done": "Measure for Measure"
57 Minute

## DOWN

1 Shady spots
2 Bly who traveled around the globe in 72 days
3 Set of programs including Drive and Docs, once
4 With 16-Across, championship-winning head coach of the Golden State Warriors
5 Stun, in a way
6 Compliment to the chef
7 Entertains
8 Bond
9 Really impress?
10 Emulate Olympian Lindsey Vonn
11 Visual effect from a partial eclipse
12 With cunning
13 Moved en masse
15 Brood
21 Springtime forecast
24 Monitor, e.g.
26 Digs, so to speak
28 They have many small teeth
29 Freak out
30 "Lincoln in the ___" (2017 best-selling novel)
31 Stuff in stuffing
32 Main course?
33 Nickname for the White House Correspondents' Dinner
35 Part of a company
36 Popular ice drink
39 Redeem, as at a casino
40 Gets ready for a date, maybe
41 Morning omen for sailors
43 It's not a good look
44 Apt rhyme for "stash"
47 Something an ascetic might fight
48 Actress Blanchett
50 Sister channel of Flix, for short
52 Kind of milk

*by Will Nediger*

## ACROSS

1. Leading lady?
12. Depiction on the Australian coat of arms
15. Popular orders at beachside bars
16. U-Haul option
17. Comment before indulging
18. Some theft targets
19. Protrusions near a trunk, maybe
20. Sticks
21. Whizzed (by)
22. Word sometimes substituted for "your"
23. Killing a mockingbird is one, per Atticus Finch
24. Prepare for court, in a way
26. Tamagotchi, once
27. Modern lead-in to speak
28. Park ranger's handout
29. Stayed out of sight
31. Bouquet
32. Palindrome with an apostrophe in the middle
34. Contents of some wells
35. Sleeveless top, informally
36. Approached quickly
37. Complete set in musical comedy?
39. Psych up
41. Bill that's half a 52-Across, informally
42. ___ Short, pioneer in West Coast hip-hop
45. Reroute
46. The sun or the moon
47. Ganja
48. Whizzed (by)
49. "The Virtue of Selfishness" essayist, 1964
51. Pal of Seinfeld and Costanza
52. See 41-Across
53. Way of Life?
55. Stir
56. Helen of Troy, e.g.
57. Lip
58. Some reference works in newsrooms

## DOWN

1. Not very much
2. Missing portion of a manuscript
3. Gradually stopped, with "out"
4. Hair pieces
5. Qts. and pts.
6. Way out
7. Onetime Food Network show featuring Creole and Cajun cuisine
8. Kind of jar
9. "Go placidly ___ the noise and the haste . . ." (start of Max Ehrmann's "Desiderata")
10. Louise of TV's "Mary Hartman, Mary Hartman"
11. Ballpark fig.
12. It's a bad sign
13. Raked in the dough
14. Messy, as a floor
21. Tussle
23. ___ protein
25. Parent company of Gerber and Lean Cuisine
27. Dorothy of old "Road" films
28. 13, for many
29. Shaped, as wood
30. Singer/songwriter of 1980's "Kiss Kiss Kiss"
32. Popular salon option, informally
33. Toxin that might contain formic acid
36. Symbol associated with Communism
38. Go out
40. Houston or Washington vis-à-vis Manhattan
42. Tightened (up)
43. Threatening words
44. Hyperfocus
46. Buck ___, Major League Baseball's first Black coach
47. Gardner of "S.N.L."
50. General assembly?
51. R&B singer Erykah
53. Burnable items
54. Burnable item

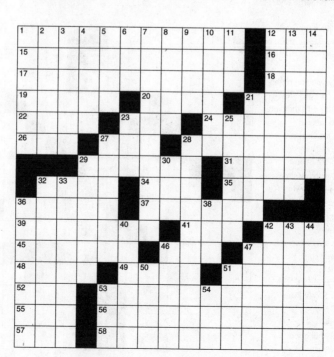

by Amanda Rafkin

## ACROSS

**1** Requirement
**7** Wage conflict, say
**13** Things often hit during rush hour
**15** "I Wish" rapper, 1995
**16** Subj. of the 17th Amendment
**17** Bit of inside info
**18** Cold War missile type
**19** Believer in the Horned God
**21** Excellent
**22** Campaign figure, informally
**23** Front on the waterfront
**24** Out of one's head, in slang
**25** Sci-fi portals
**29** Fairy tale villain
**30** ". . . unless I'm mistaken"
**31** Writers George and T. S.
**32** "You have my vote!"
**35** Jeering words after a prank
**36** Clear
**37** Things you can barely see at art galleries?
**38** Time for an exhibition
**42** Word derived from the Greek for "age"
**43** Rafter neighbor
**44** Org. with resources on smart growth
**45** Fashion inits.
**46** Do a favor
**48** Reclined
**49** Uses a stylus on a credit card reader, e.g.
**51** Role in 2012's "The Dark Knight Rises"
**53** Take on
**54** Whole
**55** Really not good anymore
**56** Specialty of Aristophanes

## DOWN

**1** Supporting character?
**2** ___ von der Leyen, first female head of the European Commission, who negotiated Brexit for the E.U.
**3** Remove one's coat?
**4** Wealth
**5** It adds one point to a soccer team's standing in the English Premier League
**6** Proceeding very, very quietly
**7** "Poppycock!"
**8** Singer whose name becomes a city if you add an "R" in the middle
**9** As ___
**10** Reaction to some P.D.A.
**11** Port of SE Spain
**12** Restaurant chain originally called Chicken on the Run
**13** Borders
**14** Protective suits?
**20** Trig function
**24** Sevastopol is its largest city
**26** Humorist Leo who wrote "The Joys of Yiddish," 1968
**27** Shades, as with a pencil
**28** "The Queen's Gambit" actress ___ Taylor-Joy
**29** Thick as thieves
**31** Reigns, say
**32** "Sure, it could be"
**33** One might have a bunch of errands
**34** Anticonsumerists aiming to help the environment
**35** 12 months from now
**38** Homie
**39** One doing some stitching
**40** Methadone or oxycodone
**41** Kind of state
**43** Buddy of "Barnaby Jones"
**46** "This one's ___"
**47** "___ Is Betta Than Evvah!" (1976 album)
**48** Actress Petty
**50** Make extremely upset
**52** Card

by Ali Gascoigne

## ACROSS

1 Bit of strategy
7 Painting technique used in van Gogh's "The Starry Night"
14 Good as gold, and others?
15 High-m.p.g. vehicle
16 One having a certain video chat
17 This just in!
18 What happens while you're busy making other plans, it's said
19 Italian architect Ponti
21 ___ and Ole (stock characters in Upper Midwest jokes)
22 Revolution around o sol
23 Makers of parts
25 Be present
28 Expression of support
30 Expression of contempt
31 One who might meet with angels, for short
32 Things used by star witnesses?
38 Meet somebody you've heard lots about
39 Creator's leeway
40 Jill Biden ___ Jacobs
41 Mauna ___
42 Something found after many years?
43 Fencing sport with bamboo swords
46 Film composer Morricone
48 Seat occupier, for short
51 Stylish
53 Like 2021
54 It has its faults, informally
55 Club's premier venue
58 Bring aboard, sci-fi-style
60 How many Amish barns are raised
61 Robinhood competitor
62 Patronized, in a way
63 Indenting aid

## DOWN

1 Producer of 15-Acrosses
2 Oscar nominee for "Argo"
3 Narcissist's ploy
4 It's on a roll
5 Follower of McCarthy
6 Boatload
7 Levin who wrote "The Stepford Wives"
8 Team with "Mr." and "Mrs." mascots
9 Irritant
10 Appropriate
11 What Grand Canyon tourists enjoy
12 Large marble
13 Choice words
15 Capital of every country?
20 Dolt
23 James Beard award winners
24 Northernmost part of the U.K.
26 "___ legit"
27 "Lovely ___ You" (song by the Moody Blues)
29 Flavoring of Cedilla liqueur
32 Defeat soundly, slangily
33 Setting for a blender
34 Pic on a pec, say
35 Amour de ___ (self-love: Fr.)
36 Equatorial plantation crop
37 Force on Earth, in brief
44 "Go, and catch a falling star" poet
45 Stop here ___ (traffic sign)
47 "Intuition tells me . . ."
49 Sidestep
50 Lab tube
52 Diminutive master of film
54 Potato or pasta, informally
55 Prefix with century
56 What Friday has, unlike any other day of the week?
57 ___ of This Swirled (Ben & Jerry's flavor)
59 Pilot's info, for short

by Chuck Deodene

## ACROSS

1 Hoopster's mantra
11 Two-time FIFA Women's World Player of the Year (2001, 2002)
15 "My point is . . ."
16 Like castaways, before being cast away
17 Set for the afternoon?
18 Clinches
19 A couple of dollars?
20 Material whose name is a Scandinavian country in French
21 Moves like a butterfly
22 Countenance
24 Stingray feature, once
25 Pioneer in 35mm cameras
26 School softball?
28 Singer Braxton, sister of Toni
30 Its birthstone is peridot: Abbr.
31 "Let's get ___!" (party cry)
33 Individually
35 In the cloud, say
38 Title character in a "Sgt. Pepper" song
39 Night light
41 Wiz Khalifa's "We ___ Boyz"
42 Ron who played Tarzan on old TV
43 Moving
45 Some didy changers
49 Fare from some bars
51 Smart ___
53 "Au revoir!"
54 Letter to the editor, often
55 Atomic clock timekeeper
57 Prefix with binary
58 Kind of bowl ordered at a juice bar
59 Opposite of cheap eats
61 Actress/YouTube star ___ Condor
62 Whole
63 "East of Eden" twin
64 #1 on a list, maybe

## DOWN

1 "Buzz off!"
2 Renato's wife in Verdi's "Un Ballo in Maschera"
3 Some deals from dealerships
4 "___ Mañanitas" (Mexican birthday song)
5 Woman's name that's also a plural suffix
6 Work it, on the runway
7 Four-time Grammy winner Lyle
8 George Sand title heroine
9 [I'm such an idiot!]
10 Inspect
11 Selassie of Ethiopia
12 What this is an example of: \_(^.^)_/
13 Trope seen in rom-coms
14 Rub the right way?
21 Switched (on)
23 Alternative to polyester
27 Home for a drone
29 Jokester
32 Props of sorts
34 Target
35 Vehicle equipped with photovoltaic cells
36 Schroeder plays one, in the comics
37 Dig for insights, digitally
39 Annual N.Y.C. event hosted by Vogue
40 Some Pepperidge Farm cookies
44 Begrudge
46 "Get Out" star Kaluuya
47 Like, now
48 Birth control pioneer Margaret
50 Like some drones
52 Forfeits
56 What comes before old age?
59 "Of course it looks good on you!," maybe
60 Zip

by Yacob Yonas

## ACROSS

1 Like faces around a campfire at night
6 One whose business is home-based?
9 Part of a diplomatic address, maybe
14 Spot for an umbrella
15 Pickup line?
17 Perfectly timed
18 Fluffy four-footed friend
19 Fire ___
20 Smart remarks?
22 Popular camp assemblies
23 Aid in preventing a soup stain, maybe
26 Passes
28 They're worn on the road
30 Seljuk Empire citizen
31 Cozy chairs for pairs
33 Word with base or combat
34 Side dish in Cajun cuisine
36 Vaccine target
39 Acute bronchitis, familiarly
41 Bill
43 Motif in much Christian art
45 Squirt-squirt-squirt-squirt
47 Screwballs
49 W.W. I headgear
51 "It's just OK"
52 With 60-Across, East Asian cuisine style
53 Print source
55 Go off with a hitch?
57 Former home of the San Antonio Spurs
58 "Ha, fell right into my trap!"
59 Neuter
60 See 52-Across
61 Sudden blasts

## DOWN

1 In-depth subject for a war historian?
2 Tip with ink
3 Milk-producing
4 Frequent setting on "Chicago Med"
5 Historic London venue
6 ___ triple play, baseball feat rarer than a perfect game
7 Chaps
8 Cello quartet
9 Comedian Marc
10 Peak overlooking Armenia's capital
11 Backgammon accessory
12 2019 sci-fi film starring Brad Pitt
13 Came across
16 Break
21 Where many a drive ends, unfortunately
24 Hunk
25 Pursues for food, say
27 Hit high in the air
29 Old-timey hearing aid
32 Deep-fried British treat wrapped with sausage and bread crumbs
35 Essayist who wrote "Newspapers always excite curiosity. No one ever lays one down without a feeling of disappointment"
36 Focus of middle management?
37 Skink or gecko
38 Places where things are all tied up?
40 Throw back some Jack, say
42 Checkers cry
44 Online companion animal
46 2021 Chinese zodiac sign
48 Inhibits
50 Classic moonroof alternative
53 44-Downs, once
54 Online qualifier
56 ___ Hoover, first lady before Eleanor Roosevelt

by Ryan McCarty

## ACROSS

1 Tinder and others
5 Appeal
9 Costa ___
14 Activist Copeny known as "Little Miss Flint"
15 City SW of Pyramid Lake
16 Chilled
17 Kind of device used in filmmaking
18 Jafar's parrot in "Aladdin"
19 Big name in kitchen appliances
20 Unexpected
23 Rhythmic
24 Constellation that Regulus is part of
25 Decision-making time
26 Smartphone pop-up
27 Rotation calculation
29 "That fits perfectly!"
31 Cosmopolitan
35 Sarcastic punch line to an insincere remark
36 Energize, with "up"
37 City whose name means "spring hill"
38 Total wrecks
40 Reciprocal of cosecant
41 Best-selling video game that takes place in space
44 Lets, say
45 Running apparel?
46 "Well done!"
48 Endangered
50 Liquor brand that inspired the name of a Grammy-winning rapper
54 Nonkosher deli order
55 Something of interest to a business?
56 Mathematician who lent his name to a test

57 Singer who was an original judge on "The Voice"
58 Flies
59 Ab ___ (absent, in Latin)
60 Good to go

## DOWN

1 Hype (up)
2 Home of many a tech start-up
3 ___ moment (crowning achievement)
4 Stay-at-home workers
5 Meaning
6 Heartfelt
7 "Just Give Me a Cool Drink of Water 'Fore I Diiie" poet
8 Low speaker
9 Mouth part
10 Esoterica
11 Word that becomes its own synonym when RED is inserted between its first two letters
12 Train that serves three Union Stations
13 Wonkish
21 Relevant
22 Parts of a restaurant's overhead?
23 Caleb represents him in "East of Eden"
27 Part of a ship's rigging
28 Something bookmarked in a bookmark bar
30 Wishes
32 Voracious
33 Young 'un in Yucatán
34 Anticipatory times

37 Common items at merchandise stands
38 Giveaway
39 Banned refrigerant, for short
41 Common items at merchandise stands
42 Build muscle
43 Having the same number of karats, e.g.
44 Coors Field athlete
47 Roman god of beginnings and endings
49 Tear
51 Some deer
52 Truth's counterpart
53 ___ the finish
55 Sweetie

by Brooke Husic

# 37

## ACROSS

1 Supreme court member?
11 III, e.g., in "Richard III"
14 Number of days it takes Mercury to orbit the sun
16 It becomes another question when its first letter is moved to the end
17 "Wall Street" catchphrase
18 Chump
19 Just a bit
20 Like the last in a line
21 Wear
23 Day to post a throwback picture on social media: Abbr.
24 What a nod might mean
27 ___ bowl
28 Perfumery compound
30 Actress Shields, mother of Brooke
31 One stoner to another
32 Satisfied sigh
34 What a shrug might mean
36 Was up, in a sense
39 Nibbles
40 Cheap cab, perhaps
42 Org. with an annual Codebreaker Challenge
43 More than suspicious of
44 Be in the works
46 Irish name that's a Slavic name backward
50 The old you?
51 Like some unpleasant comments
53 Kind of trip taken solo
54 Utah's "Industry," e.g.
56 Camper's gear chain
57 Throw (together)

58 It can lay a one-and-a-half-pound egg
59 "Hold on!"
63 Calculator button next to cos
64 Words after "The end"?
65 Lead-in to stars or daylight
66 Soft, green food

## DOWN

1 Void
2 Once-in-a-lifetime events
3 Get too old
4 "I'm right here"
5 Business letters
6 Horizontal
7 Walt Whitman wrote one beginning "Lo, 'tis autumn"
8 Turn right, say
9 Years ___
10 Sorority letter
11 "How adorable!"
12 It involves much ear-tugging and head-shaking
13 Grade-A
15 Notable examples of crossing a line, in brief
22 Noodle dish whose name indicates its cuisine
24 Steaming
25 Club type
26 Pumbaa's friend in "The Lion King"
29 Goes on a dinner date, e.g.
33 They may be used in a pinch
35 Composition test
36 Easy friendliness

37 Correction for a wild pitch
38 "Marriage Story" Oscar winner
40 Dumpster fire
41 Lacks
45 Ring in the holiday spirit?
47 Flood
48 Annual genre writing award
49 Common complex rule
52 Celebrity portmanteau beginning in 2012
55 Accept the blame for
57 Impertinent sort
60 Archery need
61 Grocery store found in Michigan?
62 Pete Buttigieg's home state: Abbr.

*by David Steinberg*

# 38

## ACROSS

1 Gold Coast port
6 Grade
10 Certain hieroglyphs
14 Snacks known as "student fodder" and "scroggin" in Germany and New Zealand, respectively
16 Home of the Starzz, one of the original eight W.N.B.A. teams
17 What few fliers desire
18 Michael of "Scott Pilgrim vs. the World"
19 Bug expert?
20 Winter Olympics equipment
21 See 44-Down
22 Old Forester and Old Overholt offerings
23 Ethereum or Bitcoin, for example
25 Shame
27 Site of an underground pool, maybe
28 Get an 800 on the G.M.A.T., say
29 Animal that comes to shore to lay eggs
32 Bel ___ (Italian cheese)
33 One of the Kennedys
34 Single-___
35 Leftovers from a doughnut, say
37 Easy two-pointer
38 Deep cuts
39 Bad sorts to be stuck talking to at a gathering
40 Savory Scottish delicacy
41 Go down
42 Drug kingpin on "The Wire"
43 Coffee spot?
45 Comedian Margaret
48 Actor who played Senator Vinick on "The West Wing"
49 Historic Charleston site

51 St. ___, locale in an English nursery rhyme
52 One way to crack a code
53 Studies
54 "Got it"
55 People

## DOWN

1 You can bank on them
2 "___ Camp," 2020 Oscar-nominated documentary
3 Women's rights pioneer Elizabeth ___ Stanton
4 Clear
5 Words from Mission Control
6 Stops lying
7 Cut
8 Things that pique your interest on TV
9 14 billion years, for the age of the universe: Abbr.
10 "You thought wrong!"
11 Judge unfairly, say
12 Person in a contract
13 Bygone potentate
15 Hockey game highlight, for some
21 Unsatisfactory
22 Begin the toasting process
24 Zinger
25 Kind of berry
26 Oktoberfest locale
27 Does a deep dive on a topic, with "out"
28 Inclined
29 They can cause anxiety
30 Gifts that are usually scented
31 West end?

36 Bigeye tuna
39 U.S. city that's home to the largest Basque population outside Spain
40 Split, in a way
41 Tall order?
42 One of eight in "The Twelve Days of Christmas"
44 With 21-Across, straight up
45 2017 double-platinum debut album for SZA
46 "Shucks!"
47 Raw materials
49 Govt. org. whose director serves a 10-year term
50 "How now?," to a cow?

by Yacob Yonas

## ACROSS

1 Event with kings and queens
9 Avon lady, for one
15 Beverage such as huangjiu or cheongju
16 "We absolutely aren't doing that!"
17 Put off paying, say
18 What might go through the wringer
19 "Dumb and Dumber" duo
20 Odorless hydrocarbon
21 Runs or walks
22 Willing participant?
24 Dome of Notre-Dame?
25 Iconic sports cars, for short
27 Jolly laugh
29 Worked in Starbuck's business
33 Patronize farm stands and farmer's markets, say
35 Co-star of TV's "thirtysomething"
37 Terra firma
38 Apocalyptic event in Norse mythology
40 Revises
41 Lumber
42 Locks you pick?
44 Took some steps
46 Word on a Champagne bottle
47 Triangular sails
51 "___ Twain" (platinum album of 1993)
53 iPhone on display at an Apple Store, e.g.
55 Rise
56 "You don't need to tell me . . ."
57 Fixed
58 Moonstone, for Florida
59 No fans
60 Hip joints

## DOWN

1 Rubbish
2 Smack a baseball hard
3 What's on the fast track?
4 "The Balcony" playwright Jean
5 Lead-in to son or song
6 Drop down suddenly
7 With money at stake
8 Safari destination
9 Who defeated Holyfield to become the world heavyweight boxing champion in 1992
10 Butler in the old South
11 Short
12 Incapable fighter, in boxing slang
13 Start of a two-part thought
14 Informal denial
23 Perceptive sense
25 Soccer star Carlos
26 Halal cart fare, informally
28 Mother and father, slangily, with "the"
29 Sitcom station
30 Where some sweaters hang
31 Pet breed from Turkey
32 Sight from Big Ben
34 ___ disease
36 One getting pwned in online gaming
39 Language spoken in Iraq
43 ___ Vallarta (popular gay vacation destination)
45 Where a "houseboat" is a banana split
47 Southern refreshment
48 ___ Montoya, swordsman in "The Princess Bride"
49 "Carmen" composer
50 Sticks in the mud?
51 It's fit for a queen
52 Puts on
54 Overnight ___ (trendy breakfast)

by Sam Trabucco

## ACROSS

1 Schooner feature
5 Shock treatment, for short
10 Subject of the 2011 Jon Roberts memoir "American Desperado," with "the"
13 Tongue-in-cheek
14 "So sad . . ."
15 Stamp collector's purchase
16 Impetus behind a prank, maybe
17 One going the distance?
19 Refuse to talk
21 A ton of bricks?
22 Source of heart-shaped leaves
23 Like water at the shallow end of a pool
25 Name on a vintage red, white and blue cap
27 Weighs (down)
28 Lead-in to a crazy idea
29 Part of an old circus act
32 Realm of the Valkyries
33 2007 film with the tagline "The last man on earth is not alone"
34 Competitor of Dick's Sporting Goods
37 Be a rat
39 Dish rack accessories
41 Eel order at a sushi bar
44 "Land sakes alive!"
45 Severely self-disciplined sort
46 Appear
47 Men's grooming items
50 "Sir" might be found at the start of it
51 Colleen

52 Investor's "No deal"
53 Mario who wrote "The Godfather"
54 5-Across administrator
55 Makeover result, maybe
56 Go on and on bitterly

## DOWN

1 Eccentrics
2 Victim of a 20th-century environmental tragedy
3 Small but full of fight
4 Some bars returned to again and again?
5 Conducive to mold, maybe
6 Org. established partly in response to Rachel Carson's "Silent Spring"

7 The "Tannen" of Tannenbaum
8 One might consist of a primo, secondo and digestivo
9 Data base?
10 Quarters that could be worth a lot
11 Brownie mix add-in, often
12 Playoff positions
15 Muckety-muck
18 Fig. on a driver's license
20 Sleep aid brand
23 Prognosis that a problem has only just begun
24 Sunburn-soothing substance
26 Lead-in to P or C on a PC
30 Peer of Ibsen

31 Where the Ring is destroyed in "The Lord of the Rings"
32 Constant reminders?
33 Recovering orthopedically, maybe
34 Get back together
35 Write à la Thomas Gray or John Donne
36 "Ahhh"
37 Fit to be tried
38 Line at a clothing store
40 Gives birth to, as puppies
42 "___ be nice if . . ."
43 Toxic protein prepared on "Breaking Bad"
46 "Qué es ___?" ("What's this?": Sp.)
48 Run, like a Deere?
49 Homie

by Sam Ezersky

## ACROSS

1 Regarding
6 Take back, in a way
10 Start of an aside
14 Omega competitor
15 Something hitting a nerve?
16 Papyrus, e.g.
17 "Take me with you!"
18 Begin flirting with someone, so to speak
20 Assign
21 Hoth, in "Star Wars"
22 ___ rule
23 They don't hold water
24 Feudal figure
26 Panegyric, e.g.
27 Sci-fi enemy collective, perhaps
31 Ones born beginning in the early 2010s
37 They might cut to the chase
38 Electrically balanced, in chemistry
42 Leaders at the Kaaba
43 "Things are going great for me!"
46 Muscle worked in rowing exercises, for short
47 Portmanteau coinage for the uneducated and uncultured
48 Touches, e.g.
51 Special pawn move in chess
52 Many a Madrileño
53 Enemy of Wonder Woman
54 Best Picture-nominated 2011 film based on a children's book
55 Certain Caribbean, informally
56 Self-___
57 What might help you get out of a rough spot?
58 Is just awful

## DOWN

1 Home to 41-Down
2 Convince
3 "I wanna know all the details"
4 Start of a modern inquiry
5 Drink similar to sarsaparilla
6 Co-star of 1984's "Ghostbusters"
7 Right on
8 Aces with aces?
9 Like some households
10 Designer with an eponymous hotel in the Burj Khalifa
11 Currency units in West Africa
12 Grievous
13 "Golden Boy" playwright
19 Actress Shawkat of "Arrested Development"
24 Assignment for an anchor
25 "___ noticed . . ."
28 Great Hindu sage
29 Late-Triassic flier
30 It can be found right on a clock
32 "100 Years . . . 100 Stars" and others, in brief
33 The world's largest desert capital, after Cairo, Egypt
34 Like a relationship with an ex, maybe
35 Utterance while chewing on a pencil
36 One often sent packing?
38 Deity that becomes a given name when its fifth letter is moved to the front
39 Beat
40 Looking to steal, say
41 So-called "Land of a Million Elephants"
43 Building support
44 Words not everyone understands
45 Intimate
49 Hit on the head, in slang
50 Indian honorifics

*by Sid Sivakumar and Matthew Stock*

## ACROSS

1 Building with many drafts
8 Got clean
14 "Heavenly" dessert with a lemony filling
16 Space between the ribs of an insect wing
17 Unresolved detail
18 One-pointer in horseshoes
19 Woman's name that sounds like two letters of the alphabet
20 Pad
22 Without a match
23 Econ. stat
25 Enticing spot
27 Gay rights pioneer Marsha P. Johnson, for one
31 Bud's place
32 "I'm ___, she's mine" (repeated lyric in "Do Wah Diddy Diddy")
33 Movement to reduce frivolous lawsuits
37 Early p.m.
38 Renowned football club founded in 1899
39 Golfer's concern
40 "Vice" principal?
42 T-Bonz treats brand
43 Bob ___, Canadian ambassador to the U.N.
44 Curve cutter
46 "Isn't that strange?"
49 Collar
50 Resort with a "no snowboarders" policy
51 More than outstanding
53 They produce results
57 Discipline based on the principles of yin and yang
59 White House reception locale
61 Leaves a grave impression, perhaps
62 What's not working?
63 Protester's cry
64 Brand whose famous slogan contains a double negative

## DOWN

1 Roll in the hay?
2 905-year-old in Genesis
3 Clash of the titans?
4 Throws in the towel
5 Runs
6 Great ___
7 Tough skin
8 Model's makeup, often
9 Is for more?
10 Bit for a fortuneteller
11 90s groups?
12 First name on the Supreme Court
13 Had the gall
15 Post master?
21 Not so hard
24 Topic for a voice coach
26 Taken in
27 Jazz trumpeter Jones
28 Offer you might have less interest in, for short?
29 Ones who might use oils in a pan?
30 Surfaces
34 Fabric made from cellulose
35 Seacrest's partner on morning TV
36 Cat's 'sup?
38 Didn't just excel on
41 Home of Jinnah International Airport
42 Province named for a daughter of Queen Victoria
45 Second
46 Word with hold or holy
47 Lift up
48 Job that usually requires a face covering
52 Parts of roller coasters
54 Potter's substance
55 Antithesis of light reading?
56 Aide to Captain Hook
58 "___ Your Dog, Charlie Brown" (TV special)
60 "Finding Nemo" setting

by Andrew J. Ries

43

## ACROSS

1 Protection of a protagonist for narrative purposes, in slang
10 Rum-soaked treats
15 Get in the pool, say
16 Actress Grant of "Weeds"
17 "Not always"
18 Water from a water fountain
19 Judge
20 Help out with a job
21 Frequent book setting
22 Elicit an "Oops!," maybe
23 Goad
24 Chuck at a high speed
25 Timely question?
27 Hot Chelle ___, rock group with the 2011 hit "Tonight Tonight"
28 Have a sneaking suspicion
29 Tuck's partner
30 Nickname for a toy
31 All knotted up
33 Key arrangements made for house sitters?
35 Lose one's vigor
36 Latin possessive
38 Subj. for the 2009 Nobel Prize winner Elinor Ostrom, the first woman to receive it
39 Typical taxi toppers
40 Big names in the news
42 Really into
44 Father of Jörmungandr
45 Inflation stat, for short
48 Source of honeydew
49 Ginger at a sushi bar
50 Ones who've split
51 Who can get in the way of what Alicia Keys feels for you, in a 2007 hit
52 Rude question following an unsolicited idea
54 Dummkopfs
55 Aid in getting a smooth shot
56 Email ___
57 Lines of communication in schools?

## DOWN

1 Annual June celebration
2 About two-thirds of a 7-Eleven Double Gulp
3 Farther out there
4 Brim
5 Spreader of venom
6 Four-time Emmy winner from Coney Island, N.Y.
7 Bunch of hipsters?
8 Use Uber Eats or DoorDash, say
9 Break
10 ___ hound
11 α
12 Like some tropical seas
13 Caulking might prevent them
14 Release
23 Carpet type
24 Exclamation popularized by "Die Hard"
25 Said, informally
26 Start of a cheer
28 Blind optimist's downfall
30 Goad
31 Habitat for a starfish
32 Roger's equivalent
34 Fruit rich in antioxidants and vowels
35 Source of Vibranium in the Marvel universe
37 Home to the world's busiest airport
40 Low-key
41 Packs
43 Montana, e.g., informally
45 "Ciao"
46 "Get out!"
47 Subjects for gossips
49 [I'm in shock!]
50 Fit
53 Some E.R. cases

by Adam Aaronson

# 44

## ACROSS

1. Hot pot spot
5. Thriller with a two-note theme
9. Certain fund-raising orgs.
13. Something said while nodding
15. Or
16. "Quit looking at me like that"
17. Actor and L.G.B.T.Q. rights activist George
18. A child who's lying might make one
19. What's always found in bed?
20. More than suspicious of
21. ___ bar
23. ___ bar
26. Bigwigs
29. Bread crumbs used as a coating
30. Mythological figure who nearly managed to flee Hades
31. Anxiety condition, for short
32. Measure of a heart rate
34. "Pachinko" author ___ Jin Lee
35. Tight squeezes for Santa
38. Riffles (through)
40. Small organic food producer
41. One whom you might tell "everything"
42. Fixes, as unruly hair
43. Hardly a long shot
44. Spectacle
46. Not all it's cracked up to be
51. Honor . . . or a goner
52. Genre for "The Truman Show" in 1998's "The Truman Show"
53. Actor Elba
54. Space out?
55. Time out?
56. Manual part
57. Sequel to Pearl S. Buck's "The Good Earth"

## DOWN

1. Jokes
2. Words after walk or cash
3. Jay between Johnny and Jimmy
4. Business school alumni, collectively
5. Cheerful and self-confident
6. "Wait for it . . . wait for it . . . now!"
7. Pay
8. Explicit, to a Brit
9. Sign
10. Sets sights on
11. Befuddled
12. Well-guarded area in sports?
14. 2012 title role for Jamie Foxx
15. Drop in
22. Loan figs.
23. Anthropocene, for one
24. Guac go-with
25. Turn out badly for everyone involved
26. Rib
27. Bookstore section, informally
28. Savvy
32. One in the care of una madre
33. Concerns for homeowner associations
36. Is serious
37. Queens squad, for short
38. Unleash
39. They get left behind
41. Gunny
43. "See ya later!"
44. Hubbub
45. Veiled language
47. Common item of fishing apparel
48. Cars for cats, say
49. One of the schools named in the Public Schools Act of 1868
50. Certain Netflix offerings

by Nam Jin Yoon

## ACROSS

**1** Basketball game in an arcade
**9** Bad spot for a date?
**15** Death stare
**16** Bug's place?
**17** Popular dish in Seville
**18** Kind of duck
**19** ___ Morris, lead character on TV's "Saved by the Bell"
**20** Expecting, informally
**21** Heavy metal band that earned a Grammy Lifetime Achievement Award in 2019
**26** Bar food
**27** Palter
**28** Third-tier caste member in "Brave New World"
**32** Low stats for some M.V.P. winners
**33** Newspaper designer's responsibility
**35** Inspired stuff
**36** Qualities in music
**37** Brand of cashmere pronounced "say"
**38** Climactic court moment
**40** Actress Seehorn of "Better Call Saul"
**41** Way
**42** R&B group ___ Hill
**43** Sta4nce, for instance
**44** Took things to a whole new level
**47** NorCal daily
**50** Assessment, for short
**51** "My schedule permitting"
**52** Nail-biter
**56** Explosive cited in "Hamlet"
**57** Qualifying phrase
**58** Some ice cream orders
**59** Fly from Honolulu to Tokyo, say

## DOWN

**1** Marker in the game Battleship
**2** Ingredients in Caesar's salads?
**3** Social event in which the food is usually ordered in
**4** Sources of hypoallergenic fiber
**5** Casual wear
**6** Pawns
**7** "You're in such trouble!"
**8** Ringside call
**9** Prince William's sister-in-law
**10** It won't react well
**11** Take advantage of the situation
**12** Moralizing sort
**13** Pulmonologist's study
**14** Toaster Strudel alternative
**21** They're brought in for starters
**22** Aid in rounding up
**23** Like some desserts
**24** 8'2" children's character
**25** Bar tidbit
**29** Postponed indefinitely
**30** Sight along the National Mall in Washington
**31** Unstressed
**33** Spot on a face
**34** Cause for a replay
**36** Steinbeck novella
**39** Commuter's amenity
**40** They're fit for a king
**43** Rail against
**45** Has yet to be decided
**46** Opening of a toaster
**47** Tests one's spirit?
**48** Not lots
**49** Credit card name
**52** As late as
**53** World's first TV channel to be transmitted via satellite
**54** NASA spacewalk, for short
**55** Palpatine's granddaughter in "Star Wars" films

by Peter Wentz

## ACROSS

1 "I literally ___" (millennial's overstatement)
5 First country to discover water on the moon
10 Criticize forcefully
14 Nirvana, e.g.
16 Part of the eye
17 Computer file arrangement
18 Sharp
19 Manhattan, for one
20 Former major-league slugger Adam nicknamed "Big Donkey"
21 Best Actor winner Malek
22 "I'd love to!"
23 [Is this thing on?]
25 Moving option
26 Celebratory shout
27 Bud
28 Cause of a 2014 scare
30 "Rabbits" in a race
34 Sobriquet for international hip-hop star Pitbull
35 Scorsese film added to the National Film Registry in 1997
36 "I want it!"
37 "Minari" director ___ Isaac Chung
38 It doesn't last long
41 Bit of royal regalia
42 Abjure
46 Olympic figure skating commentator Johnny
47 Spencer of "Good Morning America"
49 Goddess whose Roman counterpart is Victoria
50 This and this
51 Big Apple
52 They may have lots of steps
54 Windmill part
55 News headlines
56 "I like texts from my ___ when they want a second chance" (Cardi B line)
57 Absinthe flavoring
58 Site for crafty sorts?

## DOWN

1 Start to squat?
2 Covered, as by insurance
3 Being
4 ___ list
5 Investment opportunity, for short
6 Jokey response to an overly technical explanation
7 Prevent from running
8 "Sorry, unavailable"
9 Hartford-based health care company
10 Leave damaged
11 Many a farmer's market attendee
12 Members of a certain kingdom
13 ___ Spirit, winner of the 2021 Kentucky Derby
15 D.C.'s ___ Stadium, opened in 1961
23 Dish that can be prepared al pastor
24 Small
27 Put in hock
29 They might be twins
30 Tot toter, in Tottenham
31 Canon offering, in brief
32 "Blossom of snow," in song
33 One studying for a bar or bat mitzvah, say
34 Cell boundary
35 Studio with "Chicago" and "Chocolat"
36 Start a stream, say
38 Get into a rhythm, informally
39 Long divisions?
40 Not casual
43 Pic that may have millions of likes
44 Keep under wraps
45 "African unicorn"
46 Question in a shell game
48 Las Vegas W.N.B.A. team
50 "Arguing with a fool proves there are ___": Doris M. Smith
53 U.S. 1, for one: Abbr.

by Matthew Stock

# 47

## ACROSS

1 One with a train, maybe
6 Stick around on July 4?
14 Shake
15 Lincoln, for one
16 Middle name of the writer born Nelle Lee
17 "Unbelievable!"
18 Maintains
19 Regulator of IUDs
20 Rep
21 Prefix with -graph
22 Prefix with -graph
23 Hotel room extra
24 "Star Trek" catchphrase
27 Nursing ___
30 Carefully exiting a parking space, say
31 Compile
32 Fragrant rice
33 Zooms past
35 Dendrogram, more familiarly
36 Hit below the belt
38 Part of P.S.T.: Abbr.
39 Comes around, say
40 Do nothin'
41 "How Long ___ Black Future Month?" (N. K. Jemisin short-story collection)
42 Scoop
44 Word with secret or source
46 Order for a big party, maybe
47 Pumped
48 "There's no hope for me now"
50 Kind of flour used in marzipan
51 Elbows, e.g.
52 Appropriates
53 It covers the field
54 Minute, informally

## DOWN

1 Cause of an uptick in Scottish tourism beginning in 1995
2 Like albums that include bonus tracks, often
3 "Let's see what you've got"
4 They might go for a few bucks
5 Overthrow, e.g.
6 Tied the knot
7 Sponsor of Usain Bolt
8 ___ distance
9 Setting for a meet cute
10 Retailer originally named the S. S. Kresge Company
11 Do nothing
12 Just got (by)
13 What those with protanomaly have difficulty seeing
14 Word uttered while pointing
19 Like eggshells
22 Very low stake?
23 Acropolis, e.g.
25 ___ de los Reyes
26 Hold together with duct tape, maybe
27 Orchestra that performs an annual Fireworks Spectacular
28 First and last name of Rihanna
29 ___ Raisman, third-most-decorated Olympic gymnast in U.S. history
31 Fruit that's a major Chinese export
32 Best-selling K-pop group
34 Org. with operations
37 Obelix's friend in comics
39 Some Spanish titles
40 Home of the Strat, the tallest observation tower in the U.S.
43 Some calculations in 40-Down
44 Actor ___ Benson Miller
45 Rate
46 Numbers game
47 Ingredient in some gel face masks
48 Puck, for one
49 San Francisco's ___ Hill
50 Asexual, informally

by Brooke Husic and Brian Thomas

## ACROSS

1 Bill Bryson book subtitled "Rediscovering America on the Appalachian Trail"
16 Give a scolding
17 Show whose logo replaces an "o" with a diamond ring
18 Actress Rowlands
19 Look after
20 Head for a cow, horse or lion?
21 Book often stored horizontally
23 Put a strain on
24 Short jazz riff
25 Johnny with 10 World Series of Poker bracelets
26 Reading area
27 Spoils
29 Mother of the four winds, in myth
30 Cut off the back
32 High-risk game
37 Many national anthems
38 "Errare humanum ___"
39 "Whatever works"
42 Indifferent remark
43 Hurdle for a future atty.
44 Something you're not likely to fork out?
45 Seventh word of the Gettysburg Address
46 Home to the Imam Ali Mosque, built in the seventh century
47 ___ Reactor (Iron Man's power source)
48 Weathered, say
50 "Je t'___"

51 Products of Under Armour and Nike
56 "Could you give more detail?"
57 Certain summer attire

## DOWN

1 Enter the picture?
2 Muted trumpet sound
3 Pub container
4 Claim to fame for Freeport, Me.
5 Zen riddles
6 People who built the Qhapaq Ñan, or "Royal Road," which stretched roughly 3,700 miles
7 High degree
8 1960s spy series
9 Path an electron may take moving in a constant magnetic field
10 Nobel Prize subj.
11 City section
12 Lucky strike
13 Gets on a mailing list, say
14 Pick up
15 Hearty dinner entrees
21 Big name in laptops
22 Grand
23 Much of Gen Alpha, now
24 Train route
26 Hon
27 Unsparing response to a complaint
28 Isn't 100%
30 Slant
31 Not a company person?
33 Substitute
34 Mosaic tiles
35 Romanov V.I.P.
36 ___ Candy, best friend of Wonder Woman

39 Jason who played Lucius Malfoy in Harry Potter films
40 Plaything for a Greek god
41 Trump is named in it
43 Delilah player in 1949's "Samson and Delilah"
45 Large bay window projecting from a wall
46 Two-legged stand
48 Cable channel owned by AMC Networks
49 Great Plains people
50 Police dept. alerts
52 Rebecca ___ Crumpler, first African-American female physician in the U.S.
53 Small cells
54 Org. that administers the G.R.E.
55 French article

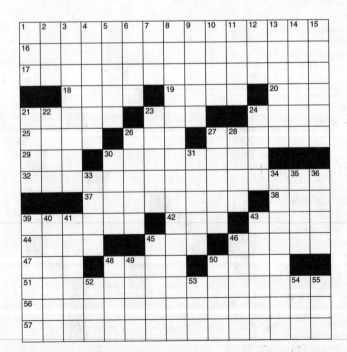

by Daniel Larsen

## ACROSS

1 Take pregame shots?
10 "The Metamorphosis" protagonist
15 Person who will do anything for you, in modern slang
16 "You caught me"
17 Cold, caramel-colored concoction
18 Sephora product
19 Literary utopia
20 Bridge, e.g.
22 Locale of an early 20th-century gold rush
24 "Homeland" home, in brief
25 Phisher's "catch," for short
26 ___ check
29 Letter between Oscar and Quebec
31 Davis who said "I am no longer accepting the things I cannot change. I am changing the things I cannot accept"
33 With it
35 Things not allowed in New York's Central Park
37 Birthplace of Ivan Turgenev
38 Babbled
39 Singer Rita
40 Character who can be played in every installment of 26-Down
41 Opening settings for "The Canterbury Tales" and "Treasure Island"
42 It's elementary
43 Ordered from Grubhub, say
44 Show-offy kind of push-up
46 "What's the ___ ?"
48 Abbr. in an office address
49 Tampon alternative
50 Contents of some chats, in brief
52 Name derived from the Latin for "to be born"
54 Smirnoff Ice, e.g.
56 Keynotes, e.g.
60 Ancestry
61 Firewall target
64 Mexican sandwich
65 Leave space for someone running late, say
66 "See what I'm sayin'?"
67 2004 comedy written by Tina Fey

## DOWN

1 Magician's favorite cereal?
2 Villa ___ de la Vera Cruz (historic city name)
3 Mideast port
4 Kia Rio, e.g.
5 Not close
6 Hospital specialty
7 Big inits. in home security
8 Hoppin', in modern lingo
9 Something you might play for
10 Suppresses
11 Bunches
12 It goes for a short run
13 "Can't argue that"
14 Something released while skydiving
21 Mental sparks
23 Home of the World Showcase
26 Nintendo offering with more than 10 installments
27 "Lemme see!"
28 Del Monte or Green Giant product
30 Elder brother of Moses
32 Affliction of Benjamin Franklin
34 "Brooklyn Nine-Nine" detective Diaz
36 Dish that might come with a flavor packet
40 Team game played in the dark
42 Snowballs, in a snowball fight
45 Toolshed tool
47 Warm, in a way
51 Jerk
53 Indian drink made from yogurt
55 Italian number that's also a man's name
57 Piece of cake?
58 Bibliographic abbr.
59 Where scenes are made
62 Actor Daniel ___ Kim
63 Cavaliers' sch.

by Sophia Maymudes

## ACROSS

1 Presses (down)
6 Org. for the Houston Dynamo and Austin F.C.
9 Along for the ride, say
14 "Yeah, lunch now works for me"
16 Taurasi who leads the W.N.B.A. in career scoring
17 Showing promise
18 Tag
19 What you'd love to own and drive
20 Acknowledgment with a shrug
21 "This ___ here!"
22 Partner of day
24 2014 Television Hall of Fame inductee
25 Spirals out over the winter holidays?
29 Endorsement, for short
31 Gymnast Mary ___ Retton
32 Its members were collectively awarded Time magazine's 2017 Person of the Year
35 Unearned advantage based on sex
36 Hit HBO series based on a Liane Moriarty novel
37 What "minuscule" is often misspelled with
38 Stub hub?
39 Prep class subject, for short
40 Costa ___
42 Activity common in nightclubs, in brief
44 Italian for "so"
48 Tab on a Google search
50 Band together against
54 Lite
55 Question that's rarely a sign of good news
56 Buncha

57 Get overly personal, perhaps
58 Environmentalist Adams
59 They're good to know
60 Compound with a fruity smell

## DOWN

1 Key symbol near "!"
2 Tough nut to crack
3 Sang part of "Old MacDonald"
4 Beadlike bit on a surfer's necklace
5 Improbable
6 Ginormous
7 ___ Bassi, first woman to earn a doctorate in science (University of Bologna, 1732)
8 Garage brand
9 Like some threats
10 "Slow Hands" singer ___ Horan
11 Four on the floor?
12 Like tutoring, typically
13 Peaceful protest
15 Party org.
20 Pests for a grain farmer
23 Be sycophantic
26 Had quite a trip?
27 Styles associated with the Beatles
28 Taken care of, with "out"
30 ___ Cruz, so-called "Queen of Salsa"
32 Hat tricks are seen in them
33 "Thanks a ___!"
34 Parts of many rom-coms
35 Quick post-wedding getaway

36 World's largest pasta producer
41 Fire ___ (gemstone)
43 "Wasn't the first time enough?!"
45 Genre for Bridget Riley's "Shadow Play"
46 Crack
47 Aide for a cartoonist
49 It doesn't offer flights on Saturday mornings
51 Workers you wouldn't want to see in the office?
52 Group co-founded by Eazy-E
53 Splicing target
55 X

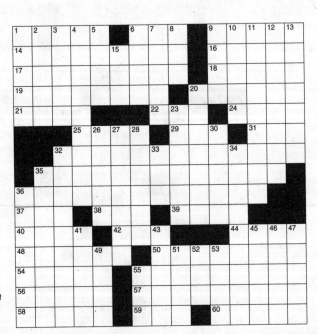

by Scott Earl

## ACROSS

1 Test that uses radioactive tracers
8 Behaves badly
15 Hyperbole from one approaching the buffet
17 Literary team playing in front of "ten thousand eyes"
18 Zoom call figure
19 Jack-in-the-box part
20 Goes along with the party line?
21 They're searched for in a rush
23 When "Ma is gettin' kittenish with Pap," in "Carousel"
24 Like some mail and laundry
27 Reduction indicators
31 Central event in 1960's "Inherit the Wind"
32 English football powerhouse, to fans
33 HI ring?
34 Like popping bubble wrap, for many
38 File size unit, informally
39 Speeds through Shakespeare?
40 Give away
41 Digital applications?
44 Certain Girl Scout cookies
45 Serenade need, perhaps
46 Cause of a feeding frenzy
47 Go to
50 Occupied leader?
51 Toponym in the dairy aisle
55 "Can you be less cryptic?"
58 Times when NPR listeners are engrossed enough to linger in their idling cars
59 Gloucester setting
60 Some bachelorette outings

## DOWN

1 Crux
2 Second, so to speak
3 Answer that would be more apt at 10 Down?
4 Entirety, redundantly
5 Actor Gulager of TV's "The Tall Man"
6 Mixed up
7 Tropical island whose name comes from the Spanish for "snows"
8 Home to the Trap Music Museum: Abbr.
9 It has its limits
10 Romantic's dream
11 "Ozymandias," e.g.
12 Master: Abbr.
13 Jimmy Carter's alma mater, briefly
14 Popular reunion swag
16 Backing
22 Count
23 ___ Ian, "Mean Girls" revenge seeker
24 Annoy downstairs neighbors, maybe
25 Opposite of 54-Down
26 Topographical map feature
27 Stuffs
28 Self-described "practical originalist" of the Supreme Court
29 City where Marco Polo was held as a prisoner of war
30 "Stop" and "Open," e.g.
32 Noted producer of blueberries
35 Discredited
36 German title
37 Went on and on and on and . . .
42 Labor-intensive tattoo type
43 Beverage steeped outdoors
44 Ungrammatical title of a 1984 Cyndi Lauper hit
46 Stuffs
47 Kind of power supply
48 ___ Westover, author of the 2018 best-selling memoir "Educated"
49 Junket
50 Thickness
52 ___ Owens a.k.a. Queen Latifah
53 Court fig.
54 Opposite of 25-Down
56 Suffix with Jacob
57 German granny

by John Lieb and Brad Wilber

## ACROSS

1 Has nowhere to go but down
6 Scepter topper
9 It's just the wurst!
13 Northernmost land in the Inner Hebrides
16 Prefix with nautical
17 Cut-and-paste tool for language learners
19 Piece of sensitive info, for short
20 Average
21 Name that sounds like two of its letters
22 Garden figure
25 Stoke
26 What a fitness coach likely leads
32 One-named rapper with the 2019 video "Can't Explain It"
33 Puts on the line, say
34 Word after dead or data
35 Browser button
36 Bedouins, e.g.
37 Post-punk sort
38 Squeeze (out)
39 Classic Disney character who never speaks
40 It can come as a relief
41 In-N-Out Burger's "Animal Style" burgers and fries, e.g.
44 [Gulp!]
45 Plus
46 Part of a church chorus
47 Theravada or Mahayana vis-à-vis Buddhism
49 Japanese assent
52 Like some headphones
56 People of northeastern Canada
57 Eagerly starting, as one's work
58 Streaks on the side of a wineglass

59 Word that becomes its own synonym if you change its first letter to WI
60 Bring to a boil

## DOWN

1 Gluttons
2 Those: Sp.
3 Well overdue
4 Powder holder
5 G, in a C major scale
6 West African food staple
7 "Star Trek" actress Jeri
8 Big ___
9 In which you might see an échappé sauté
10 Out of the ordinary
11 Pretentious, in a way
12 The point of 9-Down?
14 Queer designation

15 Instrument played by a pannist
18 Dr. for kids
23 Daughter of Styx
24 Things sometimes frozen
25 Requirements with some applications
26 Can't move a muscle, say
27 Crack under pressure
28 Boiling
29 Eponym for a mathematical pattern identified centuries earlier in India
30 "Eh, they can do that"
31 Spirit of a people
36 Range for a viola
37 Box-office revenue
39 Mostaccioli relative

40 Lead-in to male or female
42 Kind of monkey
43 Hwy. through Fargo and St. Paul
46 Tops
47 Fly (through)
48 "Our ___ always lasts longer than the happiness of those we ___": Heraclitus
50 Request a hand, say
51 Composer Stravinsky
52 Love of the game?
53 Their sales were surpassed again by phonograph records in 2020
54 Inits. near New York's Flushing Bay
55 Jeremy ___, first Asian-American N.B.A. champion

by Brooke Husic and Adam Nicolle

## ACROSS

1 What may need to be kneaded
9 Warning made with H.R. in mind
13 Dish that may be made in its own pan
14 ___ Lederer, a.k.a. Ann Landers
15 Test out
16 College in Poughkeepsie, N.Y.
17 Trace evidence?
18 Monopoly token
19 Shaded from the sun
20 Longtime "60 Minutes" correspondent
21 Hit taken willingly
22 Where cc's are seen
23 Radio amateur
26 It's often seen beside art
29 "Beg pardon . . ."
30 More than just moi
31 "The Fly," "The Host" or "The Thing"
34 "___ Nobody" (hit for Rufus and Chaka Khan)
35 Cereal container
36 D.___ (doctor of letters deg.)
37 Boston's flagship medical center, familiarly
40 Listing near a club?
41 ___ Ishii, Lucy Liu's character in "Kill Bill"
42 Demand during a gossip sesh
46 Blast furnace input
47 One is depicted on the Oregon license plate
48 McCarthyite called out in Billy Joel's "We Didn't Start the Fire"
50 Took shots with?

52 Metal oxide in dental crowns
53 Latin "between"
54 Plato is considered the father of it
55 Stadium in the Billie Jean King National Tennis Center
56 Artistic imitation

## DOWN

1 Soaks
2 Drops
3 Strengthen, as an embankment
4 ___ Gilbert, "The Vampire Diaries" protagonist
5 Cabana
6 Verdi opera set during the fifth century
7 & 8 Part of some shortcuts

8 See 7-Down
9 Glass home?
10 "Just say what you're going to say!"
11 Govt. body that approves warrant requests for spies
12 Milk provider
14 Word with man or fire
16 Defiant response
18 Desire
21 Edgar Allan Poe poem written for a woman named Jane, despite its title
24 Member of the only M.L.B. team never to have played in a World Series
25 Hardly a pro

26 Tests
27 Proverbial rarities
28 Sea ___ (grass seen in sand dunes)
31 Country that celebrates the new year ("Choul Chnam Thmey") in April
32 Log-in component
33 Street prowler
38 Many an intern
39 Could gobble right up
43 Cause to recall?
44 Invigorating substance
45 Literally, "skewer"
48 Rapper Flo ___
49 Receptionist's query
51 "BlacKkKlansman" director
52 Jack squat

by Kameron Austin Collins

## ACROSS

1 Spelunker's aid
5 Went (for)
10 Club alternatives
14 Home of the Polka Hall of Fame and Pro Football Hall of Fame
15 Interpret the parts of
16 Line for a sleigh ride
17 Olympics haul of fame?
19 European royal capital
20 Images that are nice and easy to look at
21 Master negotiator
23 Move named for the 19th-century skater Paulsen
24 Most milquetoast-y
25 Skill for a good physician
29 Heritage
30 Folk rock band with two 1965 #1 hits, with "the"
31 Org. with an Office of Air and Radiation
34 Some Tripadvisor listings
35 Light brown seals
36 "Frozen" character with antlers
37 It's not the final number: Abbr.
38 Skier's problem
39 Equanimity
40 Accept things as they are
43 Nurse's office supply
45 Sassy
46 Sport that made its first Olympics splash in 1904
47 Slot machine bonus
51 Piece of mind?
52 Crawl
54 Stretched out
55 2x

56 International grp. that's well financed?
57 Pump up
58 Did some crew work
59 Kind of force

## DOWN

1 Box on Broadway
2 Shouted greeting
3 Word with air or square
4 "This American Life" and others
5 Led the way
6 People-powered vehicles
7 It helps make waiting easier
8 Common night school class, for short
9 Goes to hell?
10 TV journalist Baldwin
11 Choice made while thinking "ugh"
12 Mahjong set
13 Ungenteel laugh
18 Long dresses
22 You can see right through it
24 On menus, it's often by the lobster
25 Big wheel at a party?
26 Millennia
27 "Keep on keepin' on!"
28 Biblical birthday gift
32 Capital of the Philippines
33 Over
35 Doesn't surrender
36 Charming vulnerability

38 Journalist Ifill who was depicted on a postage stamp in 2020
39 Israeli P.M. between Rabin and Netanyahu
41 Oxymorphone, for one
42 Followed
43 "Downton Abbey" daughter
44 Irrational thing to celebrate?
47 "Not ___!"
48 Follower of Oscar in the NATO alphabet
49 Snacks that drip
50 Head turner
53 Group depicted in the 2015 biopic "Straight Outta Compton"

*by Robyn Weintraub*

## ACROSS

1 Goof
16 Mischievous character in West African folklore
17 Hosts
18 David who took 15 years to write "The History of England"
19 Cut into
20 Andy Capp's wife in the comics
21 Somme times
22 Fabergé egg recipient
24 "The pretty worm of Nilus . . . that kills and pains not," per Shakespeare
26 Concept in Hinduism, Buddhism and Jainism
30 Swashbuckler's implement
32 Course
34 "You couldn't be more wrong!"
35 Diplomatic successes
39 Find inner strength
41 ___ Island
42 Will can change it
44 Total package?
46 Shameless sycophant
49 Doubly hyphenated fig.
50 Book it
52 Where the idiom "on a roll" comes from
55 Self starter?
57 Attendant of Dionysus
60 New Balance competitor
61 Passive-aggressive tactic
64 Renter's amenity
65 Gaze at with appreciation

## DOWN

1 Computer store
2 Have ___ (be able to save face)
3 Hit hard
4 Snarl
5 Sch. whose yearbook is the "Gumbo"
6 Strauss's "___ Nacht in Venedig"
7 Brouhaha
8 Aim for
9 Sets right
10 "Seriously!"
11 Place of salubrity
12 Two in a row, say?
13 Capital city near Kangaroo Island
14 It's called paraffin oil in the U.K.
15 Starts of hedges
23 Unkempt
25 Hold (up)
27 Unfulfilled duty
28 Staff
29 Sine qua non
31 What a whale watcher may watch
33 Mystery writer Buchanan
35 Doesn't go straight, in a way
36 Birthplace of Lewis Carroll
37 Julius Caesar's first wife
38 Wordsworth wrote one about a cuckoo
40 Web access co.
43 It has furrowed gray bark
45 Came in behind
47 ___ Brown, Whoopi Goldberg's role in "Ghost"
48 Established facts
51 Like some 44-Across
53 Part of mayo that's most popular?
54 No longer on the table
56 Cranks (up)
58 Urges
59 Play a critical role?
61 Block letters?
62 Bryce Harper when he won a 2015 M.V.P. award, e.g.
63 Tax

*by Trenton Charlson*

## ACROSS

1 Cases of false incrimination
9 Groom
14 Band featured in Disney World's Rock 'n' Roller Coaster
16 Bumper adornment
17 Last of the Ptolemys
18 Train through eight states
19 Thin in tone
20 Supporting
21 "Alas . . ."
22 Ford vehicle, familiarly
23 Black Sea resort town
25 Splitting of hairs?
26 Word with over 400 definitions in the O.E.D.
27 Sweat ___
29 When doubled, a 2010s hip-hop fad
30 Draws
31 Bites, in a sense
33 Gaffer's supply
36 Most sacred
37 Low draw
38 Scholarly work
39 O'er and o'er
40 Big name in pizza rolls
42 Cardinal pts.?
45 Thick manes
47 Certain gown wearers
48 River past Louisville
49 Rolls, e.g.
51 Partner of all
52 Heard, but not seen
53 Last of the Greeks
54 She's the responsible one in the group, colloquially
56 Whiz

57 Not the glamorous sort
58 Sanctify
59 Animal in the suborder Vermilingua ("worm tongue")

## DOWN

1 "Truth be told . . ."
2 Fix, as a winter coat
3 Hannah who wrote "The Human Condition"
4 Distracted, as with romantic feelings
5 Best Driver, for one
6 Actress Thurman
7 Hidden dangers
8 Perambulates
9 Palms, e.g., for short
10 Run through
11 Winter Olympics pairs event
12 1995 cult classic directed by Kevin Smith
13 Try out before release, as a game
15 Short-story writer Bret
23 Holiday hearth feature
24 One of the Fates
27 Muscly
28 Tennis great Monica
30 Home/school link, for short
32 Word with hot or fresh
33 Make an unwanted appearance in a video call

34 Not requiring a suit, say
35 Loud chewing, for many
36 Mr. Fixit
38 Roll player
41 March
42 "If you don't tell them, I will," e.g.
43 Senator Feinstein of California
44 Do some bonding
46 Wise guys
48 Spirited message board?
50 Dojo levels
52 "Rule, Britannia" composer
55 Muscly, say

by Sophia Maymudes and Kyra Wilson

## ACROSS

1 High branch, for short
7 "Don't make me laugh!"
13 Library of Alexandria collection
14 It reaches Washington heights
15 First name in flight
16 Boxer whose full name is made up of only three different letters
17 Pea piercers
18 Endangered wetlands reptile of the northeastern U.S.
19 Name in a noted '90s breakup
20 Back up
21 Bagel variety
22 Pull (out)
23 Sterling Cooper ___ Pryce ("Mad Men" ad agency)
25 Pig tail?
26 Break down for closer analysis, as data
30 Iconic iPhone addition of 2011
33 Ones exploited in a capitalist system, per Marx
35 Corvine cry
38 First international rock band to play in Cuba (2016), with "the"
39 Raider's grp.
40 Hardly klutzy
43 Christine ___ Whitman, first female governor of New Jersey
44 Victorian greeting
45 Dead tree edition
47 Hat tips
48 "Anyhoo . . ."
49 Shout from a teen's bedroom
50 Petty tyrants
51 Green party?
52 Diamonds used in fashion
53 Places of rest

## DOWN

1 Whirlpools
2 Sleeveless undergarment
3 Family time at the pool
4 Shortest-serving U.S. vice president (31 days)
5 "Exodus" novelist
6 "Cheap Thrills" pop star
7 Dressage criterion
8 Grease
9 Snafu
10 Having a gap
11 "Whoa, ___!"
12 Position
14 Inductee into the National Toy Hall of Fame five years after his sister
16 They go around in circles
18 High-flying picnic game
20 "___ Wife," Pulitzer Prize-winning George Kelly play
23 Already: Fr.
24 Like corduroy
27 Yoga pose done on hands and knees
28 Acts lovey-dovey
29 Lent feature
31 Topping brand with multiple misspellings in its name
32 Proposed legislation often debated alongside the DACA program
34 Goes along
35 Literally, "heads"
36 Moroccan resort city on the Atlantic
37 Clearing
41 Like herons and flamingos
42 Documentarian Morris
44 Unexpected windfall, figuratively
46 Give up
47 Insensitive sort
49 Major vitamin retailer

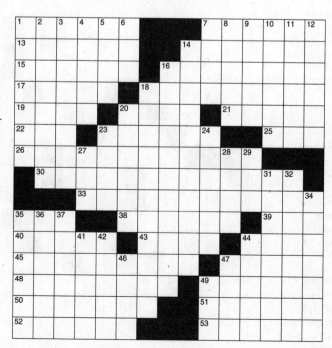

*by Ryan McCarty*

# 58

## ACROSS

1 Thrilled
12 Browsing inits.
15 Suitable for printing
16 Fig. in annual reports
17 Shows respect, in a way
18 Rocket Mortgage FieldHouse athlete, for short
19 Hydroxides, e.g.
20 Line on a bill
21 "No way" man
22 Brainiac, stereotypically
23 Lead-in to one or time
25 Group that grows every May
27 Numero su un orologio
28 Master
29 Windblown
30 Lushes
32 Targets of snuffers
33 Home of a Big 12 school
35 Unhealthy
36 Rest
37 Place of rest
38 Singer Womack with the 2000 hit "I Hope You Dance"
40 Heighten
42 Depot info, for short
43 [That was bad of you!]
46 Synagogue holding
47 Lifeguard's concern, in brief
48 Elisabeth of "CSI"
49 "___ shut me up in Prose" (Emily Dickinson poem)
50 Key on a keyboard
52 Block
54 Frosted ___ Flakes (breakfast cereal)
55 Period following the Renaissance
57 Healthy
58 Get 10 from one?
59 Fish ___
60 In this world

## DOWN

1 One eighth
2 More prideful
3 Hit Fox drama starting in 2015
4 Maintain, in a way, as a lawn
5 "___: Legacy" (2010 film sequel)
6 "Birds in an Aquarium" artist
7 "Thanks in old age— thanks ___ I go": Walt Whitman
8 Chaotic
9 National Memorial Cemetery of the Pacific locale
10 Whoopi's "Ghost" role
11 Weekly magazine publisher since 1896: Abbr.
12 Flash source
13 Venomous swimmer
14 Peaceful protests
21 Kind of calendar
24 Without regard for privacy
26 Close to the bottom
28 Ovary's place
29 Out
30 Place in battle formation
31 Cry after a score, maybe
33 Critic's place, so to speak
34 What the Wicked Witch of the West called Dorothy
37 Discard
39 Originally
41 Mead holder
43 Argument
44 Numbers game?
45 One of the Wayans brothers
47 Lifted
48 Get 10 from two?
51 Blue
53 Kind of lab
55 "Aladdin" character who's transformed into an elephant
56 Distant

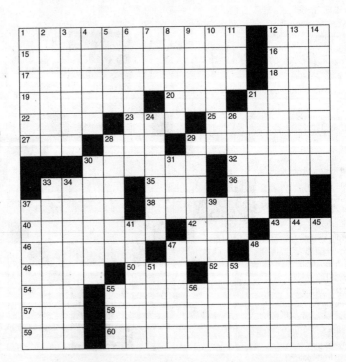

by Jacob Stulberg

## ACROSS

1 Barbecue chef's coat
8 Angry Birds starting in 2010, e.g.
15 Pick up
16 Something on a ticket
17 Deeply felt
18 Small stabs
19 Overused
20 "Kinda"
22 Company with a buck in its logo
23 Literary character self-described as "poor, obscure, plain and little"
24 Ostracized sort
26 Plane wing part
27 Inits. after a big media merger of 1958
28 All-weather convertible?
30 Alternative to Food Lion or Piggly Wiggly
31 1990s "caught on tape" series
33 Vagaries
35 "No hard feelings?"
37 Query about a phone call
40 Many a maid of honor
44 Roach of old comedy
45 In the dictionary, say
47 Mitsubishi sports car, for short
48 Some thirst quenchers
50 Shrinking
51 Seed coat
52 Something water lacks
54 Tranquil and minimalistic
55 It might reveal what you've lost
56 Up to speed, musically
58 Something to pick a number from
60 One taking heat at work?
61 Synthetic dye compound
62 "Talk to the hand"
63 Gives a number?

## DOWN

1 One pressing the flesh
2 Subspecies of a distinct geographical variety
3 Features of many doctor's office waiting rooms
4 Veil material
5 Widespread
6 Latin American soccer powerhouse: Abbr.
7 It's what you think
8 Assured
9 [Take THAT!]
10 Within
11 Banquets
12 Not merely good
13 Aristocracy
14 Pre-euro money
21 What a wormhole is a tunnel in
24 Court blowout
25 Took it easy
28 Pricey strings
29 iPhone rival
32 Brief topic
34 D.M.V. demands
36 Hot spot
37 Thoughts of wishful thinkers
38 Imbibed modestly
39 Ingredient in Pringles Light
41 Unit in superfast data transfer
42 Old Scratch, with "the"
43 Wearable status symbols
46 Stealth fighters
49 Provide direction
51 Express starting in 2000
53 Model who wrote the 1996 book "True Beauty"
55 Fall rapidly, as sales
57 Grocery brand that's also a girl's name
59 "Les Mille et ___ Nuits"

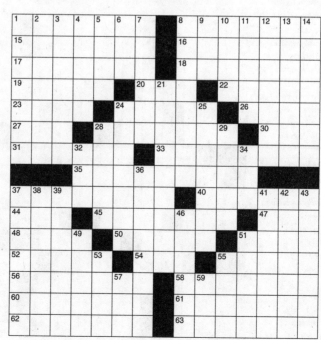

by Roland Huget

## ACROSS

1 After the hour
5 Lou who wrote "Exporting America"
10 Plague, with "at"
14 Instrument with a bent neck
15 Key
16 Defraud, in slang
17 Very much
18 Recreational sites not designed for walkers
20 Is a bad loser, say
22 Family name in Sir Walter Scott's "The Bride of Lammermoor"
23 Fr. title
24 Zimbalist of old TV
26 One of the renters in Steinbeck's "Tortilla Flat"
30 Founder of the American Shakers
32 Sweet pitcherful
34 Important word to a marriage counselor
35 New homeowner's feeling, maybe
39 @fakechucknorris, for one
40 Diorama, maybe
41 Updated art?
42 Wrap (up)
43 Things to do after dinner
46 Painter's primer
48 President who said "If you want to see your plays performed the way you wrote them, become president"
51 Secret ending
52 Word before or after state
54 Ricoh rival
56 They're "family"
60 Pride : lions :: parliament : ___
61 God for whom a weekday is named

62 Real stinker
63 All-nighter, maybe
64 Like high school and college students of the '80s–'90s, e.g.
65 Competitive and outgoing, say
66 Views

## DOWN

1 Bank deposit
2 Fall
3 Record stat for major-leaguer Rickey Henderson
4 Running event
5 Slam
6 Title role in a 1993 film . . . which sounds like a prize the film won
7 Unimpressed

8 Character who dies at the end of "Little Women"
9 Editorial reversal
10 Burkina Faso neighbor
11 Here-there connection
12 Require (of)
13 Jazzman Montgomery
19 The first one was a modified Ford D-Series truck
21 "Toodles"
25 What a meow may mean
27 Grammy-nominated 2011 Lady Gaga album
28 Aphrodisia
29 Dug stuff
31 Bonus upon signing, e.g.
33 Adjudicate
36 George Dickel product

37 ___ and violins (music pun)
38 Some French votes
39 Without any filler
40 Newsstand offering, informally
44 Change with the times
45 Intuits
47 Big name in shapewear
49 Start to malfunction
50 Author with a restaurant at the Eiffel Tower named for him
53 Like Hansel and Gretel in the forest
55 Bead producer?
56 Part of the works
57 "How Sleep the Brave," e.g.
58 28-Down, e.g.
59 Handle preceder

by Andrew J. Ries

## ACROSS

1 Back in
10 Golf or tennis lesson topic
14 Time Lords, e.g.
15 Kimchi solution
16 Something that may help control the border?
17 Shop item
18 Roast figures
19 Anchovy or sand eel
20 Same old
21 Fix permanently
23 X factor?
24 House flip, e.g.
25 Very loud
27 Celebrity ex of Bruce and Ashton
29 With 26-Down, bit of winter fun
30 Really hot
32 1978 Nobel sharer
34 Requisite
36 Like some extreme diets
39 Part of a Guardian Angel's attire
41 Roast figures
43 Comic who was the 2012 presidential nominee of the Peace and Freedom Party
46 Bangkok banknotes
48 Join the club, in Canterbury
49 "Either way works for me"
51 Mother of the wind gods
53 One of two in a tournament
54 Cousin of ibid.
55 Run
57 Follower
58 Davis of "The Accidental Tourist"
59 "Shh!"
61 Mock wedding setting in Shakespeare
62 Words before a business's date of establishment
63 Bracket position
64 Person on a quick vacation, maybe

## DOWN

1 Carpaccio, e.g.
2 Tiny orbiter
3 50-50, e.g.
4 Like the lower half of Haiti's flag
5 Georges
6 Game with an official called a stickman
7 It "paralyzes life," per Martin Luther King Jr.
8 Tools descended from alpenstocks
9 Warrant, e.g.: Abbr.
10 They often turn knees green
11 Initiation, e.g.
12 Yoga class directive
13 Like bananas in banana splits
15 Like the upper half of Haiti's flag
22 Cockamamie
24 Free from
26 See 29-Across
28 "Wowser!"
31 Topper for Chaplin's Tramp
33 Parcel portion
35 Org. concerned with some labs
37 Thrill during an excavation
38 Bond seen in "Wayne's World"
40 Obviously Catholic person, in a snarky rhetorical question
42 Ending with gun or mud
43 Manure byproduct
44 Coulomb per second
45 What coastlines may do
47 Perfectly
50 N.B.A. coach Van Gundy
52 Was lousy
55 Put one over on
56 Instead
60 Blood group?

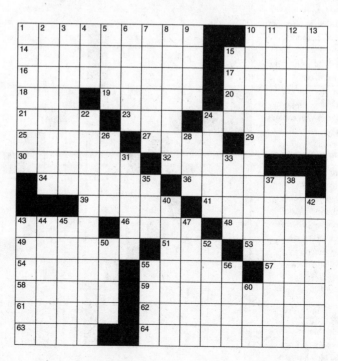

by Andrew Kingsley

## ACROSS

1 "The Great" or "the Terrible"
8 Have more stripes than
15 Yankees closer Rivera
16 "Not gonna happen!"
17 Senselessness
18 Authentic
19 Like pork pie and clotted cream
21 Femme with a halo
22 Hustle
24 Eponymous physicist Ernst
25 Training tally
29 John with an Oscar
31 Bewildered
33 Turnpike ticket listings
35 Best Actress nominee for "Philomena," 2013
37 Sorority character
38 Better adversary to deal with, in a saying
41 Unlikely husband material
42 Looks like a 41-Across
43 Name on an excavator
44 Old blacklisting org.
46 Brownies with cookies, maybe
48 Fostered
49 Turnovers, e.g.
51 Absorb
53 Activate, as a wah-wah pedal
55 Husband material
59 Genre for Ladysmith Black Mambazo
61 1984 biography subtitled "The Man, the Dancer"
63 Royal Stewart and Clan Donald
64 Bugs
65 Needs blessing, maybe
66 They play just north of the Ravens

## DOWN

1 Queen's longtime record label
2 Postal sheet
3 Only remaining home of the Asiatic cheetah
4 Sound repeatedly heard at a wedding reception
5 Flags down
6 Decoy
7 Little green men
8 Has way more than enough, for short
9 See 50-Down
10 Approximate end of a rush hour
11 Like some census data
12 Spot for spirited worshipers
13 Cape Ann's area
14 It's capped and often slapped
20 Something to enter with a card
23 TV character who fronted as a waste management consultant
25 [Gag!]
26 Aid in clearing the air
27 Apartment that's a second home
28 No-frills: Abbr.
30 "Junior" or "senior" mil. figure
32 Like some stalled vehicles
34 French seasoning
36 Ginnie Mae's dept.
39 One who might drug a boxer
40 ___ Mo', five-time Grammy-winning bluesman
45 Hoffman won Best Actor for playing him
47 Chief flight attendant
50 1967 Cold War suspense novel by 9-Down
52 Florence's ___ Palace
53 Scores of these may plague high schoolers
54 Less than slim
56 Chat, across the Pyrénées
57 Setting of Sisyphus' perpetual rock-pushing
58 Almond or pecan
60 Additions after closings, in brief
62 One of three for Sisyphus?

by Angela Olson Halsted

## ACROSS

**1** Popular playground pastime
**9** Pacific demonstrations
**15** News source with a "For the Record" feature
**16** "Oh yeah!"
**17** Remarkably rapid
**18** Overall
**19** Producer of boxing rings
**20** City in Central Macedonia
**22** Permanent marker
**23** Violinist Kavafian
**24** Looks down
**25** Actress Campbell
**26** "Dear ___" ("Double Fantasy" song)
**28** Actress Thurman
**29** Charles who starred in the 1938 drama "Algiers"
**30** Slightly
**33** Prized game fish
**35** He played Ant-Man in 2015's "Ant-Man"
**36** Place
**37** Come out on top
**40** Betraying extreme embarrassment
**43** Prepare, as some Mexican food
**44** Movie-archiving org.
**46** Bulbous perennial
**47** Women's issue?
**48** Series finale
**50** Partner of 9-Down
**51** Downwind
**52** What small cranes may produce
**53** Tourist haven with the capital Denpasar
**54** Home to the Zapotec people
**56** Politician's accessory
**58** Letter closing
**59** Share confidences with
**60** He wrote "Lust's passion will be served; it demands, it militates, it tyrannizes"
**61** Warm, inviting facial feature

## DOWN

**1** Camp classic
**2** Words of understanding
**3** They result in very fast response times
**4** "Superhits of the Superstars" label
**5** Reaction from a tough crowd
**6** Seller of TV and magazine spots, informally
**7** Knocked senseless
**8** Oration location
**9** Partner of 50-Across
**10** College just north of New York City
**11** Squirt
**12** "Nice going, jerk!"
**13** "Far less than that"
**14** Longhorns' rivals
**21** Blocks, e.g.
**25** Common beach policy
**27** Works of a lifetime
**29** Imported wheels?
**31** Xmas, for Jimmy Buffett
**32** First name in infamy
**34** It may be labeled "XXX"
**37** Install, as software before shipping
**38** Software event
**39** Sorry
**40** 2013 World Series M.V.P., to fans
**41** French motto part
**42** Restaurant with a "playful" name
**45** "How ya holdin' up?"
**48** United base
**49** "Dumb and Dumber" drive destination
**52** Looped in, in a way
**53** Midnight, e.g.
**55** Seat of Missouri's Douglas County
**57** Appropriate answer for this clue

*by James Mulhern*

## ACROSS

1 Feature of the European Union
12 Half a ten-spot
15 Slipped
16 Loafer alternative, for short
17 "Definitely not that!"
18 Part of a press kit
19 Flat, e.g.: Abbr.
20 See 34-Across
21 Grave robbers
23 Land in which political parties are banned
24 She created a monster
25 First name in hot dogs
28 Goes from stem to stern, maybe?
29 Off
30 Fix, as some neckwear
31 Bambino
32 Nix
33 Sound of the Northwest
34 With 20-Across, relocate
35 Many a large desk or sofa
36 Ingredients in the national drink of Puerto Rico, to Puerto Ricans
37 An elephant seal will fight for one
38 Vassal
40 Part-human gods
41 "Be my guest!"
42 Moors
43 Melodious
44 Romance novelist Tami
45 TV band
48 Part of some punt returns
49 Like marriage supported by Loving v. Virginia
52 End of the King James Bible?

53 Fixer-upper, often
54 Unlikely to change
55 Course that offers mixed results?

## DOWN

1 Bradley with many medals
2 One getting framed
3 Brand with the flavor French Silk
4 It gets tons of traffic
5 Where many Loyalists resettled after the American Revolution
6 Real name of Ben, in a sci-fi classic
7 Actress Saoirse with two Oscar nominations
8 Stray calf: Var.
9 Decline
10 Camps in the wild

11 "Told ya!"
12 Not bedridden
13 Blew a gasket
14 Caves and coral reefs, for example
22 Cry when un gol is scored
23 Exceedingly
24 The 4-Down has millions of them
25 Is way too introspective
26 Take the edge off
27 Someone gets belted at the end of it
28 Actress Mullally with two Emmys
30 Rush
33 Red stuffing?
34 Sights at a martial arts center
36 What a bad cold may do

37 Places to fix flaps
39 Too-sweet sentiment
40 Prepared, as some scallops or tuna
42 Strength
44 For the goose, not the gander?
45 Alto clef instrument
46 Mie ___, actress who played the Bond girl Kissy Suzuki
47 Turned tail
50 Figures in some univ. classes
51 Dance bit?

by John Guzzetta

# 65

## ACROSS

1 "The Haywain Triptych" painter
6 Classic novel written under the nom de plume Currer Bell
14 Its logo consists of a pair of calipers in an oval
15 Present some opportunities
17 Officially prohibit
18 1998 Spike Lee movie
19 Gesture of razzle-dazzlement
21 System developed by Bell Labs
22 Strict limitation, of a sort
23 Italian brewery since 1846
25 Wine aperitif
26 Sister and wife of Cronus
28 Dish often served with applesauce
29 Friendly introduction?
30 "
32 4.5 billion years, for the age of the earth: Abbr.
33 "So soon?"
34 "Gotcha"
37 Opposite of slow
38 Texter's "Oh, yeah . . ."
41 "Gotcha"
43 A cry of relief
45 It's searched for in a rush
46 Some dispenser items
47 Agitated
49 "Outside the Lines" airer
50 Heck of an effort
52 Web deposit?
55 It may be used by a person who is bowing
56 One with many enemies
57 Young migratory fish
58 Harbinger of spring
59 Narrow apertures

## DOWN

1 Something a bomber delivers?
2 Vast
3 C-c-c-cold
4 Rage
5 Sarcastic response to a 1-Down
6 "Steel-driving man" of African-American lore
7 Took off on
8 Sources of prints, for short
9 "Another Day on Earth" musical artist
10 Setting for Yankees home games: Abbr.
11 Dish eaten with a spoon
12 Lost Colony's island
13 Royal wraps
16 Like some pigs
20 Victim of Paris
23 Activity in a drive
24 "Don't get all worked up!"
27 Nail the test
31 Not dead yet
33 What tipplers may have
34 Value
35 Impetuous person
36 Scuba gear component
38 "Blaze of Glory" band, 1990
39 Eight-line verse form
40 Luxury home features
42 Like finished wood
44 Matisse, Derain and fellow artists, with "les"
48 A biker may have a nasty one
50 Recipient of a royal charter, with "the"
51 Commercial lead-in to Bank, in many Midwest states
53 Miss the mark
54 Chi-___ (religious symbol)

*by Damon Gulczynski*

## ACROSS

1 Call from a bar, maybe
10 Allied (with)
15 She played Odin's wife in "Thor"
16 Key ingredient?
17 App with an envelope icon
18 Warren with the 1978 platinum album "Excitable Boy"
19 Onetime label for the Beatles
20 Pickup line?
21 Pre-euro money
22 Is no longer good
24 Wreck locale
26 Arm muscles, in bodybuilding lingo
27 "Your Movie ___" (Roger Ebert book)
29 Served whoppers?
30 Lout's lack
31 What's exited in Brexit
33 Sci-fi shocker
35 Bastes, e.g.
37 Penguin's perch
38 [I can't believe that just happened!]
42 Somewhat
45 Somewhat
46 Whole bunch
48 "Specifically . . ."
50 Ned's adoptive son on "Game of Thrones"
51 Town where "Parks and Recreation" is set
53 Roman-Parthian War figure
54 1965 hit for the Yardbirds
56 Salad dressing brand
58 Juan Perón's second wife
59 Real shocker
60 Features of some city streets

62 They come before deals
63 "Keep your pants on!"
64 Put on the line
65 Crying for attention?

## DOWN

1 Tumbling equipment
2 Tear into
3 Disconnect, as a trailer
4 Lead-in to Luddite
5 Fast-food empire builder
6 "The Black Tulip" novelist, 1850
7 Juan Perón's third wife
8 "Since you weren't listening . . ."
9 Twitter titter
10 Measured (up)
11 "Riders in the Sky" singer, 1949
12 Something cold from Mars
13 Blue prints
14 Power line?
21 Piano parts
23 Not straight
25 Grievance
28 Creep out?
30 Best Actress winner for "Monster"
32 Jazz devotee, most likely
34 Road rage sound
36 Whole bunch
38 Alternatives to chimichangas
39 Superhero with the foe Professor Von Gimmick
40 Game in which jokers and twos are wild

41 Guy's sling swimsuit
43 Many a Taylor Swift fan
44 Part of a circulatory system
47 Check out quickly
49 Warm and cozy
51 Break down in school
52 Newman, to Seinfeld
55 Easy to walk all over
57 Spill (over)
60 Marcel Marceau moniker
61 Caregivers' org.

by Paolo Pasco

## ACROSS

1 You'll see things in them you can't handle
13 Best-selling celebrity tell-all book of 1978
14 Something work-related
15 Forgivable
16 Answer rudely
17 Inflexible, as rules
20 Stock market events
21 Edited for television, maybe
22 Sitcom set in Lanford, Ill.
26 Ben-___ (N.F.L. cheerleading squad)
27 Final car built in Buick City before its shutdown
28 Estadio cheer
29 A little cleaner
30 Fish ladder site
33 Physicist who formulated the two laws of electrolysis
34 What bugs are found in
35 Completes the purchase of
37 Gas in an ion thruster
38 Medieval invader of Spain
39 Tops of the Mounties
41 Onetime White House family
44 Parlor fixture
45 They're known as "Viennese bread" in Scandinavia
49 Helped someone move into an office, say
50 Common baby food

## DOWN

1 "___ vobiscum" ("the Lord be with you")
2 Influence
3 Minor
4 One rolling dough
5 Plumeria creation
6 Stir
7 Wants
8 ___ Bill Weedles (Land of Oz character)
9 "Bacchus and ___" (Titian painting)
10 Gradually become noticeable
11 Slip away
12 Changes back
13 Item worn by the Count on "Sesame Street"
14 Post box's contents
15 Spica's constellation
18 Concert venues
19 Back-to-back moves
23 Eminent scholar
24 Company that bought (and later sold) Skype
25 Cannonball's path
27 Old Roman coins
29 More south of the border?
30 Stood for
31 Makes up (for)
32 Parson's residence
33 Over-the-counter product?
34 Inseparable duo
35 Permanent magnet metal
36 Repair shop amenity
37 Nissan model discontinued in 2015
38 Statistical calculations
40 Name on a bottle of Pleasures perfume
42 City near Turin
43 Hebrew letter on a dreidel
46 Noted writer who married his first cousin when she was 13
47 Along with
48 National Grandparents' Day mo.

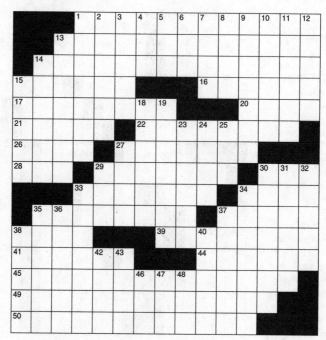

*by Patrick Berry*

## ACROSS

1 Epiglottis, for one
5 Doc's subscription
9 Navy enlistee, informally
13 Seducer of Josef in Kafka's "The Trial"
14 C.D.C. concern
16 Like some plugs
17 Let out
18 "You know so-and-so, too? How about that!"
20 Tony's cousin
21 ___ for life
22 One involved in job cuts?
23 Alternatives to plugs
25 D.C.'s ___ Memorial, site next to West Potomac Park
26 Assent for 61-Across
27 Discounted
28 Medieval entertainer
29 Does some hosting, briefly
30 Stat for David Ortiz
31 Egg: Prefix
32 Lamb, e.g.
33 "Sexiest job of the 21st century," per Harvard Business Review
37 Wee
38 Graze, for example
39 Blood
40 Far out
41 Reverse
42 Concerns for sociologists
46 Chin-___
47 "NewsHour" airer
48 "Peanuts" alter ego
49 Leave the country?
51 One might be made with a handshake
52 Europe's Gulf of ___
53 Comedian with the 2016 memoir "Born a Crime"
55 Mideast's Gulf of ___
56 Actress Suvari

57 Planning to, informally
58 Coup
59 Sistine Chapel depiction
60 Enemy of ISIS, with "the"
61 Ones whose assent is 26-Across

## DOWN

1 Seek refuge at
2 Co-star of "Some Like It Hot"
3 Ill feeling
4 Bout of feeling sorry for oneself
5 Oscar-nominated actor who has written several humor pieces for The New Yorker
6 Tops
7 Certain barrier to entry
8 Completely
9 It's hardly a breath of fresh air
10 Practice for combat
11 Waiter outside a seafood restaurant, maybe
12 Doctor's prescription
15 "You said it!"
19 "You said it!"
24 Historic isle in the Tyrrhenian Sea
25 Top go-to
28 Librettist for Verdi's "Otello" and "Falstaff"
32 After Tetris, the second-best-selling video game of all time
33 Tended to, as a baby
34 Director's cry that's said with a pause
35 Boors
36 Run low on juice
37 "I'm telling you the truth"
41 Beehive, for one
43 "Beats me"
44 Fold, in a way
45 Skews
48 Wardrobe item for which Obama claimed he was "unfairly maligned"
50 Actress ___ Rachel Wood
51 Radius, but not diameter
54 Present

by Kyle Mahowald

## ACROSS

1 War game
9 Short write-ups
15 "Time was . . ."
16 Treat eaten with a spoon
17 2007 N.A.A.C.P. Image Award winner for "Inside Man"
18 Top-notch
19 Baseball's Martinez
20 They're on the books
22 Deducts from
23 Like a zebra's mane
25 Détentes
27 Language traditionally written without spaces between words
28 Cardinal topper
30 Wharf workers' grp.
31 "Nuts!"
32 "Holy cow!"
34 "Her ___" ("Miss Saigon" song)
35 Resident of the Corn State
39 Challenge for a barber
41 Lovesickness, e.g.
42 1973 Tony nominee for "A Little Night Music"
44 Power-packed engine
45 ___ comparison
46 Contractual problems?
51 The end of Caesar?
52 Barrymore and more
54 Not easily moved
55 E'en if
57 City on Utah Lake
59 Fuss
60 One of two party leaders
62 Browns, in a way

64 Full circuit
65 High-rise pants and horn-rimmed glasses, say
66 "Deliciously Different" sloganeer
67 "Sit tight"

## DOWN

1 Satiny quality
2 Be a wannabe
3 Netted, in a way
4 Key figure in saving New York City from bankruptcy
5 GPS generation: Abbr.
6 Something needed to raise the bar?
7 Not miss ___
8 "You don't say!"
9 Old map abbr.
10 Squats strengthen them
11 "___ a broken heart": Dickinson
12 "You don't say!"
13 Just deserts for misconduct
14 Salted away?
21 Part of many a submarine
24 "Rent" actor Diggs
26 Shouts heard at a rodeo
29 Hot Wheels product
31 "How stupid am I!"
33 Sneak
35 Flip
36 Have no accomplice
37 Response to "Not now," often
38 Perception
40 Things weighed in pounds?
43 Distinctive features of tamago gohan servings, in Japanese cuisine
47 Clip, say
48 Palliate
49 Like some catches and crashes
50 Keeper of the flame?
52 "Tell me more"
53 Unit of rain or ice
56 Ship or plane part
58 Virginia willow's genus
61 Covers with some rolls
63 It's way over your head

by Frederick J. Healy

## ACROSS

1 Its ribs stick out
11 "Fiddlesticks!"
15 First Chinese-American cabinet member
16 Seeing through
17 Where to stick a stick
18 Owner of the horse Sleipnir
19 Latin 101 word
20 Abbr. before Friday
21 Improvised jazz strain
23 Surrender
25 Showing signs of age
26 Rapidly down
29 Artsy L.A. district
31 Washington Post competitor: Abbr.
32 "Jurassic Park" co-star Sam
33 Teddy material
34 Not to, say
35 Omen
36 Like the function $ax^3 + bx^2 + cx + d$
37 Come up with
38 Word sometimes elided to its middle letter
39 Thwarts
40 [!!!!]
41 The Romans obtained a purple one from snails
42 Draw money?
43 They're often drawn at night
44 Base order
46 Mar. figure
48 Record of the year?
50 Castigate
51 Colosseum crowd?
54 Dropped, as poll numbers
55 Certain Internet hoax
58 Take a hit
59 News of flight delays, say
60 Sources of ricotta cheese
61 Unwavering look

## DOWN

1 First name in country
2 Occasional "S.N.L." host, to "S.N.L."
3 Who wrote "Wise men learn more from fools than fools from the wise"
4 Vixen's offspring
5 "110%" effort
6 Vocalist for the Black Eyed Peas
7 Flat tube?
8 Tuna type
9 Button-___ (hit everything at once, in gamer lingo)
10 Hippie-influenced fashion trend
11 Grace ___, servant in "Jane Eyre"
12 Curries, samosas, etc.
13 Staple of Thai cuisine
14 Dives
22 Suffix with magne-
23 Corduroy rib
24 Turns on
26 Vulgar
27 Highlighter color
28 Bug
30 Big name in escalators
33 Diamonds, e.g.
36 Smartphone heading
37 Some back-and-forth
39 Mythical piper
40 Voluptuous
43 Kind of column
45 Another name for Pluto
47 Used too much
49 Jazzman Baker
51 Reid of "Sharknado"
52 Luxury hotel in London's Piccadilly district, with "the"
53 Word after who, what or where
56 Hacker's tool
57 Part of a gig

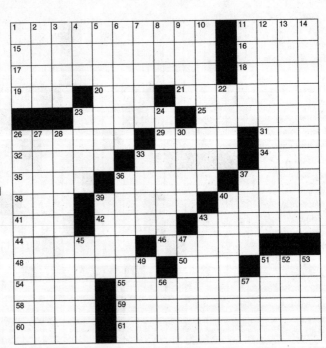

by David Steinberg

## ACROSS

1 Was almost, with "on"
9 New England staple
14 Owing
16 Brand with a "PM" variety
17 "Bow your heads . . ."
18 Strength
19 Loyal subject
20 Can
21 Hacker's success
22 Things are unlikely when they are long
23 Prohibition's beginning
25 Prince George's mom
26 Day spa treatment
27 Many a promotional media giveaway
29 Not as shy as one might think
30 Bad feeling
31 Title nickname of filmdom's Lt. Jordan O'Neil
33 Raising hell
36 In stitches
37 Prison in which Timothy Leary was housed next to Charles Manson
38 Asks a loaded question, say
39 Antipiracy grp.
40 "Ain't gonna happen"
42 Lame
45 One may make tracks
47 Alternative to a "Psst!"
48 They click
49 Barbershop part
51 Transcription product
52 "Silence is golden," e.g.
53 Floor
54 Exploits
56 Like some communities
57 Something to work out in
58 When to wish someone un prospero año nuevo
59 10 years, for example

## DOWN

1 Puff out
2 The so-called "People of the Standing Stone"
3 Like "Last Tango in Paris," initially
4 Therapy group?
5 Cousin of Manx
6 Single curl or crunch, in the gym
7 Beam's path?
8 Really ready to rest
9 Aid for an ed.
10 Sound heard shortly after "Here's to . . ."
11 Dollar, for one
12 Suggestion
13 Innocent
15 Diocesan assembly
23 "Ain't gonna happen"
24 Desi Arnaz Jr. was on its first cover
27 It has a chilling effect
28 "That makes two of us"
30 Danger while drying out
32 ___ d'orange
33 Like many lines fed to actors
34 Lady's counterpart
35 Put off
36 Cold wine-and-nutmeg drink
38 "You'd better brace yourself for this . . ."
41 Rennin results in them
42 Western heat?
43 Cutting
44 Bump down
46 Demolition site sight
48 Shepherd's home
50 Fresh styling
52 Something catching?
55 Led

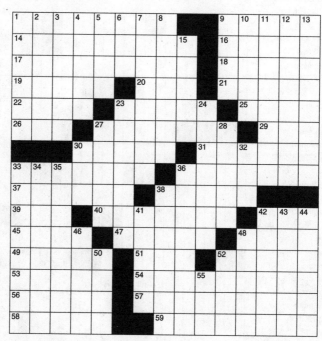

by Steve Overton

## ACROSS

1 Take a while to wear off
5 Bird food holder
9 Allow through
14 Big dog
16 "It Is Never Too Late to Mend" novelist, 1856
17 The Fab Four kicked it off
19 Like many sub-Saharan languages
20 What often follows grace
21 Their tops can produce "power output"
27 Nitrogen source for plants
28 Put in firmly
29 Michelangelo and others
34 With nothing on
35 Title mankini wearer in a 2006 film
36 Woman often depicted 34-Across by 29-Across
37 Didn't release
38 Astronomical discovery initially called Xena
39 Ingredient in some mulled wine
41 File menu option
43 Locale of Franklin County . . . or of Aretha Franklin's birth: Abbr.
44 Workout area?
50 Music direction to stop playing
51 Celebrity astrologer Sydney ____
52 Usually anonymous newspaper worker
57 They're more important than quarters
58 Bavaria, per part of its official name
59 Seahawks stadium name before 2011
60 Twitter feature
61 Something pulled uphill

## DOWN

1 Orientation letters?
2 Orientation aid
3 River that Henry Miller likened to "a great artery running through the human body"
4 Golden Horde member
5 They may be stored in towers
6 Match noise
7 Darth Vader's childhood nickname
8 Darling of literature
9 It's between Navarre and Catalonia
10 Co-star of a #1 TV show for four seasons in the 1950s
11 Artery
12 "Yes, agreed"
13 X
15 Attacks medieval-style
18 Things picked up by the perceptive
22 High-five go-withs, maybe
23 Certain white-collar criminal
24 Hoist
25 Pinheads
26 Angioplasty device
29 Like cartoondom's Peter Griffin or Chief Wiggum
30 Once-ler's opponent, in children's literature
31 Rush hour, on the airwaves
32 Their grilles have trident ornaments
33 Actor Auberjonois and others
37 Upper class
39 Wickerwork material
40 Co. with the longtime slogan "Live well"
42 Waylay
45 Joe Blow
46 Broadcasts
47 From one's earliest days
48 Where the Linear A script was unearthed
49 Was immoral
52 Lawyer's title: Abbr.
53 Beads on petals
54 Were present?
55 Spike in direction
56 Say 12-Down

by Andrew Zhou

## ACROSS

1 Reject someone, in a way
10 Reject
15 Mammal that jumps vertically when startled
16 Kind of seating
17 Sociopathic role for Alain Delon (1960), Matt Damon (1999) and John Malkovich (2002)
18 Went without
19 Face-planted
20 Vegas hotel with a name from English legend
22 "Cheese and rice!"
23 1,000 baisa
24 Without having a second to lose?
25 Wee, informally
26 Present from the start
28 Iowa college
29 First Indochina War's Battle of Dien ___ Phu
30 Ones taking a lode off?
31 Worry
32 Streak breaker, maybe
33 Puts down
36 Corrupt, in British slang
37 Car ad letters
40 Giovanni da Verrazano discovery of 1524
42 "Get a ___!"
43 Made like
44 Users' resources
45 Stays out all night?
46 Like dollhouse furnishings
48 Keynote, e.g.
49 Former employer of Keith Olbermann
50 Number of bacteria living on a surface that has not been sterilized
52 ___ des Beaux-Arts
53 Bubbling over
54 Aglisten, in a way
55 60s sorts

## DOWN

1 Hellish
2 Emailed, say
3 Dunk
4 All things being equal?
5 Cross-outs and others
6 Impudence
7 Linda ___, "Girl Reporter" series author
8 Bodybuilder's pose, e.g.
9 Matchbox item
10 Satirist who said "If you were the only person left on the planet, I would have to attack you. That's my job"
11 Trail mix ingredients
12 Hunting dog breed
13 Shaped like Cheerios
14 Keeps the beat?
21 High cost of leaving?
26 Sport similar to paintball
27 Essence
29 Seat in court
31 Having a ring of truth
32 Offer on Airbnb, say
33 Taken to the cleaners
34 "Ya got me?"
35 Note in a Yelp business listing
36 Entree often served with a moist towelette
37 Popular California winemaker
38 Boy Scout shelter
39 Is rankled by
41 Applied, as face paint
42 Stephen King's first novel
45 Had the know-how
47 Slipped one by, in a way
51 Primary color in italiano

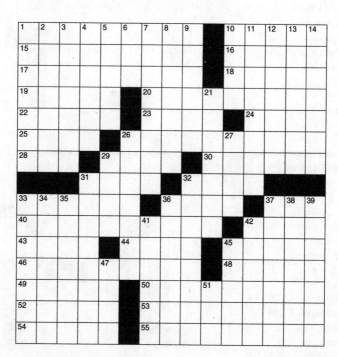

by Mark Diehl

# 74

## ACROSS

1 Entanglement
4 Brings down
10 Hold up
13 Heady stuff
14 Mortal sister of the immortal Stheno and Euryale
15 Jumpsuit-wearing music group
16 He's taken
18 Place whose population was 1, then 2, then 0
19 Champagne grape
20 Attack ad accusations
21 Management
22 Take the wheel?
25 Left port
27 Unrebellious
28 Sir in the Ruhr
30 Attack ad tactic
31 Where Alice is asked "Why is a raven like a writing-desk?"
33 Rock groups that are far out?
36 Sobriquet for the woman who said "Only the little people pay taxes"
37 Global support?
38 Daredevil's highlight
39 Whole bunch
43 Tip of a wingtip
45 Visited unexpectedly, as a town
47 Prefix meaning "extreme"
48 Ocean floor burrower
50 Office supply brand
51 Be critical of?
52 Dachshund, colloquially
55 Boardwalk treats
56 Cuisine that includes trout meunière
57 ___ Simbel (Egyptian landmark)
58 Appreciate
59 Doing time
60 100% aluminum coin

## DOWN

1 Indian bread?
2 Jerry's ex on TV
3 First name in 2016 presidential politics
4 ___ Island ("Jaws" locale)
5 Orthographic competition
6 Recipe instruction
7 1958 hit song that begins "I'm a-gonna raise a fuss, I'm a-gonna raise a holler"
8 Biblical polygamist
9 Takes the edge off?
10 State of emergency
11 Has everything?
12 Waterless
15 There's a point to it
17 Shift in one's seat, perhaps
23 Her albums include "Cuchi-Cuchi" and "Olé, Olé"
24 Was first to go
26 Tree known scientifically as Populus tremuloides
29 Casino correction
31 Sharp club
32 Lose intensity
33 Talladega event
34 Chosen one
35 Trains
36 Residents of the world's richest country per capita
39 Center of activity
40 Sometime in the future
41 Flickering light
42 Cap holder
44 De Niro's "Raging Bull" co-star
46 Bucks on a horse, e.g.
49 Pull down
53 Soak
54 "The Greatest"

by Patrick Berry

## ACROSS

1 Figs. in many police procedurals
5 Roma's Fontana di ___
10 Split ticket?
14 Cotillard won Best Actress for playing her
15 Flier with an S-shaped neck
16 Where lines are drawn?
17 "Is this thing on?"
20 He played the "King" opposite Deborah's Anna
21 Sports item with a sensor
22 Like stones in a cairn
23 Website offering "mentally stimulating diversions"
25 Corporate department
26 Moneyed, in Madrid
27 They can be found next to six-packs
28 Lead-in to Pen
31 "That's cheating!"
34 Gone badly?
35 Untalented writer
36 Letter in the NATO alphabet
37 British thrones?
38 "Draft Dodger Rag" singer
39 Yosemite's range
41 The Eagles, for short
42 Cavils
43 Source of chips
44 Drain away
46 "I've had enough!"
49 Fortunate
51 South ___ (Polynesia's locale)
52 TV series that spawned an exhibit at Chicago's Museum of Science and Industry
53 First black woman elected to Congress, 1968
56 Uffizi Gallery's river

57 Manuel ___, German soccer star called a "sweeper-keeper"
58 India with four Grammys
59 G.I.'s wear
60 Fulfills
61 Group of 435 pols

## DOWN

1 Fixes
2 Excite
3 Actress on "Orange Is the New Black"
4 Trans-Pacific flight destination, for short
5 Exclamation after more information is revealed
6 Noted Civil War signature
7 It's down the lake from Buffalo

8 "Ara ___ Prec" (T. S. Eliot poetry volume)
9 Targeted
10 Unesco World Heritage Site on the Arabian Peninsula
11 Red square
12 Eric of magazine publishing
13 Longtime Cotton Bowl home, informally
18 Big maker of candy hearts
19 Thought patterns, in brief?
24 Places for curlers
25 ___ Mercer, originator of the palindrome "A man, a plan, a canal—Panama"
27 Fast results?
29 Lame
30 "Play it, Sam" speaker

31 "Eat up every moment" sloganeer
32 Part of a dashboard, for short
33 "Taking the first step even when you don't see the whole staircase," per M.L.K.
34 Many a Nikolskoye native
40 Bridge call
42 Deicer formula
45 Capital of France
46 Laughter sound
47 Neighbor of New York's Bay Shore
48 ×
49 Attends
50 Dragsters' grp.
51 ___ work (tedious tasks)
54 Senate affirmation
55 Laughter sound

by Mary Lou Guizzo

## ACROSS

1 Powerful singer's asset, informally
11 Prophet in the Book of Mormon
15 Gelato alternative
16 Open ___ of worms
17 Pioneer in heliocentric theory
18 Fishing floats
19 Baht : Thailand :: ___ : Laos
20 +, $ or @
21 Observed visiting
23 Imperial sticks, say
25 San Francisco's ___ Tower
27 Dismal turnout
28 End of a letter
30 Backstage Broadway worker
32 Unmitigated disaster, in slang
35 Jeanne d'Arc, e.g.: Abbr.
38 Raptors' home: Abbr.
39 Shoebox spec
40 Second-in-command at a corp.
41 Leonardo da Vinci drawing featuring superimposed body positions
45 Very light
46 They roll in
50 Erie or Miami
51 D.C. tourist destination
54 Senate majority leader who succeeded Dole
55 The house of Versace?
57 Vanquish
59 Bucolic expanse
60 Having a scrap
61 John Nash's field of mathematics
64 Narrow margin
65 A question of cosmology
66 Mime and puppetry, e.g.
67 Went door to door?

## DOWN

1 Twisted types
2 Cannes star
3 CNN newsman Jake
4 Copa Mundial cry
5 You may visit a lot of them before Christmas
6 Kind of attack
7 Covent Garden architect Jones
8 Spreads out in a park?
9 Euro forerunner
10 Time in therapy, e.g.: Abbr.
11 Shia who's not a Muslim
12 Cost-effective
13 Cayenne's hotter cousin
14 Like much FM radio
22 Implore
24 Human appendage?
26 "Count ___" (calming advice)
29 They're traded in the Chicago Board of Trade
31 Feel
33 Affect
34 Hector's father
35 2015 Literature Nobelist Alexievich
36 Certain chemistry lab apparatus
37 Immanuel Kant, for one
42 Purchase incentives
43 In a 6-Down
44 It's nothing
47 Bit of computer programming executed repeatedly
48 Perpetual, poetically
49 Didn't take off
52 "Brigadoon" composer
53 Theorbos, e.g.
56 Ottoman chiefs
58 Soften
62 Cardinals' home: Abbr.
63 "My God!," as cried by Jesus

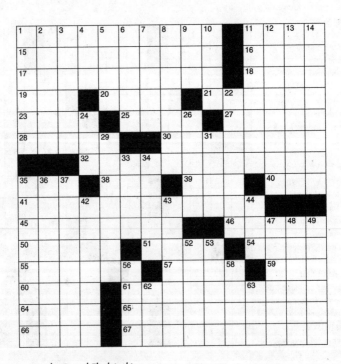

by Pawel Fludzinski

## ACROSS

1 Genre akin to indie rock
7 Fellow
12 Co-organizer of the 1970 Women's Strike for Equality
14 Modern topic in race relations
15 Sci-fi natives of the planet Kashyyyk
16 Little monsters
17 Programming keyword
18 Longtime TV tavern
20 To whom Durocher was referring when he said "Nice guys finish last"
22 Little wriggler
23 Wise one
26 Go through the roof
27 Where bows may be made
28 It's described as fine and flakelike in Exodus
29 Piece of glib journalism often written under a tight deadline
32 Theatrical hybrid
34 Insect that's born pregnant
35 8, e.g.
37 "Are you blind, ump?," e.g.
38 Course on courses, for short
39 Tearing up, say
42 Tolkien's Prancing Pony, for one
43 3, 4, 5 and occasionally more
44 Opposite of doddery
45 Quite off
47 Lover of history?
51 Field in which a helmet and gloves are often worn

53 Award-winning Cartoon Network series with Finn the Human and Jake the Dog
54 Repeated lyric in the Who's "Tommy"
55 Twist and turn

## DOWN

1 Uniform
2 "There's not a ___ can do"
3 Word with family or Christmas
4 Main, say
5 Sculler
6 Wave function denoter in quantum mechanics
7 Some Vietnam War protests
8 Disney's "___ & Stitch"
9 Corresponding exactly
10 Frat party stunt
11 Suffix in linguistics
12 Popular word game
13 Soap box?
14 Bolt (down)
15 Like Tom Thumb
19 Wired
21 What someone may be holding while waiting
23 Kind of roe
24 What had a double standard in the Bible?
25 Try to win
26 Uniform
27 Ruckus
28 Fashion designer Ecko
29 Traveler to a certain 27-Across
30 Request at the dentist's
31 "How dare they!"
33 Regret

36 "Apologies"
38 Rushed
39 Rush
40 Red ___
41 Red ___
43 Cut back
44 Snail trail
46 Paragraph in the newspaper, say
48 Look the wrong way?
49 Subject of a cellphone cap
50 Move like a fairy
51 Biological duct
52 Palooka

by Natan Last

## ACROSS

1 "Hilarious!"
5 Flight alternatives
10 Tag, for example
14 HH
15 Centipede creator
16 "Lionel Asbo: State of England" novelist, 2012
17 Some paperwork: Abbr.
18 Well-built
20 Ran
21 Foolish
22 Curriculum ___
23 Sub rosa
25 Bourbon drinks
26 Off
27 Arise
28 Amount before bonuses
32 Slips
34 Hill dweller
35 Foolish
36 Dedicated to
37 Fort ___ (Civil War landmark near Savannah)
40 Gravy go-withs
41 City on Amtrak's Boston-to-Chicago line
42 Osprey, for one
44 Once-common building material
48 Sequel
50 "Homeland" airer, for short
51 Foolish
53 Jacob's father-in-law
54 Thomas who headed the 9/11 Commission
56 Bach's "Musical Offering" includes one
58 Simple
59 Supermarket chain until 2015
60 ___ Rock, N.J.
61 Displays near gates, briefly
62 Stack of papers
63 "Who ___ ?"

## DOWN

1 When its second syllable is drawn out, "Are you out of your mind?!"
2 Skipping record?
3 Command for turning sharply right
4 Biblical mount
5 "Groundhog Day" director
6 Whatsoever
7 How one might fall in love
8 Hunted
9 Be idle
10 Region bordering Lebanon
11 Recreational soccer, to Brits
12 Embezzles, e.g.
13 ___ Park
19 Sex-ed subject
21 Foolish
24 "___ thee to hell for shame": "Richard III"
25 Beatitude
27 Jon of "Two and a Half Men"
28 Comic book sound effect
29 Question in response to an insult, maybe
30 Some wax
31 Phone inits.
33 Top class: Abbr.
38 Be idle
39 Grammy category
40 Off
43 ___ Alto
44 "Shoot!"
45 Byes
46 The "O" in television's OWN
47 Title locale
49 Foolish . . . or, when read as three words, how this puzzle's other four "foolish" answers are arranged
52 Robe-wearing trainer of cinema
55 Dr. Mario console
57 Abbr. in a beach bag

by Jacob Stulberg

## ACROSS

1 Even faster than overnight
8 Creator of Bluto and Wimpy
15 From the heart, in Latin
16 Heart
17 He played an escaped convict in "We're No Angels"
18 Bad representation?
19 Bucket of bolts
20 Central U.S.'s ___ Plateau
22 Keys are found in it: Abbr.
23 So-called "Caput Mundi" ("Head of the World")
24 Phrase usually abbreviated
25 Longtime Cunard flagship, for short
26 Polymer add-on?
27 The Allegheny and Wabash, to the Ohio: Abbr.
28 Succession in a board game
29 One for the record books
31 "Clearly!"
32 "How ludicrous!"
34 Town in Connecticut's Gold Coast
37 Tweak
41 Rte. that ends in 22-Across
42 Lounge piece
43 Competitor of Baker's Joy
44 River of York
45 "Death and the ___" (Bosch painting in the National Gallery of Art)
46 Confusion
47 "The Cocktail Party" inits.
48 With 9-Down, hit sitcom of the 1980s–'90s
49 Prepare for a close-up
50 It could be a blooper
52 Like stars in a review
54 Longtime locals
55 School address
56 Commoner contemner
57 One of a pair a gardener might wear

## DOWN

1 Marine 10-legger
2 "Welcome to the Jungle" singer, 1988
3 Marie Curie and Irène Joliot-Curie, e.g.
4 Line online
5 More than serious
6 Org. for many residents
7 Go in and out of middle management?
8 Mid-luxury Mercedes-Benz line
9 See 48-Across
10 Be lousy
11 Form of the Italian verb "to be"
12 Set electricians
13 Crow's-foot, e.g.
14 Aggressive poker play
21 Aquarium denizen with horizontal stripes
24 1991 Daytona 500 winner Ernie
25 Classroom command
27 Tickling response
28 Coin at an arcade
30 Packing supply
31 Whale facility
33 Cat's tongue
34 Photoshop color effect
35 Predictably
36 Mozart contemporary Antonio ___
38 Honest or respectable course
39 It ended after W.W. II
40 Like first drafts, usually
42 Think over
45 Studio equipment
46 "The Outcasts of Poker Flat" author
48 Pandorans in "Avatar"
49 Distance unit of about 30 inches
51 European crested ___
53 ___ Jiabao, 2003–13 premier of China

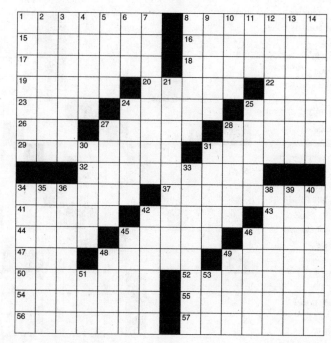

*by Roland Huget*

## ACROSS

1 Indications of one's qualifications?
10 They can be found in two different sections of home-improvement stores
15 Men's fashion shortcut
16 Completely wiped out
17 Bad occasion for an anchor to drag
18 Like many beta programs
19 Burrowing sea creature
20 Practically begs to be hurt
22 Through the roof
25 Clip art?
27 ___ George H. W. Bush
28 1982 Disney film
30 Hybrid business entity: Abbr.
31 Ancient Roman citizenry
34 Traveled in trunks, say
35 Ritual drink in Shintoism
36 Diamond delivery
39 Judith with two Tonys
40 Metal finish?
41 Turns off
42 "___ for Alibi"
43 Become attentive, with "up"
44 Stop working for good
45 Tizzy
47 Protectors sent packing?
51 Foiled
54 Blues group, in brief
55 "___ true"
56 What'll give someone a bleeping chance?
59 Writer/director of "The Evil Dead"
60 Stiff material under a ball gown
61 Novelist Hammond ___
62 Proved sound

## DOWN

1 The Bronx Zoo has 265 of them
2 Aerodynamic
3 1985 Oscar nominee for "Agnes of God"
4 Wetlands regulator, for short
5 Jazz trumpeter Hargrove with two Grammys
6 Shabby
7 Sniffer dog's discovery
8 Thrill
9 Grasps
10 Uncivilized sort
11 Flip-flop
12 Take care of bills
13 Boastful sort
14 Challenge for a housecleaner
21 It might be caught by a 56-Across
23 One of a hitched pair
24 California congressman Darrell
26 People with decorating tips?
28 Do some dirty dancing
29 Like walk-off touchdowns
31 Hospital vessel
32 Moby Dick, e.g.
33 Reading problem
34 One receiving top billing
35 "In Luxury Beware" painter, 1663
37 Punk
38 Nike alternative
43 Tab alternatives
44 Hang (on)
46 Request for a card
47 It grows in the dark
48 Dark
49 Banquo, for one
50 Better with trickery
52 Really impress?
53 Test of one's backbone
55 Prefix with athlete
57 Giant in chemicals
58 She, in Rio

by Michael Hawkins and John Guzzetta

## ACROSS

1 2016 #1 Kanye West album, with "The"
12 Rave's opposite
15 Treat on a stick
16 Time of one's life, maybe
17 Coffee, in military slang
18 Container whose letters appear in "container"
19 Abbr. for a two-striper
20 False modesty, e.g.
21 Torrent
23 Gray matter
24 "Get a ___!"
25 Cry of denial
26 Running slowly
28 Move
30 Finished elegantly
31 Seder celebration
33 Classic case of making life choices?
35 Rate of speed
37 Have a bad view?
38 Raised sharply
42 Diving athlete
46 Company investing in self-driving cars
47 Literary waiter
49 Aid package component
50 Locale in two James Bond films
52 British ends
54 ___ big
55 Freebie at a rally
56 Director DuVernay
57 Text ___
58 Printer setting: Abbr.
59 "Frankenstein," e.g.
63 Exotic jerky meat
64 Species of the Liberty Tree
65 Wiz Khalifa's "We ___ Boyz"
66 "Just stop talking already"

## DOWN

1 Justin Trudeau's party: Abbr.
2 "Got it"
3 Gets
4 Prefix with -derm
5 Extractions are made from it
6 Unbroken
7 Bad job news
8 ___ hour
9 Media inits. since 1922
10 Failed ignominiously
11 Group of families
12 Tobacco flower relative
13 Movie agent on "Entourage"
14 Broadway title character who runs off to Atlantic City
22 Hose and such
23 It may raise its hood
24 Washer/dryer unit?
27 Hoarder
29 Joey of children's literature
32 Pitcher who was the 1995 N.L. Rookie of the Year
34 Some YouTube uploads
36 "Horse voice," e.g.
38 Mixed up
39 Introduction to bio?
40 Supplement brand
41 Conqueror of Cuzco
43 Part of many international flights
44 Banished
45 Supposed end of a flight, for short
48 Missing, with "of"
51 Subject of the 1942 film musical "Yankee Doodle Dandy"
53 Proud "Pride and Prejudice" character
57 ___ fide
60 Fort Sumter victor, informally
61 Bub
62 What moms have that dads don't?

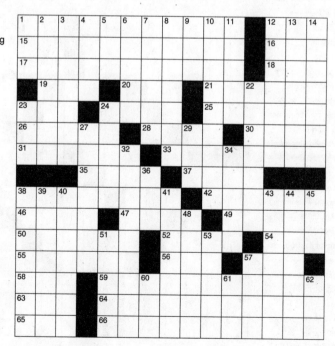

by Sam Ezersky and David Steinberg

## ACROSS

1 "Don Juan," for one
9 Look a little here, look a little there
15 Old means of getting discovered
16 Mammals using echolocation
17 Stayed the course
18 Like biorhythms
19 "The Flowering Peach" playwright
20 Moo ___
22 Hayek of "Grown Ups"
23 John of pro wrestling
24 Hard stuff to swallow
26 Dunderhead
27 Nancy Sinatra's "If ___ Love Me"
28 Brown Betty, e.g.
30 Org. with a campaign called "Degrees Not Debt"
31 Options in a catalog
32 In a sound bite, say
34 Jet stream locale
37 Romantic visionary
38 N.B.A. Hall-of-Famer Mourning
39 Oscar-winning role in "Life Is Beautiful"
40 ___ system (GPS device)
41 Romantic liaison
43 Real pal, for short
46 Many of its products have legs
48 Lacking focus
49 Noah of "Falling Skies"
50 Plants of the arum family
52 Ft. Sumter battler
53 Pet shop purchases
54 Range that's home to Ha Ha Tonka State Park
56 Units in modern film ratings?
58 Convertible
59 A trivial sum, informally
60 Like cream cheese on a bagel
61 Shady bunch?

## DOWN

1 1980s big-city mayor
2 Alphabetically rhyming river name
3 Loom
4 Baked, in Bologna
5 Grps. supporting the 30-Across
6 Wild thing?
7 Series opener
8 Modi operandi
9 Common four-year deg.
10 Novelist Jean with the 1966 best seller "Wide Sargasso Sea"
11 Things in a pod
12 Not near the beginning of
13 What has different strokes for different folks?
14 Bit of antics
21 AK-47 alternative
24 "Go away!"
25 Probe, to Brits
28 ___ topping
29 Leading figure
31 Light of the world
33 Big name in kitchen utensils
34 Cleanup crew
35 "Presto chango!"
36 Media attention
37 Good practice for the show "It's Academic"
39 Montreal daily
42 Winter coat lining
43 Past
44 Winter coat lining
45 Spills it, with "up"
47 Trunk in the trunk
49 Well-kept resource
51 Hershey bar
53 Airline V.I.P.: Abbr.
55 One wearing sunglasses, stereotypically
57 Pop enthusiast?

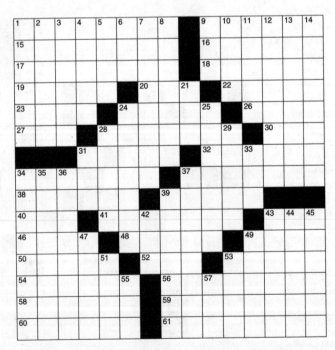

by David C. Duncan Dekker

## ACROSS
1 One of the Great Lakes
5 Menacing cloud
10 Sony offering
14 Saint's home, for short
15 Place for a barbecue
16 Rich finish?
17 "Don't give up"
19 Rather powerful engine
20 Brown
21 Some plants
23 Value
25 Spooky quality
28 Smoothie fruit
29 Popular cookie
31 Taking things for granted on April Fools' Day and others
32 "Time ___ . . ."
33 Track, in a sense
34 Not wait for Mr. Right, say
35 Huuuuuuuuge
37 Loose, now
40 Powerful D.C. lobby
41 Raiser of awareness, for short
44 Not accidental
45 In opposition
46 Guru, maybe
47 Straightens
49 Firm parts: Abbr.
50 Hockey team, e.g.
51 Words on a jacket
53 Risked a ticket
55 Construction staples . . . or a hint to this puzzle's theme
59 Famous Amos
60 Rocker Steve
61 "Don't go!," e.g.
62 Obnoxious one
63 Subject of some codes
64 Scandinavian capital

## DOWN
1 Vase style
2 Compatriot of Mao
3 Noted father-or-son singer
4 Ancient New Mexican
5 Part of a crib
6 Living ___
7 Major Asian carrier
8 Attire
9 Like melancholy musical keys
10 The poor
11 Not go along
12 Prefix with lateral
13 Bedevil
18 Girl's name that may precede Ann
22 One may be starting in sports
23 What's shaken when you say "Shake!"
24 Big letters in electronics
25 Ones moving far from home
26 Fifth in a group of eight
27 Saginaw-to-Flint dir.
29 Bit of beachwear
30 ___ way
33 It may be added to alcohol
34 Pitiful
35 Hit the gas pedal hard
36 Actress Wilson of "Mrs. Doubtfire"
37 Sch. with the George W. Bush Presidential Library
38 Corral
39 Strips at breakfast
41 Tough, tenacious sorts
42 Wild blue yonder
43 Features of Boston accents
45 Milieu of the FX series "The Americans"
46 Poetic stanza
48 Like government bonds
49 German preposition
51 Oil qtys.
52 They burn
53 Racing letters
54 Author who wrote "I became insane, with long intervals of horrible sanity"
56 Buried treasure
57 Pull (in)
58 Noted pseudonym in short story writing

by Howard Barkin

# 84

## ACROSS

**1** Hopes not to be called, say
**7** Market figures
**13** Came to an end
**14** Harpers Ferry river
**15** Storehouse
**16** "Brace yourselves . . ."
**17** Rock music?
**19** Bunk
**20** 1963 western based on Larry McMurtry's "Horseman, Pass By"
**21** Prep before playing
**22** Like a well-written thriller
**23** Onetime Chicago Outfit establishment
**27** Wallops
**28** Many first graders
**30** Heat shields, of a sort
**31** Treatment
**32** Boy Scouts founder Robert ___-Powell
**33** Drivers in cabs
**37** History course topics
**38** Herring relative
**39** Up-to-the-minute
**40** Singer Winehouse
**41** Druidic monument
**45** Rafter connectors
**47** Bird whose name means "golden"
**48** Say repeatedly
**49** Result of one too many misdeeds
**50** Wagner's Tristan and Parsifal, e.g.
**51** Cynical responses

## DOWN

**1** American candy company since 1904
**2** Beat soundly
**3** Like a bed you're in
**4** It's picked up in a mess
**5** Roll up
**6** Ophthalmological ailment
**7** 20th-century comedian who was known as "The Clown Prince of Denmark"
**8** Runnin' ___ (N.C.A.A. team)
**9** Shriek of pain
**10** Green valuables
**11** Dishes that might be prepared in Crock-Pots
**12** Sister brand of Ortho
**14** Retro amusement center
**16** Minds one's place?
**18** Doesn't go out
**22** Obsolescent online connection provider
**24** Parts of a rambling oration
**25** Popular Japanese beer
**26** Fortune reader, maybe
**27** Orange Free State founders
**29** Enlarge, in a way
**30** Gaza Strip guerrillas
**31** Bread spread whose tagline is "Love it or hate it"
**32** 1983 Record of the Year
**34** Added numbers?
**35** Brush alternative
**36** When people meters are used
**38** Trading card figures
**41** Brown
**42** Ear parts
**43** 1979 revolution site
**44** Tease relentlessly
**46** Mate

*by Patrick Berry*

## ACROSS

1 Subject of plays by Sophocles, Euripides and Cocteau
9 Inventor with three steam engine patents
13 Sitter's charge, maybe
14 Philanthropy beneficiary
15 "You get the idea"
16 They're filled at factories
17 Squeaks by
18 One of a pair of drawers facing each other?
19 Tear
20 Fabric shop collection
21 Hires for a float?
24 Gas: Prefix
25 One who might recall action on Iwo
26 Bonehead, to Brits
27 Hotel offering for an extra charge
30 YouTuber or eBayer
32 It was often accompanied by a lyre in ancient Greece
33 Component of the pigment Maya blue
35 Divorced
37 Fictional mariner also known as Prince Dakkar
38 Necessitates
40 President between two Williams
42 G.I. Joe and Cobra Commander, e.g.
44 Grandma Moses' output
45 Tender spot?
48 Round bump on a cactus
49 Emulate Bonnie and Clyde
50 Problem to address
51 Croatia is on it
52 To avoid the risk that
53 Ineffective pill

## DOWN

1 "Hello . . . I'm right here"
2 Like herbal cigarettes
3 Wear (out)
4 Words accompanying a head slap
5 Tears up the dance floor
6 Slanted paper lines?
7 First-century megalomaniac
8 Adding a "z" to its front forms its preceder
9 Head scratcher?
10 Gordon Gekko or Rooster Cogburn
11 Entertainment enticement
12 Bikini, notably
14 Soprano + tenor, maybe
16 68 works of Haydn
18 Guitarist Zappa
20 "Rabbit of ___" (Bugs Bunny short)
22 50-50, say
23 It's just a line or two
27 Guaranteed-to-fly
28 Jerkwater
29 Suitable for all ages?
31 "I'll shut up now"
34 Member of a heist crew
36 Muckety-muck
39 Commercial enticement
41 Counterpart of a rise
43 Court colleague of Ruth and Elena
45 What's often debugged
46 "East of Eden" girlfriend
47 Award-winning webcomic about "romance, sarcasm, math and language"
49 Def

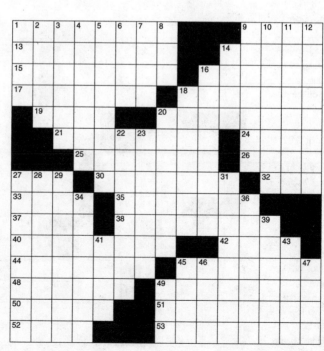

by Jeff Chen

## ACROSS

1 Yankee fare
9 Order to go
13 "I meant to tell you . . ."
15 Verona vino
16 A good bawling-out might be an example of it
17 World leader who's a judo master
18 "I'm with ___"
19 Word after light or fire
20 Kendrick and Paquin
21 June honorees: Abbr.
22 Provision for an outdoor event
24 Family-friendly diner choice
27 "The Blacklist" network
28 Followed closely?
29 Some long sentences
32 Floor support?
34 Arrive on the sly
35 Brewski
39 Then
40 Kayak alternative
41 Big hit
44 Spiked punch?
46 "Napoleon Dynamite" star Jon
47 Vernacular
49 Bud source, perhaps
50 16 things in "Don Giovanni"
51 Take up again?
53 These, in Toulouse
56 Culture ___
57 Foreigner's genre
59 Ancient mountain climber
60 Instrument with a three-sided body
61 Seasonal transport
62 Show room?

## DOWN

1 It may be beaten
2 Instrument with octave keys
3 Museum offering
4 Persian, e.g.
5 Husband or wife
6 Statue at Rockefeller Center
7 Opportunity
8 Place where people make the rounds?
9 Out
10 Siesta
11 Play an ace?
12 Flinched, e.g.
14 Big data unit
15 Cross
21 Very conservative
23 Climber's tool
24 Cheap shot?
25 Muesli morsel
26 One begins "Thou still unravish'd bride of quietness"
30 Fibonacci, by birth
31 Catch on TV's "Deadliest Catch"
33 Leader of the pack
36 Whimsical
37 German "never"
38 Piece in Mr. Potato Head
41 Jerks
42 Creator of the 1966 underground film "Chelsea Girls"
43 Melodic
45 Check out, in a rude way
48 Poses
49 1000, familiarly
52 Prefix with pad
53 "When we have shuffled off this mortal ___": Hamlet
54 Fashion designer Marc
55 Game in which sevens are low
58 Aides at M.I.T. and U.S.C.

by Andrew Kingsley

## ACROSS

1 Walks or runs
5 3D White brand
10 Some TVs
14 Formal guarantee
15 Microwave no-no
16 Try to contain, in a way, as a spill
17 Rich dessert
19 Hockey legend Jaromir
20 Colbert competitor
21 ___ ears
23 Place to work up a sweat
24 Metaphorical rock of Matthew 16:18
26 Auntie Em, e.g.
28 Org. with biennial bids
29 Band that shares its name with a film canine
32 Get on
33 Skedaddle
36 Ones counting down to vacation time?
38 It's included in many bundles
39 ___ compound
40 What you can expect
41 Joe
44 Place for a decal, maybe
46 1988 N.F.L. M.V.P. from the Cincinnati Bengals
49 Epithet for Louis VI, with "the"
50 Mitts
53 Pick up quickly
54 Like many canine tails, quaintly
56 Object of envious comparison
58 Hideout
59 Benzene or lead
60 "How ___!"
61 Sandy who won the 1985 British Open
62 "Man, I did good!"
63 Chips, initially

## DOWN

1 Clobbers
2 Stop for James Cook when circumnavigating the globe
3 Getting back to speed, musically
4 2011 Jason Statham action flick
5 Dishes often served au fromage
6 ___ hall
7 Slightly
8 Reservoir, e.g.
9 Dim or grim
10 U.T.'s ___ Library
11 Very fair, admirable sort
12 Urban exercise areas
13 DNA pair
18 Ready follower?
22 Chintz, e.g.
25 Lacking scruples
27 Annual party favors
30 Sweeping, for short
31 Works of a lifetime
34 Feature of Earth, Mars and Pluto
35 Symbol of biblical wrath
36 Wave off
37 Women's World Cup sight
38 Unforeseen trouble
42 Runs through
43 School closing?
45 In serious disrepair
47 Swimmer Thorpe with five Olympic gold medals
48 Looked (around)
51 Cousin of "OMG!"
52 Hot
55 Inits. on a master's application
57 "Star Trek" captain, to friends

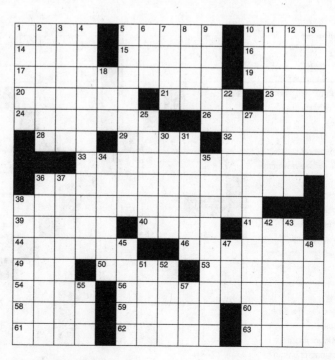

by Peter Wentz

# 88

## ACROSS

1 Talk
7 Driver's hazards
15 Not divisible, as a job
16 Amelia Earhart, e.g.
17 Good news for wage earners
18 Far Eastern city whose name means "long cape"
19 Org. that covers Springfield in a dome in "The Simpsons Movie"
20 Torpedo
22 Black
23 Office monitor
25 Dough made in the Middle East?
26 Lane in a strip
27 Wedding keepsake
29 Long-running Vegas show
30 Even's opposite
31 Gravy goody
33 Mississippi feeder
35 Backslash neighbor
39 Buddhist memorial dome
40 Like motets
42 Cross words
44 One-on-one basketball play, slangily
46 Sound
47 Feature of un poema
48 Accomplished
50 Damage done
51 It welcomes praise
52 "Wouldn't think so"
54 Pixar specialty, briefly
55 City called the Bush Capital
57 2006 musical featuring a vampire
59 Light blue partner of Connecticut and Vermont
60 Crazy Horse, e.g.
61 "It was my pleasure"
62 They're drawn by the bizarre

## DOWN

1 Green grocery choice
2 Brazilian city name that sounds like a U.S. state capital
3 Some southern cookin'
4 Alternative to SHO
5 Celebrate
6 Rapping response
7 Its rosters aren't real
8 1997 comedy with the tagline "Trust me"
9 Odysseus' faithful dog
10 Clout
11 Christmas trio
12 Key of Chopin's étude "Tristesse"
13 Collect lots of
14 Cross states
21 Word with a 35-Across before and after it
24 Separator of the Philippines and Malaysia
26 "Incoming!"
28 Charcuterie, e.g.
30 Nut-brown
32 Tony-winning title role of 1990
34 Country's ___ Brown Band
36 Aid in labor management?
37 One handling an OD
38 Get too close, in a way
41 Teases, in older usage
42 French daily, with "Le"
43 Lackey's response
45 Pick
47 Casing job, for short
48 Big supply line
49 Bill collectors?
52 Dimple
53 Something farm-squeezed?
56 Arthur with a Tony
58 Genre for Reel Big Fish

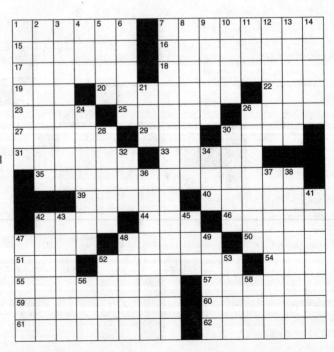

by James Mulhern

## ACROSS

1 Postprandial woe
9 Fight memento
15 "That's it . . . too rich for me"
16 Classical record on Norman Bates's turntable in "Psycho"
17 Licorice candy that was originally raspberry-flavored
18 Ross and Spencer
19 John of the Velvet Underground
20 Berlin's ___ Nationalgalerie
22 Promised lands
23 Alex's mom on "Family Ties"
25 Totes
27 Tía's title, perhaps: Abbr.
28 Brought (up), as from the distant past
31 Get in the end
32 Gladiator type
36 Classic song with the lyric "Let's get together and feel all right"
38 Rays are in it
39 Browns
40 Head honchos
42 Pie slice, so to speak
43 Disney aunt
44 Most insensitive
46 "___ Theme," tune from "Star Wars: The Force Awakens"
48 Change colors
49 Oyster cracker?
54 No longer crisp, in a way
56 Two-time All-Star Martinez
58 Half of a comic strip duo
59 Put an end to
61 2008 Tina Fey/Amy Poehler comedy
63 Words said in a rush
64 Small show of one's feelings
65 Considered to be
66 Barren, in a way

## DOWN

1 "Broad City," for one
2 N.B.A. star with size 22 shoes
3 "___ enough . . ."
4 Low bars
5 10th-century year
6 Chaplin of "Game of Thrones"
7 Robert ___, F.B.I. director from 2001 to 2013
8 Like many retired Derby winners
9 Like parking meters
10 Singer India.___
11 Pride : lions :: knot : ___
12 It may be a credit to the band
13 "This is too much"
14 Prove one's worth
21 Something that may pop up in the morning
24 Who said "Opportunity is missed by most people because it is dressed in overalls and looks like work"
26 Some claim to have six of them
29 Poor spirits?
30 Loved by
32 Has fun getting towed?
33 Recharging period
34 Like debts
35 Old dope?
37 Director Jacquet of "March of the Penguins"
41 Blue books?
42 Ann Landers, for one
45 Sweeteners
47 M.I.T.'s ___ School of Management
50 Linguistic origin of "mulligatawny"
51 Whisper
52 Ticklish dolls
53 They have coats with white hairs
55 ___ noche (tonight: Sp.)
57 Something that may be found in a pit
60 "___ Mine" (hit of 1957 or 1995)
62 Accounting abbr.

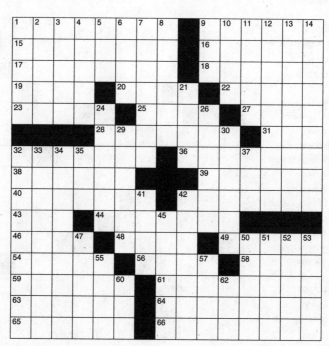

by Erin Rhode

## ACROSS

1 Preceder of 64-Across on the calendar
12 It may justify things
15 Ilmenite is the chief one
16 Winner of the first three Fiesta Bowls, for short
17 Airport terminal feature
18 Radio frequency abbr.
19 Scrap
20 Discoverer of New Zealand
21 "I can't believe that!"
22 Liberty's home, for short
23 4-Downs, south of the border
25 Site of Akbar the Great's tomb
28 Article in El País
31 Release?
34 Parts of cross-shaped churches
37 He worked for Hershey in the 1910s–'20s
38 Quaint getaway destination
40 Bring down
41 Officially gives up
42 More compact
44 Dutch oven, e.g.
45 1995 Emmy winner Sofer
46 Less adorned
48 Highway hazard
50 Laverne and Shirley, e.g.
52 Lumber mill employee
55 World of Warcraft figure
58 Bud abroad
59 Port authority?
61 World of Warcraft figure
62 Name that went down in history?
63 Buns, for example
64 Follower of 1-Across on the calendar

## DOWN

1 Vitamin a.k.a. riboflavin
2 Story teller
3 Having a scrap
4 Stealthy sort
5 Sweaters and such
6 Got via guile
7 Kirmans, e.g.
8 Certain prayer leader
9 Rapper wrapper?
10 22-Across and others
11 Motion supporter
12 Departs
13 Court legend
14 Dreaded game show sound
21 Antedate
22 Civil War battle site
24 Largest minority in Bulgaria
25 Single chance?
26 Duck lookalike
27 Spots for air traffic controllers
29 They may precede high-speed chases, in brief
30 Peel
32 European city whose name means "eat"
33 Bright swimmer
35 Part of a mean mien
36 One of Utah's state symbols
39 Civil War battle site
43 Like hashish or shoe wax
47 Soul mate?
49 Philosophy
50 Bookkeeper's stamp
51 It's loaded
53 "___ live!"
54 W.W. I battle site
55 With 60-Down, gotten by great effort
56 "Eri tu," but not "Eres Tú"
57 Oz salutation
59 New Mexico State's athletic grp.
60 See 55-Down

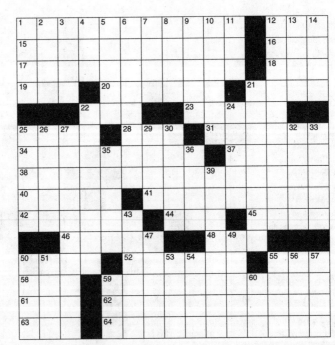

by Barry C. Silk

## ACROSS

1 One might have black-and-white standards
11 Treasure hunter's loot, maybe
15 Stay off the water?
16 Unconventional and hippielike, informally
17 Some juvenile records
18 Way: Abbr.
19 Developers work on them
20 Wrong
22 Jazz great Montgomery
23 More than a fraction of a cent
25 Responsibility
26 Outfits for big parts?
29 Station display
31 "The perfect idiot's profession," per Katharine Hepburn
34 Certain upper-growth limit
36 Orange snack in a red box
38 Where the Lost Battalion got lost
39 Doesn't go off as expected
41 Flip-flop, e.g.
42 Crooked joint
43 Boxing ring?
45 Religious figure from on high?
47 Set at sea?
48 Small vault
51 One of 20–30 "genius grants" awarded annually
54 ___ soup
55 Impulse transmitter
56 North Carolina vacation area
59 Gaiman who wrote "American Gods" and "Coraline"
60 Film about rock groups?
61 Without much effort
62 Bellini and Botticelli

## DOWN

1 "Yeah, right!"
2 [Fingers crossed]
3 Wins easily
4 War force
5 Pro ___
6 "Out of the Blue" group, for short
7 "Hockey sticks," in cards
8 Buzz, e.g.
9 2011 Best New Artist Grammy winner Bon ___
10 Philippine money
11 His last play was "When We Dead Awaken"
12 "Excuse me?"
13 Classic folk number
14 Heaps
21 Bouquets, quaintly
23 Island known for its spices
24 This year's starlet
26 Sphere of control
27 Org. in "Patriot Games"
28 Like Hemingway vis-à-vis most other writers
30 Exfoliation
31 Tiptop
32 Hung around casually?
33 It may cause sparks to fly
35 Isolated
37 It may be in the bag
40 Went looking for places to shoot
44 First name on the 1970s–'80s Lakers
46 Rugged
48 Swinging joint
49 "The Tin Drum" boy
50 Duck faces, e.g.
51 Salon job, informally
52 Land on the Gulf of Guinea
53 Project with a lot of momentum
54 Like Colt 45 and Mickey's
57 Kind of virus
58 Not haut

by Josh Knapp

## ACROSS

1 Insincerely polite
7 13-Down natives, e.g.
15 Hugh who played TV's House
16 Laid into
17 Wool source
18 Subcontinent-wide
19 One for whom 36-Across has four syllables
21 Many new car drivers
22 Island west of Mull
23 Red stuff to cut through
25 Dim bulbs
26 Off
28 Compromise
30 Trial cover-up
31 Gray head
32 Has the stage
34 What exterior doors typically do
36 See 19- and 57-Across
38 Lyricist who adapted "Pygmalion"
41 Clubs to beat people with?
42 Chrome runners, maybe
45 x, y and z
46 Mozart title starter
48 Devil's deck
50 Lawyer's workload
52 Admission evidence
54 Musical group known for wearing red hats called "energy domes"
55 Recycling bin fill
57 One for whom 36-Across has three syllables
59 Figure-changing agent
61 Calmer?
62 Lesser "Seinfeld" role played by Len Lesser
63 Bomb
64 Early Beatle
65 Going rates

## DOWN

1 Beyond slow
2 Sought safety, say
3 Princess in line to the British throne after Beatrice
4 Agents in some therapy
5 When told "I'm sleepy," she sometimes says "I hope you're not driving"
6 Rising generation?
7 The Era of ___ (1964–74 Notre Dame football)
8 Like some angels and arches
9 Really bug
10 Paris fights in it
11 Like many bad words
12 Appended
13 Safari Capital of the World
14 Nine-time presidential contender of the 1940s–'90s
20 Shaving the beard with a razor, in Jewish law
24 Bit of décor in a sports bar
27 It makes a wave
29 Nap
33 Top of the line?
35 Tick, e.g.
36 Fill with anxiety
37 Freeze
38 Like skates and corsets
39 Scrutinize
40 Word repeatedly spelled out by Franklin
42 Make as a heat-and-serve product, say
43 Much-sought-after
44 British floors
47 Time after Time?
49 Think much of
51 Backtrack?
53 Calligraphic messes
56 Creator of the lawyer Perry
58 "Superman" catchphrase starter
60 Grokked

by Matt Ginsberg

## ACROSS

1 School for Rory Gilmore of "Gilmore Girls"
5 Item that became trilingual in the late '90s
15 Slavering toon
16 Captain
17 Salty drink?
18 She was "the answer to a prayer" in a 1941 #1 Jimmy Dorsey hit
19 1983 hit for Rufus and Chaka Khan
21 French pronoun
22 Pitch successfully
23 Like salsa
25 Ingredient in a Baltimore Bracer
26 Pros at settling disputes
27 Auto option patented by 3M
28 Cast mate?
30 Italian term of address: Abbr.
31 Leaves out in the open?
33 "No ___!"
36 Shower component
37 Apparent flaw
38 Confessed statements
41 "Wake Up on the Bright Side" sloganeer
44 Louses
45 Medical term for lead poisoning
46 "___ word?"
47 Pool cover
48 Film animation technique
51 Drug smuggler
52 Governor who was the father of another governor
53 Yank with 25 grand slams
54 Polysomnogram finding
55 Bird with a resonant "ha-wah" call

## DOWN

1 Balance sheets?
2 Ninth-century pope who was married with a daughter
3 Simba sobriquet
4 A migraine sufferer might have one
5 Level best
6 Aeschylus' play "The Persians" is about one
7 Crossing state lines, perhaps
8 HC(O)NH$_2$, for one
9 Kill
10 Grasp
11 Companion
12 "Swan Lake" heroine
13 "Claude Monet Painting in His Garden at Argenteuil," e.g.
14 Drills
20 Scottish refusal
23 Magazine that published Harry Truman's memoirs
24 Kill
26 Worthless amount
29 2005–07 sitcom about the Gold family, with "The"
31 RICO enforcers
32 They may end with golden goals, for short
33 Job for which you give someone a hand
34 Exhibition locale
35 Rush
36 Former Florida senator Martinez
37 Support for a pilot
38 Gulfs
39 Zipcar alternative
40 Kid-lit character who says "The nicest thing about the rain is that it always stops. Eventually"
42 Trendy pseudocereal
43 Cinerary item
45 Suddenly took notice
47 Locale of the Evert Tennis Academy, familiarly
49 Word that follows pot but precedes pan
50 Clean (up)

by Byron Walden

# 94

## ACROSS

1 Sharp projections
5 What a capt. may aspire to be
8 Service provider
14 Much-photographed mausoleum site
15 1978 Grammy nominee Chris
16 Be faithful (to)
17 Blotchy, in a way
18 Blotchy, in a way
20 Mimicking
21 "Enfantines" composer
22 "Join the club"
23 Lifesaver, at times
24 Book and film title character surnamed Gatzoyiannis
25 Flame proof?
26 Fancy wrap
28 Measure of econ. health
30 Gear protector
33 Got rich
39 Depression era?
40 One with a smaller Indian relative
41 Hurtful pair in a playground rhyme
42 Show celerity
43 Flop's opposite
44 Mil. roadside hazard
45 78 letters
48 Dixieland sound
51 "10-4"
54 Cole Porter topic
56 "To Helen" writer, in footnotes
57 Feedable thing
58 Abstract Expressionist who married Jackson Pollock
60 Cannery row?
61 Iris feature
62 He's unrefined
63 They're unrefined
64 Brokerage come-on
65 Suffix with green
66 Big name in Renaissance patronage

## DOWN

1 Follower of a diet system
2 Twinkle-toed
3 Only living thing that can be seen from outer space
4 Blue
5 Alternative to Geneva
6 Al ___
7 Appearing with fanfare
8 Back stroke?
9 "Battlestar Galactica" role
10 Starts suddenly
11 What "Banzai!" literally means
12 Food brand since 1912
13 Fresh styling
19 Who called a date "a job interview that lasts all night"
21 Green around the gills, maybe
27 Shakespearean duel overseer
29 They're often struck in studios
31 Combined
32 Temporary quitting times?
33 Make ___ of (botch)
34 Civvies
35 What Google Wallet uses
36 Eternal water-pourers in Hades
37 Chameleon, e.g.
38 Literally, "big water"
46 What some caddies hold
47 ___ Norman (cosmetics franchise)
49 21-Across's "Three Pieces in the Shape of ___"
50 Circumlocutory
52 Target of the plume trade
53 Western union?
54 War room development
55 Wind-cheating
59 Some camera cells
60 ___ College

*by Martin Ashwood-Smith and George Barany*

## ACROSS

1 Those falling head over heels?
9 Little rows
14 Ones with love-hate relationships, say
16 Pop singer Goulding
17 Show on which Adam West voiced Mayor Adam West
18 Actress Balaban of "Supernatural"
19 Make a measure of
20 Shift specification: Abbr.
21 Some temple figures
22 César subject
23 Measure (up)
25 Press target, informally
26 Soupçon
27 Is a kiss-up
29 Org. awarding 5-Downs
30 Bass brass
31 Foreign aide
33 Reduced
36 Guts
37 Do-it-yourself wheels
38 W.W. II landing site in Italy
39 Hookups on "House"
40 Tough
42 Malfunctioning
45 Like venison
47 First division, maybe
48 Hindu embodiment of virtue
49 Procedure improving one's looks?
51 "Let me ___ pray thee": Exodus 4:18
52 Picks nits
53 Golfer's error
54 Some small tablets
56 Power of two
57 Hesitant
58 Something to believe in
59 Princess and angel, e.g.

## DOWN

1 Move
2 Holders of thoughts?
3 Order back
4 Shelved
5 Supporting strip
6 She anchored "Weekend Update" with Tina, then Seth
7 Scrooge
8 "Bathers at Asnières" and "Parade de Cirque"
9 Game giveaway
10 24-book classic
11 What a troll may perpetuate
12 Preceder of the sound of a gavel
13 Be in shock from a sock
15 Biggest rival of US Foods
23 Recover after being wrecked
24 Year-end tradition since 1966
27 Half of a 2000s stoner-film duo
28 Longtime hair lightener brand
30 Alternative to Flix
32 Kung ___ beef
33 Things that one is good at
34 Be what one isn't
35 Prognostication proclamation
36 Start
38 Music genre for Miriam Makeba
41 Charley Bates's mentor, in literature
42 Musical with the song "There's a Sucker Born Ev'ry Minute"
43 One often accused of being blind
44 Rank and file
46 Something to carve out
48 First lady Barbara's Russian counterpart
50 Last name in the funnies for nearly 50 years
52 "Let's go!"
55 Ariz. doesn't observe it

by Debbie Ellerin

## ACROSS

1 Gets steamy, with "up"
5 Order to go away
9 Ever
14 Letters on a crucifix
15 Rabbit's friend
16 Grit
17 Teen's fender bender, maybe
20 2001 fantasy/adventure film with three sequels
21 Many an étagère display
22 Gush
23 Lab housing the world's largest machine
24 Luca who "sleeps with the fishes"
25 Symbol of virility
30 Don't delay
31 However
33 "Frozen" princess
34 Match makeup
36 Match
37 "Ellen's Design Challenge" airer
38 One of the eight points of contact in Muay Thai
39 Least apt to offend
41 "Life of Pi" director
42 Longest word in English containing only one vowel
44 Many gases lack them
46 R&B/pop singer Aubrey
47 Readies for an operation
48 Therapist's image
52 Some miniature hors d'oeuvres
54 Concern in family planning
56 Inuit for "house"
57 Simon of the stage
58 Hostile to
59 Roughhouse?
60 Eponyms of the week?
61 270°

## DOWN

1 Goes on perfectly
2 Target of the Occupy movement
3 Brains
4 Twisted sorts
5 Figure in a dark suit
6 They're held at both ends when eating
7 Sister co. of Verizon Wireless, once
8 "How Deep Is Your Love" Grammy winners
9 Principal, e.g.
10 Catacomb component
11 Turn and a half on the ice
12 Shoppers' headache
13 "I'm in!"
18 Cry after "One, two, three," maybe
19 Rail hubs?
23 Intolerantly pious
24 Takes pleasure (in)
25 Deep in thought
26 "Yeah, right!"
27 Like the Bahamas, Barbados and Belize
28 Cuts through
29 "Two thumbs way up!" and such
32 Like losers' looks
35 Get
40 Doughnutlike
43 Kind of pass in basketball
45 Make furniture-safe, in a way
47 Relatives of sprains
48 Relative of a spoonbill
49 Just about
50 African tree cultivated for its nuts
51 Like-minded voters
52 Muslim judge of North Africa
53 Bit of improv
55 Driver of a bus.

by John Guzzetta

## ACROSS

1 Ridiculous imitation
8 Basis of a patent
15 Traffic report source, often
16 Something John Adams and John Quincy Adams each had
17 Change, as allegiances
18 "Mean Girls" screenwriter
19 Close to, colloquially
20 Sell
21 Means of communication since 1817, in brief
22 Some receptions
24 Wonder
27 Surgeon's tool
29 Charles who created murals for Harlem Hospital and the American Museum of Natural History
32 Start of many a romantic comedy
34 1922 Kafka short story
35 Hematologist's measure
36 Pioneer in New Journalism in the 1960s–'70s
37 Author who shares his name with a German state
38 Fire away
39 Pet name meaning "faithful"
40 Michael Moore offering, for short
43 Sea ___
47 Part of a hit 1940s–'50s film trio
50 Has dreams
52 Completely surpass
53 It doesn't have much to say
54 Armful for Moses
55 Slide presentations?
56 Hedge fund employee

## DOWN

1 Santa ___
2 They might be ill
3 Feature of CNN or Fox News
4 Hindu goddess often portrayed with her husband Shiva
5 Work on a lead, maybe
6 Part of a square
7 That there
8 F and G, but not H
9 Wife in Jonathan Franzen's "The Corrections"
10 Meander
11 It adds stress: Abbr.
12 "Glass half empty" sort
13 Emily Dickinson's "Ended, ___ it begun"
14 Writer Sedaris
20 Like motel walls, it often seems
23 Host
25 Refuses to
26 Grade sch. class
27 Ladder's counterpart
28 Track things
29 Sprayer
30 "___ pray"
31 Author of the "Mostly Ghostly" book series
32 Attribute as the cause of
33 Sprayed, in a way
34 Start of a Hamlet monologue
35 Child support, for short?
39 Sparring partners?
40 Dull-witted
41 Boots
42 Peak
44 Ready
45 Zodiac symbol
46 One sitting on a celestial throne
48 Goya's "Duchess of ___"
49 Grind down
50 Legal org.
51 Kind of card
52 Itinerary abbr.

by Lily Silverstein

# 98

## ACROSS

1. Conflicts with combat
8. TED talk, e.g.
15. Going around the world?
16. Where people live well beyond the city limits
17. Eponym of an annual Golden Globe award for lifetime achievement
18. Parts of abdomens
19. Event where kids ask lots of questions, informally
21. Hardly deliberate
24. Female antelope
25. Student monitors, for short
26. Like the tops of many porticoes
28. Crib piece
30. Home of Charlie Chan
34. Mortal
36. Recited prayers
38. Second City subway org.
39. You might be thrown on it
41. Narrow inlet
42. Average producer
44. Paradise
46. Recital numbers
47. Sammy who wrote the lyrics to "Ain't That a Kick in the Head"
49. Italian dictators
50. Frustrated cry
52. Impressed cry
54. Dunham of "Girls"
55. Real hack?
60. Resembling a heavy curtain, say
61. Christie's event
65. Temple of Artemis city
66. "Ah, got it"
67. Least hopping
68. Chameleon, e.g.

## DOWN

1. Put away
2. "Army of ___" (recruiting slogan)
3. "Spotlight" director McCarthy
4. Twists
5. ___-bodied
6. Sore
7. Some women on "Mad Men"
8. Injured: Fr.
9. Added cost of selling overseas
10. Confessional word
11. Charge that may be high
12. "Evolving the way the world moves" sloganeer
13. Compost heap bit
14. Undemanding
20. Colorful swallow?
21. Some mixtapes
22. Playground comeback
23. Opposite of fine print?
27. Locale for a 39-Across
29. Direct
31. Shooting star?
32. U.S. athlete who won more gold medals at the 1980 Winter Olympics than all but two non-U.S. countries
33. Patriotic chant
35. Martial arts weapons that are two sticks connected by a chain
37. Somewhat
40. Div. of the Justice Department
43. Moved like a 20-Down
45. There's nothing to it
48. "I was robbed!"
51. Come about
53. Mount
55. Armisen of "Portlandia"
56. Hip-hop's ___ Fiasco
57. Ottoman honorific
58. Start and end of many a flight
59. The Miners of the N.C.A.A.
62. What makes nose noise?
63. :-D alternative
64. Source of fleece

by Brendan Emmett Quigley

## ACROSS

1 Spontaneous public gathering
9 Balance sheet data
14 For whom the Collegiate School was renamed in 1718
16 Sushi bar brew
17 Like Cirque du Soleil performers
18 Paris attraction?
19 Coin collectors?
20 As follows
22 Co. with the slogan "We move the world"
23 Precisely
24 Chuckleheads
26 "Red, White & ___" (2005 rock album)
27 Canonflex or Leicaflex, for short
28 1,000 or 1,000,000
29 Profits
31 Manipulative use of the Force
34 Coup d'___
35 Like a young Jay Gatsby
36 Someone always good for a few pints?
42 Boehner's successor as House minority leader
43 The Japanese captured it in 1941
44 Flight component
46 Procrastinator's favorite word
47 Jay Gatsby's beloved
49 New brunette, say
50 Terminal requests
51 Coup d'___
52 Dwarf warrior in "The Lord of the Rings"
53 Part of many a diary
55 Sticker in a nursery
58 Feeling toward a supervillain
59 Activity for when there's nothing going on?
60 Dapper
61 Back in the day

## DOWN

1 Saturnalia events
2 2012–16 host of the Grammys
3 Soaring expense?
4 Certain weanling
5 Nerve centers
6 "Lady Marmalade" Grammy winner of 2001
7 ___ bread
8 Member of a holiday team
9 Morse "Toto," totally
10 Telegraph extension?
11 Shoulder-to-hip belt
12 One who's green after seeing red
13 Stain-free
15 Auto-reply message?
21 Media giant since 1982
24 Get some help with transportation
25 21-Down runs them
26 Shaggy Scottish dog
28 Gives credit
30 Sound of power
32 Red English cattle
33 Figure in the high 60s
36 Y lookalike
37 Genre of some of Yoko Ono's art
38 "My anger got the best of me"
39 Nimbleness
40 Scandalous Manet painting of 1863
41 Knocked for a loop
45 Yank, in Yucatán
48 Facilitates
49 Relatives of stilettos
51 Cry of surprise
52 Ski boots and such
54 Like bodybuilders' bodies
56 Is for a group?
57 Word with soup or salad

by David Phillips

# 100

## ACROSS

1 Porcine paramour
11 Yesterday, so to speak
15 Product with a Crispy Buffalo variety
16 Underwater breather
17 Tremendous
18 Beginning to morph?
19 Brady bunch, briefly
20 Some zoo employees
21 Harmonious
22 Blubbers
23 Some red giants
24 Little 'un
27 They had rolls to play, once
29 Disappearing exclamations
30 Foe of Big Boy and Little Face
33 Tremendously
34 Bothers
35 Bothers
36 Good news for business
38 Combined
39 Turn on
40 Shot measure
41 Meshes
43 One for whom "hello" is "hej"
44 Geezers
45 Tough spots
46 What "it" is found in
49 Symbol del cristianismo
50 Haughty
53 Artist Magritte
54 It takes turns making dinner
55 Extra, in ads
56 Reminder that sticks?

## DOWN

1 Sound from a cheater
2 Israel's Olmert
3 Staple of Memorial Day services
4 Instrument that's cradled, for short
5 Full of butterflies
6 Under water
7 Touches
8 Mushy foods
9 '50s campaign nickname
10 2014 World Cup winner: Abbr.
11 Weapon used in the Vietnam War
12 Seriously under the weather
13 Fix as 20-Across might do
14 Schemes
21 "And who ___?"
22 Hot, salty snack
23 Lord & Taylor rival, informally
24 Go over
25 John Paul II, e.g.
26 Do some ferreting
27 Magical duster
28 Founder of Rhyme $yndicate Records
30 Webster wrote many of them: Abbr.
31 Traffic director
32 Nieuwpoort's river
34 Counterpart of moi
37 Some antlered animals
38 "No, no, really . . ."
40 He succeeded two queens
41 Capital up the coast from Cape Coast
42 Hurt with a horn
43 Hoist on a ship
45 Dashes off
46 Pacific dietary staple
47 Settled
48 Jubilation
50 "Leaves and Navels" artist
51 Comic's nightmare?
52 Eli Manning, on the field

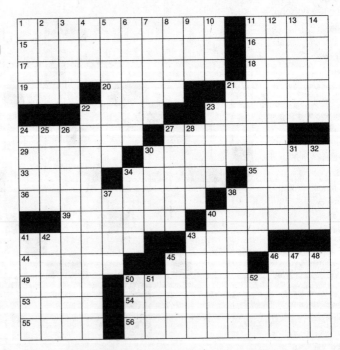

by Kelly Clark

## ACROSS

1 Player's fee
5 Plant used in tanneries
10 Topps tidbit
14 Bandleader whose band was the New Orleans Gang
16 River into which the Big Sandy and the Little Sandy flow
17 It goes station to station
18 Private jet, maybe
19 Flummoxed
20 Delights
22 What many do at tax season
23 Cough drop brand
25 Nerves-of-steel type
27 Human member of an old TV trio
28 Sixth graders, typically
32 Whatever
33 Filing centers
34 Jailer, sailor and tailor
35 Book collection?
37 Charlton's "The Ten Commandments" co-star
40 1979 film that ends with Peter Sellers walking on water
41 Big do
42 Long-distance call?
43 Albert Einstein and others
45 Rush
46 Address loudly and at length
50 "People who fight fire with fire usually end up with ___": Abigail Van Buren
51 Oscar nominee for "The Aviator"
53 Actress sister of Francis Ford Coppola
55 Disorderly conduct
56 Balanced
57 Door plate, maybe
58 Aid for the forgetful, maybe
59 CAT scan units

## DOWN

1 Fodder for dairy cattle
2 Junction injunction
3 Super ___
4 With 41-Down, women's fashion brand
5 Luxury hotel facility
6 Some garden ornaments
7 Lapel attachment
8 Religious agreement?
9 Deep scarlet shade
10 Pacifier
11 Horror film remake released on 6/6/06
12 They feature dogfights
13 Game pieces
15 Eminem song about an obsessed fan
21 Device used by Anubis to determine a soul's fate
24 Hymn set to music by Vivaldi and Haydn
26 Psychic mediators
29 Casting lady
30 Olympic-level
31 Ethyl acetate, for one
33 Hillary's mate
34 Eldest Bennet sister in "Pride and Prejudice"
35 1970 Simon & Garfunkel hit
36 Joined the force
37 "Yentl" setting
38 Came out with
39 Dials down
40 Note that sounds like a direction to think
41 See 4-Down
44 Far ___
47 Flatten, in a way
48 ___ Ramsay, hero of "The Black Stallion"
49 Brown of publishing
52 Put away
54 Symbol of Tut's power

by Patrick Berry

# 102

## ACROSS

1 "Come again?"
10 They're put in for work
15 Brand whose first commercial featured a cable car
16 Large-scale detail
17 Trust issue?
18 "Bleeding Love" singer Lewis
19 Non-humanities acronym
20 When repeated, spouse's complaint
21 Walter ___, Dodgers manager before Tommy Lasorda
22 "The Fox and the Hound" fox
23 Dish that often has pea pods
25 Medium for many 13-Down
26 Emmy-winning Susan Lucci role
28 "On the hoof," in diner lingo
29 "Yeah, why not!?"
30 Kim Jong-un, for one
32 Gendered "Seinfeld" accessory
34 Shake off
36 Sticky stuff
37 Person with a lot on his plate?
41 [I find this mildly amusing]
45 Confederate
46 Rush, e.g.
48 Corners
49 Federal div. concerned with gas consumption
50 They may be settled over drinks
52 Burn
53 Shakes off
55 "If you ask me . . . ," for short
56 Give a Yelp review, say
57 Hometown of Columbus
58 "Let's do this!"
60 Secluded spaces
61 "Let's do this!"
62 Yom Kippur War leader
63 America, informally

## DOWN

1 Took by force
2 Done for
3 Was on the cast of
4 ___ U.S.A.
5 Sr. stress source
6 Reznor of Nine Inch Nails
7 What blowhards blow
8 On end, to Donne
9 Concert needs, for short
10 Good for sledding, say
11 Gender-neutral possessive
12 Entertainment for general audiences?
13 Collection at the Musée d'Orsay
14 Nonactor with cameos in more than 20 Marvel movies
21 Playground comeback
23 ___ Fierce (onetime Beyoncé alter ego)
24 Certain grenade, for short
27 Batman?
29 "Neat-o-rific!"
31 Aquarium fish
33 People thinking on their feet?
35 Road sign silhouette
37 No-goodniks
38 Song that starts "Hate New York City / It's cold and it's damp"
39 Slowly picked up
40 Comeback
42 Battled
43 Model
44 Early Judaic sect
47 End
50 The Antichrist, with "the"
51 They may grab a bite
54 Lisbon lady
56 Beatles title girl with a "little white book"
58 Boring thing
59 Came down with

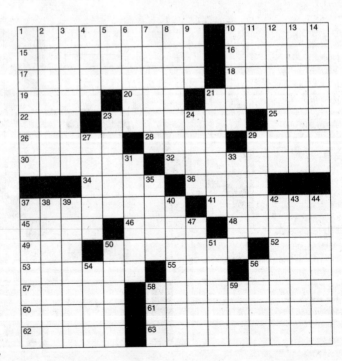

by Paolo Pasco

## ACROSS

1 Like a Navy seal
11 Tall tale producer?
15 Colorful ornamental with a trunk
16 Very large, informally
17 One-stop shopping spot
18 Battleship guess
19 Advance look, commercially
20 Backing for a cartoonist
22 ___ Williams, Potsie player on "Happy Days"
24 ___-on-Thames (regatta site)
25 Little bits
27 Wet blanket?
29 Subject of the biography "Lightning in His Hand"
30 Girl's name in which the last three letters are equivalent to the first?
31 Quality wool source
33 It's an imposition
34 Acupuncturist's supply
36 Feeling
38 "OMG, that's enough!"
39 Came (from)
41 Hawkeye State city
42 John Wayne title role
44 Quick on the uptake
45 Washington Sq. Park squad
46 One not yet one, say
48 Something to live for
50 Primitive
52 Marcos of the Philippines

56 Minor flaw
57 Old-fashioned auto feature
59 Front money?
60 Obama's first Homeland Security secretary
61 Supportive cries
62 Dark brown quartz sometimes sold as a gemstone

## DOWN

1 One might be involved in a sting
2 Like la mer
3 Stick with it
4 High
5 Most TV Land programming
6 Paralyzes, in a way
7 Education's ___ Tech

8 "What do you call a fake noodle? An impasta," e.g.
9 Foreign term of address
10 Ones put on retainer?
11 "Not another bite for me!"
12 Imprinting tool
13 Like Alzheimer's disease
14 Plot lines
21 Believe in
23 Frederick Forsyth thriller "The ___ File"
25 Four-for-four Super Bowl-winning QB
26 2.5%
28 Seeing right through
30 Thus
31 All the suspects in "The Usual Suspects"

32 ___ Land, 1954 Kirk Douglas sci-fi role
35 Currency in Freetown
37 Accept
40 Animato
43 Edmond ___, the Count of Monte Cristo
45 "Your call"
47 Mountain lakes
49 Lollapalooza
51 53rd "state quarter" locale
53 Capriole
54 "Two Years Before the Mast" author
55 Leaving nothing out
58 ___ Tower Gardens, National Historic Landmark in Florida

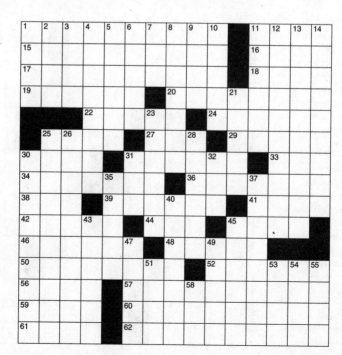

by Mark Diehl

# 104

## ACROSS

1 Social app with the slogan "the world's catalog of ideas"
10 City with the world's largest clock face
15 Hypnotized
16 Joan of Arc quality
17 Kale or quinoa, it's said
18 Phone charger feature
19 Father of Fear, in myth
20 Many sisters
22 This, in Taxco
23 A crane might hover over one
24 "Good thinking!"
26 Active ingredient in marijuana, for short
28 City in central Israel
29 Through
31 Place for bowlers
35 Ornamental garden installation
37 Quick tennis match
38 Part of a devil costume
39 Fuming
41 "You don't want to miss it!"
42 Bit of bronze
43 Statue outside Boston's TD Garden
44 Lunk
45 Watering holes
48 Eye-opening problem?
52 First name in gossip
53 Knee jerk, perhaps
55 Political accusation
56 Bill Clinton or George W. Bush, informally

58 Only highest-grossing film of the year that lost money
60 Stocking stuff
61 Spots that might smear
62 Pirouetting, perhaps
63 Bought or sold, e.g.

## DOWN

1 Fibonacci, notably
2 Temper
3 Pickup points
4 Statistician's tool
5 Say irregardless?
6 Nickname for a two-time Wimbledon winner
7 State
8 Variety of quick bread
9 Multimedia think piece
10 Stephen Curry was one in '15 and '16
11 Like some seals
12 Feature of the 1876 or 2000 presidential election
13 Cup or bowl, but not a plate
14 2012 thriller with John Goodman and Alan Arkin
21 Straight men
25 Boobs
26 4.0, maybe
27 They're straight
30 Chick's tail?
31 Party person
32 Bacteriologist's discovery
33 What emo songs may convey

34 Org. doing pat-downs
36 "Tommyrot!"
40 Large letter in a manuscript
41 Hare-hunting hounds
46 Painter Veronese
47 European country whose flag features a George Cross
48 Relieve, in a way
49 Child of Uranus
50 Passing concern?
51 Off
52 Informal move
54 It's water under the bridge
57 Successful campaign sign
59 Cut of the pie chart: Abbr.

by Andrew Kingsley

## ACROSS

1 Where to belt one down and belt one out
11 Latch (onto)
15 Not-so-firm affirmative
16 Yasmina ___, two-time Tony-winning playwright
17 Ones hitting snares
18 Fabric finish?
19 Political pundit Perino
20 "Qué ___?" ("How are you?": Sp.)
21 Demanding occupations?
23 Means of forecasting
25 It may be spiked in winter
27 Hamper
28 Sushi order
30 ___ Minor
32 Owner of Flix, in brief
33 Airhead
37 Mo. with All Saints' Day
38 Cleans up
39 Way down in Wayne Manor
42 Relative of -ish or -ory
43 Deliverer of the U.N. General Assembly speech "Atoms for Peace"
45 Musician with the 2016 album "The Ship"
46 View from the Ponte alla Carraia
47 On, in Orléans
48 Lugs
50 Terrain maker
52 Belt
56 Bandage
58 Monogram for Christ
60 Postcard printing process, for short
61 Essential element
62 Essential element
65 Treat since 1912
66 Popular ice pop
67 Danny Ocean's wife
68 Group that rejected its 2006 Rock and Roll Hall of Fame induction

## DOWN

1 Little buddy
2 Biblical name meaning "exalted father"
3 Get together after school?
4 Often-replaced reference works
5 Suffix with Québec
6 Last name of a comic strip title teen
7 Alternative to Dasani or Deer Park
8 Obscure
9 Put it to
10 ___ Sea (Bay of Whales locale)
11 Hibachi feature
12 Song lyric following "But as long as you love me so"
13 Opening for an E.P.A. worker?
14 Opportunity, e.g.
22 Title princess of a comic opera
24 Wooley of "Rawhide"
26 Helldiver, e.g.
29 Like the Arctic Ocean vis-à-vis the Atlantic
31 Set of seven countries, informally
33 Great point
34 Something hammers hit
35 Gives a gloss
36 Gerontologist's subject
40 Accordingly
41 Landscape alternative
44 Alternative to Nytol
46 11-Down buildup
49 Community spirit
51 Like talk, it's said
53 Maker of the Pocket Fisherman and Electric Food Dehydrator
54 Midway, e.g.
55 Dixie cakes
57 Some PC keys
59 One of about 1,000 in Lux.
63 Severe soreness
64 ___ Midway

by Jim Page

## ACROSS

1 Ultimate necessity
8 Needs grease, maybe
14 Cup holder
15 School whose mascot is Riptide the Pelican
16 Became untied
17 Intro to Comp Sci, for Data Structures, e.g.
18 Push away
19 Giant in sports entertainment
20 Made new?
21 Something you might take a pass on
22 Valuable diamond
24 Hosp. readout
25 Bigwig
28 One ___ (multivitamin)
29 Highly sought-after things
31 Foucault's "This Is Not ___"
32 This
36 Certain powerful engines, briefly
37 Warrants
38 Newswoman Burnett
39 Guiding light?
40 Writes to briefly?
43 Replies of understanding
44 Month with two natl. holidays
45 Auto name discontinued in 1986
48 One is a prize for scoring
50 Endowed with from the start, as money
52 Nobody special
53 Mace and shield, e.g.
54 Took for a ride
55 Hopeful
56 Closely following
57 Order that's rarely followed?

## DOWN

1 Play
2 Fair, e.g.
3 Key
4 Gem
5 Place for a long run, maybe
6 Big ___ Conference
7 Summer Olympics event
8 "A Prairie Home Companion" broadcast site
9 Becomes a traitor
10 "Where Is the Life That Late ___?" ("Kiss Me, Kate" number)
11 One with connections to traveling speakers?
12 Largest sesamoid bones
13 Et ___ (footnote abbr.)
14 Not one's best effort, in coachspeak
21 Ache
23 They can turn red in a flash
26 Contract employee?
27 Actor with the title role in "Robin Hood: Men in Tights"
28 Loan figs.
29 Beam
30 Some linemen: Abbr.
31 Just do it
32 Baseball exec Epstein
33 What to call Judge Judy
34 Words of longing
35 Some help from above
39 Southernmost city on I-35
40 Looms
41 Wolverine of Marvel Comics, e.g.
42 Derisive reaction
44 Reno, for one
46 They're not pros
47 Animal in un parc zoologique
49 Old "Red, White & You" sloganeer
50 Small nail
51 River to the Seine
52 "What you can get away with," according to Andy Warhol

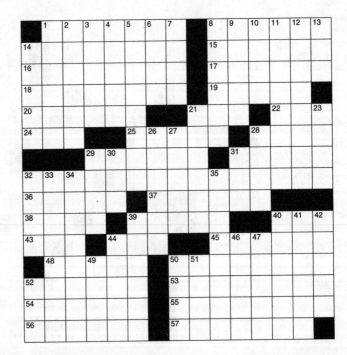

by David Liben-Nowell

## ACROSS

1 They get picked up at clubs
5 Engages in a bit of back-and-forth
10 Bread and drink
14 First name in court fiction
15 Goddesses guarding the gates of Olympus
16 Mediterranean pizza topping
17 V feature
19 Charlie Bucket's creator
20 Double-dipping, e.g.
21 One on the Lee-ward side?
22 Not working
24 Political writer/blogger Klein
25 Hits with a big charge
26 Name-dropper's word
27 Volunteer's place: Abbr.
28 Lib. arts major
30 Start to drift, say
32 Wacky morning radio team
36 Refuse
37 Like many roasted potatoes
39 Pollen ___
40 Secluded spot
41 Up until, in poetry
42 "Dona ___ Pacem" (Latin hymn)
46 Man-to-man alternative
47 Kind
50 Blow away
51 Buddy from the block
52 Homologous
54 Singer with the 1954 album "Frontier Ballads"

55 Nascar Hall-of-Famer Jarrett and others
56 Lack life
57 Means of inheritance
58 Waxed
59 Hopper full of dirt?
60 Latin word on Missouri's state seal

## DOWN

1 Something to get a spot out of?
2 Secrets
3 Utters unthinkingly
4 Give background information
5 Refuse
6 Key to the city, e.g.

7 Courtroom activity
8 Oversize hip-hop tops
9 Witness
10 Old letters in the mail
11 Starting time?
12 Alternative to Wi-Fi
13 Four-time All-Star third baseman of the 1960s–'70s
18 Dump, e.g.
23 Some sorority women
24 Historic institution on the Jubilee River
29 One of Us?
31 Slightly
32 Chess situation in which any move is a bad move

33 Witness
34 Directive that has some teeth to it?
35 Visitors' announcement
38 Signaled
43 Light shades
44 Motivate
45 Not one-sided, in a way
48 Free from faults
49 Second-largest body in the asteroid belt
53 Neighbor of Victoria: Abbr.
54 "Poppycock!"

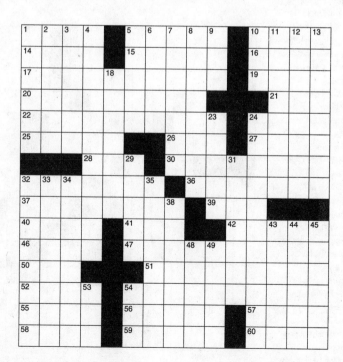

by Damon Gulczynski

# 108

## ACROSS

1 Really huge number
10 Bridge pair, briefly?
15 In a foreboding manner
16 Bane of cereal grain
17 Sufficiently good
18 Sauce often made with lemon juice
19 TiVo remote button
20 Not go to
21 Jerks
22 Lose, as a carrier might with a call
24 New York restaurateur with a Tony Award
26 Doomed
27 Round of four
29 B-ball
31 ___ Dolly ("Winter's Bone" heroine)
32 Contraction in Hamlet's soliloquy
34 1972 blaxploitation film with a soundtrack by Curtis Mayfield
36 Gun point?
40 Fur-lined cloak
41 Tight hold
43 A.L. or N.L. East: Abbr.
44 Some sports cars
45 Six-time U.S. Open champ
47 Get one's fill?
51 "That was exhausting!"
53 Ammonia and others
55 Longtime TV figure known for his garage
56 Dawgs
58 Liver by the Loire?
60 Sculptor who described art as "a fruit that grows in man"
61 "A Dog of Flanders" author

62 Bails
64 Beehive Blender brand
65 It fell in 2016 for the first time since 1919
66 Reviewers of scientific papers
67 Cause of rebellion, maybe

## DOWN

1 Thanksgiving table decorations
2 A in physics class?
3 Adolescent program, slangily
4 Goddess who saved Odysseus
5 Records
6 Doesn't show oneself, say
7 So-called "Shakespeare of the Prophets"
8 Veterans
9 Host of the web series "Emoji Science"
10 Junior posthumously inducted into the Football Hall of Fame
11 Victorians
12 Searches for oneself
13 Mustard and others
14 Dirty look
21 Rewarded for waiting
23 Climber's aid
25 Decorate
28 Blacken a bit
30 Baseball commissioner during the steroid era
33 Robot arm movers
35 Navratilova, to 45-Across, e.g.
36 "Well, la-di-frickin'-da!"
37 It has big screens for small films

38 Apple operating system that's also a geographical name
39 One to one, say
42 Seemingly everywhere
46 ___ l'oeil
48 Hideous foe of Popeye
49 Strips, as a ship
50 Valve with a disc at the end of a vertically set stem
52 Like the Atlantic Ocean, slightly, from year to year
54 Barely drink
57 They may ring after parties
59 She, in Venice
62 Project
63 Stop: Abbr.

by Kristian House

## ACROSS

1 Got smart
10 Section of a golf bag
15 Capital where "hello" is pronounced "johm riab sua"
16 Two cents' worth
17 He played Moe Greene in "The Godfather"
18 "Capeesh?"
19 Title for Romulus
20 Block at an airport, perhaps
21 Move very freely
22 Very dark
24 Drone base
25 Animal whose name is derived from the Latin for "ghosts"
26 Breakfast offering
28 March Madness conclusion
30 It's a natural
32 Burrow
33 "Tabs"
34 Suit
36 Grab (onto)
38 Like distant stars
41 One rarely seen outside its shell?
43 It's around a foot
47 Batting a thousand, say
50 Scratch
51 Insurance company symbol
52 "No ___!" ("Sure thing!")
54 Noah of "ER"
55 Twisting the knife, say
56 Kennedy who won a Medal of Freedom
58 Fracas
59 Needing guidance

60 Brand once pitched with the slogan "You're soaking in it"
62 Currency in 15-Across
63 Regional IDs
64 The Devil, e.g.
65 "Ha ha, what a dork!"

## DOWN

1 Comment made with an eye roll
2 Soil scientist's measure
3 Banished
4 Object of controversial hunts
5 Modern brain-scanning procedure, for short
6 Late Jurassic, e.g.
7 Cheating

8 Lacking courtesy
9 Frustrating exchange
10 Leeway
11 What a goose may stand on
12 Unbeatable
13 Small lollipops with collectible wrappers
14 Exercised control over
23 Dearest
27 Like Y's
29 Gentle rising and falling, of a sort
31 In the offing
35 Piece of brunch-making equipment
37 "Look who's being catty!"
38 Light carriage

39 Trouble getting started
40 Non-PC sort
42 Rarer than rare
44 Going out with a hot model?
45 Everywhere
46 She famously said "I'm single because I was born that way"
48 Rapper with the 1995 hit "I Wish"
49 Faucet brand
53 "If you want to sulk, go right ahead"
57 Crazy, in a 2010 Shakira hit
61 Common palindromic text

by Peter Wentz

## ACROSS

1 Handle things
5 Try out
9 Additional
14 With nobody playing, say
16 Retro stereo component
17 Life preserver?
18 Katherine of NBC's "State of Affairs"
19 Observes closely
20 Girl adopted by Silas Marner
21 Anxious
22 Anti-___ League (Progressive Era organization)
24 Blade brand
26 On the program
28 Feels deep sympathy
32 Site of Oscar Wilde's trials
34 By and by
35 Sound effects pioneer Jack
36 Mandatory courses
37 Eponym of Bible history
39 Ehrich ___ a.k.a. Harry Houdini
40 Was unconsciously disturbing?
41 "I, Claudius" figure
43 Blathers
45 Component of some biodiesels
50 Ones coming ashore
51 Put away for someone
53 Drafted
54 One with changing needs
55 It may be off the charts
56 Like some physicians
57 Fuses

58 Person offering you a fortune
59 Command that a dog shouldn't follow

## DOWN

1 Section of a botanical garden
2 School zone?
3 Top of the winter
4 Swords, in Sèvres
5 PC-linking program
6 It's hard to find in a crowd
7 8:00–9:00 on TV, e.g.
8 Proverbial certainty
9 Shakespeare character who coins the term "primrose path"

10 Winner of back-to-back Best Rock Instrumental Grammys in 1980 and 1981
11 The ordinary folk
12 "Scientists dream about doing great things. ___ do them": James A. Michener
13 Capacity
15 Gigli and pici, for two
23 "Dear ___" (1960s–'70s radio program)
25 Longtime "Voice of the New York Yankees"
27 Easter stock
28 Does some grilling
29 Quarters' quarters?

30 Group that almost can't fail?
31 Added to a plant
33 Treat with violent disrespect
35 Become dull
38 Lives the high life
39 Go downhill
42 Chicago Sun-Times columnist Richard
44 Soft options?
46 Brainy high school clique
47 Cosmic path
48 Former Trump Organization member
49 Like Ziegfeld girls
50 Thick of things, in a manner of speaking
52 Kid Cudi's "Day 'n' ___"

by Patrick Berry

## ACROSS

1 First name in fantasy fiction
6 Payola payoff
10 Branch extension
14 Subject for une chanteuse
15 When repeated, singer of the 1987 #1 hit "Head to Toe"
16 Exclamation sometimes said with a hand over the mouth
17 One in la-la land
19 Clichéd gift for a prisoner
20 Christ's end?
21 For instance
22 Snack brand first produced at Disneyland in the 1960s
24 Street ___
26 Alternative to a snap
28 Asia's ___ Darya River
29 Structural support
31 Stephen who was nominated for a 1992 Best Actor Oscar
32 Title sometimes shortened by removing its middle letter
34 Dish that often includes anchovies
37 Website for people interested in "cultivating" a relationship?
38 "Lemme be straight with you . . ."
39 Good-for-nothing
40 Letterhead abbr.
41 5½-point type
45 Falcons, on scoreboards
46 Staple of Victorian architecture
49 Square
50 McCarthy in Hollywood
52 Break down, maybe
54 Terse admission
55 For the ages
56 Some kitchen utensils
59 Court psychologist's ruling
60 Where Arthur Ashe played college tennis
61 Book before Philemon
62 Summer coolers
63 Round end, of a sort
64 Curry of the N.B.A.

## DOWN

1 Educational foundations
2 Lend
3 One day's drive, maybe
4 N.F.C. South pro
5 They're graded in geology class
6 Spot for autograph seekers
7 Top
8 One who works a lot?
9 Bulldog rival
10 Spelling with lines
11 "Whew!," upon arriving home
12 Cry before rage-quitting
13 Plaster of paris, essentially
18 King James, e.g.
23 Country that's home to Dracula's Castle
25 Tickets, in slang
27 Pupil
30 They're often said to be sitting or moving
33 Claim
35 Angst-ridden and moody
36 Currency of Peru
37 Place to do some shots?
38 It has rules for writing
39 San Diego suburb known as the "Jewel of the Hills"
42 Wing it?
43 Get misty
44 Catch in a net
47 Deplete
48 One exposed by a flip-flop
51 Summer coolers
53 Counter orders?
57 Bitter ___
58 Card

by Andrew J. Ries

## ACROSS

1 One making waves over the waves
10 Bridge support
14 Lothario's activity
16 Wearing red to a Chinese funeral, e.g.
17 It has no life
19 Very well-pitched
20 Become flowery
21 Fat: Fr.
22 Cuff
23 Company that makes Tamiflu
24 Mailed or faxed
26 Head of Hogwarts
28 Salon job
30 Says "Top o' the morning," say
32 Shoshone language relative
33 Quite removed (from)
36 Manager honored at Cooperstown in 2013
40 Marker
41 Kitchen drawers?
43 Pilates class sights
45 Southern African game
46 Give a raise?
50 Zoom (along)
52 Many are named after M.L.K.
54 Sit (down) heavily
55 Bond femme fatale
57 Prestidigitator's word
58 Summoning statement
60 Cousin of a kite
61 Modern parents may try to limit it
62 Jazz combo?
63 Broadway star who was on Nixon's list of enemies

## DOWN

1 Playground set
2 Painter Jean-___ Fragonard
3 Certain Cornhusker
4 Film setting?
5 Drawn together
6 "Huckleberry Finn" character
7 Conductor who has a hall at Tanglewood named after him
8 Worthy of reference
9 Lego competitor
10 Administer, as a shot
11 "The Consolation of Philosophy" author
12 Aeschylus, Sophocles and Aristophanes
13 College recruitment org.
15 Camera manufacturer whose slogan is "Be a Hero"
18 Shout of surprise
22 Genre that "The Long Goodbye" is based on
25 "Cake Boss" network
27 World capital with 40 islands within its city limits
29 Breakfast spot?
31 Cannon shot in Hollywood
33 Word shouted before "Fire!"
34 Material for mounting photos
35 Get perfectly pitched, in a way
37 Midwest college town
38 Farm butter
39 Openings in the computer field?
42 Longtime "Meet the Press" moderator
44 Places for pilots
45 Digs around
47 Cesario's lover in literature
48 Serious
49 Worked the field, in a way
51 "Yet that thy brazen gates of heaven may ___": Shak.
53 Pianist McCoy ___, member of the John Coltrane Quartet
55 Hearing command
56 Brief moments
57 Start of a classic boast
59 c, in a text

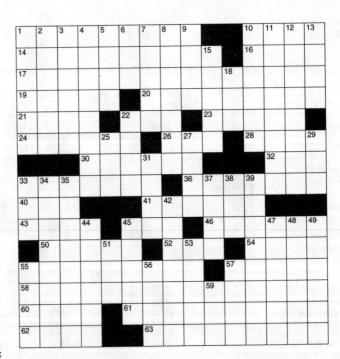

by Andrew Zhou

## ACROSS

1 Collection of high lights?
8 Something a dog might fetch
15 Capital of the French department of Loiret
16 Smokeless explosive
17 Youngest-ever Nobel Prize recipient
19 Pennsylvania county named for an animal
20 Delights
21 Cab alternative
22 Cold shower?
24 Missouri and Arizona
25 Fast-food menu information: Abbr.
26 ___ dirt
28 Mich. neighbor
29 "Love Is Strange" actress
30 In a ball
32 Frickin'
34 Things discussed at une académie
36 Like safeties vis-à-vis field goals
37 Missed a lot
40 Got rid of
43 Hot
44 Science fiction author Stanislaw
46 Indian-born maestro
47 Spanish pronoun
48 Head of an Indian tribe
50 Hold
51 Mil. figures
52 Colloquy
54 Pennsylvania and others: Abbr.
55 Was brutally honest
58 Firedog
59 Electron's area around an atom
60 Easy shoes to put on
61 Makes secret again, as court documents

## DOWN

1 "I wasn't expecting it, but . . ."
2 Skipping sounds
3 "Seriously . . ."
4 New Deal power agcy.
5 Colt 45, e.g., informally
6 Writer Nin
7 Classic film whose soundtrack is famously composed entirely of strings
8 One going around the block?
9 Shakes
10 Portfolio parts, for short
11 Many an email attachment
12 Italian food named after a queen
13 Amazon, e.g.
14 Curbs
18 Clearing
23 Things corporations and fire trucks both have
25 [Emergency!]
27 Like kiwi fruits
29 Engine sound
31 Cool, in slang
33 Drain
35 Pacific Island group
37 Dishes sometimes served with Riojas
38 Blink of an eye
39 ___-A
41 Like the Olympic flame
42 Fairy tale figures
45 "Someone who allows you to see the hope inside yourself," per Oprah
48 Dakota dialect
49 Olympic skier Phil or Steve
52 Modern know-it-all
53 Bull Run victors
56 Double ___
57 "I already have other plans," often

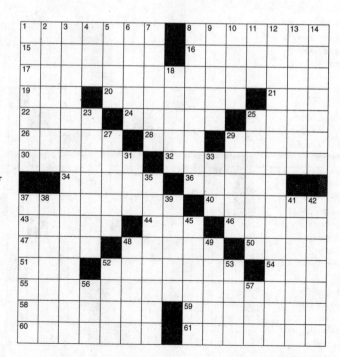

by Mary Lou Guizzo

## ACROSS

1 Golf handicap of zero
8 Like some garages
14 Where Forrest Gump played college football
15 Everything included
16 "Funky Cold Medina" rapper
17 Gives a walk-through, say
18 Fig. on a quarterly report
19 Test pattern?
21 Certain flight pattern
22 1970s TV spinoff
24 Some mouse cells
25 Broadway score?
26 Weigh station sight
27 Place to go when you're not going to the races, for short?
28 Joneses (for)
29 Creamy chilled soup
33 Source of break-dancing beats
35 N.B.A. M.V.P. who has hosted "Saturday Night Live"
36 Inroad
37 New Agey sounds
38 Facial option at a spa
42 "Everyone's private driver" sloganeer
43 Kind of walk
45 River of forgetfulness
46 Jerk
47 "The Chalk Garden" playwright, 1955
49 Shipload
50 1983 hit song that mentions Santa Monica Boulevard
52 Arcane matters
54 Lazy bum
55 Access
56 Playwright Eve
57 Pinch-hitter

## DOWN

1 Figures in ribald Greek plays
2 Make a decent person out of?
3 Stochastic
4 Vigoda of "The Godfather"
5 Shire of "The Godfather"
6 "Get outta here!"
7 Collaborative computer coding event
8 Plants sometimes used to make flour
9 Letter of the law?
10 Not you specifically
11 Exchange words
12 Creature that Dalí walked on a leash in public
13 Puts back in the original state
15 Weapon that's thrown
20 Swedish-based maker of infant carriers
23 Seedy place to drink
25 "I'm down with that"
27 Quattuor doubled
28 Rip off
30 Reply that's a bit of a humblebrag
31 Contestants in a war of words?
32 BJ's competitor, informally
33 Major blood protein
34 Cry before taking the plunge
36 Pointless
39 Make it
40 What it always starts with?
41 College where Rutherford B. Hayes was valedictorian
43 Less tanned
44 "OMG!," old-style
45 Component of the combo drug Sinemet
47 Actress Daniels or Neuwirth
48 Practice exam?
51 ___ d'Isère (French ski resort)
53 Spam's place

by James Mulhern

## ACROSS

1 One of a pair of cuddlers
9 Desired response to a 3-Down
15 Handel bars
16 Bartender's stock
17 Participates in quid pro quo
18 Edward Gorey's "The Gashlycrumb ___"
19 In trouble for base violations?
20 1982 international chart-topper by Trio with a repetitive title
21 Digits in flats, maybe
22 Noted challenges for movers
24 About 92% of britannium
25 Start of a lawyer's conclusion
27 Tar liquid
28 One getting hammered
29 Some workers along Chesapeake Bay
31 Roman soldier who became a Christian martyr
33 Very long span
35 Grinder
36 Call to someone on deck
40 Like sand dunes
44 G.I. portions
45 Symbol of happiness
47 Iraklion is its capital
48 First Chinese dynasty
49 Relating to the abdomen
51 Just those of Juan's things?
52 It's on track to serve people
54 Showy and sudden
56 Like live-blogged sports updates
57 Everything must go in it
58 Deceitful sorts
59 Basic count
60 Three-footers
61 Hoarder's squalor

## DOWN

1 Western wear
2 Major export of Western Australia
3 Series of bloopers
4 Puts away under pressure?
5 ___ deck
6 ___ deck
7 Where a mud engineer works
8 Awful rating
9 Showboat
10 Billy the Kid, e.g.
11 Rear
12 Howard Hughes, for one
13 Taking seriously
14 Subject of the 2013 film "The Fifth Estate"
23 Chris of CBS's "The Good Wife"
26 Kind of diagram
28 Motive that makes sense
30 Spelling pro?
32 Decker or Dickerson of the N.F.L.
34 { }, in mathematics
36 Off-road racer
37 Huffington of The Huffington Post
38 March interrupter, maybe
39 Purchased
41 Take to term
42 Headliners at le Palais Garnier, e.g.
43 Spelunker's activity
46 Place for an anchor
49 Brand once advertised with the line "They never get on your nerves"
50 Addition sign
53 Give up
55 Subway Series squad

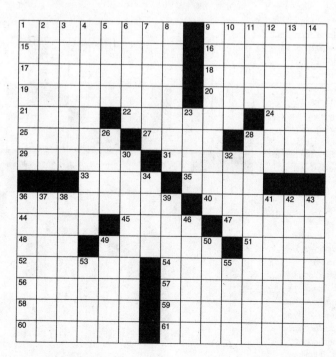

by David Woolf

# 116

## ACROSS

1 Yoda, e.g.
11 Communication problem?
15 Last of a series of nicknames
16 Zero
17 Billy Crystal's role in "The Princess Bride"
18 Enigma machine decoder Turing
19 It's not a welcome sign
20 Facebook and others
21 Primary funding sources, briefly
22 Facebook, for one
23 Org. whose symbol is an eagle atop a key
24 How garden vegetables may be planted
26 Upset
28 Manicure destroyer
29 Hot Wheels garages?
33 Rhoda's TV mom
34 Emerald ___ borer
37 Expert savers
38 Constitution Hall grp.
39 Marathon champ Pippig
40 Mesozoic Era period
42 Home of Queen Margrethe II
44 Rank below marquis
47 "Let's do it!"
48 Sch. whose first building was Dallas Hall
51 Matches, at a table
53 "Caravan of Courage: An ___ Adventure" (1984 "Star Wars" spinoff)
54 Some Siouans
55 Bayh of Indiana politics
56 Flock gathering place
57 Group getting its kicks?
59 Rep
60 "I could use some help here . . ."
61 First name in architecture
62 Place to test the water

## DOWN

1 Harry Potter's father
2 Alchemist's concoction
3 Frito-Lay chip
4 "Bleah!"
5 El Capitan platform
6 Literary hero whose name is Turkish for "lion"
7 Parts of a flight
8 2012 Republican National Convention host
9 Connection concerns, for short
10 "Toy Story" dino
11 Show impatience with
12 Developing company?
13 Wrapper that's hard to remove?
14 It's tailored to guys
24 Drinks with domed lids
25 Interest for a cryptozoologist
27 Impasse
28 Quadrant separator
30 "___ serious?"
31 Lab report?
32 Pay termination?
34 Nielsens measure
35 Fancy glasses
36 Malady with many "remedies"
41 Legal precedents
43 Get by
45 Awaken
46 Get support from
48 Photosynthesis opening
49 Interest of a mycologist
50 Quotidian
52 Old dummy
54 "Wait, I know that!"
57 Some savers' assets
58 Main hub for Virgin America, for short

by Robyn Weintraub

## ACROSS

1 Eighty-sixes
7 Rhetorical creation
15 Green
16 First Palme d'Or-winning film directed by a woman (1993)
17 "That thought already occurred to me"
19 Let fate decide, say
20 Subatomic particles with zero spin
21 Kind of cabbage
22 Pillory
26 Pump option, for short
27 Marinara sauce ingredients
32 Structures with excellent insulation
34 Telemarketing tactic
36 Try to find oneself?
38 Warming
39 David Fincher thriller of 2014
41 Had a list
42 Bid on a hand unsuited for suit play, maybe
43 Cusk-___ (deepest living fish, at 27,000+ feet)
45 Rockets
46 Leaders in robes
48 Screens
53 Onetime Fandango competitor
58 One with a long stretch to go?
60 Blaring
61 Fisher for compliments on one's dress?
62 "Les Misérables" extra
63 Managed

## DOWN

1 Infatuated, old-style
2 Italian city where Pliny the Elder and Younger were born
3 Matrix specifications
4 "Sob"
5 Type of mobile phone plan
6 Take to living together, with "up"
7 Austrian philosopher Rudolf
8 "Phew!"
9 One might turn on it
10 Per
11 Modern flight amenity
12 Main ingredient of rémoulade
13 Composer of many limericks, for short
14 "À ___ la Liberté" (1931 René Clair film)
18 Period of a revolution?
22 San ___
23 Urge
24 It's all the same
25 Einstein-___ bridge (wormhole)
27 Game's turning point?
28 Brand of sponge
29 Cousin of a skate
30 Neuter
31 Places for runners
33 First word in many temple names
35 Something odd in roulette?
37 Pricing model for many apps
40 Newspaper name that becomes a beverage if you insert an "a" after its fifth letter
44 "___ a little!"
47 State fair attractions
48 Uphill climb, say
49 Drone's place
50 Breaking a comb, in Japan, e.g.
51 "I agree," in slang
52 Toni Morrison novel
54 Menu bar heading
55 Plot feature in "Hansel and Gretel"
56 Old brand in the shaving aisle
57 Puzzle designer Rubik
59 Young women's grp.

by Julian Lim

## ACROSS

1 Connections
4 Connections to the sternum
8 Not assured at all
13 "You can figure as well as I can"
16 Treasure
17 Cream song with the lyric "Dance floor is like the sea, / Ceiling is the sky"
18 Things that may be compressed
19 Excluded category in the Paleo diet
20 Little treasure
21 Now
22 Kind of wave
23 Wasabi go-with in sushi meals
24 List heading
25 People who are in them are out, in brief
26 Shavit with the 2013 best seller "My Promised Land"
27 Where Spike Lee earned his M.F.A.
30 Little: Fr.
31 Not identifying with one's assigned sex
34 1851 Sojourner Truth speech
35 Online addresses, in part
36 "Ur hilarious!"
37 Bit of evasion
38 Still
39 Two or three sets, say
42 Where the Taj Mahotsav festival is held
44 Either director of "Inside Llewyn Davis"
46 Part of MSG
47 Fit

49 Info in a Yelp listing: Abbr.
50 Either half of a 1973 "duel"
51 Lacked options
52 Ask
54 Tribe whose name means "long tail"
55 Dessert so-called for its portions of flour, butter, eggs and sugar
56 Purchase at a golf pro shop
57 Purchases at a golf pro shop
58 Flushed

## DOWN

1 "Don't you doubt me!"
2 "You cheated!"
3 Round containers?
4 Bet (on)

5 Subj. of many antiglobalization protests
6 Threat of a strike, in labor negotiations
7 Lead
8 Birdbrained
9 Birdbrain
10 Typical "S.N.L." start
11 Something you can control the volume with?
12 "Me?" follower
14 "___, boy!"
15 Terse and unadorned, as writing
23 Part of MGM's motto
26 "Babalú" bandleader
28 Ones ranking above knaves
29 Not realized
31 Fashion mogul Gunn
32 ___ Marcos, Tex.

33 Some "CSI" figs.
34 App with over 200 free stations
35 Place to play with toys
36 Things that might be batted at a ball
39 Approach
40 Something not many people laugh at
41 Blew it
43 Floral symbol of patience
45 ". . . but I could be wrong"
46 Comedian Maron
48 Superlatively
50 Contends (for)
53 Clément Marot poem "A ___ Damoyselle Malade"

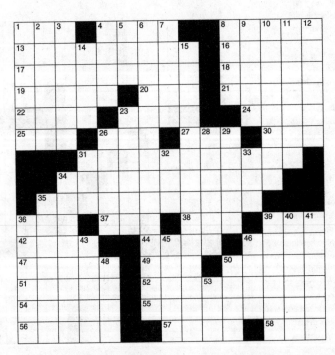

by Natan Last

## ACROSS

1 Something that might be built around a police station
8 Hen tracks
15 Came aboard, in a way
16 Long-running Joel McHale show on E!
17 Not free
18 Seedy place
19 Bengali who won the 1913 Literature Nobel
20 Small glass disk used as an ornament in a stained-glass window
21 Melted munchie
22 Kind of bean
23 Follower of a team
24 Rear
25 Source of anago sushi
27 Golf units: Abbr.
28 Roughly half of all binary code
29 "Friendly staff" or "For a limited time only"
31 Swallowing worry in an old wives' tale
36 Potential libel defendant
37 Next ___
38 Latin trio leader
41 No-brainers?
42 Call from the lobby, perhaps
43 "Utopia" writer, 1516
45 "___ thou love me?": Juliet
46 Completely block
47 "The difference between ordinary and extraordinary," per Vladimir Horowitz

49 Steve Buscemi's role in "Reservoir Dogs"
50 Reveal
51 Triple-platinum Lady Gaga hit of 2011
52 Longtime fitness guru Jack
53 Keep close relations?
54 Part of a physical
55 Common dorm room decorations

## DOWN

1 Words of explanation
2 Something sweet potatoes provide
3 Brightly colored marine fish
4 Three albums bound together, e.g.
5 Hero-worship, say
6 Jazz pianist Allison
7 Raid target
8 Forte
9 Directive in tennis after odd-numbered games
10 On a pension: Abbr.
11 Lent symbols
12 Unclear, as thinking
13 Put off guard
14 Blender settings
20 Goes without a leash
22 A child can have a blast with it
25 People ruled by an elective monarchy
26 ___ al Khaymah (one of U.A.E.'s seven emirates)

30 Isolate
32 Go head-to-head with?
33 Doctor's patient, e.g.
34 Create a tunnel beneath
35 "The Brady Bunch" bunch
38 Shot glass?
39 Béchamel sauce with Gruyère added
40 Font of knowledge
44 Brilliance
46 Easily outscores
48 What calisthenics improve
49 One up front?
51 High-pitched cry

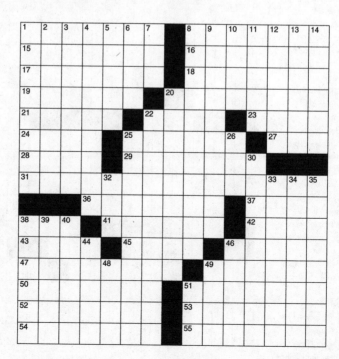

by Mark Diehl

## ACROSS

1 Ones making the rules?
16 "Thanks"
17 Passage between Sicily and the toe of Italy
18 Laughfests
19 Take home, perhaps?
20 ___ scripta (statutes)
21 Blyth of "Mildred Pierce"
22 Word before or after "what"
23 Org. opposed to weaving?
25 Scottish refusal
27 Band from the East
29 "1984" concern
38 Pre-buffet declaration
39 Take legal action, say
40 Sheep-counting times
41 Gendered Spanish suffix
42 Prize for Pizarro
43 Gulf War ally
46 Occasion for dragon dances
48 Cousin of a zebra
51 Something that might interrupt a flight, for short
53 "Little ___"
55 Frequent flier
57 Didn't mince words
60 It's of no concern to a usurer
61 Showed caution, in a way

## DOWN

1 Perfume named for Baryshnikov
2 Shirley of "Goldfinger"
3 It comes with strings attached
4 Cross words
5 "Mila 18" novelist
6 Abbr. after many a military name
7 Twenty: Prefix
8 Faboo
9 Go, for one
10 Whistle blower?
11 Model X maker
12 "___ complicated"
13 Labor day highlight
14 Batman co-creator Bob
15 Memphis-based record label
22 Large beer mug
24 "Stay"
25 Ad follower?
26 Hopeless
28 Doesn't need a thing
29 Server's bread and butter
30 Round openings in domes
31 Shredded
32 French thinker?
33 Sounds during a massage
34 Arteries: Abbr.
35 Definitive disclaimer
36 Just slightly
37 Seas overseas
44 "Bird on ___" (Mel Gibson/Goldie Hawn comedy)
45 Picked up on
46 Tin anniversary
47 ___-deux
48 Fictional title character who declares "How puzzling all these changes are!"
49 Sub standard?
50 Way up
51 Hit the ground
52 Transparent sheet
54 More than more
55 Org. with many banned Super Bowl ads
56 "Before ___ you go . . ."
58 Clue follower: Abbr.
59 What's left on a farm?

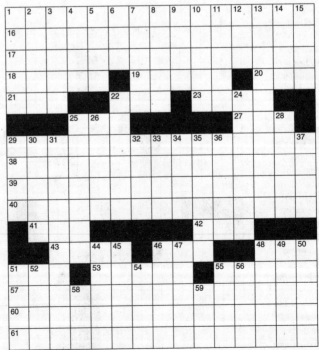

by Martin Ashwood-Smith

## ACROSS

1. Rugby rival of Harvard
7. It operates Hamburger U.
15. Like many offshore rescues
16. Visiting only a short time
17. 1955 R&B hit for Bo Diddley
18. "Ri-i-ight"
19. Buff
20. 17-Across, to the self-titled "Bo Diddley"
21. Took care of
22. Free of shampoo, say
24. Shut (up)
25. "Cleopatre" artist
26. Directory listings: Abbr.
27. A place antelope lope
29. Kittenish
30. Maugham's title girl of Lambeth
31. Suspicion
32. Live
34. Uses without sharing, in slang
37. What there often is for improvement
38. Golfer nicknamed Long John
39. Interruption of service?
40. Model material
41. Translation material
42. Website used by a lot of artisans
43. Breeze (along)
44. "Huh . . . never mind then"
46. One of "the highest form of literature," per Hitchcock
47. They're "made by fools like me," per Kilmer
49. Parades, with "out"
51. Rollback events
53. Start, in a way
54. Squeaker
55. Lift one's spirits?
56. Subterranean scurrier
57. Played first

## DOWN

1. Unhand or disarm?
2. Oscar winner before "Grand Hotel"
3. 1974 National Book Award winner by Thomas Pynchon
4. Daughter and half sister of Oedipus
5. Shows a preference
6. Shared computer syst.
7. One who goes on to try to conquer the Universe?
8. Language akin to Yupik
9. ID
10. End of a lap
11. They may reduce sentences, for short
12. "And how!"
13. Four-time N.B.A. scoring champion in the 2010s
14. Vessel opener
20. Still matter?
23. Tough nut to crack
24. Court position
25. Prefix with village
27. Front-and-center section
28. Like fringe festival fare
30. It has a Marxist-Leninist ideology
33. Car payment?
34. Bêtes noires
35. Aid in studying a culture
36. Dump
38. Equipment for a rock band
40. Gewgaw
42. Coat
43. Design info
44. Davis of film
45. Really put one's foot down
47. Berth place
48. Repute
50. Was reckless, in a way
52. K'ung Fu-___
53. 41-Across is a topic in it, briefly

by James Mulhern

# 122

## ACROSS

1 Like the national currency known as the tala
7 Axilla
13 "Hold on there now!"
15 Chasm
16 Powerful pitch
17 Settled with
18 London locale: Abbr.
19 Like the outer core of the earth
21 Certain logic gate
22 One Direction member Payne
24 The Flying Dutchman, e.g.
25 Limb-entangling weapon
26 One nearly cut Bond in half in "Goldfinger"
29 Rise up
30 1983 double-platinum album by Duran Duran
31 Everyday productivity enhancer, in modern lingo
33 Fictional character whose name is French for "flight of death"
36 Leading newspaper that took its name from a stage comedy
37 It's nothing, really
38 One making introductions
39 "You can't make me!"
44 Queen dowager of Jordan
45 Beyond repair
46 Ago, in an annual song
47 Animal with horns
48 Norman ___, first Asian-American to hold a cabinet post
50 Abbr. in an office address
51 Princess cake and others
53 Simply not done
56 Show disdain for, in a way
57 Subject of some PC Magazine reviews
58 Mixed forecasts?
59 N.F.L. Hall-of-Famer nicknamed "The Kansas Comet"

## DOWN

1 Singer Twain
2 Blood lines
3 "Are you ___?!"
4 Cries that might be made while hopping on one foot
5 Slight interruption
6 Sure-to-succeed
7 One with commercial interests, for short
8 Nothing, in Nantes
9 Chant often heard toward the end of an N.B.A. season
10 Rick's, for one
11 Speech habits unique to an individual
12 The first one was delivered in 1984
13 "___ Stop the Rain" (1970 hit)
14 Fright night?
20 Pusillanimous
23 More festive
25 Views
27 Hiker's climb
28 Six-time Hugo Award winner Ben
29 Invoice word
32 Actress Sherilyn who was an Emmy nominee for "Twin Peaks"
33 Common ingredient in furniture polish
34 "No doubt!"
35 NASA spacecraft designed for travel to Mars
36 Units at a horse race
40 Whiskered animals
41 With 54-Down, longtime Long Island home of Theodore Roosevelt
42 Lays to rest
43 Frigid temps
45 They may have bullets
48 Main thrust
49 Field
52 The Nikkei 225 is one of its indexes: Abbr.
54 See 41-Down
55 Some lines of Milton

by Mary Lou Guizzo and Jeff Chen

## ACROSS

1 Pickup trucks from a foreign-owned company made and sold only in North America
13 Familiar story line
15 Durable, as a wristwatch
17 Goes no further
18 Moon, in Montreuil
19 Imitation
21 Ford contemporary
22 To some degree
23 Jugged ___ (old British delicacy)
24 Jazzman Montgomery
25 White sheets
26 Second part of a historic trio
27 Some prizes on "The Price Is Right"
28 Dance with high kicks
29 They're put in barrels
32 Keeps a mock rivalry going, say
33 "___ in Moscow" (1959 children's book)
34 Funereal tempo
35 Air spirit, in folklore
36 Metallic stickers
37 "Golly Gosh Oh ___" (Conway Twitty song)
40 Entertainment Weekly interviewee
41 Niche religions
42 Low lament
43 ___ Parker, director and star of 2016's "The Birth of a Nation"
44 Not staged
45 Land line?

46 Sitcom mom whose kids were named Becky, Darlene and D.J.
49 $100 purchase in Monopoly
50 Something played at 1980s parties

## DOWN

1 Ticket waster
2 Eat fast, slangily
3 Dresses down
4 Niche religions
5 Dovekies, e.g.
6 "This is ___"
7 Single-rotation skating jumps
8 Covers
9 Ruins the reputation of
10 Discombobulated
11 Small carp
12 Hit hard
14 Add value to
16 Winemaking byproduct
20 Monetary resources
22 Go down toward home?
25 Campus newbie
26 Symptoms of guilt
27 Liqueur in a margarita
28 Bready bunch?
29 Pitch, e.g.
30 Affirmed's rival for the Triple Crown
31 Protégé of Stalin
32 Compiler of an 1855 reference work
34 "The Jack ___ Show," 1959–85
36 Start of a Spanish greeting
37 Australian monitor lizard
38 Show some leniency
39 Starter follower
41 Is a quick learner?
42 His house in Giverny is now a museum
45 Smuggler's hideaway
47 Monarch's reign, perhaps
48 Cool ___

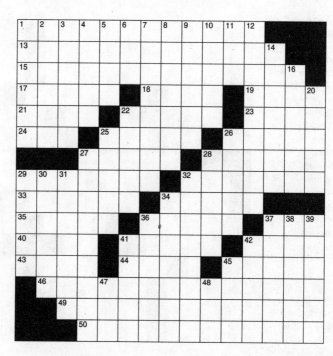

by Patrick Berry

# 124

## ACROSS

1 Brand of headphones
11 Sellers of buckets
15 Brought about
16 Smooth
17 Annual fashion event since 1948
18 ___ torch
19 Put in the trash
20 One hanging around in a deli?
22 Queen Elizabeth spells her name with one
23 Romanian currency units
24 Use Venmo, say
25 Mozart's "Le ___ di Figaro"
27 Imprecise stats: Abbr.
29 File folder part
30 One taking a survey
31 Taking on a new identity, in a way
34 Once-standard subject no longer taught in most schools
36 "That must be the case"
37 One of 32 for Beethoven
39 Harmless
40 Daytime star
41 Temper tantrum outbursts
45 To whom "Matchmaker, Matchmaker" is sung
46 Abbr. on old Eurasian maps
47 Play-___
48 Health abbr.
49 Measure the length of again
52 Game in which it's illegal to play left-handed

53 Crushed cacao beans used to make chocolate
55 Leave one's drawers in the drawer, say
57 Posthuman race of literature
58 Secret society invoked in many conspiracy theories
59 Match up
60 Participates in combat

## DOWN

1 Fifth place?
2 Offers a similar opinion to
3 Nails a test
4 Hats in the Highlands
5 Navigation abbr.
6 Parts of an "S.N.L." audition

7 Athleisure wear
8 Police department resources
9 Something no one person can run
10 Eponymous Dutch town
11 Baby skunk
12 Makes curly
13 Soda debut of 2005
14 Baseball Hall-of-Famer Duke
21 Privy to a practical joke, say
26 "Don't count your chickens before they hatch," e.g.
28 Tough situation
29 Something to do to a shoulder or the brakes
30 Corolla part

32 Someone who's really too good to be competing
33 Hu-u-uge
34 With alacrity
35 Seller of calorific pastries
38 Anvil, hammer or stirrup
39 James F. ___, Truman secretary of state
42 God, in Hebrew
43 Maintain, as standards
44 Sure winner
46 Fancy wrap
50 Protection: Var.
51 Stone that's cast
52 Gasp
54 Word usually written in brackets
56 ___ drop

by Caleb Madison

## ACROSS

1 They may require more than one return
16 Subject for James Beard or Emeril Lagasse
17 Not fade
18 Loosen, in a way
19 Viking poet
20 Account
21 Cutting comments
26 Descendant of Ishmael
27 When le jardin is at its height
28 Untouchables
30 Who said "The serpent deceived me, and I ate"
31 Practical-minded
34 Stuff used in some nasty pranks
35 Race day opening event
41 "Hey!," to Jorge
42 Relatives of guppies
43 Windjammer's setting
44 Element in traditional medicine
46 Safari sighting
47 Some referee calls, for short
48 Something one can be knocked for
50 ___ plane
51 The glow of a glowworm
57 Fed decision that spurs growth
58 Explored before making a commitment

## DOWN

1 Soldier, at times
2 Issue
3 Tools for pharmacists
4 "Glee" character in a wheelchair
5 Confirmation, e.g.
6 Haus call?
7 ___ kwon do
8 Tip
9 Common French word that sounds like two letters of the alphabet
10 Greek consonants
11 Residents: Abbr.
12 Home of the first Universal Studios outside the U.S.
13 Source of some Mideast calls
14 West Berlin used to be one
15 Makings of a plot
21 Feature of Wayne Manor
22 Magazine
23 1942 Abbott and Costello comedy
24 Three-for-two, say
25 Shamelessly promoted, with "for"
28 Zaftig
29 Popular author most of whose work is written in anapestic tetrameter
32 Put mileage on
33 ABC or Fox, in Variety-speak
35 Be roommates
36 Middle of a field of vision
37 Gets accustomed to a transplant
38 Suspiciously
39 Come back
40 Plate armor designed to protect the thighs
45 Pianist Jorge
47 Exercise in economy of language
49 Unalloyed
50 Court proceedings
52 Doc's recommendation
53 Final finish?
54 Utmost
55 Now or long lead-in
56 Prop for a classic magician's trick

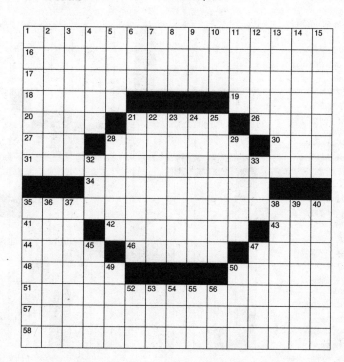

by Roland Huget

## ACROSS

1 Unfamiliar and unsettling
6 Muslim V.I.P.
13 Ones sticking around a desert?
14 Like the Trix rabbit
16 Word on many campaign stickers
17 Press orders
19 "Stop! Turn your papers over"
20 Some bread loaves
21 With 29-Down, what someone who's a natural has
22 Award for mystery writers
24 Classic clown name
25 Singer with the 2007 autobiography "Out of Sync"
29 Wreck
30 Pac-Man was its "Man of the Year" in 1982
32 It counts down to disaster
35 Perform a disco dance
36 Early conqueror of Valencia
37 Ancient land of Sidon and Tyre
42 "Oh, by the way . . ."
43 1960s TV unit
44 Parking space
45 Places for aces or cases
50 Let it all out
51 Place to watch a game
53 Expression of grief
54 Literary stigma
55 Bone that's better known as the anvil
56 "Star Wars" villain
57 Force for change

## DOWN

1 Perfumery compound
2 Spanish pro soccer association
3 Hired gun, in underworld lingo
4 "You get the point"
5 Critic's pick?
6 River running "down to a sunless sea," in "Kubla Khan"
7 Carnage
8 Polynesian capital
9 Surname at the Daily Planet
10 "___ off to you!"
11 Pirate's exclamation
12 Overly anxious
15 Modern sort of "Noah's Ark"
18 Very muscular, in slang
20 Border river in the Midwest
23 Spoke with hesitation
24 Classic clown name
26 Make sense
27 Flop's opposite
28 Tell
29 See 21-Across
31 Symbols near key signatures
32 Large spoonfuls
33 Investor's purchase outside an exchange, informally
34 Where I-70 meets I-75
35 Negotiates
38 John who wrote "The Cider House Rules"
39 Pressure
40 Futuristic weapon
41 Source of springtime stress for a H.S. student
45 Part of many common shortcuts
46 World capital with a nearly car-free city center
47 Commercial lead-in to X
48 Figure on a utility bill
49 Second-most common family name in Vietnam, after Nguyen
52 Certain stinger
53 One of 30 in junio

by Sam Ezersky

## ACROSS

1 Luxury Hyundai
6 Villain's part, often
10 Letters before Q
14 Get going
15 Comment after a burp
17 Sing to a baby, maybe
18 Antibiotic ointment
19 Court interruption
21 Former reality TV show first hosted by Anderson Cooper
22 Ancient Greek colonnade
23 Good time to build a castle?
25 John, overseas
26 Hero of New Orleans
27 Big gulp
31 Doctors' orders?
32 Classic paperback publisher
33 Touching, maybe
35 "House of Cards," e.g.
38 Oneirologist's study
39 "Pulp Fiction" actor Rhames
40 9-Down selection
41 Class
42 Ministers (to)
43 Starter for starter?
44 Embiggen
47 Cool, colloquially
48 Flawlessly styled, in modern slang
51 Hopes, with some effort, that one will
53 Major thoroughfare in Rome
55 Sticky patch
56 Real lifesavers
57 Tub-thump
58 Sediment
59 "___ Funny That Way" (old song standard)
60 Apollo played with them

## DOWN

1 Vacation destinations off the coast of Venezuela
2 Path of an overnight star
3 Compliment, typically
4 Red Spanish wine
5 Member of the British royal family
6 Japanese lunch option
7 Paleolithic relic
8 Role on the 1960s "Star Trek"
9 Some rolls
10 Argentine soccer star, informally
11 Rocket stabilizer
12 Be hot
13 Something carried by a singer
16 Tore
20 First king to unite all the Frankish tribes
24 Successfully wooed
26 Image on the South Carolina flag
28 What every actor would probably like to do
29 School in the Big Sky Conference
30 Comfy shoe features
33 Back-to-school purchase
34 Vegan no-nos
36 The King, late in his career
37 Fair game
42 ". . . the Lord ___ away"
45 Must get
46 "Jay ___ Garage" (Emmy-winning series)
47 Like pub patrons
48 Indianapolis Motor Speedway, e.g.
49 Highest score in baccarat
50 Writing on the wall, so to speak
52 Teen ___
54 Polo alternative

by Sam Trabucco

# 128

## ACROSS

1. Something to keep a watch on
6. Veal or chicken dish, for short
10. Hard-core
14. Like much of Shakespeare's and Sappho's love poetry
16. Show of hands?
17. Utopian
18. Actress Sedgwick in Warhol films
19. Fall back
20. Wise
22. What drivers try not to go over
23. Guest's sleeping spot, maybe
24. Peter or Paul, but not Mary
27. Wood used to make electric guitars
30. Hunk
32. Sine, cosine or tangent
33. What Christine is in the book "Christine"
34. Medal, e.g.
36. Take heat from?
37. Polish-language film that won a 2014 Oscar
38. Margarita garnishes
39. Ailment spreadable through kissing
40. TV character with a rippled snout
41. Facebook calendar addition
42. Facebook photo addition
43. Ready for renting
45. Part of CBS: Abbr.
46. Boutonniere's spot
48. "2 Broke Girls" actress Dennings
50. Cold-blooded sorts
52. Behind the eight ball
57. Action film weapons
58. Lacking hormones, say
60. King Lear's loyal servant
61. Service with a Street View option
62. Lip
63. They're of little use unless they're cracked
64. Horse ___

## DOWN

1. Fan sound
2. Heckled
3. "___ her in a club down in old Soho" (opening lyric of "Lola")
4. Not just increase
5. Orator's aid
6. Like a society in which people are said to be colorblind
7. Many a role on TV's "Suits": Abbr.
8. Pioneering photojournalist Jacob
9. Big espresso purveyor since 2001
10. Wiped out
11. Subject of some parental restrictions
12. "Hey, don't look at me!"
13. Trademarked repellent
15. Pirate-fighting org.
21. They can swing left or right
24. Dangled a carrot in front of
25. Some late-night viewing
26. Suffix for the 1%
28. Consommé server
29. Fantasy sports site
31. Sunday ___
32. Lack of practice, metaphorically
35. Writer on the history of Rome
44. Senescence
47. Ctrl+V command
49. Beyond stuffy
50. Longest book in the New Testament
51. Tough going
53. Brit discussing American politics
54. Algerian city where Camus's "The Plague" is set
55. Passes, in a way
56. Something ___
59. Record

by Andrew Kingsley

## ACROSS

1 Recruits
8 They're covered by boards
15 Commercial break?
17 Problem in the Tower of Babel story
18 Gets into the game
19 Depart unceremoniously?
20 Female koala
21 Depart unceremoniously, in slang
22 Mountain ridge
23 Be down with
24 School extension?
25 Copies illegally
26 Circumflex lookalike
27 Passé, so to speak
29 Tunneling machines
30 Fully in agreement
32 1991 self-titled debut album
35 Microsoft Surface surface
39 ___ acid
40 Manufactured drug, for short
41 Speed
42 They're answered once and for all
43 Manages to avoid
44 Basic spreadsheet command
45 Japanese carrier
46 Dulce de ___ (Latin American confection)
47 "A Room With a View" clergyman
48 Montreal's Bell Centre and others
51 Fierce opponent of patriarchy
52 Crack filler
53 Gets clean, in a way

## DOWN

1 Prepare for return shipping, say
2 Song that debuted on Saint-Jean-Baptiste Day in 1880
3 First name in the Gospels
4 Foreign news correspondent Richard
5 Under: Fr.
6 "___ Ramblin' Man" (#1 Waylon Jennings country hit)
7 Naira spender
8 Ones hoping for prior approval?
9 Flip out
10 Lake ___, Australia's lowest point
11 Big A.T.M. maker
12 Timorous question
13 Dined at someone else's place
14 Composition of some grids
16 Childlike personality?
22 Specializations
23 Abrasive
25 One "whose faulty vision sees things as they are, not as they ought to be," per Ambrose Bierce
26 Express carefully
28 Capital where the Arab Spring began
29 Card makeup
31 Fiddled (with)
32 Business, either personal or otherwise
33 Limitation for borrowers
34 Literally, "the foundation"
36 Renaissance symbol
37 Starting site for sorties
38 Can't take
40 Nurse
43 Football helmet item
44 "___ Evil" (1971 Mia Farrow thriller)
46 Overwhelming favorite, informally
47 "Blimey!" sayer
49 Fruit juice brand
50 D.C.'s historic Metropolitan ___ Church: Abbr.

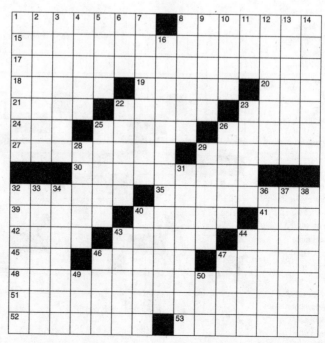

by Byron Walden

# 130

## ACROSS

1 "Voilà!"
17 Invisible social group
18 Napoleon's foe at Waterloo
19 "Telephone Line" band, informally
20 Knighted conductor
21 Reserve squad
22 Head of Napoleon's army?
24 They provide quarters for dollars
26 ___ leches cake
28 Some bucks
30 2014–15 dance craze
33 "Yeah, yeah, little ___" (repeated line in a 1964 hit)
34 Underground crop
36 7-Eleven treats
38 Hannibal's foe in the Second Punic War
41 Package of Linux software, informally
42 Decide randomly
45 Amusingly ironic
46 Kind of financing
47 Anastasia ___, woman in "Fifty Shades of Grey"
49 "This is killing me!"
53 Romney's 2012 running mate
55 Lover of Aphrodite
56 Contraction that's also a past-tense verb
57 Development phases
60 Golden ___
63 Ink container
64 Field for a Hollywood agency

67 Athlete for whom Portugal's Madeira Airport was renamed
68 Overseer of all other systems

## DOWN

1 Luxury bathroom features
2 Charm
3 ___ Territory
4 122 is a record one
5 Features on some jackets, in brief
6 Dope
7 Where po' boys are eaten
8 ___ Green, historic eloping destination
9 Journalists' credits
10 Former workers' or sports org.
11 Tiny bit
12 "___ It Fun" (2014 Best Rock Song Grammy winner)
13 Sire
14 Accurate
15 Middle of a dash?
16 Browser option
23 Land known in the Bible as Mizraim
25 Show filmed in Studio 8H, for short
27 Just fine
29 Wind catchers
31 Parent company of Lamborghini
32 TV journalist Hill
35 No longer important
37 "Phooey!"
38 Memorable line?
39 Cousin of a guinea pig
40 Knesset assembly

43 Sweet ___
44 Mouth-burning chili pepper
45 Shutdown alternative
48 Get support from
50 List on eBay, say
51 Starbucks order size
52 Badger
54 Much-criticized trial, briefly
58 Pot grower?
59 Rouse
61 Horror movie assistant
62 Prefix for vintners
64 Channel for cinephiles
65 Buddy
66 French ailment

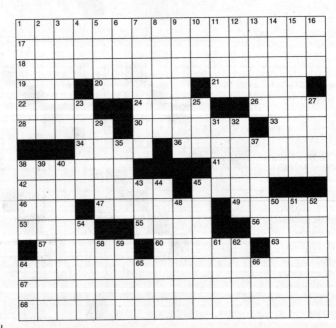

by David Steinberg

## ACROSS

1 Yellowed or grayed, perhaps
5 Decorated military pilot
11 Cold response?
14 One end of a chess game
15 Cosmetic injections for guys
16 Former 57-Across star from China
17 Another end of a chess game
18 Grade in the high 80s or low 90s?
19 Crane arm
20 Collectively
22 Half of some matched sets
23 Sommelier's concern
24 Churro ingredient?
26 "This relationship can't go on"
28 When repeated, cry in Matthew 27
29 Parched
31 Potential source of college credit
32 Director of 2018's "A Wrinkle in Time"
35 Vaping needs
37 Mr. Television, by another nickname
39 Tex-Mex offering
42 1941 Welles role
43 Late sixth-century year
45 Ones making periodical changes
47 Reason to bow
49 Sluggish
50 Do 80, say
52 Ford in the Country Music Hall of Fame
53 Sites of many -ectomies, for short
54 Accidentally got soaked at a pool
56 Scintilla
57 See 16-Across
58 They're on your side
59 Curtail
60 Nairobi-to-Johannesburg dir.
61 Position in a prosecutor's office: Abbr.
62 Doc's orders

## DOWN

1 Put on a pedestal
2 Bar food?
3 Really trounce
4 Linger (on)
5 Grp. recognizing international titleholders in 18 different weight classes
6 Primary competitor
7 Mechanical
8 Retro console giant
9 Emperor who called the First Council of Nicaea
10 Common PC file extension
11 "I say!"
12 End-of-year requests
13 Abstract Expressionist Rauschenberg
21 Provide a smooth transition for
23 "Wait for it . . ."
25 Competing groups in Mexico
27 German wine made from late-harvest grapes
30 John who directed "Tarzan, the Ape Man"
33 Sharpness
34 Like Frank Sinatra, three times
36 Tangential remark
38 Pumped
39 Penmen?
40 Totally cute, in slang
41 Fitting pastime?
44 Backups' backups
46 Moves
48 Certain decorative paperweight
51 Set down
54 Air safety org.
55 Org. in the documentary "Citizenfour"

by Andy Kravis

# 132

## ACROSS

1 Ruler who died in 30 B.C.
10 Panic button
15 Ticket request
16 Alice with a Nobel Prize in Literature
17 Weave
18 Co-star of Wood in "The Lord of the Rings"
19 Land of ___ (where 1-Down lived)
20 Legal conclusion?
21 Doesn't get involved
22 Cajolery
25 One of two polar opposites
28 Standard product, once
29 "___ It Time" (1977 hit for the Babys)
33 Unlikely Top 40 songs
34 More au courant
36 Find common ground
39 Ironic reaction to dry humor?
40 Has a great night at the comedy club
41 Tribe encountered by Lewis and Clark
42 One of the jacks in cribbage
43 Dearies
44 Much of the text of a Supreme Court decision
47 Big gaps
50 Hawaiian souvenir
51 Floppy disk creator
54 River of forgetfulness, in myth
55 Image on the Maine or South Carolina flag
58 Some "Monty Python and the Holy Grail" costumes
59 Trades
60 Pallid and unhealthy in appearance
61 Sizable ordinal

## DOWN

1 Problematic firstborn
2 Lead-in to type
3 Abbr. on a city boundary sign
4 Pamplona plaudit
5 /
6 Out
7 Rib
8 Competition that hurts everyone
9 Got into a pickle?
10 Some WikiLeaks leaks
11 Words after "Ha, ha"
12 Drs. that see head cases
13 Home, in slang
14 Orlando, in the music world
21 State capital that was a boyhood home of Herbert Hoover
22 Lacking focus
23 "You sure about that?"
24 Weary
25 Kid's proud retort
26 Moved furtively
27 Letters sung as mi, mi, re, re, do
30 Move furtively
31 Nervous ___
32 Lock
35 Olympus rival
37 Pram pushers, perhaps
38 Ring data
43 Intimate
45 ___ board
46 Civil rights org. since 1909
47 Thunderous sound
48 Goddess of marriage
49 Some bill collectors
51 Decrease?
52 Like lop ears
53 Go well (with)
55 Long-running drama set in N.Y.C., informally
56 When la Bastille was stormed
57 Word with black or blood

*by Robyn Weintraub*

## ACROSS

1 Loud, as a radio
7 What stars do
14 Repeatedly hit
15 Some petroleum
16 Play out, as events
17 "I wanna hear everything"
18 Pioneer in steam engines
20 Complete coverage?
21 Early people who used a base-20 numerical system
22 Sorrowful cries
23 Rapper ____ Rhymes
24 What closes on Sundays?
25 Cut
27 Fun bit of trivia
32 ____ Tech (former for-profit school)
33 Olympic gymnastics gold medalist Raisman
34 "Children of the Albatross" author
35 Vietnamese soup
36 Doesn't snap
40 Billies
41 Packing ____
42 They may have stained-glass windows
45 Playbill bit
46 Police line?
47 Cut
48 Internet in-jokes that have gone viral, in modern lingo
50 Individual's unique use of language
52 How dishes are usually sold
54 Martial arts holds that are hard to escape

55 President Bartlet on "The West Wing"
56 One waiting for the captain?
57 Invites out for

## DOWN

1 ____-Bakr, longtime adviser to Muhammad
2 Any member of Saul's tribe, in the Bible
3 Close friend of Hamilton, in "Hamilton"
4 Fighter of Ferocious Flea in 1960s cartoons
5 Hamilton and 3-Down, in "Hamilton"
6 Quashes
7 "Absolutely unacceptable!"
8 Cartoonist Kelly
9 Breed

10 Travel from site to site?
11 Screwballs
12 Calculus calculation
13 Multi-time W.N.B.A. All-Star ____ Delle Donne
15 Be a homebody
19 Mary Jane
21 Zayn formerly of One Direction
23 "____ chance!"
25 Bud inducted into Cooperstown in 2017
26 Belts
28 Performs some light surgery?
29 Loss of a sound at the start of a word, as "opossum" to "possum"
30 Spot in the third balcony, say

31 Trespassing and defamation
37 Chemical compounds in so-called hospital smell
38 Poisons
39 1994 Jim Carrey comedy
42 2007 #1 Alicia Keys album
43 Man of the cloth
44 Moves at a crawl?
46 Mexican bread
48 Art ____
49 Goya subject
51 Alley-oop starter
53 Tennyson's "You Ask Me, Why, ____ Ill at Ease"

by Ryan McCarty

# 134

## ACROSS

1 Ride
5 Trattoria offering
10 Effervescence
14 Natural pain reliever
15 West Indian sorcery
16 Dirt pie ingredient
17 Amorphous mass
18 5-Across unit
19 Days long gone
20 Inept.sorts
22 One low on dough
24 Aziz of Netflix's "Master of None"
25 Loft addition
26 Bush animal, for short
27 "Still, after all this time . . ."
31 Film speed letters
32 Cross to bear
34 Somewhat icy
35 What old records and happy-go-lucky people may do
36 Fore-and-aft-rigged vessel
38 Stoppage
39 Geoffrey of fashion
40 "Sup?"
43 Meritorious
45 Picked up on
48 Subject of the 2008 biography "Woman of the House"
49 Annual event that includes snocross and ski superpipe
51 Number two
52 Rock band whose name is suggested by the first row of this puzzle
56 "The Burning Giraffe" artist
57 ___ school
58 Martial art whose name means, literally, "sword way"
59 Sophocles tragedy
60 Best, but barely

61 Language from which "kayak" comes
62 Paint swatch selection
63 Go-getter
64 Pours on the love
65 "The Garden of ___" (Oscar Wilde poem)

## DOWN

1 Apocalyptic event predicted in Norse mythology
2 Like a shampoo/conditioner
3 Expands one's view, in a way
4 Referee, in slang
5 Pink, for one
6 Sacred symbol of ancient Egypt
7 The Hudson's Tappan ___ Bridge
8 Galifianakis of "The Hangover"
9 Leading
10 Place for an umbrella stand
11 Heavyweight champion who defeated "Bonecrusher" Smith
12 Gets closer and closer
13 Old-fashioned image projector
21 Fractions of a krona
23 Word
28 "Beowulf," essentially
29 Eating with one's elbows on the table, e.g.
30 Meeting places
33 "Peanuts" boy
35 Makes plans to tie the knot
37 Intense attraction, with "the"
39 Google alternative
41 Tiny brain?
42 Vamps
43 Odd duck
44 What "education is the best provision for," per Aristotle
46 Key for "Spring" in Vivaldi's "The Four Seasons"
47 Roosevelt predecessor?
48 Summoned
50 Yahtzee scoresheet row
53 Founder of Stoicism
54 Hardware bit
55 Comics character who once, surprisingly, solved a sudoku puzzle

by Trenton Charlson

## ACROSS

1 Really busy
7 Ban from argument
13 Greasers' loves
15 According to schedule
16 Bar bowlful
18 Banana Republic's parent company
19 Either of two extremes in an orbit
20 CD follower
22 Symbol of change, in math
23 Picks
24 Pick
26 First pope to be called "the Great"
27 Jr. and sr.
28 City license once needed to work in an establishment serving alcohol
30 Photogenic, informally
31 Get all twisted up
32 Itches
33 Part of what makes you you
35 Decline
36 Stock letters
39 Ancient city rediscovered in 1870
40 Blackballs
41 Royal Catherine
42 "Duck ___" (classic Warner Bros. short)
44 Its business is booming
45 Nerve
46 Expired
48 Term of respect in old westerns
50 Wrap up
51 Loan specification
52 Boil
53 Piano trio?

## DOWN

1 "Hummina hummina!"
2 Onetime Ebert partner
3 Sources of some tremors
4 "Mrs. ___ Goes to Paris" (Paul Gallico novel)
5 A bushelful
6 See 7-Down
7 With 6-Down, what may follow Indiana or Illinois
8 Like the best streams?
9 Protection from a shark, maybe
10 Bad things to blow
11 Like valentines
12 Settled
14 Party flasher
17 Up to this point
21 Source of guiding principles
24 Ova, e.g.
25 Becomes settled in a new environment
28 Speleologist
29 Minds
30 Make more palatable
31 Give up
33 Material
34 Style of Southern hip-hop
35 Things drawn by eccentric people
36 Home to the ancient Zapotec civilization
37 Like opposing groups on "Survivor"
38 Inches
41 Not natural
43 Strain of potent marijuana
45 Speck
47 Plain white ___
49 Plan out

by Kameron Austin Collins

## ACROSS

1 Dreamhouse resident
11 Food portmanteau
15 He's nothing special
16 Get fit, with "up"
17 It gets you what you need
18 Analogous
19 Schooner feature
20 Secretary of state after Muskie
21 Times, Post, News, etc.
22 Stole, maybe
23 Neighbor of Djibouti
25 Gorp ingredients
29 Actress Kirsten
30 About to go
31 One might be by the water cooler
34 Title character of a 2006 mockumentary
35 ___ characters (Chinese script)
36 Israeli-born Jew
37 What can get batters out?
39 Chad's place
40 Not built up
41 Kibble form
42 From that, formally
44 Getty oil, e.g.
45 Sword grips
46 Portuguese woman's title
48 Check out, in a way
52 Hydroxyl-bearing compound
53 Like cooking that goes whole hog?
55 Warning from one holding an iron
56 Place to spin your wheels
57 Rice and Robbins
58 Skull accompanier

## DOWN

1 Topical treatment
2 Running shoe brand
3 Short spins?

4 One who's happy about acquiring a few extra pounds, informally
5 Janis with the 1975 hit "At Seventeen"
6 Activity for a basket holder
7 Bacardi brand
8 Tourist city in Ventura County
9 Got access, in a way
10 Catwoman portrayer Meriwether
11 Not bite off more than one can chew
12 Place where lots of calls are made
13 Star ___ (pho flavorer)
14 Intelligence community?

21 Colorful seasoning that originated near the Himalayas
22 Pipe fittings and such
24 Play from which the word "robot" comes
25 Alternatives to marinades
26 For one
27 At one's best
28 Creatures that divers sometimes swim with
31 "Time ___ . . ."
32 Pleasant pace
33 Chuck wagon fixin's
35 Divided barrier
38 Language similar to Thai
39 Knocks loudly?
41 Storyboard parts
42 "Five-finger discount"

43 Five-letter capital written as two words in its native language
47 2017 Tony winner for Best Play
48 Other: Sp.
49 Appreciation
50 A cameo might have one
51 Group to which five U.S. presidents have belonged, from Harding to Ford
53 Government org. concerned with radioactive waste
54 Scepter accompanier

by Robyn Weintraub

## ACROSS

1 Performers taking bows onstage?
16 Saw around a locker room?
17 Picked individually
18 Does another walk-through of something
19 Informal agreement
20 Start of the name of many a French band
21 Time to buy back-to-school supplies: Abbr.
22 Something tanned at a tanning salon, informally
23 One-eyed god
25 "Ooh-la-la!"
27 Plus
29 Cherry or raspberry
32 Pioneering infomercial company
35 Fit the bill
40 Good name for a model?
41 Big name in casualwear
42 It can cover a lot of ground
43 Road divider
44 They may be bummed
46 Sports org. since 1916
48 Come to know
50 Bamboozled
53 Speaks honestly and forthrightly
57 What keeps you going when everything seems lost
58 AARP base
59 Factors in some work reviews

## DOWN

1 Low-end smoke
2 Spasm
3 Try again, with a bounced check
4 Inflames
5 Common perfume oil
6 International group whose leaders meet once a year
7 French waves
8 Not just laugh
9 20 lashes, maybe?
10 Break
11 Put behind bars
12 Unaccompanied
13 Large storage units
14 What gears in a gear assembly have
15 Add to the bill, perhaps
24 Sign of the times?
26 Classic Jaguar
27 Pose
28 Parisian pronoun
29 Line for a show in New York?
30 Musician Brian
31 Characterizes
33 Shogunate capital
34 Cause of some flashbacks, for short
36 ___ rating system (chess standard)
37 Angels
38 No-goodniks
39 Blood-typing abbr.
43 Meriting more Pinocchios
45 Like most Iranians
46 Noted Obama portrayer
47 Big name in air fresheners
49 Unaccompanied
51 Enjoyed a traditional family dinner
52 Rough piece of land?
53 De ___ (excessive)
54 Marsh bird
55 Ancient land located in what is now southwest Iran
56 State couple: Abbr.

by Jason Flinn

# 138

## ACROSS

1 Website revenue source
8 Sequel
14 Introduce
16 "Blah, blah, blah"
17 From which Sadie Hawkins dances come
18 Sandpaper category
19 Like seven candles on the first night of Hanukkah
20 Egyptian deity
22 Grand Central scene at rush hour, e.g.
23 Is on the run?
24 Senate attire
26 Opportune
27 Outcry
28 Actress who co-starred on "That '70s Show" at age 14
29 Lost cause
30 He might say "A day without you is like a day without sunshine"
33 Style influenced by Cubism
34 Plant in the lily family
35 He might say "A day without sunshine is like, you know, night"
41 Mountain nymph
42 Singer K. T.
43 Setting for part of "Forrest Gump," for short
45 Singer k. d.
46 Permanently, say
47 Italian artist Guido
48 Oscar nominee for playing Mia in "Pulp Fiction"
49 Jonathan Safran ____, "Everything Is Illuminated" author
50 Bit of wisdom
51 Trendy male hairstyle
53 English king nicknamed "the Unready" (ooh, that hurts!)
56 Like Miss Congeniality
57 "I dunno"
58 One of two in "Hamlet" or three in "Macbeth"
59 "Nature" or "Frontline"

## DOWN

1 Visibly embarrassed
2 "Cheers!"
3 More slapstick
4 Novelist Nin
5 Prideful grp.?
6 Ages
7 Go after
8 River to the Rio Grande
9 Heaps
10 Memorable demonstrator at the 1939 World's Fair
11 Ends
12 Response to a knock
13 A little one is called a calf
15 Star-crossed, say
21 BuzzFeed competitor
24 Stanley of "The Lovely Bones"
25 Private meeting
26 Whose last words are "Thus with a kiss I die"
28 Work
29 ____ pull
31 Collar attachment
32 Toon rodent
35 38 things in the Lincoln Memorial
36 Speech in the Bible
37 Amends
38 U.S. military aircraft
39 Expose
40 Tourist spot on the Mediterranean
44 Shower problem
46 Broadcast network originally known as Pax
47 Moves, in slang
49 Item in a box in the basement
50 Classifies (as)
52 Big ____
54 Big ____
55 Relatively easy city to fly into and out of

by Bruce Haight

## ACROSS

1 Astaire with steps
6 Onetime Virginia senator Jim
10 "My Two ___" (1980s sitcom)
14 French parish priests
15 Piece of merchandise
16 "___ homo"
17 Camaraderie
19 Autumn spice
20 Words to the disloyal
21 Cheryl of "Curb Your Enthusiasm"
22 Binge-watch, maybe
23 Like a Hail Mary
25 "By the way . . ."
27 "Nothing Feels Good: Punk Rock, Teenagers and ___" (2003 book)
28 Channel with several spinoff channels
30 Pay
32 Ones who may dress down those dressing up?
36 Some detox diets
37 Modern college major
38 Former Giants G.M. Al
39 Big name in Art Deco
40 Many a time suck
41 Social reformer Dorothea
44 Comment after a bump
49 Caustic soda, chemically
51 What you might charge for a ride
53 Onetime Korean statesman Syngman
54 Movie villain whose first name is Julius
55 Part of many an N.Y.C. subway station wall
57 Lip
58 Video game neophyte, informally
59 Mod bottoms
60 Kvass grains
61 Workers on the hill
62 Brno-born, e.g.

## DOWN

1 Made (like)
2 On account of
3 Mythical figure often depicted holding a lyre
4 Arboreal primate
5 Largest section of the dictionary
6 "Dunkirk" and "Pearl Harbor," for short
7 Merit
8 Court submission
9 She convinced George to switch to five-pointed stars, in American legend
10 Show
11 Places of learning
12 Distributor of Penguin classics?
13 What an asterisk may mean
18 "Nigerian prince," often
24 Sink
26 Some of life's twists and turns
29 Nick of Hollywood
31 Part of a programmer's conditional
32 One who sucks the joy out of the room
33 Worker on the Hill
34 Places where brain waves are analyzed
35 Panang curry alternative
36 Show that once had an April Fools' Day episode hosted by Pat Sajak
37 More sweeping
42 Book that's the basis for the movie "What's Love Got to Do With It"
43 Gas in arc lamps
45 Actress Ana of "Devious Maids"
46 River crossed in 1945's Operation Plunder
47 Thing often described redundantly as "of the past"
48 "Gimme a break!"
50 Prepares a bed?
52 Tab's counterpart
56 Hip-hop's Run-___

*by Natan Last, Andy Kravis and the J.A.S.A. Crossword Class*

# 140

## ACROSS

1 Take into account, as contingencies
8 Highly revered one
15 Delta factor?
16 Comment from one who's just getting by
17 Cover
18 Subject to change
19 Piece of gladiatorial combat gear
20 Cliffhanger locale?
22 Bugged out
23 Decrees
25 Pollen count plant
28 2011 Emmy-winning MSNBC host
30 Like many neglected pets
31 Sturdy as ___
32 ID tag?
35 Wide-beamed vessel
36 Way out there
37 "Laughable Lyrics" poet
38 Evil eye, e.g.
39 Fizzy drink measure
40 Roger's relative
41 Absence without leave?
43 Ecosystem-replicating facility
45 Absence with leave?
46 Detectives connect them
47 Benjamin
49 Q-Tip specialty
51 Not freelancing, say
54 Get ahead of
56 Kind of artery or vein
57 Works on a plot
58 Semi-opponent
59 It's impractical to live in

## DOWN

1 What a dolorimeter measures
2 The Stroll, e.g.
3 Tundra hunter
4 Grp. whose members 28-Down
5 Bearing the blame
6 Baptism by fire
7 Bit of thatching
8 Common
9 Source of extra-large eggs
10 Something to flip on
11 "Soon"
12 Mansard alternative
13 Checked out impolitely
14 It's signed, sealed and delivered
21 Their contents have been threshed
24 Think (on)
26 Barbie greeting
27 Bowl on a range
28 Charge on a field
29 Time-traveling 1980s film character
32 Common soap ingredient
33 They make people jump at picnics
34 Home of Paris
36 "I'm gone"
37 Highly revered one
39 Honorary law deg.
40 "Seriously?!"
41 Three-time "Newhart" Emmy nominee
42 Oscar, e.g.
43 Screw-up
44 Answer at the door
46 Remove out of respect
48 Sentry's station
50 Slug, e.g.
52 Modern art form?
53 Pop is part of it: Abbr.
55 Zing

*by Josh Knapp*

## ACROSS

1 HanesBrands brand
8 Exercise in a pool
14 General goal?
15 Tribe whose name means "those with many tattoos"
17 Feeler, of sorts
18 Title under which "The Lion Sleeps Tonight" originally charted, in 1952
19 Name for the T. rex at Chicago's Field Museum
20 23-Across's target reader
22 Chaps
23 Bygone 20-Across fashion magazine
25 Musical intensifier
28 Mythical predator of elephants
29 Numerical prefix
33 Stations
34 Highway sections
36 Skating gold medalist of 1928, 1932 and 1936
37 Figure in a beret
38 ___ Derby, annual sporting event since 1866
39 Grub sellers
41 ___ Park
42 Geneva-based org. encouraging healthy living
43 One of 100 in un siglo
44 Word appearing 39 times in the King James Version of Matthew 1
45 Composure
49 Genre of the double platinum box set "Songs of Freedom"
52 One going to court?
53 Utmost
56 Post, e.g.

58 Napping
60 Job-like
61 City where Jonah preached
62 Cote d'Azur town
63 Nightwear

## DOWN

1 E-1s and E-2s, in the Army: Abbr.
2 Place
3 High school spots?
4 Financial statement abbr.
5 They bite but don't have teeth
6 Great Lakes natives
7 Upward-flowing plant vessels
8 Black bird
9 Pore, e.g.
10 Popular Debussy piece

11 Fictional boxer a.k.a. The Count of Monte Fisto
12 Machine part connecting to a gearwheel
13 New York Jets' home from 1964 to 1983
16 Quizzical cries
21 Top of the charts?
23 Amount of appreciation, maybe
24 Is piercing
25 "Shampoo" director
26 Tick off
27 Sega mascot
30 "I ___"
31 Unit of magnetic flux density
32 Have ___ at
34 Latte go-with

35 Hip-hop producer for Jay-Z, LL Cool J and Missy Elliott
40 "Try it!"
46 Not left over
47 Frequent
48 "Journey to ___" (recurring "Sesame Street" segment)
49 Criticize
50 "M*A*S*H" maneuver, for short
51 Bhagavad ___ (Hindu scripture)
53 Riders on Direhorses in "Avatar"
54 Certain diagram
55 Little chortles
57 Some football linemen: Abbr.
59 Jump the broom, so to speak

by Gareth Bain

# 142

## ACROSS

1 Heavenly measurement
8 Be unable to stand
15 Primary figure
16 Hand sanitizer ingredient
17 Five-star
18 Against all standards of decency
19 1964 album that was #1 for 11 weeks
21 Political blogger Klein
22 Sound
23 What many an amusement park has
24 Projecting corner
26 Johnny Fever's station
28 Old laborer
29 Hide
31 Fielding percentage factor
33 Yogi's sounds
34 London's ___ Palace
36 Corral O.K.?
37 3-D picture producer
40 It may be seen with a 37-Across
42 Capital on the Sava River
44 2002 Literature Nobelist Kertész
47 Michael Jordan teammate Steve
49 Break in concentration
50 Scratch
52 What a bottom may be on top of
54 Religious leader with a pet elephant
55 Jack regarded as an object of devotion
58 Like orthorhombic crystals
59 Not recognizable by
61 Rattle
62 Hijack, maybe
63 What might be treated with vitamin A megadoses
64 One with a booming voice

## DOWN

1 Minute marcher?
2 Car ad catchphrase
3 Threatens
4 Car ad datum
5 Soldier's assignment
6 Like the Mets in every season from 1962 to 1965
7 Act like an ass
8 Bramble with edible purple fruit
9 To be very far away?
10 Sty youngster
11 Apple product before Tiger
12 It's spoken in los Estados Unidos
13 Grave
14 The Republican Guard guards it
20 Sommer of Hollywood
21 Returned waves?
25 Zap
27 W., once
30 Mountain climber's conquest
32 Australian export
35 Puts a hold on, say
37 Mascot since 1916
38 Employ as plan B
39 Bearded mountain climber
40 Slinkys, e.g.
41 Loser in war, usually
43 Spanish Main crosser
44 Declaration after "Hallelujah"
45 Illinois home of the John Deere Pavilion
46 Curia ___ (body assisting the pope)
48 Storm trackers
51 "Image of ___" (1960 hit by the Safaris)
53 Flat sign
56 Experience
57 Old Italian capital
60 Anthem preposition

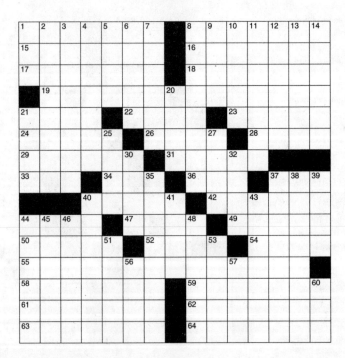

by Barry C. Silk

## ACROSS

1 Setting for part of "A Tale of Two Cities"
9 "Awww!"
15 Aces, with "the"
16 What a mass of footballers do after a tackle
17 One getting poked in the eye?
18 Smell like
19 Punches, informally
20 Psychologist Alfred
21 Jaunty
23 Not taking a loss well, say
24 High, in a way
25 Its positions are labeled North, South, East and West
29 Number of Planeten
30 Ones who are counter-productive?
32 Funny Margaret
33 Completely covers
34 Nag (at)
35 Microwaveable food brand
37 Centimeter-gram-second unit
38 Dead duck, maybe
39 Union V.I.P.
40 One might be performed en avant
41 Grow more and more irksome
42 Country music's Carter
44 Architectural base
46 Film hero chasing a motorcycle gang

47 Put on the line
50 "Let's do it!"
51 Chatted up
52 ___ Puffs
53 Target of thrown bricks, in early comics

## DOWN

1 N.C.A.A. football ranking system
2 "Now I see!"
3 Picture on file
4 "The Hippopotamus" writer
5 "Wait, this isn't making sense"
6 Separate through percolation
7 Sure thing
8 Milk sources

9 Concorde features
10 Rare driving choices
11 Like some flexible mortgages
12 Exercise ___
13 Loads
14 "___ Poetry Jam"
21 Raid target
22 Position in a relay
23 Historical community
25 Rap's Biz ___
26 Last name in women's skin care
27 "Pretty obvious, huh?"
28 Certain coffee order
30 I.R.S. settlement
31 Take turns?
33 Part of a cover

36 Some silk threads
37 Trounce
39 Cuban-born Baseball Hall-of-Famer José
41 Terra ___
42 "Baa, Baa, Black Sheep" figure
43 Threshold
44 Load
45 One who's incredible
46 Peace abroad
48 Listing that can change based on the weather, for short
49 Flyspeck

by Peter Wentz

# 144

## ACROSS

1 Smelting ended it
9 Latin pop Grammy winner Jon
15 Intellectually stimulating
16 Drive
17 Traditional
18 Scam
19 Pringles Light ingredient
20 Roster shortener
21 Bach wrote three for violin
25 Impenetrable
26 Thornton Wilder, while earning his B.A.
27 Debt memo
28 Mower handle?
29 Close match point?
32 Knuckles the Echidna's company
33 Crayola color introduced in 1958
34 Wishy-washy reply
38 Variable pay schedule
41 Put away one's own groceries?
43 Nagg's wife in Samuel Beckett's "Endgame"
44 Ziploc bag introducer
45 They have their own kingdom
46 Whisk clean
48 Procured unlawfully, old-style
49 What Montana was in the '80s
50 CW series based on a French film
51 "Piranha" director, 1978
54 One of the Wayans brothers
55 Wicker seat place?
56 As far out as possible
57 Blooms named for their scent

## DOWN

1 Ice cream store employees
2 Invent something
3 Activity for diners and list makers
4 Just starting to learn
5 Controversial school language subject
6 Weather might delay it: Abbr.
7 Square dance partner
8 Antiquity, in antiquity
9 Like a snow angel maker, at times
10 1890–1941 Italian colony
11 Ducky
12 Like hydra neurons
13 Characterize
14 Caine character who's left wondering
22 Now
23 Served
24 Quaint undies
30 It works via a series of explosions
31 Resilient strength
35 Paintings often including an infant
36 Kindergarten song
37 Some graveyard flora
39 Figure of speech like "not unlike"
40 Not unlike a ballet dancer
41 Acting as one
42 Named names, say
45 McCarthy-era epithet
47 Source of grand sounds?
51 Extrude
52 Relative of -ish
53 Spanish demonstrative

by Tom Heilman

## ACROSS

1 Help for someone just browsing?
8 1-Across source
15 Raving
16 Buds
17 Stimulant
18 "The Consul" composer
19 What a screen may block
21 Submitted
22 Noggins
24 Mouth filler
25 Zulu's counterpart
29 "___ Arizona Skies" (early John Wayne film)
31 Giveaway
33 Stimulate
35 Shadows
37 Creature whose genus name and English name are the same
38 Dare to put in one's two cents
41 Tool shed tool
42 Flip
43 Clipped
44 Number of strings on a Spanish guitar
46 Tourney round
48 Some homages
49 Bush whackers?
51 Actress Berger
53 Not strictly adhering to tempo
55 Part of an ice pack?
59 Simian
61 Series begun in 2007
63 Bet everything
64 Midday appointments
65 Like some director's cuts
66 Wraps

## DOWN

1 Goliath, e.g.
2 "Suicide Blonde" band
3 Torment
4 ___ Railroad, 1832–1960
5 Like a lot?
6 Shipping weight
7 They might include BMX and wakeboarding, informally
8 Year "Tosca" premiered
9 Sources of iron and manganese
10 Defensive strategies
11 Part of a plot
12 Source of a secret, in a phrase
13 Triple-platinum Gloria Estefan album with "Rhythm Is Gonna Get You"
14 Alphabet book phrase
20 Spies often don't use them
23 Queued
25 Eastern generals
26 Stockpiled
27 Orange children's character
28 Actor Butterfield of "Hugo"
30 Fielder's challenge
32 Pool parts
34 Bit of work
36 Alma mater for McDonnell and Douglas of McDonnell Douglas
39 Bashes
40 Prefix with realism
45 Part of an "@" symbol
47 Board
50 Supporting post
52 Temporarily formed
53 ___ Bolognese
54 Sooner alternative
56 Spanish title
57 "Your" alternative
58 "Days of Heaven" co-star, 1978
60 Wideout, in football
62 Stovetop sound

*by Michael Ashley*

# 146

## ACROSS

1. B.M.O.C., typically
5. Aids in keeping up with the daily grind?
14. Biblical figure believed to be buried near Basra
15. Yucca named by Mormon settlers
16. Handel work featuring David
17. Poorly educated
18. Pleasant surprise for a buyer
20. Cretan peak
21. Have chops, say
22. Its purpose is in sight
23. Papuan port
25. Phishing string: Abbr.
26. Lee in Hollywood
27. One of Steinbeck's twins
29. Coiner of the phrase "global village"
38. Group that might perform 16-Across
39. Cubs may play in it
40. Frequent American flier?
41. Hill person: Abbr.
42. Pros in power: Abbr.
43. Texting qualifier
46. W. Coast setting, more often than not
48. Now, in Italy
49. "Live at the Apollo" airer
52. Key name
54. All-day sucker?
57. He played Casey Kelso on "That '70s Show"
59. Linchpin locale
60. Fading out
61. Sixth in a series
62. "Tin Cup" co-star
63. Aforetime

## DOWN

1. General Reno for whom Reno, Nev., is named
2. 1994 Emmy winner for "Dvorák in Prague"
3. Oil vessel
4. Moola
5. Gifted person?
6. Creta, e.g.
7. Beach house?
8. Apply
9. Quaker offering
10. Keep in order?
11. "Mrs." in a Paul Gallico novel title
12. City called "Knightsbridge of the North"
13. Auto suggestion?
15. "Judgment at Nuremberg" Oscar nominee
19. Like some outboard motors
24. Getting in gear
26. Noted Titanic couple
28. Nintendo's ___ Mansion
29. Delivery people?
30. "How now! ___?": Hamlet
31. Delhi cheese?
32. It may be on the house
33. Bridge designer's concern
34. Email, e.g.: Abbr.
35. Mountain
36. "Look ___ now"
37. Bill ___ Climate Lab (Oakland science exhibit)
43. Cooler, in the 'hood
44. Violet relative
45. Like Mork
47. Puts soft rock on?
48. Black Bears' home
49. Lord of the ring?
50. They get nuts
51. Grip improver
53. Characteristic dictator
55. Electric flux symbols
56. Throw for a loop
58. Cyclones' sch.

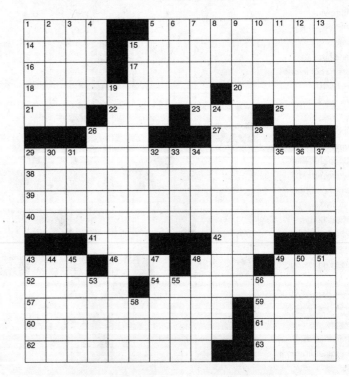

*by Martin Ashwood-Smith*

## ACROSS

1 Dragging vehicles
10 Massachusetts governor after John Hancock
12 One who was very successful with numbered balls
14 Advance man?
15 Some clouds
17 Cerebral canals
18 Crook's mark
21 Apostle of Ire.
22 Plate setting
23 Board game found in Egyptian tombs
25 Group led by a Grand Exalted Ruler
26 "The Chronicles of Vladimir ___" (hit young adult book series about a vampire)
27 Feature of some televised debates
29 Spanish demonstrative
30 Long and twisty
31 "The L Word" network, in listings
32 Survey militarily
34 Canvas in a wooden frame, of sorts
35 Yeomen of the Guard officer
36 Ready to play
37 Number one, to some
38 Old letters
40 "Combats avec ___ défenseurs!" (line from "La Marseillaise")
41 In a way, informally
42 Some Japanese-Americans
44 Period of slow growth
45 One who is very successful with numbered balls
49 One getting laughs at others' expense
50 Exercise leader

## DOWN

1 Stopped flowing
2 Exeunt ___ (stage direction)
3 Violin virtuoso Leopold
4 French preposition
5 Street caution
6 Part of an equitable trade, figuratively speaking
7 Writer LeShan and others
8 Bundles of logs, maybe
9 Not so dim
10 Dublin-born singer with a 1990 #1 hit
11 Kings' home
12 GQ sort of guy
13 Part-owner, say
14 Mess makers
16 "Just a few more miles"
18 Hit show
19 Chemical used in dyes
20 Dress store section
23 Weary
24 Reproved, in a way
27 Sessions in D.C., once
28 Battle of ___ (first Allied victory of W.W. I)
33 Like some shopping
37 Luster, e.g.
39 Gripping parts of gecko footpads
41 "Roots" family surname
43 Superlative suffix
44 ___ list
46 Map abbr.
47 Soprano Sumac
48 Mil. branch disbanded in 1978

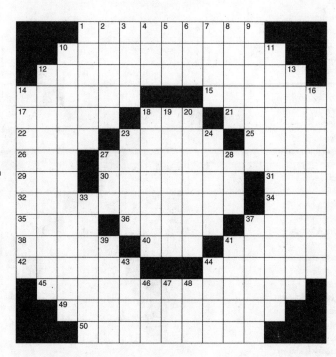

by Todd Gross

# 148

## ACROSS

1 Game with the figures "soldier's bed" and "fish in a dish"
11 Real estate mogul Olenicoff
15 Superpower with which Clark Kent shaves himself
16 Boulevardier's accessory
17 Waffling
18 Fangorn Forest denizens
19 Source of the line "Hope springs eternal . . ."
20 Larder lineup
21 It moves along via a series of belts
22 Greg Evans comic strip
24 Dental patient, often
25 Daughter of Zeus and Leda
28 Drum that might accompany a fife
30 First carrier to offer regular in-flight movies, 1961
31 Garment made of Gore-Tex, maybe
33 They're no longer tender in a typical trattoria
34 Yellowfin, on some menus
35 Tangles with, in the country
37 Classic Chrysler
39 Lead characters in "Mork & Mindy"?
40 Impart
42 Coaching concern
43 Tillis or Tormé
44 Place to moor
46 Full of adrenaline, informally
47 West Point newcomers
49 Aids in marketing?
51 O. Henry is known for one

52 Baccarat cousin
53 Estrangement
57 Zip
58 1971 film with the tagline "You don't assign him to murder cases. You just turn him loose."
60 Like shellfish
61 Regime change catalyst
62 Hard worker
63 Site near an outdoor recording session in "Help!"

## DOWN

1 Pot item
2 Prefix with -stat
3 Pool protector
4 Six-time Lombardi Trophy winners

5 Rx chain
6 Spanish wine
7 Leaning
8 Like the snowy owl
9 Very much
10 Shanghai-to-Tokyo dir.
11 Block during a blizzard
12 Genre that glorifies gunplay
13 Mostly
14 Checked
21 Emergency oil rig visitor
23 Out of one's league?
24 "Whitman Cantata" composer
25 Part of an iconic Eden outfit
26 Durable kitchen items
27 Low-priced item, maybe

29 Cartoonist Keane
32 Ululates
36 TV show that has spawned many movies, briefly
38 Cold war concern
41 Yvonne of "The Munsters"
45 Striped identifier
48 Zach ___, "Garden State" actor/director
50 Early automaker Frederick Henry ___
52 Direction from on high
54 Weights, colloquially
55 "Hullabaloo" dance
56 Bang out
58 Fielding feats, for short
59 When repeated, a sneaky laugh

*by Doug Peterson and Brad Wilber*

## ACROSS

1 White-whiskered sort
10 Symbol of Einstein's gravitational constant
15 Eager
16 Tons
17 Time of one's life
18 Youngest of five famous brothers
19 Ernst associate
20 Things worth waiting for?
21 What head shots are used in
22 People pick pockets in it
23 Eddie's partner in musical comedy
24 Burial option
25 Cut out for it
28 Intentionally flooded field
30 Short order?
31 One working with magnetite
33 Minor, legally
35 "Ha! Good one!"
37 "Bummer"
38 Word below a signature on a bill
39 Zero, in 21-Across
40 They often have good rhythm
41 Mr. T's real last name
42 Julia Child worked for it during W.W. II: Abbr.
43 Lav
44 Escalator pioneer
46 Fox on Fox
48 Blast alternative?
49 Traffic court letters
52 Facilitators of cultural growth
53 Toxicodendron diversilobum
55 Yogi Bear co-creator
56 Off-roading option
57 Fire
58 Grocery product with green leaves in its logo

## DOWN

1 400-pound calf, perhaps
2 Player of a big scaredy-cat?
3 No Mr. Personality
4 Former drug czar Kerlikowske
5 Put an ___
6 Where the Blue Nile rises
7 Jellyfish and krill
8 Some are fragile
9 Bygone means of corporal punishment
10 Buzz generator
11 "I'll Be Around" songwriter Wilder
12 TV Guide crossword focus
13 Something that shouldn't scare you
14 Garnish
21 Arch
22 Marker maker
23 It features a statue of a Scottie next to his master
25 Title slave of the stage
26 First cut on the album "Sticky Fingers"
27 Home of the Ducks of baseball's Atlantic League
29 Handle on farm equipment?
30 Humdingers
32 Fr. address
33 Texting counterpart of "TY"
34 Sno-___ (winter blower brand)
36 Orwellian superstate
40 One of nine numbers on a card
42 Clarkson College locale
43 Alpo alternative
45 "___ you!"
47 1958 spy novel set in Jamaica
48 "Cannery Row" brothel owner
49 "Get busy!"
50 Boat trailer?
51 Pottery Barn competitor
53 54-Down tally: Abbr.
54 See 53-Down: Abbr.

by Barry C. Silk

# 150

## ACROSS

1 Terminal cases
8 Something to do experiments in
15 One of the Big Three in credit reports
16 Eradicate
17 Baking session
18 Old West German moniker
19 Goal of a 17-Across
20 Off the rack
22 Jewish rite
24 Tramp
25 ___ Hawkins Day
26 Bald Mountain's range
28 Often-affected outburst
30 Time to go
31 Navigator who named Natal
33 Nice things to be massaged
35 Adoption option
36 "The Whiffenpoof Song" ending
39 Slush-pile pile: Abbr.
42 ___ cellar
43 Imitated a wound-up toy
47 Schlemiel's cry
49 Providers of football game coverage?
51 Title woman in a J. P. Donleavy novel
52 Big name in water filtration
54 Charge
56 Shot after a break?
57 Bar glasses?
60 Goal
61 Recreating, maybe
62 It smells on a bug

64 More dear
65 Sponge
66 Advanced photocopier features
67 Synchronized

## DOWN

1 One of a tight pair
2 Some zoo attractions
3 Really going after, with "for"
4 It was ceded to Brit. in the Treaty of Utrecht
5 Way off
6 Racetrack array
7 Don't hold your breath
8 Star of 2009's Fame Ball Tour

9 Assist with a job
10 Parts of the Big Apple
11 Try to scratch
12 Greasy, perhaps
13 Subject of the 2009 biography "Puttin' on the Ritz"
14 What "they say our love won't pay," in "I Got You Babe"
21 Ruthless
23 Try
27 Latin trio member
29 Behave with respect to
32 Small cells
34 Take the junk out?
37 Post masters?
38 There's nothing above it

39 Icing supervisor?
40 Kia model
41 One going over telemarketing lines
44 Ruthless sort
45 Eatery seen in a "Manhattan" scene
46 Light fright?
48 Part of many a grid
50 Torpedo layer
53 Yawning
55 Construction piece with a mate
58 See 59-Down
59 With 58-Down, drop by
63 Command level: Abbr.

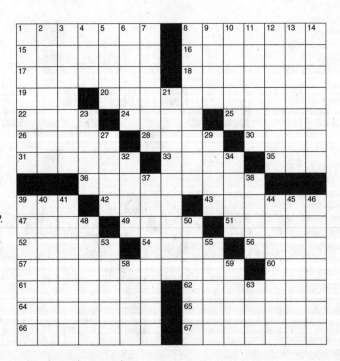

by Paula Gamache

## ACROSS

1 "8mm" star, 1999
12 "Applesauce!"
15 It has a Snapshot Tool command
16 Irish ___
17 His 1978 album "Excitable Boy" went platinum
18 Marathoner Pippig
19 Mrs. Gorbachev
20 Bicycle support, informally
22 1956 Santos rookie
23 Groupie's trait
25 Past-tense verb that is the same as its present-tense form minus the fourth and fifth letters
26 Jane who was Chicago's first female mayor
28 Title science teacher of an old sitcom
31 Mud
32 Place for locks and pins
34 ___ fide
35 Gets in a lather
37 Won't allow
41 Mrs. Grundy type
43 Far East capital
44 Kind of root in math
45 Milk producer
49 Circus Maximus stars?
51 Soviet attack sub
52 Gardener's purchase
54 Bait thrown overboard
55 Wine-tasting accessory
58 Pair in an average-sized orchestra
60 Get an edge on?
61 One stoked to provide warmth
64 A simpler one may be recalled
65 Black-and-white, say
66 Typical house on "Hoarders"
67 Flashlight alternatives

## DOWN

1 Sticks nix
2 "Go ahead and try!"
3 Orange relative
4 Inner Party member in "1984"
5 Sake brewery byproduct
6 Star with two stars on the Hollywood Walk of Fame
7 Informal remarks?
8 Image on a denarius
9 Sominex alternative
10 Storms, e.g.
11 Cousins of kites
12 Bagatelle
13 Pioneering microcomputer
14 Rakes often break them
21 Shrilly talk to
22 Many tykes' lunches
24 Potential throat clearer, briefly
27 Filing aid
29 Hangover?
30 Justice Kagan
33 "Highly doubtful"
36 Baltic Sea swimmer
38 Live, maybe
39 Ancient dweller in the Po Valley
40 Comforter go-with
42 Lugs
43 First name on the 1954 album "Mambo!"
45 Five of them represent a zero
46 The "A" of A&M Records
47 Polite cut-in
48 Chaucer's "Merciless Beauty," e.g.
50 Its contents are often wicked
53 Be a blessed person, per Matthew 5:4
56 Skinny-minny
57 Princess in Donald Duck cartoons
59 Certain pack member
62 Abbey title
63 They have high stations

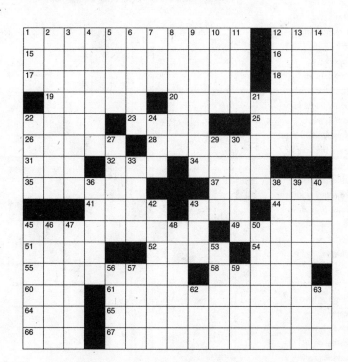

by David Steinberg and Barry C. Silk

## ACROSS

1 One looking out for #1
8 Fair way to be judged
15 Doris Day film with the song "Ten Cents a Dance"
17 Peoria resident's representation
18 They often pass through needles
19 Place for a butler
20 Spanish body of water
21 ___ corde (piano pedaling direction)
22 Rounded-up numbers?
23 Driver's invitation
24 Flashes
26 What a biblical black horseman symbolizes
27 Opposed to
28 Matadors' red capes
29 People might leave them in tears
30 Often-toasted seed
31 Year "The Tale of Peter Rabbit" was published
32 Like many sluggish drains
33 Govt. issuance
35 Life
36 Spheres
37 Cobble, e.g.
38 Small grouse
39 Things in lava lamps
40 Honey badger
41 Hostile
43 Amino acid in proteins
44 Tried to reach higher
46 Secretly plots to harm
47 More mad
48 "Jazz" artist

## DOWN

1 Pliable protein
2 1991 entrant for the Democratic presidential nomination
3 Unduly high appraisals
4 Lead-in to flops
5 Springsteen's "___ Rocker"
6 Divisions
7 How David Bowie's character fell, in a 1976 sci-fi film
8 "Miami Vice" Emmy winner
9 Aye's opposite, in verse
10 Scratch
11 It's not a good sign
12 Rundowns
13 What prosaic minds lack
14 Exchange for a Hamilton
16 Politician Paul and others
22 Big exporter of mangoes
23 Comets' head
25 ". . . ___ the bush"
26 Blue states
28 ___ Gerais (Brazilian state)
30 Some brick buildings
31 Crescent-shaped bodies
32 "Does the name Quasimodo ring a bell?," e.g.
34 Big name in frozen pizza
36 What a Pullman kitchen is built into
37 Work after the first?
39 Act to retain one's property at auction
40 Convened anew
42 "First name" in the Louvre
43 Zaxxon maker
45 '60s service site

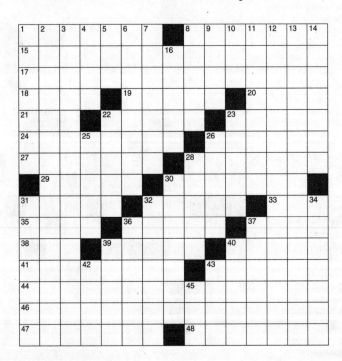

by Joe Krozel

## ACROSS

1 Increases the intensity
10 High-hatter's wear?
15 Totally plugged-in
16 Bury
17 Sheepskin source
18 Spirit, in Stuttgart
19 Maximum, nonstandardly
20 Sprites are similar to them
22 :, at times
23 "The Ground Beneath ___ Feet" (U2 song)
25 Go a long way
26 Rapper with the 2002 #1 hit "Always on Time"
28 1972 treaty subjects, briefly
31 Like many ventilation systems
35 Dress-to-impress attire
37 Singer Carmen
38 Fukuda's predecessor as Japan's P.M.
39 Italian game akin to pétanque
40 Football Hall-of-Famer who became a Minnesota Supreme Court justice
42 Thirst
43 Genre for 37-Across
44 Ice cream or pizza follower
46 Won't shut up
48 Comment while putting something away
49 Yuri's beloved, in literature
53 More prone to bellyaches
56 Growled at, say
58 Welcomed to one's house
59 One may be represented by stars

61 Plagued
62 Became fair
63 Shakespeare's Ross, e.g.
64 Gift for a TV buff

## DOWN

1 Studier of sutras
2 Final aim, to a philosopher
3 Title site of nine films: Abbr.
4 He wrote "No human thing is of serious importance"
5 Old story intro?
6 Gull's cry
7 Rip up
8 Strict follower?
9 Stamp feature, in philately lingo
10 Fierce sort
11 What a 64-Across may comprise

12 What a day trader tries to turn
13 Supervillain from Krypton
14 M.D.'s with tiny flashlights
21 Travel plans: Abbr.
24 Like 49-Down
26 Major mode of transportation?
27 Pace of "Pushing Daisies"
29 Many sit on pads
30 Start moving
31 Baroque "key of glory": Abbr.
32 Carol Burnett's 17-Across
33 It's unlikely to work
34 Like Jane Goodall's study site
36 Means of reaching a peak level?
38 "Lord," in Turkish

41 View from a pew
42 Where one may have personal reactions?
45 Put up with
47 Role for both Burton and Amos in a 1977 miniseries
49 Stuff in a swim cap
50 They're not basic things
51 Noël Coward's "Sigh No More," e.g.
52 Ace
53 & 54 Start of a historic telegraph message
54 See 53-Down
55 Invoice abbr.
57 Tutee of Seneca
60 Year in Claudius's reign

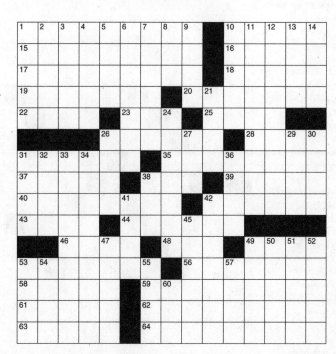

by Julian Lim

# 154

## ACROSS

1 Speak carefully
16 One of Disneyland's original attractions
17 Part of a modern address
18 Bloom who played Mary in "The Last Temptation of Christ"
19 Communicated without saying anything
20 "Not in eine Million Jahre!"
21 "Gotcha"
22 Forest climbers
23 "Hey-y-y-y!" sayer of sitcomdom, with "the"
24 The Big Red Machine, on scoreboards
25 Maisons, across the Pyrenees
26 Alternative to gunpowder
27 Charm
29 Urquhart Castle is on it
31 One often duped: Abbr.
33 Reason for denying entry, maybe
34 Attack as a cat might
38 Actress Landi of "The Count of Monte Cristo," 1934
42 ___ hammer (Mjolnir)
43 Gets something off one's back, say
45 Long, for short: Abbr.
46 Quiet
47 Swamp birds
48 Like some statues and book spines
49 Lo-___
50 Front-page New York Times addition of 1997

51 Hoops Hall-of-Famer Baylor
52 Slant in print
55 Topiary figures
56 Hoped for a miracle, maybe

## DOWN

1 Ice climbing hazard
2 Bore down (on)
3 Instrument whose name means "little goose"
4 Clearing
5 Actress Ward
6 Wheels-up announcement, briefly
7 Mexican Indians
8 Like some fees
9 Electrically neutral subatomic particle
10 Starts suddenly

11 Go along, as one's way
12 Every, in an Rx
13 The Star City of the South
14 It carries out many orders
15 Has a cold reaction?
22 Flier to Rio
23 Big name in handbags
25 Podiatric problems
26 N.L. East team, informally
28 Silk selection
30 Future alumnae, quaintly
32 Substance used in fillings?
34 Rock collections may sit beside them
35 Daughter of King Minos

36 "La Cenerentola" composer
37 Distinctive parts of some hummingbirds
39 Elegantly attired
40 Certain telecom technician
41 Suitability
44 It's turned down for extra warmth
47 Existentialist Kierkegaard
48 Blazingly bright
50 "Till the End of Time" singer
51 "___, Red-Hot & Live" (1982 blues album)
53 Jot
54 Digital ___ (high-tech shooter)

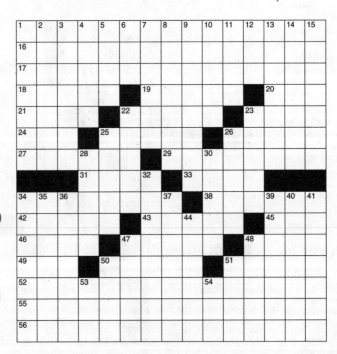

by Tim Croce

## ACROSS

1 "Another Cinderella Story" co-star, 2008
12 Focus of middle management?
15 Creator of the heroine Catherine Earnshaw
16 It's bisected by the Reuss River
17 City in the 42-Down Desert
18 Caesar's thing
19 N.Y.C. line to the Bronx
20 Race space
21 Name on a London hall
23 Poseidon's trident?
24 Channel with the tagline "Story matters here"
25 10th-century European king
26 First name in gossip
28 Like some issues
32 Like saved hockey shots
35 Gets along
36 English Channel feeder
37 Advice-disdaining sort
40 Mismatched pair?
43 Bearers of bright red arils
44 They're shortsighted
48 See
51 Neighbor of Eure-et-Loir
52 Broadway's "Never ___ Dance"
53 Shogunate capital
56 "Stuff like that"
57 One of reality TV's "Guidettes"
59 Means of enforcing compliance
60 Asian winter celebration
61 Credit card co. concern

62 Two-time Triple Crown winner
65 Operation Cyclone org.
66 Epitome of dedication, in modern usage
67 Either of two cousin Udalls, once: Abbr.
68 They're suitable to be transplanted to another bed

## DOWN

1 Not quite minor-league
2 "The American Scholar" speech giver
3 TV Guide datum
4 She, in Rio
5 Spiral-horned antelope
6 Norm of "This Old House"

7 Mean sort
8 Slow flow
9 6 string
10 View from Biancavilla
11 With fire
12 Golden
13 "Song of the South" villain
14 Raphael's "___ Madonna"
22 It's often a double-decker
27 Swell
29 Elevator of literature?
30 Add (up)
31 Look elated
33 Challenging question
34 1920–24 owner of Metro Pictures
38 What the U.S. joined in Apr. 1917
39 Bath can

40 Where future web developers develop?
41 Dessert that's out of this world?
42 ___ Desert (area with saguaros)
45 Test-record, maybe
46 Typist, at times
47 Divisions of geometry
49 Game with 59-Down cards
50 Regarding this point
54 Frank account
55 Not estos or esos
58 Pensée product
59 See 49-Down
63 "Hawaii Five-0" co-star Daniel ___ Kim
64 Trig function

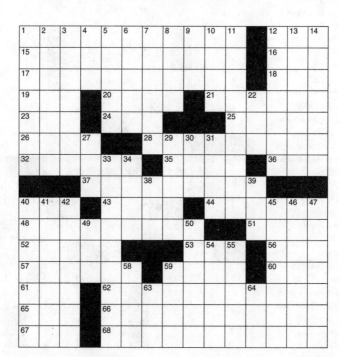

by David Steinberg

# 156

## ACROSS
1 Verbal shrug
4 Beat
9 Greets the good guy, maybe
14 Pointy-headed sort?
15 Whom Turkey's Weeping Rock is said to represent
16 Cliff hanger?
17 One of two in a plane
19 Autodom's ZR1, for one
20 Writer Moore or Moorehead
21 Where people drop off on the line?
23 Killer bees, e.g.
25 Brother
26 Cackling loon with a white coat
31 Steam up
34 Dungeons & Dragons weapon
35 With 40-Across, "Inside ___" (postgame show)
36 Goal for many a 26- or 43-Across
40 See 35-Across
41 Its products often have Allen wrenches included
42 Dueling count
43 Mighty heavy
47 "My Name Is Earl" co-star Suplee
48 One working on steps
52 Means of dropping a line
56 Victimizer of Cassio
57 "I Know Who Killed Me" star, 2007
58 Offensive play in 35-/40-Across
60 "That's ___!" ("Don't!")
61 Flip
62 Secured
63 Track lineup
64 The out crowd?
65 "Annie" characters

## DOWN
1 ___ President
2 Many a booted ruler
3 One who might do the heavy lifting
4 "Larry's Country Diner" channel
5 Greeted the bad guy, maybe
6 Churn
7 Strauss wrote a concerto in D for it
8 Doing good
9 Spineless response to pressure
10 Examine as a wolf would
11 One preparing an oil pan?
12 ___ bread
13 Forward-thinking type
18 Protective cover
22 Act the coxcomb
24 Real character
27 Strong proof
28 R. J. Reynolds brand
29 What's under an arch
30 Fox ratings
31 Stiff bristles
32 ___ Matsuhisa, celebrity chef and restaurateur
33 Small cannon balls
37 Ottoman relative
38 Capital ENE of Fiji
39 Wine colorer
44 Second-simplest hydrocarbon
45 They may be found in preserves, informally
46 Part of the total
49 Mooch
50 Impel
51 Nature life support system
52 Tire
53 Isle near Mull
54 Strong-smelling, say
55 Supervising
59 Pop-ups, e.g.

by Josh Knapp

## ACROSS

**1** In-box material for some agents
**8** Red, white and blue group
**15** Stock pantomime character
**16** Decorative server
**17** Ahead
**18** Wise words
**19** Prefix with car
**20** Boglike
**22** Puts one's foot down
**23** A cyclone is a big one
**24** Wisconsin port
**26** Bad start?
**27** Put to work
**32** Writer of the lines "Pigeons on the grass alas. / Pigeons on the grass alas"
**35** "The Mikado" weapon
**36** Emperor who built the Domus Aurea
**37** Gerontologist's study
**40** You might hear a children's song in one
**41** Some fairy story villains
**42** Dispatch
**43** Watching the big game, say
**45** Army missions
**46** Like Rome, it's said
**48** Blue, in a way: Abbr.
**51** Defiant response
**55** Skating spot, maybe
**56** Symbol of elasticity, in economics
**57** Paper work
**59** Server of food that may be steamed, fried or raw

**61** Went in tandem?
**62** Many are found on beaches
**63** Gets down
**64** Nonsense

## DOWN

**1** Door-to-door delivery
**2** Important part of mayo
**3** Plant more crops in
**4** N.Y.C. line
**5** Alpha senior?
**6** One side in the Revolutionary War
**7** Serious
**8** Common 31-Down: Abbr.
**9** Saltier
**10** Neither good nor evil
**11** Dance element
**12** Iris's location
**13** Orangish gem
**14** Wall St. manipulators
**21** 1968 #2 hit with the lyric "My love for you is way out of line"
**25** Dance elements
**26** Mustang competitor
**28** Inti worshipers
**29** End of a dictionary
**30** At one time in the past?
**31** Prescribed amount
**32** Town in '44 headlines
**33** Gracile
**34** Ones unable to swim straight?
**35** Bag
**38** "Kiss Me, Kate" song

**39** "Gimme a break!"
**44** XX
**45** Annie once played by Ethel Merman
**47** Iridescent material
**48** Messing around on TV?
**49** Members of les Nations Unies
**50** Reed section?
**51** Items in buckets
**52** Forte
**53** Privateer who captained the Blessed William
**54** Quaint shout
**58** They may be checked at an airport
**60** Part of a barn

by Gareth Bain

# 158

## ACROSS

1 Begins
9 Common sights in the Rockies
15 Expiate
16 Meaty Applebee's morsel
17 Half of an old comic film duo
18 It includes picking the place
19 Woody Guthrie and others
20 Adam Smith or Ethan Allen
22 The "needle" part of needle grass
23 Scottish sprout
25 Item on a Christmas list
26 Party person, for short
27 Horse show demonstrations
30 Desperate
31 Pop punk band with the 2002 triple-platinum album "The Young and the Hopeless"
35 Last song heard on Disneyland's Splash Mountain
36 Relatively important meeting?
37 Top
38 Take without credit
39 Ball-bearing piece
40 Field of three Nobel Prizes: Abbr.
42 Big game show prize
47 Pal 4 life
48 People without a religious affiliation, in modern lingo
51 ___ Island
52 Stops lying
54 Bug
56 Like some operations
57 Prime, as bonds
58 Works in the kitchen
59 Court luminaries

## DOWN

1 "Batman" comics sound
2 "___ your point"
3 NPR's Roberts
4 Request at a palace, maybe
5 Gives oneself something to aim for
6 Frequently, quaintly
7 Dog-ear, e.g.
8 Word on a bingo card
9 Kindergarten comeback
10 Babe Ruth mark broken by Roger Maris
11 Kegler's org.
12 Noted cliff in Yosemite Valley
13 Balance sheet figure
14 Frequent Jack Kirby comics collaborator
21 "Well, that one doesn't work"
24 Pops
28 Relative of sleet
29 Grp. whose flag has 12 stars
30 Awarder of a thimble to Alice, in "Alice's Adventures in Wonderland"
31 "Up top!"
32 Anthony's XM Radio partner
33 Samurai who's lost his lord
34 Laggards
35 "High School Musical" actor
36 Greasy part of pork
40 Mortimer of old radio
41 Figure on a manufacturer's balance sheet
43 Puffed ___
44 It's baked in Italy
45 Pioneer in psychoanalysis
46 Exemplars of thinness
49 "___ Almighty" (2007 film)
50 Q-tip, e.g.
53 Salt source
55 Bit of barnyard onomatopoeia

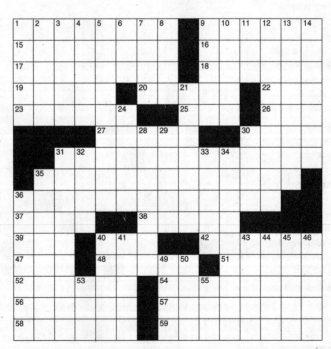

by Peter Wentz

## ACROSS

1 What many checks are for
12 Eyebrow-raising
15 One holding the line
16 Man, to Marcus
17 Alternative to lemon chiffon
18 1960s Greystoke portrayer
19 Chelsea-to-Chinatown dir.
20 Like some evidence in arson cases
21 More likely to encounter
23 Label for the Bee Gees
24 Handles
25 Rajiv's mother
28 Victor Herbert's "naughty" girl
29 Thomas called the Queen of Memphis Soul
30 Long meals?
31 Hall monitors, briefly
32 Like Bush Sr., religiously
33 Pod : whales :: knot : ___
34 Land animals?
35 Quick "ha ha"
36 Apt to strike out
37 Sidewalk scam
38 A wide variety
40 Went back and forth
41 Notably high populace
42 Joins
43 He signed 5-Down in 1940
44 Bark part
45 Bitter, e.g.

48 Chemical ending
49 London tabloid
52 Laugh, in Lille
53 1994 Olympic skating champion
54 One of a pair of fraternal twins, maybe
55 Neighbor of the Gem of the Mountains

## DOWN

1 Nicknames
2 Terminal projections, briefly
3 Cabinetry option
4 Motor additive?
5 "Witchcraft" singer
6 Minnesota county west of St. Louis
7 Large lunar crater
8 "Live at the ___" (Patsy Cline album)
9 Biblical boater, in Brest
10 Colombian cowboys
11 Mocha residents
12 Very tense
13 Dabbler
14 Like some nuts
22 Punch choice
23 Has something
24 Having missed the bell, say
25 Their anthem is "Lofsöngur"
26 Son of Marie Louise of Austria
27 Its boring bits can be quite long
28 Liver and kidney
30 Has over

33 Japanese glaze
34 Bikers' mounts
36 Finely tempered swords
37 Game requiring many plug-ins?
39 Nordic flier
40 Home to Liszt and Goethe
42 American Revolution's "Mad Anthony"
44 Pomeranian, e.g.
45 Cantatrice's delivery
46 Yahoo
47 First name in mystery
50 25-Down occupy one: Abbr.
51 Landfill visitor

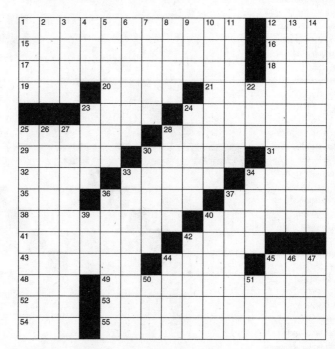

by Michael Wiesenberg

## ACROSS

1 Entree meant to be eaten with the fingers, according to its creator
12 "People's Choice Awards" airer until 2017
15 Key chain
16 Millerite, e.g.
17 In flight?
19 Late critic featured on the Hollywood Walk of Fame
20 Position of prominence
21 Vatican money, once
22 Sunbathes, informally
23 So-called "Playwright of the Midwest"
24 Out of spirits
25 Marlon Brando's role in "Superman"
26 Leave off
27 W.W. II pistol
28 Buildings with many owners
29 Post office purchase
31 Big 1970s–'80s band with a geographical name
32 Art of television
33 Innocents
34 Playing costs
35 Dear
36 What Mad magazine lacked from 1957 to 2001
39 Part of many a vegan's diet
40 Country singers?
41 Short distance
42 Goes beyond the pail?
44 Element #100 is named for him
45 It's often freely given
47 Surveillance cam location
48 Athlete who started a clothing company in 1933
49 "Fantastic Mr. Fox" director Anderson
50 Hiking guide

## DOWN

1 Dry mounts?
2 Locale for many 1-Down
3 St. Petersburg's ___ College
4 Middle-earth region, with "the"
5 "___ Nobody's Business" (old blues standard)
6 Shoulder-fired weapon, for short
7 Salt
8 Willard Scott's successor on "Today"
9 Symbol of Apollo
10 Dancer de Mille
11 Remove
12 Seeker of the Seven Cities of Gold
13 Induces
14 Victorian-era furnishings
18 Shows the ropes
22 Scorecard blemish
25 Pulitzer-winning cartoonist Feiffer
26 Bill who received a Presidential Medal of Freedom in 2002
27 Suspect groups
28 Turns up
29 Celebrated matador during Franco's reign
30 Painting and ballet
31 Be an angel?
32 Tool
33 Title maiden in a Heinrich Heine poem
35 Home of the Karl Marx Theater
36 Endangered
37 Lower
38 Brent of "Star Trek: T.N.G."
40 Company boycotter?
41 Don Quixote, e.g.
43 Kind
44 Payroll tax, for short
46 Oil in a can

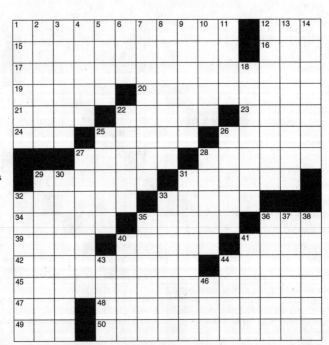

by Patrick Berry

# 161

## ACROSS

1. "Spin the Black Circle" Grammy winner of 1995
9. Sort who needs to button up
15. Buttoned up
17. Not have a hunch?
18. What shy people often have
19. Trendy tuna
20. With 22-Across, runner's woe
21. Prohibition, e.g.
22. See 20-Across
24. City near Pyramid Lake
25. Uglify
27. "Superman II" villainess
29. Atlas offerings
37. Ivory tower setting
38. Some expressions of false humility
39. Large wire
40. "Boxing Helena" star Sherilyn
41. Squad leader?
42. Comic response, in Variety
45. Greek restaurant menu subheading
48. Realization vocalization
51. Plumber's union?
52. Catcher of the rye?
53. Dipsticks
55. Part of the Ring of Fire
60. Light alternative
61. Modern resident of ancient Ebla
62. Many gallerygoers

## DOWN

1. ____-Calais (French department)
2. Imparter of fruity overtones
3. Hub for Jordan Aviation
4. Half-pint
5. Eyeshades?
6. Vingt-et-un, e.g.
7. How some instruments are sold
8. Gessen who wrote the 2012 Putin biography "The Man Without a Face"
9. Bayou predator
10. Cold war grp.?
11. "____ gather"
12. Military brass
13. Horror-struck, apparently
14. First moment
16. Goose
22. Ferry ride, say
23. Ushers in
24. Assault team
25. Depart from
26. Punish by fine
28. They get stuck in corners
29. Arizona's ____ Fria River
30. Some of a caterer's inventory
31. Upscale Italian shoe brand
32. Where Captain Cook landed in 1770
33. "____ first . . ."
34. Conductor Leibowitz
35. Crew at a pileup
36. Short term?
42. Toronto team, briefly
43. Dental gold, e.g.
44. Jacinthe or jonquille
46. Salon service
47. Late notices?
48. Peeved, after "in"
49. Play both sides, in a way
50. Pro grps.
53. Xanadu's river
54. It may have a row of 28-Down, briefly
56. William Tell territory
57. Old Eastern alternative
58. Rankin who created Inspector Rebus
59. Juice fiend

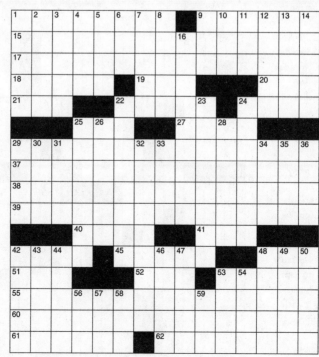

*by Martin Ashwood-Smith*

## ACROSS

1 Rob Lowe was one
11 Screen
15 It reflects radio waves
16 "Well, Did You ___?"
17 Holds water
18 She said "Don't be humble. You're not that great"
19 Many a trop. paradise
20 Unlike radio shows
21 "Scooby-Doo" girl
23 Bikini event, briefly
25 Down a sports drink, say
27 Comparison words
28 In ___ (as placed)
29 Took from the top
30 See 12-Down
33 "Love ___ Ball" (Glenn Ford film)
34 British Columbia's longest river
37 It might elicit a shrug
39 Garbage
40 Put a seal of approval on, overseas
44 "There's many ___ . . ."
46 Classic publisher of paperbacks
47 Composer Harris and others
51 Spouse's entreaty starter, perhaps
53 Giverny's most famous resident
54 Evidencing change?
55 Occasion for the fleet
57 Compass dir.
58 Not taken by
59 It's still open to investigation
62 Syllabus segment
63 Deposit memo
64 They're often ticked off: Abbr.
65 Alex P. Keaton and Marcia Brady each had two

## DOWN

1 1935–37 home for Hemingway
2 Some tributes
3 It may have its charms
4 Digital print source?
5 Covert call
6 Projection for some kneelers
7 "À bientôt," across the Channel
8 Cole of fashion
9 Sites of many revivals, briefly
10 Thin-sounding
11 Unvarying, in music
12 With 30-Across, shout of frustration
13 A bit woozy
14 Like some weekends
22 Promo team
24 ___-chef
26 Orange or plum
28 Minute Maid Park team member, for short
31 Mate via mail
32 Game stopper
34 Splendid, humorously
35 Waitress at the fictional Lobo Lounge
36 Canaries' setting
38 Flying start?
41 Make it?
42 Like some eyes and disasters
43 Sponsor of baseball's Relief Man Award
45 Reserved bars?
48 Marked down
49 Private reply
50 Pickles, e.g.
52 New York home of the painter Edward Hopper
53 Boy-girl connection
56 Year in Trajan's reign
60 Shout, to Cherie
61 Part of Fla. is on it

by Ned White

## ACROSS

1 Best-selling Apple app
11 "The Kudlow Report" airer
15 It burns quickly
16 Currency whose name can become its country's name by changing its last letter to an N and scrambling
17 Outlaws
18 Prefix with phobia
19 Like some pliers
20 Fashion inits.
21 O.A.S. member
22 Symbols of innocence
24 Some Southerners
28 Supporter to keep a watchful eye on
30 Cup, maybe
31 Shade of red
32 They're not definite
34 Wistful plaint
35 Lock that's hard to open?
36 Not procrastinating
37 Point of writing
38 ___ Club
39 Rub
40 Naturalist who coined the term "invertebrate"
42 Powerful engine
43 Music style of La Mafia
44 ___-de-Marne (department near Paris)
45 Go up against
46 Children's book ending
53 It may be pasteurisé
54 Complete

55 Colosseum cry
56 Its highest rank is Wonsu
57 Big TV announcement, informally
58 Like Barack Obama's early schoolmates

## DOWN

1 "How's it ___?"
2 Rice on shelves
3 Bundle of nerves
4 Blasted through
5 Anadem
6 Some council members
7 Comics sound
8 Western gas brand
9 What the picky pick
10 Uncheck, say

11 One may be a rocker
12 Singer with the platinum album "Pink Friday"
13 Five-time Emmy-winning role
14 Sugar sometimes does it
23 Shade of black
24 "Thief" star, 1981
25 Not recently
26 California-founded smoothie chain
27 Suffix with press
28 Open
29 "The Battle With the Slum" writer
31 Eastern ___
33 Reinstate, in a way
35 Small meat-stuffed pastries

36 Bit of resistance
38 Certain computer grouping, for short
39 Trattoria selection
41 Ready to be framed, say
42 Banging noise
43 Much lore
44 A clip may come from it
47 Part of the earth's history
48 Reddish-brown quartz
49 H's
50 Adriatic seaport
51 Italian verse form
52 Kirk ___, first actor to play Superman on the big screen

by David Steinberg

# 164

## ACROSS

1 Onetime co-host of "The View"
10 Seen-it-all
15 Did some undercover work
16 Like opals
17 "Archie Bunker's Place" actress
18 No-handed skateboarding trick
19 Cash in Cambodia
20 Some cornbreads
22 Base fare
23 Creole, e.g.
25 When repeated, response to "Who wants dessert?"
26 AARP focus: Abbr.
27 PCBs, e.g.
28 Zoom ___
29 Kind of column
30 "Forever Your Girl" singer, 1989
31 Lawsuits
34 Royal personage
36 Arizona player, for short
37 Poke
38 One of the Jetsons
39 Viagra maker
41 Kind of animation
44 Potato chip brand
45 Blasted
46 It might be spun around a campfire
47 Major education supporter
49 Some Spanish dates: Abbr.
50 Purport
51 "The Book of Eli" actress
54 Rigel's constellation
55 1985 Dennis Quaid sci-fi film
56 "___ Hope"
57 "Band" leader of the 1960s

## DOWN

1 A lot
2 More stylish
3 Marshal Dillon portrayer
4 Cinephiles' collectibles
5 Printer malfunctions
6 Not be square with
7 Actress Peeples
8 Unpredictable
9 TV set?
10 Quad standouts
11 Lee of silent films
12 What it often takes, it's said
13 Hit a lazy pop-up, say
14 Dossier stamp
21 Greetings
23 YouTube no-no
24 1940's ___ Pact
27 Bamboozled
28 "Su-u-ure"
29 Make mincemeat of, say
30 "Wearing the face that she keeps in ___ by the door" (Beatles lyric)
31 Professional claims examiner
32 Many a toy powerer
33 Land on the Indian Ocean
34 Feature on some place mats
35 Not up
37 Cursing
39 Way to stand
40 Purchase at an optician's
41 Mint family plant
42 Lady of Arthurian legend
43 Inferior
45 Hollywood father and daughter
46 Supersede
48 Bugs, e.g.
49 ___ terrier
52 Do-over, of a sort
53 Electrical unit

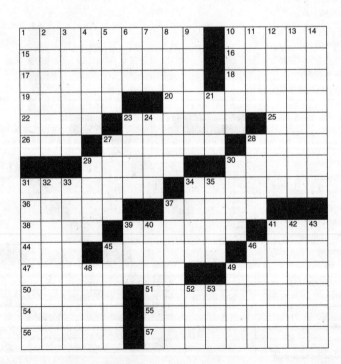

by Michael Ashley

## ACROSS

1 Stopped living the high life?
10 One paid to get shot
15 Legendary lutist
16 TV host Chung
17 Asia Minor, e.g.
18 Dumps
19 Trail rider's accessory
20 Public
21 Draft pick
22 One highly unlikely to react
24 Geneses
28 Character in "Unforgiven"
29 French verse
30 2011 All-Star pitcher Correia
31 Flow controller
32 He was born "all over like an hairy garment"
33 See 28-Down
34 Trail rider's concoction
35 Gov. Hochul's purview
36 "Bless ___" (1941 hit song)
37 Slow march, maybe
38 Player in a pocket
40 Holy smoker?
41 Title character singing in the "Tea for Two" duet
42 Not be a wallflower
43 Scrape
44 0-0
50 "Allahu ___" (Iraqi flag phrase)
51 Drill command involving a rifle
52 Whoopi's first leading film role
53 One who doesn't click in a clique
54 Graph revelation, possibly
55 Nonrevolutionaries

## DOWN

1 Easy marks
2 Olive genus
3 Ring
4 Old-time actress Bennett
5 Went long
6 Ill-fated line of the 1950s
7 Beefy Provençal stew
8 "The Producers" sex kitten
9 Landscaping alternative to sand
10 Study principally
11 Biblically named Michigan college
12 They don't do it all themselves
13 Monster
14 Common religious artwork
23 "Scratch thee but with ___ . . .": Shak.
24 Bill starter
25 Snoop
26 Like unsurprising temperatures
27 Source of 13-Down eggs
28 With 33-Across, "The Voice" vocal coach
30 Ed whose entire 18-season career was with the Mets
33 Common B-school requirement
34 Spirit in a sling
36 In the log, say
37 Right-handed
39 Hold up
40 Its patrons are usually kept in the dark
42 Blouse with a sailor collar
45 Great Seal word
46 Legal scholar Guinier
47 Symbol of love
48 Sanitization target
49 Former faves of jet-setters

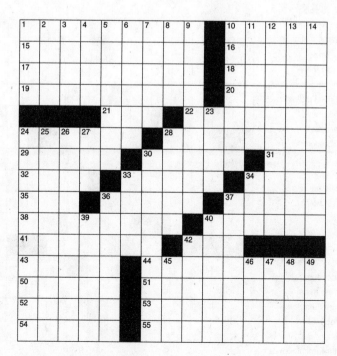

by Chris A. McGlothlin

## ACROSS

1 Singer's tongue
8 Fast delivery
15 First name in online news
16 Detox, say
17 Autobiographical book by Carrie Fisher
19 As one
20 D.M.V. offerings
21 Peace Nobelist Kim ___ -jung
22 Popcorn Nuggets offerer
24 Peace Nobelist Hammarskjöld
25 Papua New Guinea port in W.W. II news
28 "That's nice"
30 Dept. of Labor division
34 Unit of online popularity
39 "Almost there!"
40 Nice thing to hit
41 First card played in the game parliament
43 British submachine gun
44 Bog
45 Grade sch. class
46 Badge holder: Abbr.
49 Back
51 Ermine, e.g.
54 Kind of cable in TV production
58 Actress Ryder
61 Oscar-nominated Woody Allen film
63 Mythological sister of 66-Across

64 Regardless of
65 Formidable foes
66 Mythological brother of 63-Across

## DOWN

1 Went off course, as a ship
2 One of Chekhov's "Three Sisters"
3 Not accept
4 Children's author who created Miss Trunchbull
5 Scoop contents
6 Approached slyly, with "up"
7 1968 space movie villain
8 D. W. Griffith's "___ for Help"
9 "Yeah, you got me"
10 ___ -car
11 Fulfill
12 Spanish liqueur
13 "___ it?"
14 Staying power
18 Cappuccino choice
23 Not soon at all
26 Who's there
27 ___ blue (color named for a school)
29 ___ for the best
31 Be hanged after a crime
32 Throng
33 Fine things?
34 Chuck
35 N.Y.C.'s PBS station
36 Big head
37 A.L. West team, on scoreboards
38 ___ disease
42 Passed out
47 Stage directions
48 Feline in un jardin zoologique
50 Major League Baseball V.I.P.
52 Merge
53 Demolishes, in Devon
54 Govt. gangbusters
55 Put out
56 Ditto, in footnotes
57 Pupil reactions
59 ___ dixit
60 Short breaks, of a sort
62 It may be said with a raised hand

by David Kwong

# 167

## ACROSS

1 "Good point"
11 Right hand: Abbr.
15 Yarn suppliers?
16 What severe cuts may result in, briefly
17 Lacking in drawing power?
18 Succumb to interrogation
19 Roughly half of all N.B.A. M.V.P.'s
20 Will Rogers props
22 Flavoring compound
23 Resident of Angola, Brazil or Lebanon
25 Ne'er-do-well who stayed out for a long time?
29 Vader, in his boyhood
32 Mulberry cousin
33 It's marked way down
34 Sweet-tempered type
36 Argue
38 Sylvia of jazz
39 For the stated value
41 Something to believe in
43 Getaway destination
44 #5 of the American Film Institute's all-time top 100 movie villains
47 Composer who said "Give me a laundry list and I'll set it to music"
48 U.S. city that's a girl's name
52 Hole
53 Boost
55 "Alias" actress
56 Creator of Wildfell Hall
59 Different
60 Law still in effect but no longer enforced
61 Mr. ___ (moniker for Andrei Gromyko)
62 Show with a peanut gallery

## DOWN

1 Twinkling
2 Waistband brand
3 "Impossible"
4 Many a laundromat patron
5 Stopgap
6 Move around
7 Angel Clare's wife, in literature
8 Groovy track?
9 Altdorf is its capital
10 What money may be placed in
11 Stigmas
12 Quaint toe clamp tighteners
13 Green light?
14 Sounds of admonishment
21 Cow-horned deity
23 Swiss alternative
24 "Almost there . . ."
26 Super ___
27 Planet destroyed in 2009's "Star Trek"
28 Jewelry designer Peretti
29 Chiropractor on "Two and a Half Men"
30 "Of course!"
31 Be a make-up artist?
35 Where a new delivery may be placed?
37 Villain's sinister syllable
40 Ubiquitous prescription
42 Like items on Christmas lists
45 Setting of King Fahd Road
46 Fireflite of the 1950s, e.g.
49 Measures taken slowly?
50 Quiet and soft
51 Impressionism?
52 Either "True Grit" director
53 "Tennessee Waltz" lyricist ___ Stewart
54 Without fumbling
57 Con's opening?
58 Hick's nix

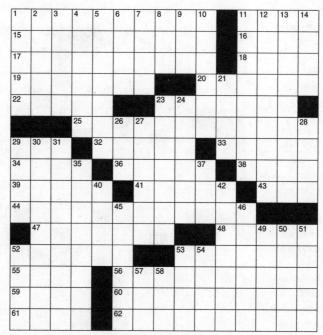

by Doug Peterson and Brad Wilber

## ACROSS

1 Finish differently, say
8 1950s backup group with four top 10 hits
14 Stars are recognized with them
17 Clear as mud, so to speak
18 It may have pop-ups
19 Scott who co-starred on TV's "Men of a Certain Age"
20 "Incredible!"
21 Not just surmise
23 Closest to zero
24 Years, in Tours
26 Oakland daily, for short
28 "Unfortunately . . ."
29 Deutschland "de"
31 Phoenix setting: Abbr.
33 D.C. nine
35 It has short shortstops
41 "What, no more?"
42 Places for a 35-Across
43 ___ other (matchlessly)
44 Satyajit Ray's "The ___ Trilogy"
45 Bill in a bow tie
46 Tarantula hawk, e.g.
49 Band options
51 DreamWorks ___
53 Phoenix setting?
55 Jacuzzi session
57 "___ of Varnish" (C. P. Snow novel)
61 Chemistry test topic
63 Cursorily
65 Certain Mexican-American
66 Where to come to grips with things?
67 Tight
68 Purports

## DOWN

1 Looking up
2 This, in Tijuana
3 Trash hauler
4 Much-filmed swinger
5 Ancient Dravidian's displacer
6 Like Chopin's Mazurka Op. 56 No. 1
7 Sony Reader competitor
8 Middle ear?
9 It's often set in a ring
10 Serve well in court
11 Come to
12 Hometown of the band Hanson
13 Party prizes?
15 "Shh! It's a secret!"
16 Hershey bar

22 Brogue feature
25 "The Moldau" composer
27 Mies van der Rohe was its last director
29 Something needing a stamp
30 Giant giant's family
32 "Giant" events
34 Be overrun
35 Party label for Brit. P.M. William Gladstone
36 Culture centers?
37 Chuck Schumer's predecessor in the Senate
38 Kids' rhyme starter
39 Congress person
40 Works for an editor: Abbr.

46 Takes orders, say
47 Concern of I.R.S. Form 8594
48 Japanese sliding door
50 Head makeup
52 Superman's name on Krypton
54 Hong Kong's Hang ___ Index
56 Polynesian drink
58 Pull felt on Earth
59 Part of a French play
60 Cher's role in "Burlesque"
62 "The Natural" hero Hobbs
64 Former Mets manager Hodges

by Derek Bowman

## ACROSS

1 Chest piece
7 St. John's, for one
15 Fish that attaches itself to a host
16 Like the Congressional Record
17 Biblical prophet whose name means "Yahweh is my God"
18 Act in "The Last Samurai"
19 St. John's, for one
20 Kneecap, e.g.
22 Joe and Mike, recently
23 Like King Sargon II: Abbr.
25 33-Down, taking into account its 61-Across
27 Author of "Herding Cats: A Life in Politics"
29 Latin rock band featured at Woodstock
33 Where the guarani is cash
37 Milk source, to a kid
38 Vein gloriousness?
39 Pope who started the First Crusade
41 Tokyo Rose's real first name
42 German chocolate brand
44 Good occasion for kite-flying
46 Shows an aptitude for
48 Mother of the Titans
49 32-Down, taking into account its 61-Across
51 Home of more than 900 volcanoes
55 2009-2017 White House girl
58 Western setting
60 Just under half a penny's weight
61 Place
63 Ostrich, e.g.

65 1950s H-bomb test site
66 Dermatological concern
67 Classic graduation gifts
68 The Missouri, to the Mississippi

## DOWN

1 ___ blank
2 Transfers often entail them, informally
3 Bahrain bigwigs: Var.
4 John Paul II, originally
5 Span of a ruler, maybe
6 First name in Chicago politics
7 Part of the coast of Brazil
8 Estée Lauder fragrance for men

9 TV or monitor part: Abbr.
10 "Beats me!"
11 Did with enjoyment
12 Ellington band vocalist Anderson
13 68-Across, taking into account its 61-Across
14 Father/daughter fighters
21 Take ___ at
24 Iran, North Korea and the like
26 Veneer, e.g.
28 Ask, as for assistance
30 It's not basic
31 Astronomical figure?
32 Out
33 Strong wine
34 "La donna è mobile," e.g.

35 Give off, with "of"
36 Not pitch or roll, say
40 Big uranium exporter
43 Twin-engine Navy helicopter
45 Site of the Three Gorges Dam
47 Hoofing it
50 Abruptly stops, with "out"
52 Like mummies
53 Instruction written in currants for Alice
54 Campaign dirty trick
55 Coast, in a way
56 1-Across, taking into account its 61-Across
57 Univ. grouping
59 Nonkosher
62 Samson's end?
64 Pal

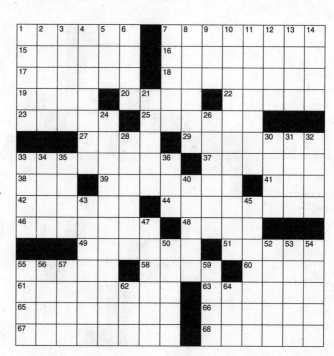

by Matt Ginsberg

## ACROSS

1 Closer to the edge, say
8 Brothers' keepers?
14 Summer time eponym
16 Peso : Mexico :: ___ : Panama
17 "NYC 22" replaced it in 2012
18 Key represented by all white keys on a piano
19 Plate holder
20 Kin of clubs
22 Sporty Spice, by another name
23 Hernando's "Hey!"
24 Batcave, e.g.
25 End point of a common journey
26 Ginnie ___
28 Darling
30 Univ. figures
31 Style of New York's Sony Building
34 '60s film character wearing one black glove
35 Literary classic featuring the teen Tadzio
36 Teen "Whoa!"
37 Grp. concerned with violence levels
38 With 43-Across, part of a squid
39 Long-running Mell Lazarus comic strip
41 What you may squeal with
43 See 38-Across
46 "Think of ___ . . ."
47 Dipped
48 Biblical waste?
50 Run one's mouth

52 Allowing no equivocation
54 Stupefying thing
55 Favor doer's comment
56 It can be dangerous when leaked
57 Like some sunbathers

## DOWN

1 Tree with large seedpods on its trunk
2 Like many older Americans' French or Spanish
3 Not given to lumbering
4 Jacob ___, South African president beginning in 2009
5 Member of the Ennead
6 Attic character
7 Movement from Cuba?
8 Brass tacks
9 Sock sound
10 Bad attribution
11 Aim
12 Where to find some nuts
13 "My heart bleeds for you," often
15 It's known for its start-ups
21 Proceed wearily
24 Unleash
25 "The Once and Future King" figure
26 Extremely
27 Albuterol alleviates it
29 Like some Beanie Babies

31 Sensible
32 Head
33 Groove on an arrow
34 Mailing to a label
35 Pie-baking giant
40 Antares or Proxima Centauri
42 Poet who wrote "Do I dare / Disturb the universe?"
43 Yes or no follower
44 Focus of stereochemistry
45 Roman Demeter
47 Neckline?
48 Union ___
49 Baby sound
51 Verano, across the Pyrenees
53 Yours, in Turin

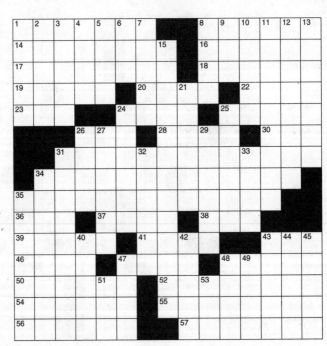

by Josh Knapp

## ACROSS

1 What you may charge with
16 Indicator of how accurate a numerical guess is
17 Bringer of peace
18 The look of love?
19 One built for Broadway
20 Intel processor?
21 Pliers part
24 "The Chronicles of Clovis" author
26 Running dog
32 Opposite of extremely
34 Curing stuff, symbolically
36 Heffalump's creator
37 Title gambler in a 1943 Cary Grant film
39 Northern game preceder
41 Waits awhile
42 Tight end Igwenagu
44 Make canning impossible?
45 Much commercial production
47 Flat
49 Some holiday honorees: Abbr.
50 Start of a Vol. 1 heading
52 Post-W.W. II fed. agcy.
54 Tone poem that calls for four taxi horns, with "An"
63 Past pump preference
64 Packing it in
65 Information information

## DOWN

1 Some of them have learned to sign
2 Blowout locale?
3 "Thou ___ lady": King Lear
4 They might design roses
5 Visual aids
6 Like bazookas
7 1930s bomber
8 Not windy at all
9 Painter Schiele and composer Wellesz
10 Life is one
11 Their caps have a stylized "C"
12 Language related to Wyandot
13 Transporter of beer barrels
14 Captive of Heracles
15 Quarter of doce
21 Window parts
22 Like some anchors and sails
23 Not just another face in the crowd?
25 "The Inspector General" star, 1949
27 Org. that publishes Advocacy Update
28 Quarter of vingt
29 "Revolver" Grammy winner Voormann
30 Split up
31 "Deirdre" playwright
33 Certain recital piece
35 Kind of chop
38 Chi setting
40 One of several Procter & Gamble products
43 Chandra, in Hindu belief
46 Like a lot without a lot
48 Boot
51 Porsche 911 model
53 ___-foot jelly
54 Many masters respond to them
55 Cross
56 Hohenberg's river
57 Like line jumpers
58 First name in '70s tennis
59 Martin Buber's "___ Thou"
60 Shore indentations
61 Thomas H. ___, the Father of the Western
62 Calls on

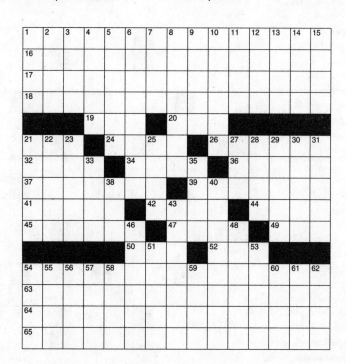

by Martin Ashwood-Smith

# 172

## ACROSS

1 Comparable in extent
6 Old White House inits.
9 Convertible setting
14 Holdings
15 "Look at that!"
16 Laughing ___
17 Is curious about
20 N.Y.C. line
21 Some bulls
22 Stranded message?
23 Place to hang something
24 Off-putting?
28 Museum funding org.
29 Scale markings: Abbr.
30 Pajama-clad exec
31 It may help you get from E to F
37 Word with place or prayer
38 Stretch (out)
39 Besmirch
40 Long time
41 Bad quality for dangerous work
45 Put away
46 Google finding
47 Cool
48 Barely lost
54 H.S. subj.
55 Rocky mount
56 ___ o menos (basically, in Spanish)
57 Pooh pal
58 Drug study data
62 '90s soccer great Lalas
63 Prince Valiant's son
64 Onetime big name in daytime talk

65 Georges who wrote "Life: A User's Manual"
66 See 67-Across
67 With 66-Across, little source of carbs

## DOWN

1 "___ of fools sailing on" (Wang Chung lyric)
2 1998's ___ Report
3 Notorious 1960s figure
4 Pension supplement, for short
5 Company of which Thomas Edison was once a director
6 Greets with a beep
7 One perhaps having one too many
8 Doctoral candidate's starting point
9 Large portion of Africa
10 Cries of despair
11 Source of hardwood?
12 18-Down, for one
13 Consumer products firm since 1837, informally
18 Dockworker's grp.
19 Infomercial pioneer Popeil
25 Fig. at the top of an organizational chart
26 Lao ___
27 Asian holiday
31 Big maker of S.U.V.'s
32 Moody's rating

33 Presidential nickname
34 It may be clicked on a computer
35 Cargo on the Spanish Main
36 Grandmother, to Brits
42 Fraternity letter
43 Start of a cheer
44 Japanese computer giant
48 Draw on again
49 Tropical lizard
50 Mauna ___
51 Mineo of movies
52 "I'm serious!"
53 Nurse, at times
59 Computer file suffix
60 ___-Magnon
61 Intl. broadcaster

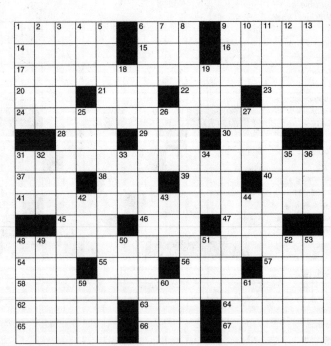

by Joe Krozel

## ACROSS

1 What's "all in my brain," in a 1967 rock classic
11 Dynasty founded by Yu the Great
15 Like some majors and wars
16 Capping
17 Be peerless
18 Blacks out
19 Little Joe's half brother of old TV
20 Einstein's death
21 Preakness, e.g.
22 Image mentale
24 First created being, in myth
26 Stand-up comic known for irreverent sermonettes
31 Form's top, perhaps
32 Make inseparable
33 River forming the Handegg waterfall
34 Having one 49-Across
35 Winner of seven tennis majors in the 1920s
38 Material in the translation process
39 Caterpillar roll ingredient
40 Operation creation
41 Java class?
43 Do a vanishing act
47 Jezebel's lack
48 One housed in a chest
49 See 34-Across
51 "Dear" one
52 Diamond stats
56 Decimal starter
57 Microsoft Office feature
60 Figure taking a bow?
61 No-strings declaration?
62 ___ deal
63 "So Wrong" singer, 1962

## DOWN

1 Labor leader's cry?
2 It may precede itself
3 Stds. for A and E, e.g.
4 Seriously thinking
5 Monitor option, briefly
6 High
7 Headbands?
8 Longtime teammate of Mr. November
9 Eastern state?
10 City near Utrecht
11 Violent sandstorm
12 Old TV show hosted by Ed McMahon
13 Makeup of some beams
14 Basilica niche
21 Submitted
23 Product named for its "'round the clock protection"
24 Broccoli bits?
25 Foil component
26 Building with many sides
27 Fifth-century invader
28 ___-one
29 Stormed
30 Winner of 14 tennis majors in the 1990s
31 Wasn't straight
36 Many a college interviewer
37 Reference
42 Cylindrical menu item
44 What outer space is that cyberspace isn't?
45 Circular stack
46 Epsom's setting
49 Leave one's coat behind?
50 Saving type
51 Performer of high-risk operations
53 Mideastern P.M.'s nickname
54 Not blind to
55 Affliction whose name rhymes with its location
57 Vegas spot
58 German granny
59 American Crossroads, e.g.

by David Steinberg

## ACROSS
1 "You doubt me?"
9 "Titus" director Taymor
14 Disappointing screen message
15 Series of movements
16 Start of a court display
17 Commensurate (with)
18 What we may be overseas?
19 Relative of a bathysphere
21 Limp Bizkit frontman Fred
23 Ingredient in some pastitsio
24 Sacha Baron Cohen character
25 Football stat.
26 21, in blackjack
28 Have words (with)
29 Earl of Sandwich, e.g.
30 What was once yours?
31 Some charge cards, informally
34 Wee
35 Florentine tourist attraction
36 Certainly didn't roar
39 Bellicose figure
40 Feature of a daredevil circus act
41 Dirt collector
44 Guinness measurement
45 Kool & the Gang's "Get Down ___"
46 Unsolicited manuscripts, informally
48 Get off the ground
51 Instruction for a violinist
52 It follows a curtain opening
53 Hood's support

55 Stir
56 Breather?
57 Gretzky, for most of the 1980s
58 Manages

## DOWN
1 Big to-do, maybe?
2 Push to the limit
3 "That cuts me to the quick"
4 Houdini's real name
5 Take the money and run?
6 J. M. W. Turner's "___ Banished From Rome"
7 YouTuber, e.g.
8 It keeps people grounded
9 "Fear of Flying" author
10 Brazen

11 Accessory to a suit
12 Many early 20th-century U.S. immigrants
13 Blend with bergamot
15 ___-law
20 Gossip column subject
22 Not live
27 Function of mathematics: Abbr.
29 It's a living thing
30 Much of the Disney Channel's demographic
31 Gets comfortable with
32 Style played on a guitarrón
33 State of stability
34 Shout repeated at a basketball game

36 ___-pedi
37 Causes of head-scratching
38 Hush-hush
40 Farrell of "In Bruges"
41 Hushed sound
42 Get high
43 Strings along a beach?
47 1972 hit that begins "What'll you do when you get lonely . . . ?"
49 "___ leads to anger, anger leads to hate, hate leads to suffering": Yoda
50 "You have a point"
54 Naked

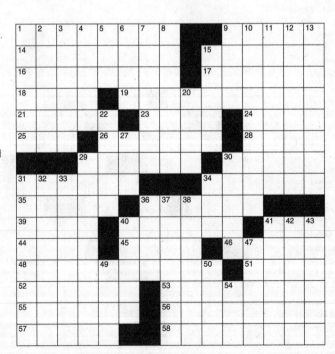

by Josh Knapp

## ACROSS

1 Stephen King horror anthology
10 Yoke attachment
15 Great depression?
16 Egg choice
17 They're available in alleys
18 Wholly
19 Short play?
20 The King's followers?
21 Like some taxes and questions
22 Considered revolting
24 Struck
25 Pick
26 Home of the Aggies of the 37-Down
31 Below the surface
34 Québec map abbr.
35 Arena support?
36 Remove, as a 45-Across
38 Grand alternative
41 Trip option: Abbr.
42 She plagues ladies' lips with blisters, per Mercutio
44 Game of falling popularity?
45 It fits around a mouth
49 Bangladesh export
50 Using
51 Aviation safety statistic
55 What's often blowing in the wind
58 Show piece
59 Floral arrangement
60 Floor plan data
61 Painful spa treatment
63 Had an inclination
64 Nevertheless
65 Roman world
66 Justice from the Bronx

## DOWN

1 What a speaker may strike
2 Nepalese bread
3 Classic Meccano toy
4 Midwest trailer?
5 Embedded column
6 Hardly any
7 Haydn's "master of us all"
8 Upstate New York natives
9 Unseld of the Bullets
10 Twist in fiction
11 Hit soundtrack album of 1980
12 Stationery securer
13 Look while delivering a line
14 Metalworker's union?
21 Leaving out
23 Grand
27 Good name for a brooder?
28 How many reach the top of Pikes Peak
29 Not grade-specific
30 Loses liquidity
31 Bellflower or Bell Gardens, vis-à-vis L.A.
32 Quaint preposition
33 Put down
37 New Mexico State sports grp.
39 "Cloth diaper" or "film camera"
40 Bullet follower
43 Frito ___ (old ad symbol)
46 Cable channel with the slogan "Laugh More"
47 Doesn't level with
48 Check out for a second
52 Certain building block, informally
53 Former defense grp.
54 Knick foe
55 One with hot dates, maybe
56 ___ Biscuit (1912 debut)
57 Spare
61 Low, in Lyon
62 Portfolio part, for short

by Barry C. Silk

# 176

## ACROSS

1 It uses liquid from a pitcher
9 Cloud maker
14 Resolve a longstanding disagreement
16 ___ 8
17 Political entity of 1854–1900
19 Tree-defoliating insect
20 Tries to ensure a hit
21 One with big hips, maybe
22 Bounces
25 They're thrown in anger
29 What keeps a camera rolling?
30 Old English recorder
31 Day break
32 Pirate's hiding place, possibly
33 "Poor Richard's Almanack" tidbit
34 Maintenance
35 Roadbed inset
36 Like the ancient Greeks
37 "Beyond the Sea" singer
38 Ones offering pass protection?
40 Designated
41 Membership list
42 Jazz trumpeter Baker
43 Largest land animal
50 Popular June program?
51 Mid 19th-century president
52 Site of Goodfellow Air Force Base
53 Spheres
54 1950s million-selling song that begins "The evening breeze caressed the trees . . ."

## DOWN

1 Chance to win
2 Shave
3 Tolstoy character ___ Ilyich
4 Arm of the sea?
5 Typical of urban life
6 Special Forces units
7 Artists' stories, maybe
8 It's at the end of the line
9 Hockey stat
10 Role in a drawing-room mystery
11 Flame Queen ___ (famous gemstone)
12 Having multiple layers of self-reference
13 Southern contraction
15 Swampland swimmer
18 Rob Roy or Shirley Temple
22 Cuts a line, say
23 Animated girl-group leader
24 Actress Corby who played Grandma Walton
25 Short-lived republic founded in 1836
26 Take a piece from
27 Madame Tussaud's first name
28 Devote
30 Elaborate spectacles
33 Cocktail often made with pineapple juice
34 Queen Dido's home
36 Handle, as paperwork
37 Where one may take the plunge?
39 Game show fodder
40 Oedipus, for one
42 Copy
43 Alan who won an Emmy for his role on "The West Wing"
44 "That little darkroom where negatives are developed," per Michael Pritchard
45 Major party
46 Conseil d'___ (French government body)
47 Make known
48 "Little" Dickens character
49 Where Patroclus met his end

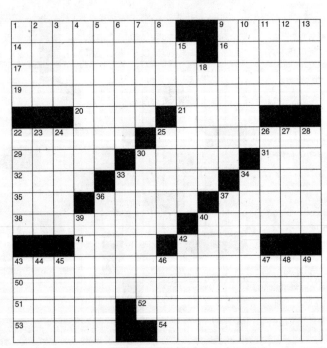

*by Patrick Berry*

## ACROSS

1 Service with many followers
8 Kettles, e.g.
15 Hair-raising stuff?
16 Where it never rains
17 With 53-Across, classic Kipling poem ending
19 Plane wing component
20 Pro team with a horseshoe logo
21 Many trial subjects
22 ___ penny (very common, in British lingo)
23 "White Writing" painter Mark
24 Penny ___
25 Quagmire
27 Unit of fun?
28 Challah form
29 Fresh
31 Attempt to enter dead space?
32 Kind of identity
36 Like many gems
37 Gershwin's first hit
38 "Ewww!"
39 Curve creators
40 Tangier location: Abbr.
41 East Coast city where tourism peaks in October
46 "___ Is Betta Than Evvah!" (1976 album)
47 Creamer who won the 2010 U.S. Women's Open
49 In case
50 Duke's setting: Abbr.
51 Talk, talk, talk
52 Barneys rival
53 See 17-Across
56 Small, simple flute
57 Casanova's first name
58 At the movies, say
59 "Without further ado . . ."

## DOWN

1 Getaways that people try to get away with
2 Like some 8-Downs
3 Creature in a Tennessee Williams title
4 Dental concern
5 Potential play prolonger
6 Put into 13-Down
7 Started over, in a way
8 One deserving a hand?
9 Apprehensive
10 Suffix with grape
11 Field work that was award-winning
12 Ruling
13 The way things are done
14 One way to take drugs
18 Brachium's end
26 Wings, e.g.
28 St. Pauli Girl alternative
30 It's between Obama and Robinson
31 Holder of eggs
32 Give a thumbs-up
33 Activate, in a way
34 Orange neighbor
35 Scored due to an error
36 Leave
38 Y.M.C.A. section?
40 River through Toledo
42 Strasbourg is its capital
43 Bait
44 Like the language Kalaallisut
45 Vt. ski resort
47 Big name in aircraft engines
48 Miss Hannigan's charge, on Broadway
54 Spanish name suffix
55 Alligator ___ (underwater menace)

by Gary Cee

# 178

## ACROSS

1 Cause of a paradigm shift
12 Prepare for pain
14 It takes a lot to get one upset
16 Stadium support?
17 Antiquity's antithesis
18 "Vox populi, vox ___"
19 Disney animator Johnston who received the National Medal of Arts
21 Civil Rights Memorial designer
22 Like some milk
24 ___ Bonn Airport
25 One of a sailing trio
27 25-Across part
28 Opting not to strike out?
30 German/Polish border river
32 24-Across article
33 Smithereens
34 Longtime guitar brand
37 "I'm with you"
41 Little belts
42 Have ___ on (monitor officially)
44 Plane figures?
45 Philosopher Kierkegaard
47 She, in São Paulo
48 Unpolished
49 Grp. with a "decent work" agenda
50 They often get incorporated into the body
53 Follower of many a mineralogist's name

54 Tendency to overcompensate for a perceived shortcoming
57 Hunter with rough hair
58 Spoke up with one's head down?

## DOWN

1 2007 Disney princess
2 Fig. at the bar
3 ___ Liebe (Dear, in Dresden)
4 To be overseas
5 Waiters in a mess
6 "World of Magic" Emmy nominee
7 Without
8 Party bowlful
9 Brief explanation

10 The Liberty Tree, for one
11 Gears up
12 X-box setting?
13 Immune system circulators
14 Doctors
15 Words that'll get you carded?
20 Extreme
23 High-tech scam artist
25 Singer with a short-lived 1950s sitcom
26 Manga set in motion
29 Image on some joke T-shirts
31 When French fans circulate?
33 Gymnast, often
34 Not righteously

35 Place for cultural studies?
36 Regarding
37 "Psycho" feature
38 Site-specific merchant?
39 Scan lines on a monitor
40 New Jersey county whose seat is Newark
43 Accessory for Sinatra
46 Actress Nita who never made a talkie
48 Prius alternative
51 Owning evidence
52 Pseudonym of a noted Freud patient
55 3,600 secondi
56 Amount to be divided

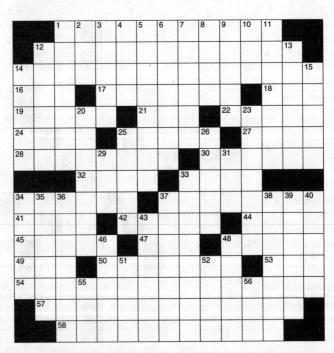

by Paula Gamache

## ACROSS

1 Outclass one's peers?
11 Round bodies
15 Stressed
16 Nutty stuff
17 Providing relief, but not a cure
18 Retreat
19 Flooring specialist?
20 Poetic work with an account of Ragnarok
21 Right on
22 "The Franchise Affair" novelist
23 It's about 5 mL
26 Pushover
28 Numbskull
29 "Too rich for my blood"
31 1,000,000,000 years
32 Sports reporter Andrews
33 See 7-Down
36 Like some insurance
38 Not at all loose
39 Scottish doctor/ explorer John
41 Teresa's home
42 "Pushover" singer James
43 Straight out of the dryer, perhaps
46 Sop for aloo palak
47 Cost-of-living no.
48 Norman ___, coach in "Hoosiers"
49 It goes from one vessel to another
51 One in 100
57 Bar closing?
58 City on the Ohio
59 ___ incline
60 "Snow-Bound" setting
61 Creatures with electrocytes
62 Spots

## DOWN

1 Takes night courses?
2 Chip, as flint, in Britain
3 Baseless
4 Athlete nicknamed "O Rei"
5 Desiccated
6 "My pleasure"
7 With 33-Across, confirmation, e.g.
8 Live
9 Religious observance
10 Its entrance was barred with a flaming sword
11 Give the twice-over?
12 Ceaseless drinking or gambling, say
13 Certain control freak
14 Artificial alternative to the sun
23 1811 battle site
24 Android runner, e.g.
25 Like rankings
26 Stop: Abbr.
27 Generative music pioneer
28 Wally's bro
30 Sch. whose alumni constitute the Long Gray Line
34 [I'm not happy about this]
35 Brandy
37 Elfin
40 Issuing forth
44 Largely green kingdom
45 Show
50 Impulses
51 Works on one's jumper, say
52 "Lift ___ Voice and Sing" (old hymn)
53 Group of pages
54 Home of the ancient Olympic games
55 Author/architect Buzzi
56 Romeo or Juliet

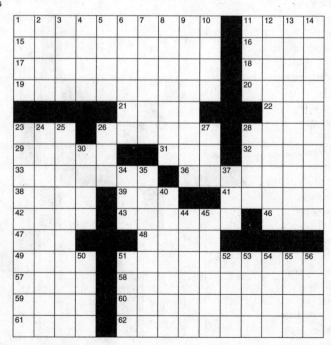

by Joon Pahk

# 180

## ACROSS

1 "Try not to stand out"
10 Call ___ to (stop)
15 Words after an insult
16 Jason who directed 2011's "Arthur"
17 Beatles song with a complaining title
18 Utah State athlete
19 I. M. Pei's alma mater, for short
20 War hero who killed himself with a onetime rival's sword
21 Rapid descent on skis
22 Hail ___
24 Unrestricted music plan
26 Burdened
28 French waters
29 "Bloody"
30 Ticket
31 Honorary deg. for many a writer
32 They're found in rock bands
33 End of a flick?
35 Letters at the beach
37 Absorbed
40 "Here comes trouble!"
44 Some stars
48 Plot segment
49 Tons of
50 Cover
51 Words accompanying an arrow
54 Kind of twin
55 Like some glasses
56 Professor 'iggins
58 Gray
59 Admit
60 Prepared
62 Levels
63 "Told you so!"
64 Suit material
65 Remedy for a tizzy

## DOWN

1 Some cracker shapes
2 Wacky
3 Fiesta food item
4 $$$ head
5 Old Spice rival
6 Conductor Ozawa
7 Like a first-time tournament player, usually
8 Type of reproduction
9 Was up
10 ___ plane
11 Very recognizable
12 Bony, as a face
13 Work's opposite
14 Locks
21 Titillating transmissions
23 One stage of development
25 Rapa ___ (Easter Island)
27 "Der Ring ___ Nibelungen"
34 Moist
36 Smartphone, e.g., for short
37 Discombobulates
38 Carry out
39 Press user
41 Cheated
42 Rule for free samples
43 Sonata maker
45 Composer known as the Red Priest
46 First name of two first ladies
47 Calf part
52 Detect
53 Old "Go from flat to fluffy" sloganeer
57 Term of address in the South
60 Open ___
61 Fire

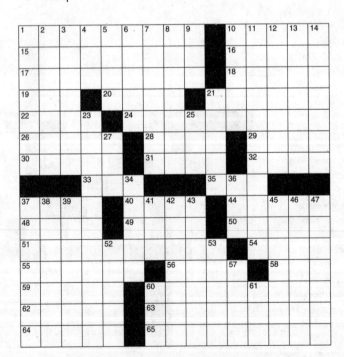

*by Milo Beckman*

# 181

## ACROSS

1 Adroitness
5 22-Across product
10 English Leather alternative
14 Interjections from the obtuse
15 Searches for signs in a hospital
16 Queen with a degree from Princeton
17 ___-Z
18 Its shadow is often cast
19 Decoration
20 "Gnarly waves, dude!"
22 Pabst brand
23 Foil
24 Like some exchange rates
26 Less like nuts?
27 Where to get a citation while surfing
28 Like two Kennedy brothers
30 Portions
31 Hang-up
34 Watt-hour fraction
35 Small team
36 You might get a charge out of it
37 Secure the aid of
39 They're lined up on a neck
41 Kind of test associated with the null hypothesis
43 Practice with the Wheel of the Year
47 27-Across, e.g.
48 Wet behind the ears
49 Directive obeyed by Alice
50 City where "Smokey and the Bandit" begins
52 Fit to finish?
53 Like many dreamers
54 Pap's son, in literature
55 La., e.g., once
56 Like la nuit
57 Scored together?
58 Brand that has Dibs
59 Telecom giant headquartered in Denver
60 Fork-tailed flier

## DOWN

1 Subjects are expected to follow them
2 Polar region phenomenon
3 Greet and seat
4 Things some cons are pros at
5 Preceded, with "to"
6 Impulse carrier
7 Van Gogh threatened him with a razor blade
8 Keep from spilling over, in a way
9 U leaders?
10 St. John's is its capital
11 Like some conclusions
12 Grooming routine
13 Missiles may be delivered in one
21 Tom Stoppard's "Travesties," e.g.
22 Chief Sassacus led one side in it
25 Nettle
27 Easily changeable locks
29 Pianist Schnabel
31 Play
32 Like many swimming pools
33 Severely sunburned, say
35 Producer for 50 Cent, familiarly
38 Atomically related compounds
39 Prize in Cracker Jacks, e.g.
40 Part of morning dress
42 Ad imperative
44 Rains in a studio
45 Go along (with)
46 Arouse
48 Massachusetts Maritime Academy student, e.g.
51 MTV generation
53 It may be judicial: Abbr.

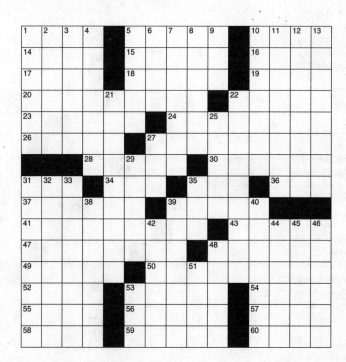

by Barry C. Silk

# 182

## ACROSS

1 It often contains "lies"
8 Person making a cameo, say
15 Start of a big 1975 sports event?
16 Tending to bring together
17 Florida's ___ Park Race Track
18 Some photography equipment
19 Priest at Shiloh
20 Genetic stuff
21 It may be pinched
22 "Do Ya" band, for short
23 Winthrop's affliction in "The Music Man"
25 One taking orders
27 Title girl in a 1990s–2000s MTV cartoon
29 Fishing tool
31 Like many blog comments, informally
33 One of eight in chess
34 2008 World Series athlete
36 Cousins of blackbirds
38 Pro-Church of England position
40 Creamlike paint shade
42 French article
43 ___ land
44 Aforementioned
46 "A little ___ do ya" (1950s–'60s slogan)
50 London borough with Wembley Stadium
52 'Vette option
54 Tart plum
55 Eastern band
56 Big 12 Conf. member
58 1-Across accompanier

60 Mama grizzly, south of the border
61 Crazy Horse, e.g.
63 Causes to take hold
65 Chanel fragrance "pour homme"
66 Astronaut's favorite dessert?
67 Indicates
68 Overruns

## DOWN

1 Rosenberg and Roosevelt
2 An apostle
3 Declaration at a poker table
4 The Everly Brothers' "(___) I Kissed You"
5 34-Across, e.g., for short
6 Alternative fallback position
7 "You think you're so funny!"
8 Popular hair care product
9 Prefix with -derm
10 Hyper
11 Normandy was in it: Abbr.
12 What's not right?
13 Story from Joyce's "Dubliners"
14 Wets again
24 Like some politics
26 Class with Browning and Golding, say
28 Home of the 42nd U.S. president
30 Salad tidbit
32 Kind of chart
35 Ja and da
37 Squalled

38 Structural piece bent 90° along its long dimension
39 Sheet music notations
40 Jostled
41 Claptrap
45 Moolah
47 Hardly line drives
48 Went bonkers
49 Papers on pads?
51 Plot element
53 New Mexico's state tree
57 Yea or nay
59 Classy sort?
62 2016 Olympics host
64 "___ moment"

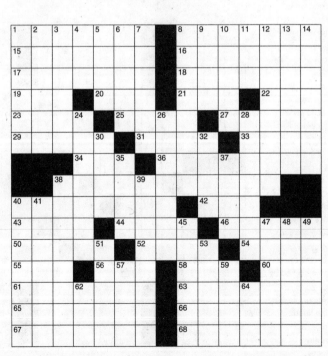

by Chris A. McGlothlin

## ACROSS

1 Makeshift mask
9 Old Navy's owner
15 Lingua di Livorno
16 Ford from long ago
17 Home of minor-league baseball's Sea Dogs
18 23-Across representing a user
19 Join
20 Rte. through 17-Across
22 It may be groove-billed
23 Desktop item
24 "Mama's Special Garden" brand
25 Old Maltese money
27 March Madness souvenir
28 Literature's Dolores Haze, familiarly
30 Most arias
31 38-Down, to a 14-Down
32 Drive in N.Y.C.
33 What may appear after washing or baking
34 Oppose authority
39 Reaction to bad news
40 Giant rival, briefly
41 Tag for some grandchildren
42 Kept in
43 Patrol boats patrol them
45 Stat on some guns
48 Casino winner, often
50 Man ___
51 Driver's alert
52 Like "Spring" from Vivaldi's "The Four Seasons"
53 Use as a crash site?
55 Where Paul and Silas were sent, in Acts

56 Stage name of entertainer David Adkins
58 Stage name of entertainer Stanley Burrell
60 Yet
61 Chemistry website?
62 Faulkner family name
63 "Don't believe it for a second"

## DOWN

1 Supply, as elevator music
2 Straightaway
3 Ape
4 Singer at Diana's funeral
5 Streamlet
6 Cry of shear fear?
7 Tomato or pea, e.g.

8 Don Juan's self-description
9 Bootlegger's bugbear
10 Dumpy dwelling
11 Writer LeShan
12 Cry to the overly amorous
13 "The Four Seasons" director
14 Métro area resident
21 One-up
24 Violinists' cake ingredients
26 Some nonnative Hawaiians
28 Coin whose original portrait was Alexander the Great
29 More affected
31 Most Prestwick Airport patrons
34 Fallacious reasoners

35 It has unbelievable news
36 Part of many a smear campaign
37 Kings Beach sits on it
38 Embroidered word, at times
44 Vaquero's charge
45 Young follower
46 Runs a bill through
47 Cry for attention
49 Really pick up
51 Bonne ___ (cooked simply)
54 13th, at times
55 Spots for shots
57 Like Bill Clinton or Jimmy Carter: Abbr.
59 ___ characters (common Chinese writing)

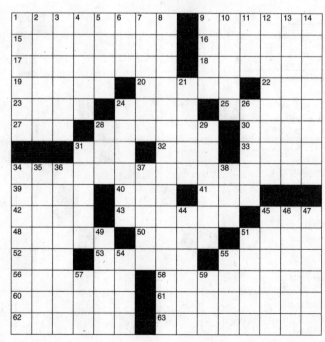

by Joel Fagliano

# 184

## ACROSS

1. Dance that simulates the drama of a bullfight
10. Chuck wagon fare
14. 1978 Bob Marley hit whose title words are sung four times before ". . . that I'm feelin'"
16. Faux Japanese reply
17. One needing kisses, say
18. Jazz duo?
19. Nooks for books, maybe
20. Furry folivores
22. It may be set with music
24. Cudgel
25. Believers' comments
27. Escaped
31. Sound at an auto race
32. It holds the line
33. Foot of the Appian Way?
34. Trouble, in a way
35. Locale of some mirrors
36. Letter-shaped girder
38. Lord John Boyd ___, winner of the 1949 Nobel Peace Prize
39. Study, say
41. Winston Churchill's Rufus, for one
42. They know the drill
44. Turned up
45. Child's play, perhaps
46. Snitch
47. Company that makes Life cereal
51. Area next to an ambulatory
55. Letter-shaped fastener
56. Daydreaming
58. Days of old
59. Worked the docks
60. Waste of Congress?
61. "You got it!"

## DOWN

1. Early Inverness resident
2. Cadaverous
3. Ticklee's cry
4. "You have got to be kidding!"
5. The Divine, to da Vinci
6. City at the mouth of the Fox River
7. Shade of red
8. "She was ___ in slacks" (part of an opening soliloquy by Humbert Humbert)
9. Baddie
10. Shady spot in a 52-Down
11. Cousin of a cassowary
12. ___ fee
13. One with fire power?
15. Trick-taking game
21. March instrument?
23. Out
25. Au courant
26. Keen
27. Nutrition units
28. Some essays
29. "A Lonely Rage" autobiographer Bobby
30. The farmer's wife in "Babe"
31. Did a farrier's work
35. Start to like
37. Energetic 1960s dance with swiveling and shuffling
40. God of life, death and fertility who underwent resurrection
41. Pattern sometimes called "Persian pickles"
43. "I'm very disappointed in you"
46. Song verse
47. Canal cleaner
48. Menu option
49. Teacher of Heifetz
50. Fashion model Wek
52. See 10-Down
53. Ko-Ko's dagger in "The Mikado"
54. Current happening?
57. Kick in

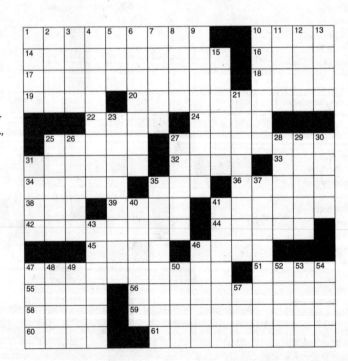

*by Natan Last*

## ACROSS

1 Place to buy a smoothie
9 Electrum and others
15 Author born Howard Allen O'Brien
16 Little show-off's cry
17 You shouldn't go through with it
18 "The Great Escape" setting
19 Went belly up
20 Subject of some amateur videos
22 World Wind developer
23 Plays for a fool
24 Crams, maybe
26 Symptom for a car mechanic
27 ___ Arcs, French ski resort
28 Los Angeles-based magazine with one-million-plus circulation
30 Trailer
32 An inset might depict one
33 10-time Gold Glove winner of the 1990s and 2000s
34 Film in which Olga Kurylenko plays the Bond girl
38 Person of great interest?
39 Suggest
40 Girl's name that sounds like two letters of the French alphabet
41 Resting place
42 Cooler
45 Genre of rock's Fall Out Boy
46 Jazz great seen in the 1967 film "Hotel"
48 Staff lines?
49 Cuffs
51 @ follower, sometimes
52 Balzac's "___ Bette"
54 Cat calls
56 Little music maker
58 Loosen, as a bra
59 Trunk item
60 Candy brand
61 Beginning of time?

## DOWN

1 Peanut butter quantity
2 Fidgetiness
3 East or West area
4 Biologists' study
5 Lake ___, home of the Bass Islands
6 Cowboys' home, informally
7 "___ was!" (German exclamation)
8 Stop daydreaming
9 Journalist Joseph
10 Studio part
11 Advance
12 Musical that won a 1944 Pulitzer
13 Singer famous for her wide vocal range
14 Long Island's ___ Hill National Historic Site
21 Elflike
24 Rhapsody, e.g.
25 Bathtub sound
28 Treasure
29 Result of a long exposure, often
31 Iago, for one
32 48-Across starter
33 "___ happens . . ."
34 The late Elizabeth Bowes-Lyon, familiarly
35 Ship with a memorial in New York City's Central Park
36 Main route?
37 Ride, maybe
41 Pal
42 Italian writer Pavese
43 Key of Beethoven's "Für Elise"
44 "You're doing it all wrong!"
47 Port containers
48 Frankie of "Malcolm in the Middle"
50 Symbol of blackness
52 "The Last of the Mohicans" girl
53 Wroclaw's river
55 Try hard to win
57 Trivial Pursuit goal

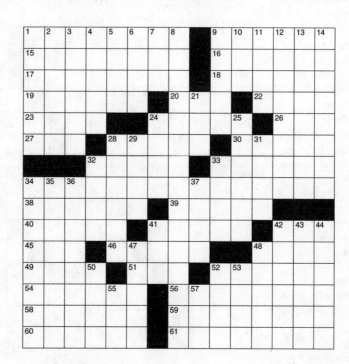

by Will Nediger

## ACROSS

1 Source of troubles
12 ___ of God
15 "Later!"
16 What the 1939 50,000-word novel "Gadsby" completely lacks
17 Bank offerings
18 "Uh-huh"
19 Turns down
20 Spirit
21 ___ leaf
22 Irritation suffix
23 Irritated, after "in"
25 Like most music
26 Persian, e.g.
27 Not yet delivered, after "in"
28 W.W. II air ace who lent his name to an airport
29 Wee hour
30 Meyerbeer output
31 ___ Day (September 19)
35 How some dares are done
36 Outline
37 Bar tenders?: Abbr.
38 Places for dust to collect
39 Assn.
42 Apparently is
43 Insurance providers, for short
44 "Super Trouper" group, 1980
45 Kind of delay
46 Poke
47 Packers QB whose #15 jersey is retired
48 LAX datum
49 One end of the Welland Canal
52 Hi-___

53 At someone's mercy
54 Ones needing career counseling, maybe: Abbr.
55 Shell locations

## DOWN

1 Eat out?
2 Hindu drink of the gods
3 Play with the line "Hell is other people"
4 Guys
5 Revolutionary patriot James
6 Start to smell, maybe
7 Union inits. starting in 1886
8 "Well, I'll be!," as it might be said on September 19

9 ___ Santiago, 1987 N.L. Rookie of the Year
10 City near Provo
11 Scratches, with "out"
12 "Later!"
13 200 milligrams
14 Like soldiers known as Gurkhas
21 Stick
23 Wiped out, slangily
24 Top
25 What debaters debate
27 Hedge word
29 "That's fine"
30 Pendant adornments
31 Some diner equipment
32 It has a long tongue

33 Student excuser
34 Live folk album of 1968
38 D.T.'s
39 Italian restaurant chain
40 TV newswoman Soledad
41 Doorstep numbers?
44 ___ 2600 (hit product of the 1970s–'80s)
46 Joe
47 "This instant!"
49 Record
50 Bit of chicken feed
51 Org. with the annual Eddie Gottlieb Trophy

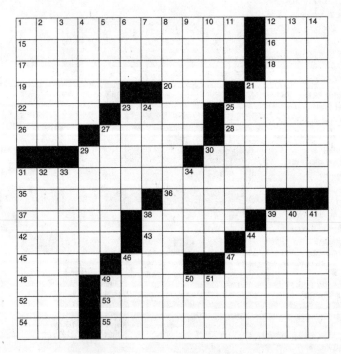

by Alex Boisvert

## ACROSS

1 Agreed
6 "Only bad witches are ugly" speaker
12 Drama queen
14 They might be weaving
16 "You ___!"
17 Asian range, with "the"
18 Break by hitting
19 Prompts
20 Apt to turn out badly
21 Trademark relatives
22 Something taken before swinging
23 Lame excuse
24 Opening and closing facilitator
25 Soon enough
26 Loafer attachment
28 Common household pest
33 "Sweet!"
35 Sports equipment wired for scoring
37 Bit of regalia
41 Mixed with something else
42 Separator of light and dark
43 "Les Mains Sales" playwright, 1948
44 Delivered by a third person, perhaps
45 Snow-covered cover-up
46 It contains the three-fifths clause
47 It's typically easier to give than take
48 Setting one back the most
49 Comparatively shrewd
50 Ecclesiastical districts
51 Trivial stuff

## DOWN

1 Founder of the Foundation for Florida's Future
2 "That wasn't a joke!"
3 Its capital is Gaborone
4 Artistic impressions?
5 Bursts open, as legume seedpods
6 Set piece?
7 Ballerina, often
8 Inactivity
9 By
10 Least exciting
11 Politico Hutchinson and others
13 Asian royal
14 Send from abroad
15 Blouse coverer
25 Heirs, legally
27 Licenses
29 Said while pounding the fist, say
30 One signing off
31 It's free of charge
32 Apartment adjuncts
34 It needs to be built up when it's bad
36 Participants in a kids' game
37 Like some nights and eyes
38 Deliver by truck
39 Lucia's brother in "Lucia di Lammermoor"
40 Opposite of turbulent
41 Singer of the 1991 hit "Wicked Game"
44 Refreshing things

by Joe Krozel

# 188

## ACROSS

1 Reversion to an earlier type
8 Shout after a knock
15 King's honor
17 Where moles may try to dig?
18 Hamburger's course?
19 Xbox 360 competitor
20 Attempt to make out
21 Actress Suvari
23 Den ___, Nederland
24 Ones at home on the range?
27 Victory celebration, of sorts
31 Integrated
32 Muralist José María ___
33 Understanding responses
34 An artificial satellite may have one
38 Before, briefly
39 Modulate
40 Yield
41 "Friends" who aren't really being helpful
44 Basis of some discrimination
45 Exceptional
46 Bits
47 Stout
50 Halo tarnisher?
51 Follow
55 Film about an aristocrat captured by the Sioux
58 Dish named for the queen consort of Italy's Umberto I
59 Ready for the bad news
60 It's a square

## DOWN

1 Clear conclusion?
2 Sweat
3 Like many of Shakespeare's rhymes
4 Very strong
5 Ithaque, e.g.
6 Generates
7 ___ circus
8 People in this are watched closely: Abbr.
9 Occasion to serve light refreshments
10 Roll top?
11 Katherine ___, 1983–89 Treasurer of the United States
12 Place for loading and unloading
13 Book concerned with the end of the Babylonian captivity
14 Kite flying destination?
16 Smog stat.
22 "A special laurel ___ go": Whitman
23 Plague
24 Beat badly
25 John of "Freaky Friday"
26 Sluggish tree-dweller
27 Models
28 Passing remark
29 Vichyssoise garnish
30 Vegetable oil, e.g.
32 Game stopper?
35 Mastered
36 Was shy
37 Was shy
42 Like the Colossus of Rhodes
43 Flock-related
44 Leader who said "There is no god higher than truth"
46 Model who wrote "The Way to Natural Beauty"
47 Occurrences
48 Release
49 Deconstruct?
50 Shooting option, briefly
52 War of 1812 siege site
53 City SW of Padua
54 One doing school work?
56 Sprout
57 Curse

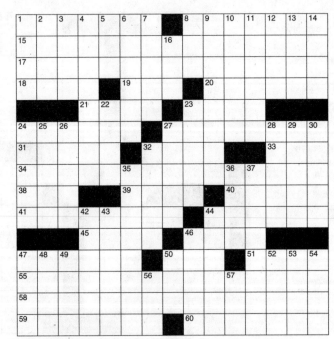

by Barry C. Silk

## ACROSS

1 Third Servile War leader
10 1970s R&B trio in the Rock and Roll Hall of Fame, with "the"
15 Driving ambition?
16 Hero
17 How a towpath proceeds vis-à-vis a canal
18 Indication of time passing
19 Credit card come-on
20 Gaming debut of 1985, briefly
21 Certain blowup
22 Fatty acid, e.g.
23 Bring up
25 Jam
27 Got a 15-Across on
31 Whence the expression "mum's the word"
35 "Hogan's Heroes" figure
36 Med. supplier?
37 Chocoholic's dessert
39 Christchurch native
40 Green patch
44 1999 film satirizing media ruthlessness
45 Half-sister of King Arthur
46 Assuaging agents
48 Black tea from India
53 Ninth, e.g.
56 Young vixen
57 First lady of the 1980s
58 Shower accessory
59 Courage
61 Former congresswoman nicknamed Mother Courage

62 Louis Armstrong's "Weather Bird" collaborator
63 David who played Bosley on TV's "Charlie's Angels"
64 Not willful?

## DOWN

1 Oscar-nominated western
2 Golf attire
3 Not grounded?
4 Richards with a racket
5 Den delivery
6 FAQs bit: Abbr.
7 Part of a pinball machine
8 Endure
9 Stays until the end of
10 ___ disk (blind spot)

11 Unite (with)
12 Early instruction
13 One placed on a team
14 Part of 20-Across: Abbr.
24 Ancestors from long, long ago
26 Vassals
28 Creator of Earthquake McGoon and Moonbeam McSwine
29 "The Silence of the Hams" director Greggio
30 Become less of a person?
31 Bank manager?
32 One of his lost works is "Medea"
33 Container abbr.
34 Supply of arrows

38 Turns up
41 Soviet premier Kosygin
42 New Brunswick's river
43 Skew
47 Sometime sampler stitching
49 Municipal dept.
50 Touristy Tuscany town
51 Thing worth keeping
52 Tricky shot
53 Outfitted
54 Great Depression figure
55 Like slime
60 Cousin of -let

by Karen M. Tracey

# 190

## ACROSS

1 Unforgettable edible
16 Concern of a certain federal commissioner
17 Fission boat?
18 Capital on the Rímac River
19 Plays
20 1040 amt.
21 Nero's buyer
23 Vehicle for an annual round-the-world trip
26 Ingredient in plastics
27 Mention casually
30 Her theme song was a 1966 hit
31 Opium product
33 Pan
34 Clash sharply
37 Be in the red for black and tans?
39 Registration agcy.
40 His chariot was drawn by four fire-breathing horses
42 Neighbor of Sunnyside in New York
44 Indication that one is just teasing
45 Occurrence after the first and third quarters of the moon
46 Nirvana
50 Mad specialty
52 Take-out meal?
53 Large copier
54 Tropical fruit, in Toledo
57 See 58-Down
58 On account (of)
62 Not so much
63 They're usually even on one side

## DOWN

1 One entering a number
2 One day
3 Defeats decisively
4 Of blood
5 Good day?: Abbr.
6 Rack up
7 Old name in news
8 Drawing device
9 Regal symbols
10 Occurrence after retiring
11 Advantage
12 They cover the ears
13 You might exchange words with them
14 Order member
15 "I don't know" lead-in
22 ___ around (close to)
23 Shoot in the garden
24 Fat, to François
25 Many skit actors
27 Not very sharp
28 Western costume accessory
29 Leading
32 N.F.L. cornerback Starks
34 Head pieces
35 Unlikely number for a rock concert
36 National service
38 Actress Andersson of "Persona"
41 One stuck in the snow
43 19th-century literary family in Massachusetts
47 They're below some chests
48 2002 Al Pacino film
49 Trackers' aids
51 Longtime "Days of Our Lives" actress Jones
52 One stripping on a kitchen counter
54 City noted for its campanile
55 Fingered
56 Square
58 With 57-Across, welcome words when the check arrives
59 Kidder's word
60 Historic barrier breaker
61 Hacker's aid

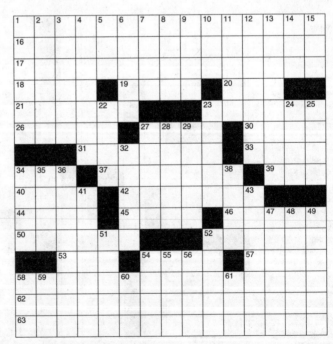

by Harvey Estes

# 191

## ACROSS

1 "Sweet!"
6 "Dial ___ Murder"
10 Touch, e.g.
14 Inherently
15 Europe's third-largest island
16 Rover's watcher
17 Rover's reward
18 Self-absorbed individual
20 Start of an Einstein quote that holds true when solving clever crosswords
22 Doesn't fall short
23 Chicken choice
26 R.S.V.P., e.g.: Abbr.
27 R.S.V.P. facilitator: Abbr.
29 Thought about Paris?
30 Gas usage units
33 City opener
34 Middle of the quote
37 Guardian spirits
38 Type A problem
39 Most ready
41 Far Eastern capital
42 Scented, medicinal plant
45 Originator of the phrase "Pandora's box"
47 Something often read from
50 End of the quote
52 Unpleasant rules to be under
54 Check box choice
55 Antony's love
56 Trix alternative?
57 Treat unjustly
58 Unable to part?
59 Scene of W.W. I fighting
60 Smart

## DOWN

1 Bests
2 "Hello, Dolly!" composer
3 Pool openings
4 County in Kansas, Missouri or Oklahoma
5 Some unsubstantiated sightings
6 Knights, e.g.
7 Order
8 Politico Hatch
9 Get back
10 Parts of many military uniforms
11 Relays
12 Pac-12's Beavers: Abbr.
13 Zeitung article
19 Gets down
21 Some W.W. II internees
24 Ger.
25 Questionnaire info
28 Drain
30 Strains
31 Big honor for a college athlete
32 One might refuse to shake hands
34 Head of state who resigned in 1974
35 Making the rounds
36 Esquire's plea?
37 M.A. hopeful's hurdle
40 Writer of "A Man Must Fight," 1932
42 Burning
43 Burning
44 It can be conserved
46 Some kitchen waste
48 Performer with a big mouth?
49 Fourfront?
51 Bogotá baby
52 Indexing aid
53 Singer who appeared with Charlton in "Secret of the Incas"

by Matt Ginsberg

## ACROSS

1 Beach nos.
5 Scorer of a record 158 goals
9 Certain dry cell, briefly
14 Bucket of bolts
15 Target of a 1989 E.P.A. investigation
16 Language related to Winnebago
17 Weapon for un soldat
18 Game in which players barely bet?
20 Makeshift
22 Drives in the country
23 Place
24 Yupik relative
26 Amateurs
28 Emphatic response during a drill
32 TV biz figure
33 Preceder of what should have been said
34 2008 French Open champion ___ Ivanovic
35 Horizon happening
37 Dealmaker's delight
39 Club ___
40 Rope fiber source
42 Beneficial thing to release
43 Gator rival
45 Having a headline?
46 Pulitzer-winning writer Sheehan and others
47 Came up with an invention
48 They don't take many tricks

50 Needs for 8-Downs
54 Much of high society
56 Knowledge of body?: Abbr.
57 Childish comeback
58 Many a team booster
59 Torch site
60 Up
61 Certified letters?
62 "Pardon the Interruption" airer

## DOWN

1 Three-time M.V.P. of the N.B.A. finals, familiarly
2 Indiana town where Cole Porter was born and buried

3 TV station?
4 Lab subject
5 Parties, say
6 Some singers
7 School concerned with classes?
8 Hand pic, perhaps
9 Macho credo
10 Knows the plans of
11 Stick together
12 Forever
13 Overseas article
19 Like apples and oranges
21 Monitors
25 Salome, to Herod Antipas
26 Spelunking aids
27 Dig deeply
29 Burial site for many French kings

30 It doesn't come out of the stomach
31 Spread unchecked
33 Above ___
36 Solipsistic sort
38 Fraternity activity
41 Pitchers, e.g.
44 Real
45 Kind of TV
48 Pop singer DeSario
49 Ways: Abbr.
51 "Rats!"
52 Way up
53 Gun of old
54 Funerary receptacle
55 ___ lepton

by Kyle Mahowald

## ACROSS

1 Routines
8 Who said "A man's kiss is his signature"
15 End up
16 Source of much talk
17 Play or movie starring William H. Macy
18 The Green City in the Sun
19 Winner of eight consecutive M.V.P. awards
21 Outsides of sandwiches?
22 See 49-Down
23 It was made to fall in 2001
26 Southwestern resort community
27 Dr Pepper Museum locale
28 One of only two women on Rolling Stone's 2003 list of "100 Greatest Guitarists of All Time"
33 Salt baths
35 Singer with the 2000 #1 hit "Be With You"
37 Anne Rice's Brat Prince
38 Active Ecuadorean volcano
39 Where you might be among Hmong
40 Swing-set set
41 Every, to a pharmacist
42 Roll up
44 Three-time NOW president Eleanor
49 Garlicky dish
51 Bachelorette party attendees
54 Ago
55 "Don't you believe it!"
56 Where Arabic and Tigrinya are spoken
57 Booty
58 Reversible silk fabrics

## DOWN

1 19th-century abolitionist
2 Shakes in the grass?
3 Small diamonds, say
4 Puerile
5 Ben & Jerry's stock
6 "___ Pow! Enter the Fist" (2002 spoof film)
7 Detail in a captain's log
8 Cousin of a cockroach
9 Stagger
10 Ballet dancer Bruhn and others
11 Gun-shy
12 Old Far Eastern capital
13 Person in a tree, briefly
14 Parisian pronoun
20 Steaminess
23 Rage
24 Scaling tool
25 Martini's partner
26 German: Abbr.
27 Thin fragment
28 It may still be moving when you eat it
29 Late late hour
30 Bad ignition?
31 Small carps
32 First three-letter White House monogram
33 They're made in short order
34 Runabout or Royale
36 Success
40 Kind of roll
42 Take ___ look at
43 1957 hit for the Bobbettes
44 Drop on a stage
45 It's north of Libya
46 Foreign dignitaries
47 Sneak ___
48 Former capital of Italy
49 With 22-Across, prepares to put on the line
50 Old-time actress Haden
51 Country stat.
52 Choice for chat
53 Sch. whose teams play at the Pete Maravich Assembly Center

by Pete Mitchell

# 194

## ACROSS

1 What boosters boost
7 Coffin nail
13 Oil-rich peninsula
14 Ready to go, you might say
15 Ancient Romans
16 Sherlock Holmes story not by Conan Doyle, e.g.
17 About whom Churchill purportedly said "A modest man who has much to be modest about"
18 Took the offensive
19 Of the north wind
20 In the buff
21 Curaçao flavoring
22 Joust participants
23 They offer rates for automobiles
25 Things that talk in sch.?
26 Isn't strict enough, say
35 Bitingly sarcastic
36 Splits with one's beloved
38 Skin soother
39 Attend to, as a loose shoe
40 Veteran
41 Plant family that includes the hibiscus
42 Special announcer
43 Not behind the defenders
44 Topmost optic in a microscope
45 Nickname for a cheater in the Oklahoma land rush of 1889
46 Most valuable, possibly
47 James in many westerns

## DOWN

1 Equatorial Guinea's capital
2 Delivery professionals?
3 It deserves to be condemned
4 Town that Wild Bill Hickok was marshal of
5 Pedigree
6 Like paintings in progress
7 Integration that exceeds the sum of its parts
8 Semitic fertility goddess
9 Price holder
10 Winner over the Patriots in Super Bowl XXXI
11 Organic compounds used as solvents
12 Swamp flora
14 Showing the most wear and tear
16 People of much experience
24 Candor
26 Servant in a cause
27 Meaningless talk
28 Thinks the world of
29 Closet hangings
30 Los Angeles County's ___ Beach
31 ___ of Aquitaine, Henry II's wife
32 Passes, as time
33 Milky and iridescent
34 Uses a key, perhaps
35 Singapore lies just off its tip
37 Offbeat Parisian tourist sites
38 Behave cravenly

*by Patrick Berry*

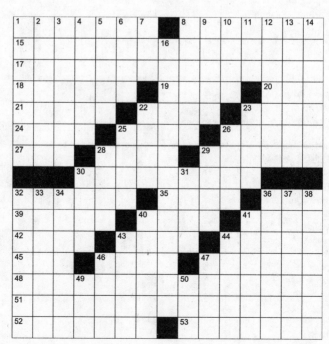

# 195

## ACROSS

1 Like Delftware
8 Robert B. Parker's private eye
15 Court slam dunk
17 Seriously deteriorate
18 Projects
19 Rubs the wrong way
20 Gathered dust
21 Rewards for good dives
22 It's in the cards
23 "The Right Stuff" subj.
24 Stucco ingredients?
25 Dotty
26 Precursor of Pascal
27 Things to rush for: Abbr.
28 It builds up in bars
29 Designing women
30 Use a metal detector, maybe
32 Bolts
35 Sound system parts?
36 Baseball positions: Abbr.
39 Wolf who wrote "The Beauty Myth"
40 Life-or-death
41 Fashion
42 2006 Grammy-winning blues singer ___ Thomas
43 Fall shade
44 See 46-Across
45 Sch. figure
46 With 44-Across, 1940 Laurel and Hardy film
47 Chemical relative
48 Writing that mixes reportage and fiction
51 It's not a total knockout
52 Writer of pieces in passing?
53 Wagner opera title role

## DOWN

1 Persuasiveness
2 Glued, in a way
3 Makes grand adjustments?
4 Magnetron parts
5 Some nags
6 Much may come after it
7 Quarantining org.
8 Corporation allocation
9 Very slow-burning, as a fire
10 Waiting area announcements, briefly
11 Big A.T.M. maker
12 It may be chain-linked
13 Star QB for the 1980s–'90s Bengals
14 Many tuxes
16 Equivocate
22 Creator of a bathroom cloud
23 Collective bargaining watchdog org.
25 Pollster's concern
26 Points
28 Important match
29 Irritated
30 Southeastern Conference team, for short
31 Online shopping icon
32 Fish by thrusting a baited hook into holes
33 Auto-rotating system
34 Bookstore section
36 Philosophical studier of the universe
37 Cousin of a crocus
38 DC Comics superhero
40 Spandex source
41 Choir robe accessories
43 Asian nobles
44 Brew from Tokyo
46 Star turns
47 Preface: Abbr.
49 Turn back
50 Letter run

by Brad Wilber

# 196

## ACROSS

1 Subject of the 1989 musical monologue "Bon Appétit!"
11 Gimbel contemporary
15 Old torturer
16 Latin trio member
17 Country whose capital is Palikir
18 Union member of the future: Abbr.
19 Start to court
20 Company that developed NutraSweet
22 Worker that never gets tired
26 Jung's feminine side
27 Big name in oil
31 Postpones
33 Spying aid
34 Yellow primrose
36 Oscar winner after "Rocky"
38 Tops
40 We
41 Does some macramé work
43 Guys who make people look good
44 View from the Arlberg Pass
45 Applied, as paint
47 Bit of biblical graffiti
48 Novelist Binchy
50 "Married . . . With Children" actress Sagal
52 Record listing
54 Mass stack
59 Genève and others
60 It's easy to burn
64 Target of un coup
65 Twin
66 Evening for Evangelo
67 Thing to swing from

## DOWN

1 Chichi-___ (largest of Japan's Bonin Islands)
2 "O'Hara's Choice" novelist, 2003
3 Sure winner
4 Obi accessory
5 Reason for a tryst
6 One whose lead is followed in the service
7 Rush
8 Some bracelets
9 Strand on an island?
10 Strands of biology
11 Bad lover?
12 1992 film directed by and starring Edward James Olmos
13 Warden player in "Birdman of Alcatraz"
14 Simplify
21 Fall off
23 Unconventional sort
24 Every, in prescriptions
25 One taking a first step
27 Sexy numbers
28 Send
29 Berth place
30 Young rivals, often
32 Cancún kinsman
35 Family of 18th- and 19th-century painters
37 Vitiate
39 Calypso relative
42 Seraglio section
46 Home of the University of Delaware
49 Third-largest asteroid
51 Supporter of the mascot Handsome Dan
53 High-end shoe and handbag maker
55 Sitcom guy with a frequently upturned thumb, with "the"
56 Sum lead-in
57 Zip around France?
58 Sun-damaged
61 It's attached to a hoop
62 A hoop may be attached to it
63 Century-beginning year

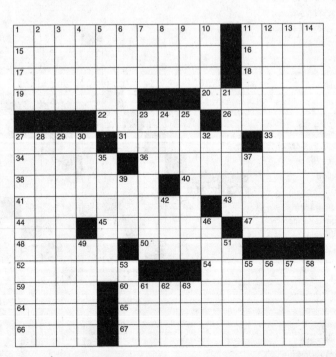

by Frederick J. Healy

## ACROSS

1 Spread choice
5 Captor of Han Solo
10 ___ 1000, annual Mexican off-road race
14 Opera singer created by Arthur Conan Doyle
16 Well out of range
17 Bypass
18 Twisted
19 Player of Danni Sullivan on "Scrubs"
20 Cords, e.g.
22 They may cover rocks
24 Princess in Mozart's "Idomeneo"
25 College Park player, briefly
28 Park in Ranger Smith's charge
31 Trucial States, today: Abbr.
32 Decks
33 Cone holders
34 Religious house
36 They lack details
37 Exert some pull
39 Generational indicator in some names
40 "Ad majorem ___ gloriam" (Jesuit motto)
41 "Guerrilla Warfare" author, 1961
43 Jazzman ___ Allison
44 Many Mexicanas: Abbr.
45 Not too rocky, say
47 Paris's House of ___
49 Brunswick stew ingredient
53 Bank opening?
54 Conspirator's cautious conversation starter
56 French "some," with "les"
57 Home of Our Lady of the Lake University
58 Starling, e.g.
59 He-Man's twin sister
60 Striplings

## DOWN

1 Roman's foe of yore
2 24-Across's "Zeffiretti lusinghieri," e.g.
3 Apt. amenity
4 Bivouac
5 Writer of the 1918 play "Exiles"
6 Steers
7 "Gilmore Girls" co-star Alexis
8 Big ___
9 They may be patronized
10 Like some lava
11 Buff
12 Whippersnapper
13 Refuges
15 Overseas capital
21 Obey
23 Professional shooter, briefly
25 First name in rap
26 Faint illumination of the moon's dark side
27 Hammers away at
29 Trailing evergreen related to savory
30 Davis who played Maggie in two "Matrix" movies
32 "Six Feet Under" star Peter
35 One may play at a ballpark
38 Knoxville-based org.
39 Tony Blair advocated it
42 Sherlock's French counterpart
43 Red choice
46 Joe's love interest in "South Pacific"
47 Measure of support?
48 Sweetheart
50 First name in Hollywood gossip
51 Vance Air Force Base locale
52 Bill Clinton and Arnold Schwarzenegger, to the stars?
55 Sound from a bowl

by Karen M. Tracey

# 198

## ACROSS

1 Take in
6 Unenthusiastic response
14 Companion of Hearst at San Simeon castle
16 Like friendship bracelets
17 Dualistic deity
18 Club restriction
19 Ordinary human being
21 Z preceder
22 Signs of disuse
23 Big exporter of diamonds: Abbr.
24 Black Forest resort
26 Maestro ___ de Waart
27 "___ It Grand, Boys" (Irish standard)
29 See 35-Down
30 Hostess's ___ Balls
31 Little something
32 Equal
33 "Easy does it!"
39 Grp. for counselors
40 Capital of the Apulia region
41 Not much at all
42 "Good Guys Wear Black" star, 1978
45 Golfer Aoki
46 Blood
47 Not worth ___
48 Private instructor: Abbr.
49 Drink with a straw
50 Box: Abbr.
51 Strength of character
54 Literally, "sheltered harbor"
57 Mean
58 Does some body work?
59 Some porters
60 Far from macho
61 Cultural doings in Cádiz

## DOWN

1 Actor who voiced the mayor on "Family Guy"
2 Aussie with purple hair and ornate glasses
3 Be too reserved?
4 Languishes
5 Stretch in a seat
6 "Easy does it!"
7 Sammy nicknamed "The Red Rocker"
8 1977 memoir set at Harvard
9 Year Marcian became emperor
10 Bud abroad
11 Open-sided porch
12 Made a long story short?
13 Sisters of Charity founder and family
15 ___ Jorge (Azores island)
20 ___ cycle
24 Chicago's Little Village, e.g.
25 Out of harm's way, in a way
27 Presently
28 Ballpark concessionaire's offerings
29 Nazareth native, e.g.
34 Win
35 With 29-Across, picnic dishes
36 Try to get dirt on, say
37 Process of grooming and dressing oneself
38 Artemis or Atalanta
42 Some chips
43 They have many suction cups
44 Capital of the Brittany region
48 Ones underfoot?
49 Hardly worth mentioning
51 Longtime La Scala music director
52 Church with elders: Abbr.
53 Topping on Mediterranean pizza
55 Connecting words in logic
56 Spend, with "out"

by Jim Page

## ACROSS

1 It's often laid on someone else
6 Gun-cleaning aid
9 Indian honorific
14 High-altitude home
15 Motel freebie
16 Take on
17 Detours
20 Its slogan was once "More bounce to the ounce"
21 Espouse
22 Panama, e.g.
23 Site for a bite
25 Calyx component
27 Béret holder
28 Onetime ring master
29 Some blemishes
30 Showed again
31 Court order
33 Decathlete Johnson
35 Many thoroughfares . . . or what this puzzle's Across answers consist of?
39 Illegal match play?
40 Infernal
42 Aid in avoiding the draft?
45 Mass communication?
47 World Cup cry
48 In case
49 Stepping-off point
50 Sailboat stopper
51 Stowe girl
52 Square on un calendario
53 Cousin of a hyacinth
55 Possible result of an appeal
60 Rhone feeder
61 Rio producer
62 Crackerjack
63 Spring Air competitor
64 Org. that may call for a recall
65 City in North Rhine-Westphalia

## DOWN

1 Comic actress ___ Lillie
2 Start of many rappers' stage names
3 Dig discovery
4 Predecessor of Thornburgh in the cabinet
5 Marshal played by Fonda, Costner and Lancaster
6 Person who's combining
7 10/: Abbr.
8 Ebbed
9 Pack
10 Seller of Squishees on "The Simpsons"
11 Like Venus vis-à-vis Mercury
12 Come up with something
13 Critic and then some
18 Cranes constructing homes, e.g.
19 Minister's area: Abbr.
23 "Le ___" (Jules Massenet opera)
24 Intoxicating round
26 Member of the carrot family
27 Fool's place
29 27-Down users, e.g.
30 ___ post (railing supporter)
32 Not keep a poker face
34 One who's more than devoted
36 Unable to hit pitches?
37 Total alternative
38 Determine
41 CD follower
42 Some pyrotechnics
43 Make a shrine to, say
44 "Yours" alternative
46 Seat of Shawnee County
49 Talk trash about
50 Canine features
52 High-culture strains
54 Not so rich, informally
56 It's somewhere in the neighborhood: Abbr.
57 Impersonated
58 Stanzaic salute
59 Staple of Indian cuisine

by Donald K. Willing

## ACROSS

1 Big name in bikes
9 Happen (upon)
15 Medal of Honor recipient, say
16 Doctrine developer of 1823
17 Hotel waiters?
18 Be a catalyst for
19 Accessories whose colors may indicate rank
20 Flavoring in a Tom and Jerry
22 Put down on the street
23 Part of a philosophical dichotomy
24 Port on Osaka Bay
25 Temper, informally
27 "Contact" author, 1985
29 Research venue: Abbr.
31 About
32 ___ Cabos, Mexico
34 Sits beside a fireplace, perhaps
36 Self-contained music equipment
40 Half a pair for pairs
41 Burns into film
42 Clammy
43 Former news gatherer
45 Space traveler of 1957
49 Grass unit
51 "Wicked Game" singer, 1991
53 Pilothouse dir.
54 Cry from a litter
55 Untimely comment?
57 Anatomical part named after the Latin for "grape"
58 Go by
60 It's heard at a slumber party

62 In it together
63 "Spamalot" lyricist
64 Depilatory equipment
65 Like some watermelons

## DOWN

1 Retail chain once popular with kids
2 Coffee source
3 Not yet full
4 Warren of the car rental business
5 Mo
6 Dryer maker
7 Drama in which male actors play both male and female parts
8 Email alternatives
9 Chérie
10 Piece of pi?
11 Yellow pages abbr.
12 Where guards are stationed
13 Highly sought shares
14 Drives
21 Bear cub mascot of the 1980 Moscow Olympics
24 Thumbing-the-nose gesture
26 Almaviva serenades her in "The Barber of Seville"
28 Its motto is "North to the future"
30 Strategy
33 Activity in which people are not playing with a full deck
35 Snail variety
36 Smaller fare, usually

37 Like many doo-wop groups: Var.
38 Big part of magazine income
39 What PayPal facilitates
44 "The Colbert Report" and such
46 Irrupt
47 Sounds ominously
48 See 50-Down
50 One who 48-Down
52 Thing to soar to and from
56 Some are covered by insurance, informally
57 Monopoly buy: Abbr.
59 Kind of filling
61 Laptop feature, for short

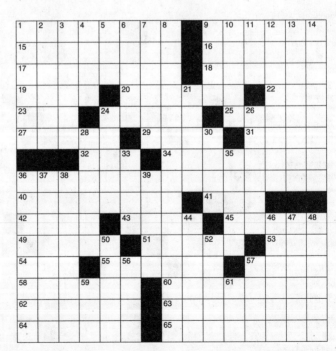

by Kevin G. Der

## 1

SANDP · SUPE · RAPS
UHURA · TREX · AURA
NAKEDLUNCH · STUB
· SEAMAN · IPHONE
· MASTERBREWER
JEWELS · QUIERO ·
AVEDA · SUITS · RAE
PER · KATANAS · KIA
ERE · SLOBS · REEDS
· AWHIRL · DEFRAY
IBLAMEMYSELF ·
CALVIN · PLEATS ·
ELSE · APPALACHIA
USER · TOES · SEALS
PATS · EXAM · EDITS

## 2

IMHO · TOSS · SITE
NOOB · SALAD · HOOD
CUTS · PRICERANGE
ANDCO · PRPERSON
STEEDS · OILUP ·
· SNOT · FLOP · WHO
JOKEWRITER · NEAT
CHILDISHGAMBINO
TINY · KNEEBOARDS
SOG · JETT · LOAD ·
· LASSO · EDGERS
BLUEMOON · SEDAN
BOCABURGER · NONE
OWLS · TRUCE · TUDE
YEAH · YEOW · STIR

## 3

THESTOOGES · TROT
HITCHARIDE · HAVE
INTHATCASE · EVEN
STAR · ACE · ARENT
· OIL · OLDWELSH
DEADCALM · ELI ·
AUDIOBOOKS · SUMP
BRENNAN · OPENSET
SONG · MICROCOSMS
· EBB · INTHERED
OVERLAIN · SOS ·
PALSY · HES · COPE
ALEC · HOMEPLANET
LUNA · SPACEOPERA
SEAT · TEXTALERTS

## 4

SUCKDRY · APPEASE
INHERED · CHANTER
THREADS · TORTOLA
SEISMS · TANLINES
HASHEESH · EOCENE
ITSADATE · SUEDES
VEINY · ESTERS ·
ADE · REMAX · TEA
· HEADUP · AWOLS
SALAMI · RIPTIDES
ALEVEL · FREELOVE
LEVERETS · LADLES
OPIOIDS · HATPINS
OPENTAP · EGOISTE
NOSEATS · LENGTHS

## 5

BOTTLES · SIDEBET
EVASIVE · PREGAME
EURASIA · ROLODEX
FLORALPRINT · MRT
EATS · GLENS · DOGE
DRS · CRAFT · TRUED
· PAINE · CHATS ·
· RUNNERSHIGH ·
· HOPES · EWERS ·
SILAS · SNEAD · LAD
ITLL · SADAT · MAGI
THE · LUNARCRATER
PODCAST · JOSHING
AMRADIO · ADVANCE
TESTEES · REPLAYS

## 6

· MCCAIN · OFFTO
· QUIZZICALLOOK
QUOTATIONMARKS
BURNER · TOPSY ·
AAA · DIPOLES · HOW
MYNA · NAMED · BABE
· SCAGGS · NOMAD
TRAIPSE · PARLEYS
HILDA · BEAPAL ·
ISLE · HOPUP · SERB
SKA · ROYALLY · MOA
· FLIES · IOMOTH
FROZENDAIQUIRI
DENOFINIQUITY ·
REEDS · ARSENE

## 7

```
BINGEWATCH ESA
ESCAPEROOM EVIL
DEATHTRAPS MAXI
SEAS NADA PANTS
PAY RELIGHT
OHSTOP FEMALES
RECUT SONIC LEE
EARTHSHATTERING
ODE OPALS BOSSA
HEALERS LOOTED
SUNDECK SOS
ANTES NACL BMWS
UTEP MAKEITRAIN
NEST IDONTWANNA
ART CONTAINING
```

## 8

```
RADISH JAMESON
ARETHA CAROLINA
GOSTAG ONENINTH
ADS GASLEAKS
EGGROLLS ICUS
PREY CEL WORST
BATE GIGECONOMY
ARM PREEMIE TIL
BEEFHOTDOG TONE
ENNUI YEN KANT
STUN LPGATOUR
KEYARENA ISM
AGERANGE OLIVIA
BOYARDEE TAMERS
STEPPES ESPRIT
```

## 9

```
PADS TEMP MIMI
COURT HAIRTONIC
ALTAR ERRORCODE
LOOFA CLOSEKNIT
TINA SEXT
OHMYGOSH AIMS
MAO HABIT BINET
IDONTHAVEALLDAY
TIRES HEAVE ILL
STEW STINKEYE
AHAB ODDS
STAGECREW ETHER
ORDERHERE DAILY
POORDEVIL ITSME
SUSS SEES NESS
```

## 10

```
MACY WRAPS DAFT
AGUE HOLEY ISAO
GOTASECOND SKIP
MOTHERHEN SCAR
ADO SEES SPONGE
PAW TWO YAK
HOMESWEETHOME
PAPERAIRPLANE
CASESENSITIVE
SYN EWE AGE
APOGEE BASH ENE
HIND FISHTACOS
CODA JELLOSHOTS
CNET REBAR ELIE
SEAS STONE MINX
```

## 11

```
VERISMO
NOTENOUGH
BOWANDARROW
PLUS FEN ESAS
LEAN PANDA ESPN
ESC ITS HIE
ACK OREOS IRA
SEA IVERSON NIP
ATNINE LONGTO
LADDER DISTAL
ORWORSE MARCONI
NIH TEAROSE NIT
GAIN ECOLI OZMA
ANTI SHOES JOAN
SEX SOL
```

## 12

```
CANDOR BOOTUP
PIERRE CATERTO
ARREST JANEDOES
JVSOCCER RINSE
DOES HASASIP
ARBYS DUMP USGA
HDL OHISEE SERB
LAO BELLLAP TAU
INCA FLICKR TVS
ASKS TAZO YALIE
KEYCARD PETS
AXMAN MRNOBODY
STENOPAD BUGOFF
IRECKON BREWER
FAKEID SPENDY
```

## 13

```
P O W E R C O R D S ■ S C O T
A T H L E I S U R E ■ H A H S
S T O L E A K I S S ■ A R G H
T O W ■ L O A N ■ H U M E R I
E M O J I ■ R O B ■ P E T E R
S A R O N G ■ U R L S ■ O A T
■ N E A ■ O N S A L E ■ E T S
■ ■ I N T R O ■ T O T A L ■
E S T ■ O D D I T Y ■ B A D
G A B ■ D O U R ■ D A U B E D
G R E C O ■ H E M ■ S T O M A
W A T U S I ■ S E A T ■ R E V
A L T O ■ T W I T T E R A T I
S E E M ■ Z A G A T R A T E D
H E R O ■ A N N L A N D E R S
```

## 14

```
S O I W A S L I K E ■ U S P S
P A R A C H U T E S ■ N C A A
C H A R L A T A N S ■ F A C T
A U N T ■ D E L T A B U R K E
■ ■ H U E ■ ■ Y U R T ■ ■
I N C O N T R O L ■ S L I N K
M E D G A R E V E R S ■ S I N
P A R ■ E L I T E ■ S E E
E L O ■ P E A N U T S A U C E
L E M M A ■ Y E S I N D E E D
■ D O U P ■ C O M ■
P U R P L E H A Z E ■ I M A C
O N I T ■ P A L I N D R O M E
T I V O ■ S W I T C H E R O O
S T E P ■ I N F I E L D E R S
```

## 15

```
S N I P S ■ A L P O ■ L A S
P O P U P S T O R E ■ L O C H
I H O P E T O G O D ■ A N T E
N O D ■ C A N E M ■ A G G I E
■ S I N E ■ N A N O B O T
T H R E A D ■ B I R D S O N G
R A O U L ■ C A G E Y ■ A I L
O V A L ■ P A T H S ■ S R T A
L E D ■ L U M E T ■ N U D E S
L I T T E R E D ■ S E I S M S
E T E R N A L ■ J U S T ■
Y E S E S ■ H A U N T ■ R E I
B A T S ■ B A L L R E T U R N
U S E S ■ M I L E A G E L O G
S Y D ■ W R A P ■ G E E S E
```

## 16

```
H O P A C A B ■ E D U ■ C D C
T H A T O N E ■ C E N T A U R
S O L O A C T ■ H A I R S P A
■ E I T H E R O R ■ A E O N
P R O ■ S O L E ■ O V I N E
C O L A ■ C O M M E N T S
S T I L E T T O H E E L S ■
■ I T S R A I N I N G M E N
■ H A U D E N O S A U N E E
S U I T C A S E ■ G S I X
O P C I T ■ C R A G ■ I N T
A L D A ■ B E T A T E S T
P A I N M E D ■ B O O H I S S
E T E S I A N ■ A N D O V E R
D E T ■ A K A ■ T E E P E E S
```

## 17

```
H I J A C K S ■ A S S N ■ Q U E
I F O R O N E ■ S P A Y ■ U N D
P S Y C H O A C T I V E ■ E P I
■ H O T S A U C E ■ F E E T
M B A ■ O T T E R ■ E R R S
P O L E D A N C E D ■ A R E S O
G O L D R U S H ■ U P T O Y O U
■ G E D ■ 2 0 P E R C E N T
F O R E V E R 2 1 ■ R E I
E V E L I N E ■ A P P S T O R E
R E V E L ■ S O L A S T Y E A R
G R O S ■ D E B U G ■ R N A
U R L S ■ O A T M E A L S
S I T ■ A P L U S A V E R A G E
O D E ■ S E E S ■ N O T I C E S
N E D ■ H Y D E ■ T W O S T E P
```

## 18

```
B L A C K C O D ■ S A S H
R O L L E R B A G ■ T H R E A D
A S T E R I S K S ■ H U S T L E
K E A ■ I M E A N T I T ■ O F F
E R R ■ I S R ■ O R I O N S
■ T U N S ■ M O S T O F I T
P H A R M A ■ A I N T ■ L I Z A
E E Q U A L S M C S Q U A R E D
G L U E ■ R A I D ■ U N L E S S
G L A S S E Y E ■ L E I A
■ A Z T E C S ■ T A N ■ S T R
E C U ■ M O O J U I C E ■ W E E
R O M P E R ■ O L D H A V A N A
G O B A L D ■ B I T E S I Z E D
■ L A T E ■ P O R T C I T Y
```

## 19

```
D O T H E D E W . . A L M A Y
U N H E A R D O F . T E A S E
B I E N V E N U E . M A N I A
L O I R E . A L T A . F I S H
I N S I S T . D E L L . P E A
N Y T . A N N . S A T E E N
. D E N O T E . H A D I D
. T H I S G U Y G E T S I T
C H A R S . N O O G I E
R E P E A L . U S A . C A V
A S P . Y O D A . N I C O L E
W H Y S . B O G S . N O O K S
D I N A R . W R I S T S L A P
A R O M A . D E T E R M I N E
D E W E Y . E S C O O T E R
```

## 20

```
J A Z Z W A L T Z . A M O N G
O N E O R M O R E . R A D I O
J U N O E S Q U E . G R E C O
O B I . S C U D . D O T T E D
B I T . T R A G I C . S O S O
A S H E . A T E O U T . J A M
. R A Y S . U P A B O V E
J A M A L . D O Y E N
O F A S O R T . C Z A R
E T S . T E E P E E . E M I T
S E T H . L E A R N S . O N O
C R O A K Y . M A M A . R B I
H Y D R A . L E M O N P E E L
M O O D Y . B L I N D D A T E
O U N C E . J A C K S Q U A T
```

## 21

```
B A T B O Y . S C H M A L T Z
I P H O N E . Q U E E R E Y E
G R E W U P . U S E D C A R S
W I R E S . D A H L S . D O T
I C O N . P I T Y . H E N S
G O B . F A S T . S M O R E
S T O L E T H E S H O W
. S T A R T E R P I S T O L
. M A I D S O F H O N O R
. F A B L E . R O T E . C O E
P O L O . F I N S . O A K S
O R C . S N A G S . J U M B O
E G O D E A T H . M E T E O R
M O V I E S E T . C A R R O T
S T E P D A D S . S N E A K S
```

## 22

```
. C A L L T H E S H O T S
. M U S E U M E X H I B I T
. L E T I T G O A L R E A D Y
G A R E T H . B R I O . M E R
A P R S . A K I M B O . A P E
G U I T A L E L E . M A S O N
S P A . F L E E . R U D E
. M E R Y L . T R A M P
S A W V . S E E P . P B S
A R E E L . S C R A P B O O K
R I B . U N P A I R . U R S I
A G S . G I L L . E A S T O N
N A T I O N A L A N T H E M
A T E A S E S O L D I E R
C O R N I S H P A S T Y
```

## 23

```
L O L C A T S . H A S H T A G
I P A D P R O . E R N U R S E
P E R S E U S . A G O N I S T
R N A . S L U M D O G . V A L
I B M S . Y E A S T . R E N O
N A I A D . M S U . M O T T S
G R E N A D E . P L A Y S E T
. D Y E . E R A
P E P B A N D . B A L L H O G
H A S O N . I R E . A W O K E
O R Y X . N S Y N C . E T S Y
T L C . H O M E G Y M . D H S
O O H L A L A . A L O H A O E
O B E S I T Y . L O C A T O R
P E D D L E S . I N K J E T S
```

## 24

```
M O O D R I N G S . S L I T S
I N D U E T I M E . M A B E L
S T A N D S P A T . A D E L E
T O Y . R E A C T . R O L L E
. W A L T . H I T L I S T
T O P O F F . B E N I C E
A P O R T . B R O K E E V E N
R E T D . H A I R Y . V E T O
O L D S M O K E Y . B I S O N
. E F I L E R . P U T O N S
A R C A D E S . K O L A
L U R I D . A R R O W . D A B
O D E L L . L A U R A N Y R O
F E M M E . E S P E R A N T O
T R E E S . S H A R K W E E K
```

## 25

```
F E Z . . E S P . S T A M P
E X E S . S L E E P E R C A R
A T R A . T E R R A C O T T A
T R O M B O N E . T R U S T Y
S A C . E V A . D E E T . .
. S H A R E . S E N T . O P T
. P A N T . P U B T R I V I A
P I N T A . E M U . E R E C T
A C C E N T R U G . C O R K
L Y E . D E P P . M I N T Y
. . L E N S . M O P . H E F
S A T I R E . D O N E D E A L
P A R E N T H O O D . A T T Y
C R I S I S M O D E . L O E B
A P P L E . M R S . P R Y
```

## 26

```
. H O A G I E . D R O I D
. R O C K E T S C I E N C E
. Y O U H A T E T O S E E I T
S A Y N O . G R A D . D O N E
C L A D . C O A T E S . F E N
A T L . S U I T E . C R U S T
B A S E L I N E . M O U S S E
. P A N G . D A U B .
C A S I N G . K I T T Y C A T
E X A C T . D U S T S . A D O
R O O . S C O N C E . K N I T
A L I G . R O D E . C E D E S
M O R E P O W E R T O Y O U
I T S N O W O R N E V E R
C L E A T . P A S T E D
```

## 27

```
I T S O N . S E E S F I T
N E W D A D . H A V E A G O
T R E E T O P . E R E C T E D
E R A . S C R O L L . R I T A
N A R C . S O I L . E M I T
D I J O N . F L O W S T A T E
. N A V E L . B U I C K .
. R E P A R A T I O N S
. R A Z O R . S T O P S
I M A L L E A R S . S C O O P
M O R E . D E L A . K I L L
P O R T . A T L A S T . L O U
A L I T T L E . T A G T E A M
C A V E A T S . P I E R C E
T H E R O O T . F A S T S
```

## 28

```
L E O . M I L . . H E Y
I N N E E D O F . H O N E
S T E P H A N I E . H E L G A
P E C S . H E R S T O R I E S
E R A . B O R S C H T B E L T
D I R G E . S T A R W A R S
. C A R P S . S P O I L
. T E A C H . E A R T H
. A T L A S . T I E I N
. S A T I A T E D . N A N O S
T H E W E S T W I N G . D U E
N O N O N S E N S E . E F T S
O V E R T . D I S H I T O U T
T E A K . N E R D C O R E
E L S . . D U O . T N T
```

## 29

```
N B A M V P S . P I E H O L E
I S R A E L I . E M P O R I A
P A I N T E R . A L I S T E R
. S T A I R C A S E
R S V P E D . O H T O . T L C
E L A L . S W A Y E D . H O O
S E G A . T A N K . I D E A S
P E R I D O T . E X C E E D S
I V A N I . C H E X . R U S E
T E N . S P H I N X . B R I T
E S T . H A C K . R A Y O N S
. D O T H E M A T H
A M M O N I A . I T S A B O Y
T O R T O N I . L E E T I D E
V E T E R A N . E D A S N E R
```

## 30

```
A N G S T Y . H U E . S P A T
R E S T A U R A N T . K E R R
B L U E S M U S I C . I N T O
O L I V E . M O T H S . U F O
R I T E . L I V E . H A M U P
S E E . Z I N E . G O B B L E
. B I Z A R R O W O R L D
. S N A P A T . O N E D A Y
P E E R P R E S S U R E
L A R D E D . L E T S . C P R
A R D O R . S U M S . C A R E
T O P . S U N R A . C A S E D
O U R S . R E P R O A C H E S
O T O H . G E E Y A T H I N K
N E M O . E R E . T E E N S Y
```

## 31

| A | L | P | H | A | F | E | M | A | L | E | █ | E | M | U |
| B | A | H | A | M | A | M | A | M | A | S | █ | V | A | N |
| I | C | A | N | T | R | E | S | I | S | T | █ | I | D | S |
| T | U | S | K | S | █ | R | O | D | S | █ | F | L | E | W |
| O | N | E | S | █ | S | I | N | █ | E | N | R | O | B | E |
| F | A | D | █ | L | O | L | █ | A | R | E | A | M | A | P |
| █ | █ | L | A | Y | L | O | W | █ | S | C | E | N | T | █ |
| █ | M | A | A | M | █ | I | N | K | █ | T | A | N | K | █ |
| R | A | N | T | O | █ | V | O | W | E | L | S | █ | █ | █ |
| E | N | T | H | U | S | E | █ | A | B | E | █ | T | O | O |
| D | I | V | E | R | T | █ | O | R | B | █ | H | E | R | B |
| S | P | E | D | █ | R | A | N | D | █ | B | E | N | E | S |
| T | E | N | █ | C | E | R | E | A | L | A | I | S | L | E |
| A | D | O | █ | D | E | M | I | G | O | D | D | E | S | S |
| R | I | M | █ | S | T | Y | L | E | G | U | I | D | E | S |

## 32

| █ | M | U | S | T | D | O | █ | P | A | Y | G | A | P | █ |
| C | A | R | H | O | R | N | S | █ | S | K | E | E | L | O |
| U | S | S | E | N | A | T | E | █ | H | O | T | T | I | P |
| S | C | U | D | █ | W | I | C | C | A | N | █ | A | C | E |
| P | O | L | █ | P | R | O | W | █ | C | R | A | Y | █ | █ |
| S | T | A | R | G | A | T | E | S | █ | C | R | O | N | E |
| █ | █ | O | R | N | O | T | █ | E | L | I | O | T | S | █ |
| █ | I | T | S | A | Y | E | S | F | R | O | M | M | E | █ |
| I | G | O | T | Y | A | █ | E | R | A | S | E | █ | █ | █ |
| N | U | D | E | S | █ | P | R | E | S | E | A | S | O | N |
| A | E | O | N | █ | E | A | V | E | █ | █ | E | P | A | █ |
| Y | S | L | █ | O | B | L | I | G | E | █ | L | A | I | N |
| E | S | I | G | N | S | █ | C | A | T | W | O | M | A | N |
| A | S | S | U | M | E | █ | E | N | T | I | R | E | T | Y |
| R | O | T | T | E | N | █ | S | A | T | I | R | E | █ | █ |

## 33

| T | A | C | T | I | C | █ | I | M | P | A | S | T | O |
| E | R | R | A | T | A | █ | G | R | E | E | N | C | A | R |
| S | K | Y | P | E | R | █ | L | A | T | E | N | E | W | S |
| L | I | F | E | █ | G | I | O | █ | S | V | E | N | █ |
| A | N | O | █ | C | O | M | B | S | █ | E | X | I | S | T |
| █ | R | A | H | █ | B | A | H | █ | C | E | O |
| S | P | A | C | E | T | E | L | E | S | C | O | P | E | S |
| P | U | T | A | F | A | C | E | T | O | A | N | A | M | E |
| A | R | T | I | S | T | I | C | L | I | C | E | N | S | E |
| N | E | E | █ | L | O | A | █ | A | G | O | █ |
| K | E | N | D | O | █ | E | N | N | I | O | █ | R | E | P |
| █ | T | O | N | Y | █ | O | D | D | █ | C | A | L | I |
| M | A | I | N | R | O | O | M | █ | B | E | A | M | U | P |
| I | N | O | N | E | D | A | Y | █ | E | T | R | A | D | E |
| D | I | N | E | D | A | T | █ | T | A | B | S | E | T |

## 34

| B | A | L | L | I | S | L | I | F | E | █ | H | A | M | M |
| I | M | E | A | N | T | O | S | A | Y | █ | A | S | E | A |
| T | E | A | S | E | R | V | I | C | E | █ | I | C | E | S |
| E | L | S | █ | S | U | E | D | E | █ | F | L | I | T | S |
| M | I | E | N | █ | T | T | O | P | █ | L | E | I | C | A |
| E | A | S | Y | A | █ | T | R | A | C | I | █ | A | U | G |
| █ | █ | L | I | T | █ | A | L | A | C | A | R | T | E | █ |
| █ | S | T | O | R | E | D | █ | M | R | K | I | T | E | █ |
| M | O | O | N | B | E | A | M | █ | D | E | M | █ | █ | █ |
| E | L | Y | █ | A | S | T | I | R | █ | D | A | D | A | S |
| T | A | P | A | S | █ | A | L | E | C | █ | T | A | T | A |
| G | R | I | P | E | █ | M | A | S | E | R | █ | N | O | N |
| A | C | A | I | █ | F | I | N | E | D | I | N | I | N | G |
| L | A | N | A | █ | I | N | O | N | E | P | I | E | C | E |
| A | R | O | N | █ | B | E | S | T | S | E | L | L | E | R |

## 35

| U | P | L | I | T | █ | U | M | P | █ | M | A | D | A | M |
| B | E | A | C | H | █ | N | E | E | D | A | R | I | D | E |
| O | N | C | U | E | █ | A | N | G | O | R | A | C | A | T |
| A | N | T | █ | O | W | S | █ | S | M | O | R | E | S | █ |
| T | I | E | C | L | A | S | P | █ | E | N | A | C | T | S |
| █ | B | A | L | D | T | I | R | E | S | █ | T | U | R | K |
| █ | L | O | V | E | S | E | A | T | S | █ | P | A | Y | █ |
| █ | █ | D | I | R | T | Y | R | I | C | E | █ | █ | █ |
| A | R | M | █ | C | H | E | S | T | C | O | L | D | █ |
| B | E | A | K | █ | A | D | O | R | A | T | I | O | N |
| S | P | R | I | T | Z | █ | N | U | T | C | A | S | E | S |
| █ | T | I | N | H | A | T | █ | M | E | H | █ | H | O | T |
| F | I | N | G | E | R | T | I | P | █ | E | L | O | P | E |
| A | L | A | M | O | D | O | M | E | █ | G | O | T | E | M |
| D | E | S | E | X | █ | P | O | T | █ | G | U | S | T | S |

## 36

| A | P | P | S | █ | D | R | A | W | █ | R | I | C | A | N |
| M | A | R | I | █ | R | E | N | O | █ | O | N | I | C | E |
| P | L | O | T | █ | I | A | G | O | █ | O | S | T | E | R |
| █ | O | U | T | O | F | L | E | F | T | F | I | E | L | D |
| C | A | D | E | N | T | █ | L | E | O | █ | D | D | A | Y |
| A | L | E | R | T | █ | T | O | R | Q | U | E | █ | █ | █ |
| I | T | S | S | O | Y | O | U | █ | U | R | B | A | N | E |
| N | O | T | █ | P | E | P | █ | T | E | L | A | V | I | V |
| █ | █ | █ | F | I | A | S | C | O | S | █ | S | I | N | E |
| S | T | A | R | C | R | A | F | T | █ | R | E | D | O | S |
| H | O | S | E | █ | N | I | C | E | J | O | B | █ | █ | █ |
| I | N | P | E | R | I | L | █ | B | A | C | A | R | D | I |
| R | E | U | B | E | N | █ | B | A | N | K | L | O | A | N |
| T | U | R | I | N | G | █ | A | G | U | I | L | E | R | A |
| S | P | E | E | D | S | █ | E | S | S | E | █ | S | E | T |

## 37

```
N B A A L L S T A R ■ ■ A C T
E I G H T Y E I G H T ■ W H O
G R E E D I S G O O D ■ S A P
A T O M ■ N T H ■ ■ S P O R T
T H U ■ I G E T I T ■ A C A I
E S T E R ■ T E R I ■ D U D E
■ ■ A A H ■ N O M A T T E R
■ B A T T E D ■ N O S H E S
H O U S E R E D ■ N S A ■ ■
O N T O ■ B R E W ■ A I D A N
T H O U ■ S N A R K Y ■ E G O
M O T T O ■ R E I ■ S L A P
E M U ■ W A I T A M I N U T E
S I N ■ N I G H T Y N I G H T
S E E ■ M A S H E D P E A S
```

## 38

```
A C C R A ■ R A T E ■ A S P S
T R A I L M I X E S ■ U T A H
M I D D L E S E A T ■ C E R A
S P Y ■ S L E D S ■ N O R T H
■ ■ R Y E S ■ E M O N E Y
■ A B A S E ■ G R O T T O
A C E I T ■ S E A T U R T L E
P A E S E ■ T E D ■ P A Y E R
T I R E M A R K S ■ T I P I N
■ G A S H E S ■ B O R E S ■
■ H A G G I S ■ L O S E ■
M A R L O ■ S T A I N ■ C H O
A L D A ■ F O R T S U M T E R
I V E S ■ B R U T E F O R C E
D E N S ■ I S E E ■ F O L K S
```

## 39

```
D R A G S H O W ■ B R I T O N
R I C E W I N E ■ O H N O N O
O P E N A T A B ■ W E T M O P
S I L E N T B S ■ E T H A N E
S T A T ■ H E I R ■ T E T E
■ ■ V E T T E S ■ H O H O
W H A L E D ■ E A T L O C A L
K E N O L I N ■ D R Y L A N D
R A G N A R O K ■ E M E N D S
P L O D ■ T O U P E E ■ ■
■ T R O D ■ B R U T ■ J I B S
S H A N I A ■ D E M O U N I T
A S C E N D ■ I R E A L I Z E
S P A Y E D ■ S T A T E G E M
H A T E R S ■ H O T S P O T S
```

## 40

```
M A S T ■ D E F I B ■ M O B
A R C H ■ A P I T Y ■ P A N E
D A R E ■ M A R A T H O N E R
C L A M U P ■ L E G O S E T
A S P E N ■ W A I S T H I G H
P E P S I C O L A ■ B O G S
S A Y ■ S T R O N G M A N ■
■ N O R S E M Y T H ■
■ I A M L E G E N D ■ R E I
S I N G ■ T E A T O W E L S
U N A G I R O L L ■ O H G E E
A S C E T I C ■ E M E R G E
B E A R D C O M B S ■ L O I N
L A S S ■ I M O U T ■ P U Z O
E M T ■ N E W D O ■ S P E W
```

## 41

```
A S F O R ■ R E P O ■ A L S O
S E I K O ■ A X O N ■ R E E D
I L L G O ■ M A K E A M O V E
A L L O T ■ I C E P L A N E T
■ M O B ■ S T R A I N E R S
L I E G E ■ P R A I S E ■
E V I L E M P I R E ■
G E N E R A T I O N A L P H A
■ H E I S T F I L M S
■ A P O L A R ■ I M A M S
I M O N A R O L L ■ L A T ■
B O O B O I S I E ■ I P O D S
E N P A S S A N T ■ S E N O R
A R E S ■ H U G O ■ T R I N I
M A D E ■ I R O N ■ S U C K S
```

## 42

```
B E E R B A R ■ B A T H E D
A N G E L P I E ■ A R E O L A
L O O S E E N D ■ L E A N E R
E S S I E ■ D I G S ■ L O N E
■ G D P ■ T E A S E R A D
T R A N S I C O N ■ E A R
H E R S ■ T O R T R E F O R M
A F T ■ A C M I L A N ■ L I E
D I C K C H E N E Y ■ A L P O
■ R A E ■ S C R O L L S A W
W E I R D H U H ■ N A B ■
A L T A ■ E P I C ■ T E S T S
T A I C H I ■ E A S T R O O M
E T C H E S ■ F R E E T I M E
R E S I S T ■ S A R A L E E
```

## 43

PLOTARMOR / BABAS
RIDESHARE / ALLIE
ITDEPENDS / SPURT
DEEM ABET SHELF
ERR SPUR YEAGER
WHENISIT RAE
FEAR NIP PEKE
TANGLY SPARES
WILT MEA ECON
ADS MASTHEAD
KEENON LOKI PSI
APHID GARI SECT
NOONE ANDYOUARE
DOPES STEADICAM
ALERT PASYSTEMS

## 44

KILN JAWS PTAS
INEEDANAP SLASH
DONTJUDGE TAKEI
SNOWANGEL OCEAN
ONTO TAPAS
ENERGY TOPBRASS
PANKO EURYDICE
OCD BEATS MIN
CHIMNEYS LEAFS
HONEYBEE BESTIE
TAMES PUTT
SCENE OVERRATED
TOAST REALITYTV
IDRIS ESCAPEPOD
REST STEP SONS

## 45

POPASHOT PIMPLE
EVILLOOK INARUG
GAZPACHO PEKING
ZACK PREGGO
BLACKSABBATH
TAPAS LIE GAMMA
ERAS PAGELAYOUT
AIR TIMBRES TSE
MATCHPOINT RHEA
STYLE DRU REBUS
UPPEDTHEGAME
SACBEE EVAL
IFICAN THRILLER
PETARD IBELIEVE
SWIRLS LOSEADAY

## 46

DIED INDIA SLAM
INNERPEACE CONE
DATAFORMAT ACID
DRINK DUNN RAMI
LETS TAPTAP VAN
YAY PAL EBOLA
PACESETTERS
MRWORLDWIDE
MEANSTREETS
GIMME LEE FAD
ORB DISOWN WEIR
LARA NIKE THESE
IMAC STAIRWELLS
VANE TOPSTORIES
EXES ANISE ETSY

## 47

BRIDE SPARKLER
TREMOR AUTOMAKE
HARPER IMAMAZED
AVERS FDA CRED
TELE TRI COT
HESDEADJIM BRA
EASINGOUT POOL
BASMATI RACESBY
TREE PLAYDIRTY
STD SEESREASON
VEG TIL INFO
OPEN KEG AMPED
IMAGONER ALMOND
MACARONI COOPTS
PRESSBOX EENSY

## 48

AWALKINTHEWOODS
CALLONTHECARPET
THEBACHELORETTE
GENA MIND SEA
ATLAS TAX LICK
CHAN DEN TAINTS
EOS BEEFLOIN
RUSSIANROULETTE
WARSONGS EST
IMEASY MEH LSAT
SOUP OUR BASRA
ARC WORN AIME
ATHLETICAPPAREL
CARETOELABORATE
SLEEVELESSDRESS

## 49

```
T R A S H T A L K . . S A M S A
R I D E O R D I E . . I L I E D
I C E D L A T T E . . T O N E R
X A N A D U . . P A S T I M E .
. . N O M E . S H O . . S S N .
M I C . P A P A . A N G E L A .
A W A R E . C A R S . O R E L .
R A N O N . O R A . L U I G I .
I N N S . A T O M . A T E I N .
O N E A R M . N E W S . S T E .
P A D . I M S . N O E L . . . .
A L C O P O P . O R A T E S . .
R O O T S . A D U L T S I T E .
T O R T A . S A V E A S E A T .
Y K N O W . M E A N G I R L S .
```

## 50

```
T A M P S . M L S . I N T O W
I C O U L D E A T . D I A N A
L O O K I N G U P . L A B E L
D R E A M C A R . W E L L O K
E N D S . A G E . L E N O . .
. H A M S . R E C . L O U . .
. M E T O O M O V E M E N T .
. M A L E P R I V I L E G E .
B I G L I T T L E L I E S . .
A N I . T O E . L S A T . . .
R I C A . P D A . C O S I . .
I M A G E S . G A N G U P O N
L O C A L . C A N W E T A L K
L O T T A . H I T A N E R V E
A N S E L . I N S . E S T E R
```

## 51

```
P E T S C A N . A C T S O U T
I C O U L D E A T A H O R S E
T H E M U D V I L L E N I N E
H O S T . L I D . C O N G A S
. . O R E S . J U N E . . . .
S O R T E D . S A L E T A G S
T R I A L . M A N U . L E I .
O D D L Y S A T I S F Y I N G
M E G . H I E S . R A T O N .
P R E S S O N S . S A M O A S
. . L U T E . C H U M . . . .
A T T E N D . P R E . E D A M
C A R E T O E L A B O R A T E
D R I V E W A Y M O M E N T S
C A P E A N N . S P A D A Y S
```

## 52

```
P E A K S . O R B . B R A T
I S L E O F S K Y E . A E R O
G O O G L E T R A N S L A T E
S S N . M E A N . E L L Y . .
. G N O M E . F U E L . . . .
A C T I V E L I F E S T Y L E
C H I K A . D R I E S . S E T
H O M E . A R A B S . G O T H
E K E . P L U T O . C A M E O
S E C R E T M E N U I T E M S
. O H N O . A S S E T . . . .
. A M E N . S E C T . H A I .
N O I S E C A N C E L L I N G
I N N U . D I V I N G I N T O
L E G S . S L Y . A N G E R .
```

## 53

```
S O R E B A C K . . N S F W
O M E L E T T E . E P P I E
G I V E A T R Y . M A R I S T
S T E N C I L . H A T . T A N
. S T A H L . T O K E . I C U
. H A M O P E R A T O R . . .
. T H O U . A H E M . N O U S
C R E A T U R E F E A T U R E
A I N T . S I L O . L I T T .
M A S S G E N E R A L . . . .
B L T . O R E N . D E E T S .
O R E . F I R . R O Y C O H N
D U E L E D . Z I R C O N I A
I N T E R . I D E A L I S M .
A S H E . P A S T I C H E . .
```

## 54

```
L A M P . O P T E D . B L T S
O H I O . P A R S E . R E I N
G O L D M E D A L S . O S L O
E Y E C A N D Y . C L O S E R
. . A X E L . M E E K E S T .
B E D S I D E M A N N E R . .
R O O T S . B Y R D S . E P A
I N N S . C O R K S . S V E N
E S T . G L A R E . P O I S E
. . G O W I T H T H E F L O W
E P I P E N S . P E R T . . .
D I V I N G . F R E E S P I N
I D E A . S N A I L S P A C E
T A U T . T W I C E . O P E C
H Y P E . O A R E D . T A S K
```

## 55

CARELESSMISTAKE
ANANSITHESPIDER
COMMUNIONWAFERS
HUME ERODE FLO
ETES TSAR ASP
DHARMA RAPIER
ROUTE GODNO
ACCORDS DIGDEEP
RHODE TENSE
CEREAL LAPDOG
SSN ROOM DICE
HER SATYR AVIA
SILENTTREATMENT
PRIVATEENTRANCE
FEASTONESEYESON

## 56

FRAMEUPS PRIMP
AEROSMITH DECAL
CLEOPATRA ACELA
TINNY FOR SADLY
INDY YALTA PART
SET BULLETS NAE
PULLS REACTS
ZIPTIES HOLIEST
ONEALL PAPER
OFT TOTINOS TDS
MOPS GRADS OHIO
BREAD ANY AURAL
OMEGA MOMFRIEND
MAVEN PLAINJANE
BLESS ANTEATER

## 57

SCOTUS GOSHNO
PAPYRI RAINIER
AMELIA LAILAALI
TINES BOGTURTLE
USSR CLOG PLAIN
BOW DRAPER LET
SLICEANDDICE
EMOJIKEYBOARD
WAGELABORERS
CAW STONES DEA
AGILE TODD GDAY
PAPERCOPY BRIMS
IDIGRESS GOAWAY
TINGODS NOVICE
ARGYLE CRYPTS

## 58

OVERTHEMOON DSL
CAMERAREADY CEO
TIPSONESHAT CAV
ANIONS SUM JOSE
NERD ANY ALUMNI
TRE PRO AEOLIAN
DIPSOS WICKS
AMES ILL EASE
CRYPT LEEANN
AMPLIFY ETD TSK
SCROLL SPF SHUE
THEY ALT IMPEDE
OAT AGEOFREASON
FIT BOWLASTRIKE
FRY UNDERTHESUN

## 59

MEATRUB IPADAPP
ACQUIRE NOMINEE
SOULFUL TWINGES
STALE ISH DEERE
EYRE LEPER SLAT
UPI SOFABED IGA
REALTV CAPRICES
AREWEGOOD
WHOWASIT SISTER
HAL DEFINED EVO
ADES TIMID ARIL
TASTE ZEN SCALE
INTEMPO JUKEBOX
FIREMAN ANILINE
SPAREME SEDATES

## 60

PAST DOBBS GNAW
LUTE ISLET HOSE
ATON SKATEPARKS
SULKS ASHTON
MME EFREM PABLO
ANNLEE ADE OUR
BUYERSREMORSE
PARODYACCOUNT
MUSEUMEXHIBIT
ARE SEW DISHES
GESSO HAVEL IVE
POLICE EPSON
COSANOSTRA OWLS
ODIN SKUNK RAVE
GENX TYPEA EYES

## 61

| R | E | T | R | O | C | H | I | C | ■ | ■ | G | R | I | P |
| A | L | I | E | N | R | A | C | E | ■ | B | R | I | N | E |
| W | E | E | D | E | A | T | E | R | ■ | L | A | T | H | E |
| M | C | S | ■ | S | P | R | A | T | ■ | U | S | U | A | L |
| E | T | C | H | ■ | S | E | X | ■ | R | E | S | A | L | E |
| A | R | O | A | R | ■ | D | E | M | I | ■ | S | L | E | D |
| T | O | R | R | I | D | ■ | S | A | D | A | T | ■ | ■ | ■ |
| ■ | N | E | E | D | E | D | ■ | N | O | C | A | R | B | ■ |
| ■ | ■ | B | E | R | E | T | ■ | F | R | I | A | R | S | ■ |
| B | A | R | R | ■ | B | A | H | T | ■ | E | N | R | O | L |
| I | M | E | A | S | Y | ■ | E | O | S | ■ | S | E | M | I |
| O | P | C | I | T | ■ | S | P | A | T | E | ■ | F | A | N |
| G | E | E | N | A | ■ | N | O | T | A | L | K | I | N | G |
| A | R | D | E | N | ■ | O | P | E | N | S | I | N | C | E |
| S | E | E | D | ■ | ■ | W | E | E | K | E | N | D | E | R |

## 62

| E | P | I | T | H | E | T | ■ | O | U | T | R | A | N | K |
| M | A | R | I | A | N | O | ■ | D | R | E | A | M | O | N |
| I | N | A | N | I | T | Y | ■ | S | I | N | C | E | R | E |
| ■ | E | N | G | L | I | S | H | ■ | S | A | I | N | T | E |
| ■ | ■ | ■ | S | C | O | O | T | ■ | M | A | C | H | ■ | ■ |
| R | E | P | S | ■ | E | L | T | O | N | ■ | L | O | S | T |
| E | X | I | T | S | ■ | D | E | N | C | H | ■ | R | H | O |
| T | H | E | D | E | V | I | L | Y | O | U | K | N | O | W |
| C | A | D | ■ | L | E | E | R | S | ■ | D | E | E | R | E |
| H | U | A | C | ■ | T | R | O | O | P | ■ | B | R | E | D |
| ■ | S | T | A | T | ■ | S | O | P | U | P | ■ | ■ | ■ | ■ |
| S | T | E | P | O | N | ■ | ■ | M | R | R | I | G | H | T |
| A | F | R | O | P | O | P | ■ | A | S | T | A | I | R | E |
| T | A | R | T | A | N | S | ■ | N | E | T | T | L | E | S |
| S | N | E | E | Z | E | S | ■ | O | R | I | O | L | E | S |

## 63

| K | I | C | K | B | A | L | L | ■ | S | I | T | I | N | S |
| U | S | A | T | O | D | A | Y | ■ | W | O | O | H | O | O |
| M | E | T | E | O | R | I | C | ■ | I | N | T | O | T | O |
| B | E | L | L | ■ | E | D | E | S | S | A | ■ | P | E | N |
| A | N | I | ■ | P | O | U | T | S | ■ | N | E | V | E | ■ |
| Y | O | K | O | ■ | U | M | A | ■ | B | O | Y | E | R | ■ |
| A | W | E | E | B | I | T | ■ | T | A | R | P | O | N | S |
| ■ | ■ | R | U | D | D | ■ | L | I | E | U | ■ | ■ | ■ | ■ |
| P | R | E | V | A | I | L | ■ | B | E | E | T | R | E | D |
| R | E | F | R | Y | ■ | A | F | I | ■ | S | E | G | O | ■ |
| E | L | L | E | ■ | O | M | E | G | A | ■ | H | A | M | ■ |
| L | E | E | ■ | C | H | E | E | P | S | ■ | B | A | L | I |
| O | A | X | A | C | A | ■ | L | A | P | E | L | P | I | N |
| A | S | E | V | E | R | ■ | O | P | E | N | U | P | T | O |
| D | E | S | A | D | E | ■ | K | I | N | D | E | Y | E | S |

## 64

| O | P | E | N | B | O | R | D | E | R | S | ■ | A | B | E |
| M | A | D | E | A | B | O | O | B | O | O | ■ | M | O | C |
| A | N | Y | T | H | I | N | G | B | U | T | ■ | B | I | O |
| R | E | S | ■ | A | W | A | Y | ■ | G | H | O | U | L | S |
| ■ | ■ | O | M | A | N | ■ | S | H | E | L | L | E | Y | ■ |
| N | A | T | H | A | N | ■ | M | I | S | R | E | A | D | S |
| A | M | I | S | S | ■ | R | E | T | I | E | ■ | T | O | T |
| V | E | T | O | ■ | P | U | G | E | T | ■ | M | O | V | E |
| E | L | L | ■ | P | I | N | A | S | ■ | H | A | R | E | M |
| L | I | E | G | E | M | A | N | ■ | S | A | T | Y | R | S |
| G | O | F | O | R | I | T | ■ | F | E | N | S | ■ | ■ | ■ |
| A | R | I | O | S | E | ■ | H | O | A | G | ■ | V | H | F |
| Z | A | G | ■ | I | N | T | E | R | R | A | C | I | A | L |
| E | T | H | ■ | S | T | A | R | T | E | R | H | O | M | E |
| S | E | T | ■ | T | O | S | S | E | D | S | A | L | A | D |

## 65

| B | O | S | C | H | ■ | J | A | N | E | E | Y | R | E | ■ |
| A | C | U | R | A | ■ | O | P | E | N | D | O | O | R | S |
| D | E | B | A | R | ■ | H | E | G | O | T | G | A | M | E |
| J | A | Z | Z | H | A | N | D | S | ■ | U | N | I | X | ■ |
| O | N | E | E | A | C | H | ■ | P | E | R | O | N | I | ■ |
| K | I | R | ■ | R | H | E | A | ■ | L | A | T | K | E | S |
| E | C | O | ■ | I | N | C | H | E | S | ■ | E | S | T | ■ |
| ■ | ■ | ■ | A | L | R | E | A | D | Y | ■ | ■ | ■ | ■ | ■ |
| A | H | A | ■ | F | L | Y | I | N | G | ■ | B | T | W | ■ |
| S | O | I | S | E | E | ■ | T | G | I | F | ■ | O | R | E |
| S | T | R | A | W | S | ■ | I | N | A | S | N | I | T | ■ |
| E | S | P | N | ■ | ■ | B | A | N | G | U | P | J | O | B |
| S | P | I | D | E | R | E | G | G | ■ | V | I | O | L | A |
| S | U | P | E | R | H | E | R | O | ■ | E | L | V | E | R |
| ■ | R | E | D | R | O | B | I | N | ■ | S | L | I | T | S |

## 66

| D | R | U | N | K | D | I | A | L | ■ | S | I | D | E | D |
| R | E | N | E | R | U | S | S | O | ■ | I | V | O | R | Y |
| Y | A | H | O | O | M | A | I | L | ■ | Z | E | V | O | N |
| E | M | I | ■ | C | A | B | S | ■ | P | E | S | E | T | A |
| R | O | T | S | ■ | S | E | A | B | E | D | ■ | B | I | S |
| S | U | C | K | S | ■ | L | I | E | D | ■ | T | A | C | T |
| ■ | T | H | E | E | U | ■ | D | E | A | T | H | R | A | Y |
| ■ | ■ | ■ | W | E | T | S | ■ | F | L | O | E | ■ | ■ | ■ |
| F | A | C | E | P | A | L | M | ■ | S | O | R | T | A | ■ |
| A | T | A | D | ■ | H | E | A | P | ■ | T | O | W | I | T |
| J | O | N | ■ | P | A | W | N | E | E | ■ | N | E | R | O |
| I | M | A | M | A | N | ■ | K | E | N | S | ■ | E | V | A |
| T | A | S | E | R | ■ | B | I | K | E | L | A | N | E | S |
| A | N | T | E | S | ■ | I | N | A | M | O | M | E | N | T |
| S | T | A | K | E | ■ | P | I | T | Y | P | A | R | T | Y |

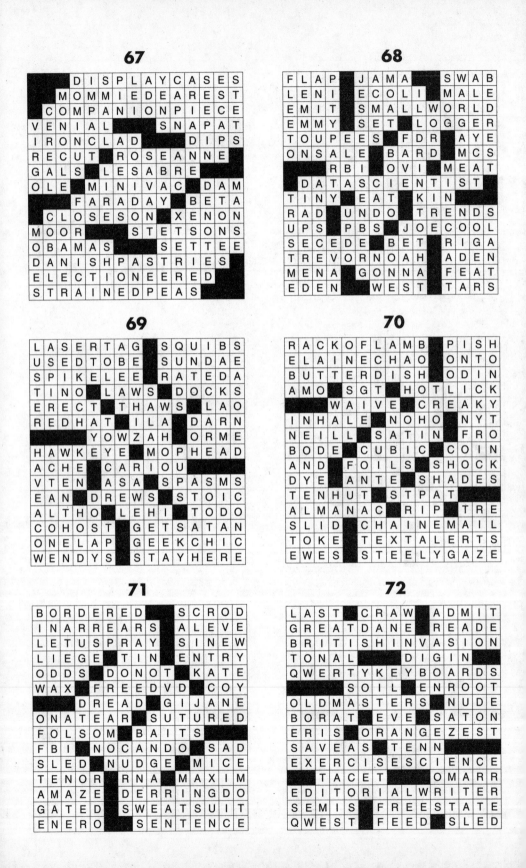

## 67

DISPLAYCASES
MOMMIEDEAREST
COMPANIONPIECE
VENIAL · SNAPAT
IRONCLAD · DIPS
RECUT · ROSEANNE
GALS · LESABRE
OLE · MINIVAC · DAM
FARADAY · BETA
CLOSESON · XENON
MOOR · STETSONS
OBAMAS · SETTEE
DANISHPASTRIES
ELECTIONEERED
STRAINEDPEAS

## 68

FLAP · JAMA · SWAB
LENI · ECOLI · MALE
EMIT · SMALLWORLD
EMMY · SET · LOGGER
TOUPEES · FDR · AYE
ONSALE · BARD · MCS
RBI · OVI · MEAT
DATASCIENTIST
TINY · EAT · KIN
RAD · UNDO · TRENDS
UPS · PBS · JOECOOL
SECEDE · BET · RIGA
TREVORNOAH · ADEN
MENA · GONNA · FEAT
EDEN · WEST · TARS

## 69

LASERTAG · SQUIBS
USEDTOBE · SUNDAE
SPIKELEE · RATEDA
TINO · LAWS · DOCKS
ERECT · THAWS · LAO
REDHAT · ILA · DARN
YOWZAH · ORME
HAWKEYE · MOPHEAD
ACHE · CARIOU
VTEN · ASA · SPASMS
EAN · DREWS · STOIC
ALTHO · LEHI · TODO
COHOST · GETSATAN
ONELAP · GEEKCHIC
WENDYS · STAYHERE

## 70

RACKOFLAMB · PISH
ELAINECHAO · ONTO
BUTTERDISH · ODIN
AMO · SGT · HOTLICK
WAIVE · CREAKY
INHALE · NOHO · NYT
NEILL · SATIN · FRO
BODE · CUBIC · COIN
AND · FOILS · SHOCK
DYE · ANTE · SHADES
TENHUT · STPAT
ALMANAC · RIP · TRE
SLID · CHAINEMAIL
TOKE · TEXTALERTS
EWES · STEELYGAZE

## 71

BORDERED · SCROD
INARREARS · ALEVE
LETUSPRAY · SINEW
LIEGE · TIN · ENTRY
ODDS · DONOT · KATE
WAX · FREEDVD · COY
DREAD · GIJANE
ONATEAR · SUTURED
FOLSOM · BAITS
FBI · NOCANDO · SAD
SLED · NUDGE · MICE
TENOR · RNA · MAXIM
AMAZE · DERRINGDO
GATED · SWEATSUIT
ENERO · SENTENCE

## 72

LAST · CRAW · ADMIT
GREATDANE · READE
BRITISHINVASION
TONAL · DIGIN
QWERTYKEYBOARDS
SOIL · ENROOT
OLDMASTERS · NUDE
BORAT · EVE · SATON
ERIS · ORANGEZEST
SAVEAS · TENN
EXERCISESCIENCE
TACET · OMARR
EDITORIALWRITER
SEMIS · FREESTATE
QWEST · FEED · SLED

## 73

```
S W I P E L E F T ■ ■ S C R A P
A R M A D I L L O ■ A R E N A ■
T O M R I P L E Y ■ H A D N T ■
A T E I T ■ E X C A L I B U R ■
N E R T S ■ R I A L ■ S O L O ■
I T S Y ■ A B O R I G I N A L ■
C O E ■ B I E N ■ M I N E R S ■
■ ■ C A R E ■ L O S S ■ ■ ■ ■ ■
S C O R N S ■ B E N T ■ A P R ■
C A P E C O D B A Y ■ C L U E ■
A P E D ■ F A Q S ■ C A M P S ■
M I N I A T U R E ■ O R A T E ■
M S N B C ■ B I O B U R D E N ■
E C O L E ■ E B U L L I E N T ■
D E W E D ■ D S T U D E N T S ■
```

## 74

```
W E B ■ A B A S E S ■ ■ R O B
A L E ■ M E D U S A ■ D E V O
M A R R I E D M A N ■ E D E N
P I N O T ■ M U D ■ C A R E
U N I C Y C L E ■ S A I L E D
M E E K ■ H E R R ■ S M E A R
■ ■ M A D T E A P A R T Y ■ ■
A S T E R O I D B E L T S ■ ■
Q U E E N O F M E A N ■ ■ ■ ■
A T L A S ■ F E A T ■ H O S T
T O E C A P ■ B L E W I N T O
A R C H ■ E E L ■ ■ A V E R Y
R A T E ■ S A U S A G E D O G
I C E S ■ C R E O L E ■ A B U
S E E ■ ■ I N S T I R ■ Y E N
```

## 75

```
S G T S ■ T R E V I ■ S T U B
P I A F ■ H E R O N ■ A R T I
A N Y O N E L I S T E N I N G
Y U L ■ E P E E ■ H E A P E D
S P O R C L E ■ L E G A L ■ ■
■ ■ R I C O ■ P E C S ■ E P I
I T S N O T F A I R ■ A W O L
H A C K ■ T A N G O ■ L O O S
O C H S ■ H I G H S I E R R A
P H I ■ N I T S ■ S P U D ■ ■
■ ■ L E A C H ■ T H A T S I T
I N L U C K ■ S E A S ■ C S I
S H I R L E Y C H I S H O L M
A R N O ■ N E U E R ■ A R I E
T A G S ■ S A T E S ■ R E P S
```

## 76

```
S E T O F P I P E S ■ L E H I
I T A L I A N I C E ■ A C A N
C O P E R N I C U S ■ B O B S
K I P ■ S I G N ■ S E E N A T
O L E O ■ C O I T ■ N O O N E
S E R I F ■ C O S T U M E R
■ ■ D U M P S T E R F I R E
S T E ■ T O R ■ E E E ■ C O O
V I T R U V I A N M A N ■ ■ ■
E T H E R E A L ■ T I D E S
T R I B E ■ M A L L ■ L O T T
L A C A S A ■ R O U T ■ L E A
A T I T ■ G A M E T H E O R Y
N O S E ■ A R E W E A L O N E
A R T S ■ S I D E S W I P E D
```

## 77

```
■ ■ A L T P O P ■ B L O K E ■
■ G L O R I A S T E I N E M ■
■ W H I T E P R I V I L E G E
W O O K I E E S ■ S N O T S ■
E L S E ■ ■ M O E S ■ O T T ■
E F T ■ S A V A N T ■ S O A R ■
■ ■ S H R I N E ■ M A N N A ■
H O T T A K E ■ D R A M E D Y ■
A P H I D ■ F I G U R E ■ ■ ■
J E E R ■ H O M E E C ■ S A D ■
I N N ■ P A R S ■ ■ S P R Y ■
■ W E I R D ■ O L D F L A M E ■
V I R T U A L R E A L I T Y ■
A D V E N T U R E T I M E ■ ■
S E E M E ■ G Y R A T E ■ ■ ■
```

## 78

```
H A H A ■ R A M P S ■ G A M E
E T A S ■ A T A R I ■ A M I S
L T R S ■ M A D E T O L A S T
L E D ■ S I L L Y ■ V I T A E
O N T H E S L Y ■ J U L E P S
■ D O I N ■ ■ C O M E U P ■
B A S E S A L A R Y ■ E R R S
A N T ■ E M P T Y ■ ■ F O R ■
M C A L L I S T E R ■ S O P S
■ E R I E ■ ■ R A P T O R ■
A S B E S T O S ■ P A R T I I
S H O ■ S A P P Y ■ L A B A N
K E A N ■ T R I O S O N A T A
M E R E ■ A A N D P ■ G L E N
E T D S ■ S H E A F ■ E L S E
```

## 79

```
SAMEDAY   ECSEGAR
EXANIMO   COURAGE
ALDORAY   LUCIFER
CRATE  OZARK  FLA
ROME  IDEST  QEII
ASE  TRIBS  TURNS
BESTEVER  SOISEE
  WHATAJOKE
DARIEN  FINETUNE
USONE  DIVAN  PAM
OUSE  MISER  HAZE
TSE  NIGHT  PANIN
OUTTAKE  AWARDED
NATIVES  LECTURE
ELITIST  KNEEPAD
```

## 80

```
ASTERISKS  BULBS
CLIPONTIE  ATEIT
RELAYRACE  BUGGY
EEL  ASKSFORIT
SKYHIGH  BONSAI
  USS  TRON  LLC
PLEBS  SWAM  SAKE
HEYBATTERBATTER
IVEY  WARE  VEERS
AIS  PERK  DIE
LATHER  PEANUTS
 TRIPPEDUP  NHL
THATS  TAPEDELAY
RAIMI  CRINOLINE
INNES  HELDWATER
```

## 81

```
LIFEOFPABLO  PAN
ICECREAMBAR  ERA
BATTERYACID  TIN
 NCO  ACT  DELUGE
ASH  CLUE  ARENOT
SEEPY  TURN  GILT
PESACH  ROEVWADE
 CLIP  OGLE
JACKEDUP  GOALIE
UBER  ENID  GRANT
MONACO  ZEDS  YEA
BUTTON  AVA  BOX
LTR  HORRORMOVIE
EMU  AMERICANELM
DEM  NOBODYCARES
```

## 82

```
EPICPOEM  BROWSE
DEMOTAPE  SHREWS
KEPTATIT  CYCLIC
ODETS  SHU  SALMA
CENA  BOOZE  SIMP
HED  PUDDING  NEA
  SIZES  QUOTED
JACUZZI  QUIXOTE
ALONZO  GUIDO
NAV  AFFAIRE  BFF
IKEA  FUZZY  WYLE
TAROS  REB  CAGES
OZARKS  TOMATOES
RAGTOP  TWOPENCE
SMEARY  ELMTREES
```

## 83

```
MICHIGAN  SWARM  HDTV
NOLA  LANAI  AIRE
GUESSAGAIN  VSIX
 SAUTE  MOLES
PRIZE  EERINESS
ACAI  THINMINT  NONOS
WAS  SONG  SETTLE
 GINORMOUS
SPRUNG  AARP  PSA
MEANT  CONTRARY  SIKH
UNSNARLS  ATTYS
 HEXAD  BLURB
SPED  TWOBYFOURS
TORI  EARLE  PLEA
PEST  DRESS  HELSINKI
```

## 84

```
BLUFFS  BUYERS
RANOUT  POTOMAC
ARMORY  HEREWEGO
CRADLESONGS  ROT
HUD  TUNE  TAUT
SPEAKEASY  BELTS
 SIXYEAROLDS
 FIRESCREENS
 MEDICALCARE
BADEN  TEAMSTERS
ERAS  SHAD  NOW
AMY  STONECIRCLE
TIEBEAMS  ORIOLE
ITERATE  BADREP
TENORS  SNEERS
```

## 85

```
A N T I G O N E . . W A T T .
H O U S E P E T . . D O N E E
E T C E T E R A Q U O T A S .
M A K E S D O D U E L I S T .
. R E N D . S W A T C H E S .
. . R O O T B E E R . A E R I
. . W W I I V E T . P R A T .
C O T . N E T I Z E N . O D E
A N I L . S P L I T U P . . .
N E M O C A L L S F O R . . .
T H E O D O R E . F O E S . .
F O L K A R T . C A S H B O X
A R E O L E R O B A B A N K .
I S S U E . A D R I A T I C .
L E S T . D E A D H E A D . .
```

## 86

```
P O T R O A S T . . . S C A T
A B O U T T H A T . S O A V E
T O U G H L O V E . P U T I N
H E R . E A T E R . A N N A S
. . . S R S . R A I N D A T E
B O O T H . N B C . A P E D .
B A D R A P S . Y E A S . . .
S T E A L I N . T A L L O N E
. . . I F S O . E X P E D I A
S W A T . A W L . . H E D E R
P A R L A N C E . T A P . . .
A R I A S . R E H E M . C E S
S H O C K . A R E N A R O C K
M O S E S . B A L A L A I K A
S L E D . . T I M E S L O T .
```

## 87

```
S T A T . O R A L B . L C D S
O A T H . M E T A L . B L O T
C H E E S E C A K E . J A G R
K I M M E L . D E A F . S P A
S T P E T E R . K A N S A N .
. I O C . T O T O . B O A R D
. . H I T T H E B R I C K S .
. S P A C E T O U R I S T S .
P H O N E S E R V I C E . . .
I O N I C . N O R M . M U D .
T O Y C A R . E S I A S O N .
F A T . P A W S . T A K E T O
A W A G . T H E J O N E S E S
L A I R . T O X I N . R U D E
L Y L E . Y A Y M E . S P U D
```

## 88

```
T A T T L E . F L A S H E R S
O N E M A N . A I R W O M A N
T A X C U T . N A G A S A K I
E P A . D E S T R O Y . J E T
B O S S . R I A L S . L O I S
A L B U M . C S I . M O R N .
G I B L E T . Y A Z O O . . .
. S Q U A R E B R A C K E T .
. . . S T U P A . C H O R A L
. F I E S . I S O . A U D I O
R I M A . A D E P T . T O L L
E G O . D O U B T I T . C G I
C A N B E R R A . L E S T A T
O R I E N T A L . L A K O T A
N O T A T A L L . S T A R E S
```

## 89

```
F O O D C O M A . F A T L I P
A N D I M O U T . E R O I C A
R E D V I N E S . D I A N A S
C A L E . A L T E . E D E N S
E L Y S E . L U G S . S R T A
. . . D R E D G E D . N E T .
W A R R I O R . O N E L O V E
A L E A S T . . S A U T E S .
T O P D O G S . P E R C E N T
E N A . N U M B E S T . . . .
R E Y S . T U R N . O T T E R
S T A L E . T I N O . A R L O
K I B O S H . B A B Y M A M A
I M L A T E . E M O T I C O N
S E E N A S . S E E D L E S S
```

## 90

```
B L A C K F R I D A Y . T A B
T I T A N I U M O R E . A S U
W A I T I N G A R E A . K H Z
O R T . T A S M A N . G E E Z
. . . M S G . G A T O S . . .
A G R A . L A S . S U B L E T
T R A N S E P T S . R E E S E
B E D A N D B R E A K F A S T
A B A S E . S I G N S O V E R
T E R S E R . P O T . R E N A
. . B A R E R . I C E . . . .
P A L S . S A W Y E R . H A G
A M I . W I N E S T E W A R D
I M P . A N D R E A D O R I A
D O S . C Y B E R M O N D A Y
```

## 91

PIRATESHIP · IDOL
SHORELEAVE · BOHO
HOMEMOVIES · SYST
APPS · ERRONEOUS
WES · ZINC · ONUS
FATSUITS · MAP
ACTING · TREELINE
CHEEZIT · ARGONNE
MISFIRES · SANDAL
ELL · BLACKEYE
LAMA · OARS · HOP
MACARTHUR · MISO
AXON · OUTERBANKS
NEIL · GREENALGAE
IDLY · OLDMASTERS

## 92

GREASY · AFRICANS
LAURIE · RAILEDAT
ANGORA · ALLINDIA
CHEMIST · LEASERS
IONA · TAPE · DODOS
AMISS · BEND · ROBE
LEE · ISON · OPENIN
UNIONIZED
LERNER · ACES · PCS
AXES · EINE · TAROT
CASES · STUB · DEVO
EMPTIES · PLUMBER
DIETDRUG · OPIATE
UNCLELEO · TURKEY
PETEBEST · SPEEDS

## 93

YALE · USPASSPORT
ODIE · TEAMLEADER
GROG · MARIAELENA
AINTNOBODY · TOI
MAKEASALE · LATIN
ANISETTE · FIXERS
TINT · TVWIFE
SIG · FOLIAGE · MAS
METEOR · WART
CREEDS · LAQUINTA
HEELS · SATURNISM
ANY · BATHINGCAP
STOPMOTION · MULE
MARIOCUOMO · AROD
SLEEPAPNEA · NENE

## 94

JAGS · ADM · PASTOR
AGRA · REA · ADHERE
PIED · INKSTAINED
ALA · SATIE · METOO
NET · ELENI · ASH
BOA · GNP · OIL
AMASSEDAFORTUNE
HURRICANESEASON
AFRICANELEPHANT
STICKSANDSTONES
HIE · HIT · IED
RPM · DRAWL · YEP
PAREE · EAPOE · EGO
LEEKRASNER · JARS
AREOLA · CAD · ORES
NOFEES · ERY · ESTE

## 95

ACROBATS · TIFFS
FRENEMIES · ELLIE
FAMILYGUY · LIANE
ENACT · HRS · LAMAS
CINE · STACK · DELT
TAD · KOWTOWS · WBA
TUBAS · AUPAIR
SLIMMED · INNARDS
KITCAR · ANZIO
IVS · RUFFIAN · BUM
LEAN · PARTA · RAMA
LASIK · GOI · CARPS
SLICE · IPADMINIS
EIGHT · NOTSOSURE
TENET · PETNAMES

## 96

FOGS · SCAT · ATALL
INRI · POOH · MOXIE
TEACHABLEMOMENT
SPYKIDS · BAUBLES
EMOTE · CERN
BRASI · CHESTHAIR
ACT · THOUGH · ANNA
SETS · AGREE · HGTV
KNEE · NICEST · LEE
STRENGTHS · ODORS
ODAY · PREPS
INKBLOT · QUICHES
BIOLOGICALCLOCK
IGLOO · NEIL · ANTI
SHACK · GODS · WEST

## 97

| M O C K E R Y | | N E W I D E A |
| A M R A D I O | | O N E T E R M |
| R E A L I G N | | T I N A F E Y |

MOCKERY · NEWIDEA · AMRADIO · ONETERM · REALIGN · TINAFEY · INWITH · PEDDLE · ASL · TEAS · AWE · CLAMP · ALSTON · CHANCEMEETING · AHUNGERARTIST · PLATELETCOUNT · TALESE · HESSE · ASK · FIDO · DOC · URCHIN · LAMOUR · ASPIRES · ECLIPSE · BITPART · TABLETS · AMOEBAS · ANALYST

## 98

HOTWARS · LECTURE · INORBIT · EXURBIA · DEMILLE · SPLEENS · TEENJEOPARDY · RASH · DOE · RAS · ARCED · SLAT · OAHU · PERSON · LITANIES · CTA · JUDOMAT · RIA · DOWJONES · XANADU · SOLI · CAHN · DUCES · GAH · OOH · LENA · FLAGRANTFOUL · RUGLIKE · ARTSALE · EPHESUS · ISEENOW · DEADEST · REPTILE

## 99

FLASHMOB · DEBTS · ELIHUYALE · ASAHI · ACROBATIC · HELEN · SOFAS · THUS · DHL · TOAT · BOZOS · CRUE · SLR · CUBE · AVAILS · JEDIMINDTRICKS · ETAT · POOR · UNIVERSALDONOR · PELOSI · GUAM · LEG · SOON · DAISY · DYER · IDS · OEIL · GIMLI · LATCH · DIAPERPIN · ODIUM · STREAKING · NATTY · YEARSAGO

## 100

PETUNIAPIG · ASAP · SHAKENBAKE · GILL · SUPERDUPER · ECTO · TDS · VETS · INKEY · SOBS · SSTARS · SPROUT · PIANOS · POOFS · DICKTRACY · ALOT · VEXES · ADOS · NETPROFIT · INONE · AROUSE · JIGGER · AGREES · DANE · COOTS · JAMS · TAG · CRUZ · ABOVEITALL · RENE · ROTISSERIE · ADDL · POSTITNOTE

## 101

ANTE · SUMAC · STAT · LOUISPRIMA · OHIO · FUELTANKER · PERK · ATSEA · SENDS · OWE · LUDENS · ICEMAN · FRAN · TWEENAGERS · ANY · NAILSALONS · JOBTITLES · CHARACTERS · YUL · BEINGTHERE · FETE · SCREAM · DEISTS · HIE · YAPAT · ASHES · ALDA · TALIASHIRE · RIOT · EVENSTEVEN · PANE · RECAP · RADS

## 102

WHATSTHAT · HOURS · RICEARONI · INSET · ESTATETAX · LEONA · STEM · NAG · ALSTON · TOD · STIRFRY · OIL · ERICA · RARE · SURE · DYNAST · MANPURSE · SHED · GOOP · BIGEATER · TEEHEE · ALLY · REED · TRAPS · DOE · BARBETS · DIS · EVADES · IMO · RATE · GENOA · BRINGITON · GLENS · ITSGOTIME · SADAT · THESTATES

## 103

```
W A T E R T I G H T ■ I M A X
A Z A L E A T R E E ■ M E G A
S U P E R S T O R E ■ D T E N
P R E V U E ■ A R T B O A R D
■ ■ ■ A N S O N ■ H E N L E Y
■ J O T S ■ D E W ■ T E S L A
I O N E ■ M E R I N O ■ T A X
N E E D L E S ■ S E N S A T E
T M I ■ E N S U E D ■ A M E S
H O N D O ■ A P T ■ N Y P D
I N F A N T ■ T O D A Y ■
S T O N E A G E ■ I M E L D A
W A R T ■ R U M B L E S E A T
A N T E ■ N A P O L I T A N O
Y A Y S ■ S M O K Y T O P A Z
```

## 104

```
P I N T E R E S T ■ M E C C A
I N A T R A N C E ■ V A L O R
S U P E R F O O D ■ P R O N G
A R E S ■ A U N T S ■ E S T O
N E S T ■ N E A T I D E A ■
■ ■ ■ T H C ■ L O D ■ V I A
H A T T R E E ■ K O I P O N D
O N E S E T ■ ■ G O A T E E
S T E A M E D ■ B E T H E R E
T I N ■ O R R ■ A S S ■
■ T A P R O O M S ■ S T Y E
R O N A ■ S P A S M ■ L I A R
E X G O V ■ C L E O P A T R A
L I S L E ■ A T T A C K A D S
O N T O E ■ P A S T T E N S E
```

## 105

```
K A R A O K E B A R ■ G L O M
I B E L I E V E S O ■ R E Z A
D R U M S T I C K S ■ A T O R
D A N A ■ T A L ■ S I T I N S
O M E N S ■ N O G ■ D E T E R
■ ■ ■ A H I ■ U R S A ■ S H O
S P A C E C A D E T ■ N O V
W I N S B I G ■ B A T P O L E
E A N ■ E I S E N H O W E R
E N O ■ A R N O ■ S U R ■
T O T E S ■ G M C ■ S T R A P
S W A T H E ■ I H S ■ R O T O
P I T H ■ S I N E Q U A N O N
O R E O ■ C R E A M S I C L E
T E S S ■ S E X P I S T O L S
```

## 106

```
■ F R I S B E E ■ S T I C K S
B R A S T R A P ■ T U L A N E
G O T L O O S E ■ P R E R E Q
A L I E N A T E ■ A N D R E ■
M I N T E D ■ B U S ■ A C E
E C G ■ W H E E L ■ A D A Y
■ ■ G R A I L S ■ A P I P E
T H I R T Y T W O A C R O S S
H E M I S ■ M E R I T S ■ ■
E R I N ■ L A S E R ■ I M S
O H S ■ J A N ■ D A T S U N
■ O S C A R ■ B O R N I N T O
A N Y O N E ■ R I O T G E A R
R O O K E D ■ A S P I R A N T
T R U E T O ■ D E S S E R T ■
```

## 107

```
T A B S ■ C H A T S ■ R Y E S
E R L E ■ H O R A E ■ F E T A
A C U T E A N G L E ■ D A H L
P A R T Y F O U L ■ ■ R E B
O N T H E F R I T Z ■ E Z R A
T A S E S ■ N E E ■ T E N N
■ ■ S O C ■ G E T B O R E D
Z O O C R E W ■ S A Y N O T O
U N P E E L E D ■ S A C ■
G L E N ■ E R E ■ N O B I S
Z O N E ■ B E N E V O L E N T
W O W ■ H O M E S L I C E
A K I N ■ P E T E S E E G E R
N E D S ■ A R E N T ■ G E N E
G R E W ■ H E D D A ■ E S T O
```

## 108

```
G A Z I L L I O N ■ S P E C S
O M I N O U S L Y ■ E R G O T
U P T O G R A D E ■ A I O L I
R E C ■ S K I P ■ T U G S O N
D R O P ■ S A R D I ■ S U N K
S E M I S ■ H O O P S ■ R E E
■ ■ T I S ■ S U P E R F L Y
B A Y O N E T ■ P E L I S S E
I R O N G R I P ■ D I V ■
G T S ■ E V E R T ■ G A S U P
W H E W ■ O D O R S ■ L E N O
H O M I E S ■ F O I E ■ A R P
O U I D A ■ J U M P S S H I P
O S T E R ■ U S P O S T A G E
P E E R S ■ T E E N A N G S T
```

## 109

| S | P | I | F | F | E | D | U | P | ■ | W | O | O | D | S |
| P | H | N | O | M | P | E | N | H | ■ | I | N | P | U | T |
| A | L | E | X | R | O | C | C | O | ■ | G | E | T | M | E |
| R | E | X | ■ | I | C | E | I | N | ■ | G | L | I | D | E |
| E | V | I | L | ■ | H | I | V | E | ■ | L | E | M | U | R |
| M | E | L | O | N | ■ | T | I | T | L | E | G | A | M | E |
| E | L | E | V | E | N | ■ | L | A | I | R | ■ | L | S | D |
| ■ | ■ | E | X | E | C | ■ | G | L | O | M | ■ | ■ | ■ | ■ |
| D | I | M | ■ | T | A | R | T | ■ | T | O | E | J | A | M |
| O | N | A | S | T | R | E | A | K | ■ | M | O | O | L | A |
| G | E | C | K | O | ■ | P | R | O | B | ■ | W | Y | L | E |
| C | R | U | E | L | ■ | E | T | H | E | L | ■ | R | O | W |
| A | T | S | E | A | ■ | P | A | L | M | O | L | I | V | E |
| R | I | E | L | S | ■ | A | R | E | A | C | O | D | E | S |
| T | A | R | O | T | ■ | N | E | R | D | A | L | E | R | T |

## 110

| C | O | P | E | ■ | T | E | S | T | ■ | O | T | H | E | R |
| A | C | A | P | P | E | L | L | A | ■ | P | H | O | N | O |
| C | E | R | E | A | L | B | O | X | ■ | H | E | I | G | L |
| T | A | K | E | S | N | O | T | E | ■ | E | P | P | I | E |
| I | N | A | S | T | E | W | ■ | S | A | L | O | O | N | ■ |
| ■ | ■ | ■ | A | T | R | A | ■ | B | I | L | L | E | D | ■ |
| A | C | H | E | S | ■ | O | L | D | B | A | I | L | E | Y |
| S | O | O | N | ■ | F | O | L | E | Y | ■ | C | O | R | E |
| K | I | N | G | J | A | M | E | S | ■ | W | E | I | S | S |
| S | N | O | R | E | D | ■ | N | E | R | O | ■ | ■ | ■ | ■ |
| ■ | P | R | A | T | E | S | ■ | C | O | R | N | O | I | L |
| S | U | R | F | S | ■ | O | N | R | E | S | E | R | V | E |
| W | R | O | T | E | ■ | D | I | A | P | E | R | B | A | G |
| I | S | L | E | T | ■ | A | T | T | E | N | D | I | N | G |
| M | E | L | D | S | ■ | S | E | E | R | ■ | S | T | A | Y |

## 111

| B | I | L | B | O | ■ | P | L | U | G | ■ | T | W | I | G |
| A | M | O | U | R | ■ | L | I | S | A | ■ | O | H | M | Y |
| S | P | A | C | E | C | A | D | E | T | ■ | R | A | S | P |
| I | A | N | ■ | S | A | Y | ■ | D | O | R | I | T | O | S |
| C | R | E | D | ■ | V | E | L | C | R | O | ■ | A | M | U |
| S | T | R | U | T | ■ | R | E | A | ■ | M | A | D | A | M |
| ■ | ■ | C | A | E | S | A | R | S | A | L | A | D | ■ | ■ |
| ■ | ■ | F | A | R | M | E | R | S | O | N | L | Y | ■ | ■ |
| ■ | ■ | N | O | T | G | O | N | N | A | L | I | E | ■ | ■ |
| L | O | U | S | E | ■ | T | E | L | ■ | A | G | A | T | E |
| A | T | L | ■ | T | U | R | R | E | T | ■ | E | V | E | N |
| M | E | L | I | S | S | A | ■ | S | O | B | ■ | I | A | M |
| E | P | I | C | ■ | E | N | A | M | E | L | W | A | R | E |
| S | A | N | E | ■ | U | C | L | A | ■ | T | I | T | U | S |
| A | D | E | S | ■ | P | E | E | N | ■ | S | T | E | P | H |

## 112

| S | H | O | C | K | J | O | C | K | ■ | ■ | I | B | A | R |
| W | O | M | A | N | I | Z | I | N | G | ■ | N | O | N | O |
| I | N | A | N | I | M | A | T | E | O | B | J | E | C | T |
| N | O | H | I | T | ■ | W | A | X | P | O | E | T | I | C |
| G | R | A | S | ■ | N | A | B | ■ | R | O | C | H | E | ■ |
| S | E | N | T | T | O | ■ | L | O | O | ■ | T | I | N | T |
| ■ | ■ | ■ | E | L | I | D | E | S | ■ | ■ | U | T | E | ■ |
| A | F | A | R | C | R | Y | ■ | L | A | R | U | S | S | A |
| I | O | U | ■ | A | R | O | M | A | S | ■ | ■ | ■ | ■ | ■ |
| M | A | T | S | ■ | G | N | U | ■ | E | M | B | O | S | S |
| ■ | M | O | T | O | R | ■ | S | T | S | ■ | P | L | O | P |
| O | C | T | O | P | U | S | S | Y | ■ | V | O | I | L | A |
| Y | O | U | V | E | B | E | E | N | S | E | R | V | E | D |
| E | R | N | E | ■ | S | C | R | E | E | N | T | I | M | E |
| Z | E | E | S | ■ | S | T | R | E | I | S | A | N | D | ■ |

## 113

| S | T | A | R | M | A | P | ■ | S | L | I | P | P | E | R |
| O | R | L | E | A | N | S | ■ | C | O | R | D | I | T | E |
| M | A | L | A | L | A | Y | O | U | S | A | F | Z | A | I |
| E | L | K | ■ | T | I | C | K | L | E | S | ■ | Z | I | N |
| H | A | I | L | ■ | S | H | I | P | S | ■ | C | A | L | S |
| O | L | D | A | S | ■ | O | N | T | ■ | T | O | M | E | I |
| W | A | D | D | E | D | ■ | G | O | S | H | D | A | R | N |
| ■ | ■ | I | D | E | E | S | ■ | R | A | R | E | R | ■ | ■ |
| P | I | N | E | D | F | O | R | ■ | P | U | R | G | E | D |
| A | N | G | R | Y | ■ | L | E | M | ■ | M | E | H | T | A |
| E | S | A | S | ■ | T | O | T | E | M | ■ | D | E | E | M |
| L | T | S | ■ | S | E | M | I | N | A | R | ■ | R | R | S |
| L | A | I | D | I | T | O | N | T | H | E | L | I | N | E |
| A | N | D | I | R | O | N | ■ | O | R | B | I | T | A | L |
| S | T | E | P | I | N | S | ■ | R | E | S | E | A | L | S |

## 114

| S | C | R | A | T | C | H | ■ | ■ | T | W | O | C | A | R |
| A | L | A | B | A | M | A | ■ | B | A | R | N | O | N | E |
| T | O | N | E | L | O | C | ■ | O | R | I | E | N | T | S |
| Y | T | D | ■ | I | N | K | B | L | O | T | ■ | V | E | E |
| R | H | O | D | A | ■ | A | A | A | S | ■ | S | E | A | T |
| S | E | M | I | ■ | O | T | B | ■ | H | U | R | T | S | ■ |
| ■ | ■ | ■ | V | I | C | H | Y | S | S | O | I | S | E | ■ |
| ■ | G | H | E | T | T | O | B | L | A | S | T | E | R | ■ |
| ■ | L | E | B | R | O | N | J | A | M | E | S | ■ | ■ | ■ |
| F | O | R | A | Y | ■ | O | M | S | ■ | M | A | S | K | ■ |
| U | B | E | R | ■ | P | E | R | P | ■ | L | E | T | H | E |
| T | U | G | ■ | B | A | G | N | O | L | D | ■ | T | O | N |
| I | L | O | V | E | L | A | ■ | E | S | O | T | E | R | Y |
| L | I | E | A | B | E | D | ■ | T | A | P | I | N | T | O |
| E | N | S | L | E | R | ■ | S | T | A | N | D | I | N | ■ |

## 115

```
BIGSPOON ■ HAHAHA
ORATORIO ■ OLIVES
LOGROLLS ■ TINIES
ONREPORT ■ DADADA
TOES ■ PIANOS ■ TIN
IREST ■ GROG ■ GONG
EELERS ■ STGEORGE
■ AEON ■ HERO ■
BATTERUP ■ RIDGED
MRES ■ CLAM ■ CRETE
XIA ■ CELIAC ■ ESOS
BARCAR ■ DRAMATIC
INGAME ■ FIRESALE
KNAVES ■ ONETOTEN
EASELS ■ RATSNEST
```

## 116

```
JEDIMASTER ■ SPAM
ALOHASTATE ■ NONE
MIRACLEMAX ■ ALAN
EXIT ■ APPS ■ PACS
SITE ■ NSA ■ INAROW
■ ROIL ■ ACETONE
■ TOYBOXES ■ IDA
ASH ■ GOALIES ■ DAR
UTA ■ JURASSIC ■
DENMARK ■ EARL
IMGAME ■ SMU ■ SEES
EWOK ■ OTOS ■ EVAN
NAVE ■ CHORUSLINE
CRED ■ DOMEAFAVOR
EERO ■ SHALLOWEND
```

## 117

```
SCRAPS ■ STRAWMAN
MOOLAH ■ THEPIANO
IMWAYAHEADOFYOU
TOSSACOIN ■ PIONS
■ SKUNK ■
DECRY ■ REG ■ ROMAS
IGLOOS ■ ROBOCALL
EGOSURF ■ DETENTE
GONEGIRL ■ TILTED
ONENO ■ EEL ■ SOARS
■ EMIRS ■
SHOWS ■ MOVIEFONE
LIMOUSINEDRIVER
OVERLOUD ■ EILEEN
GENDARME ■ SEENTO
```

## 118

```
INS ■ RIBS ■ DICEY
DOTHEMATH ■ ADORE
IFEELFREE ■ FILES
DAIRY ■ GEM ■ TODAY
SINE ■ GARI ■ TODO
ORS ■ ARI ■ NYU ■ PEU
■ TRANSGENDER ■
■ AINTIAWOMAN ■
■ DOMAINNAMES ■
LOL ■ ZAG ■ YET ■ GIG
AGRA ■ COEN ■ MONO
SPASM ■ HRS ■ BANJO
HADTO ■ INQUIREOF
ERIES ■ POUNDCAKE
SKORT ■ TEES ■ RED
```

## 119

```
TVDRAMA ■ SCRAWLS
HIRÉDON ■ THESOUP
ATACOST ■ RATHOLE
TAGORE ■ RONDELLE
SMORE ■ MUNG ■ SLED
HIND ■ CONGER ■ YDS
ONES ■ ADSPEAK ■
WATERMELONSEEDS
■ TABLOID ■ EXIT
AMO ■ MORONS ■ PAGE
MORE ■ DOST ■ DAMUP
PRACTICE ■ MRPINK
UNCLOAK ■ YOUANDI
LALANNE ■ INBREED
EYETEST ■ POSTERS
```

## 120

```
MEASURINGSTICKS
IAPPRECIATETHAT
STRAITOFMESSINA
HOOTS ■ STEAL ■ LEX
ANN ■ SAY ■ MADD
■ NAE ■ OBI
TOTALITARIANISM
ICOULDEATAHORSE
PURSUETHEMATTER
SLEEPLESSNIGHTS
■ ITA ■ ORO ■
■ OMAN ■ TET ■ ASS
APB ■ WOMEN ■ PILOT
LAIDITONTHELINE
INTERESTRATECAP
TESTEDTHEWATERS
```

## 121

```
M C G I L L   M I C K E Y D S
A I R S E A   I N A N D O U T
I M A M A N   S U R E S U R E
M A V E N   B S I D E   R A N
  R I N S E O U T   P E N T
E R T E   N O S   V E L D T
C O Y   L I Z A   I D E A
O N S T A G E   B O G A R T S
  R O O M   D A L Y   N E T
  B A L S A   R N A   E T S Y
S A I L   G U E S S N O T
P U N   P O E M S   T R O T S
E B B T I D E S   B O O T U P
C L O S E O N E   I M B I B E
S E W E R R A T   O P E N E D
```

## 122

```
  S A M O A N   A R M P I T
W H O A W H O A   D I V I D E
H A R D S E L L   R E P A I D
O N T   M O L T E N   N O T
L I A M   S H I P   B O L A
L A S E R B E A M   R E B E L
  R I O   L I F E H A C K
  L O R D V O L D E M O R T
L E F I G A R O   N I L
E M C E E   I W O N T D O I T
N O O R   L O S T   S Y N E
G N U   M I N E T A   S T E
T O R T E S   V E R B O T E N
H I S S A T   E R E A D E R S
S L E E T S   S A Y E R S
```

## 123

```
N I S S A N T I T A N S
O N C E U P O N A T I M E
S H O C K R E S I S T A N T
H A L T S   L U N E   S H A M
O L D S   S O R T A   H A R E
W E S   F L O E S   P I N T A
  T R I P S   C A N C A N
R A M R O D S   B A N T E R S
E L O I S E   L A R G O
S Y L P H   B A R B S   G E E
I D O L   C U L T S   M O A N
N A T E   R E A L   C O A S T
  R O S E A N N E C O N N E R
  V E R M O N T A V E N U E
  C A S S E T T E T A P E
```

## 124

```
B E A T S B Y D R E   K F C S
O C C A S I O N E D   I R O N
T H E M E T G A L A   T I K I
T O S S   S A L A M I   Z E D
L E I   P A Y   N O Z Z E
E S T S   T A B   P O L L E R
  T R A N S G E N D E R
  S C R I P T   I T I S S O
  P I A N O S O N A T A
B E N I G N   S O L   W A H S
Y E N T E   S S R   D O H
R D A   R E T I M E   P O L O
N I B S   G O C O M M A N D O
E L O I   I L L U M I N A T I
S Y N C   S E E S A C T I O N
```

## 125

```
S E P A R A T E I N C O M E S
A M E R I C A N C U I S I N E
L A S T T H E D I S T A N C E
U N T I E   S K A L D
T A L E   B A R B S   A R A B
E T E   P A R I A H S   E V E
R E S U L T S O R I E N T E D
  S U P E R G L U E
C E R E M O N I A L S T A R T
O Y E   P L A T I E S   S E A
H E R B   E L A N D   T K O S
A L O O P   A W A C S
B I O L U M I N E S C E N C E
I N T E R E S T R A T E C U T
T E S T E D T H E W A T E R S
```

## 126

```
A L I E N   A G A K H A N
C A C T I   L O P E A R E D
E L E C T   P R I N T R U N S
T I M E   W H E A T S   R A W
A G A T H A   B O B O
L A N C E B A S S   T O T A L
  M A D M A G A Z I N E
  D O O M S D A Y C L O C K
D O T H E H U S T L E
E L C I D   P H O E N I C I A
A L S O   F T R O O P
L O T   C O U R T S   V E N T
S P O R T S B A R   D I R G E
  S C A R L E T A   I N C U S
  K Y L O R E N   A G E N T
```

# 127

| A | Z | E | R | A |   | B | A | S | S |   | L | G | B | T |
| B | E | G | I | N |   | E | X | C | U | S | E | Y | O | U |
| C | R | O | O | N |   | N | E | O | S | P | O | R | I | N |
| I | O | B | J | E | C | T |   | T | H | E | M | O | L | E |
| S | T | O | A |   | L | O | W | T | I | D | E |   |   |   |
| L | O | O |   | P | O | B | O | Y |   |   | S | W | I | G |
| A | H | S |   | A | V | O | N |   | B | E | S | I | D | E |
| N | E | T | F | L | I | X | O | R | I | G | I | N | A | L |
| D | R | E | A | M | S |   | V | I | N | G |   | A | H | I |
| S | O | R | T |   |   | T | E | N | D | S |   | N | O | N |
|   |   |   | E | N | L | A | R | G | E |   | B | O | S | S |
| O | N | F | L | E | E | K |   | T | R | I | E | S | T | O |
| V | I | A | V | E | N | E | T | O |   | D | E | C | A | L |
| A | N | T | I | D | O | T | E | S |   | O | R | A | T | E |
| L | E | E | S |   | S | H | E | S |   | L | Y | R | E | S |

# 128

| W | R | I | S | T |   | P | A | R | M |   | A | V | I | D |
| H | O | M | O | E | R | O | T | I | C |   | T | I | M | E |
| I | D | E | A | L | I | S | T | I | C |   | E | D | I | E |
| R | E | T | R | E | A | T |   | S | A | P | I | E | N | T |
|   |   |   | P | A | R |   |   | F | U | T | O | N |   |   |
|   | T | S | A | R |   | A | L | D | E | R |   | G | O | B |
| R | A | T | I | O |   | C | A | R |   | P | L | A | C | E |
| U | N | A | R | M |   | I | D | A |   | L | I | M | E | S |
| S | T | R | E | P |   | A | L | F |   | E | V | E | N | T |
| T | A | G |   | T | O | L | E | T |   | S | Y | S | T |   |
|   | L | A | P | E | L |   |   | K | A | T |   |   |   |   |
| L | I | Z | A | R | D | S |   | I | N | A | H | O | L | E |
| U | Z | I | S |   | A | L | L | N | A | T | U | R | A | L |
| K | E | N | T |   | G | O | O | G | L | E | M | A | P | S |
| E | D | G | E |   | E | G | G | S |   | S | E | N | S | E |

# 129

| R | O | P | E | S | I | N |   | A | G | E | N | D | A | S |
| E | C | O | N | O | M | I | C | B | O | Y | C | O | T | T |
| L | A | N | G | U | A | G | E | B | A | R | R | I | E | R |
| A | N | T | E | S |   | E | L | O | P | E |   | D | O | E |
| B | A | I | L |   | A | R | E | T | E |   | H | A | V | E |
| E | D | U |   | C | R | I | B | S |   | C | A | R | E | T |
| L | A | S | T | Y | E | A | R |   | B | O | R | E | R | S |
|   |   |   | U | N | A | N | I | M | O | U | S |   |   |   |
| A | L | A | N | I | S |   | T | O | U | C | H | P | A | D |
| F | O | L | I | C |   | S | Y | N | T | H |   | H | I | E |
| F | A | Q | S |   | D | U | C | K | S |   | S | O | R | T |
| A | N | A |   | L | E | C | H | E |   | B | E | E | B | E |
| I | C | E | H | O | C | K | E | Y | A | R | E | N | A | S |
| R | A | D | I | C | A | L | F | E | M | I | N | I | S | T |
| S | P | A | C | K | L | E |   | D | E | T | O | X | E | S |

# 130

| B | A | D | A | B | I | N | G | B | A | D | A | B | O | O | M |
| I | M | A | G | I | N | A | R | Y | F | R | I | E | N | D | S |
| D | U | K | E | O | F | W | E | L | L | I | N | G | T | O | N |
| E | L | O |   | S | O | L | T | I |   | B | T | E | A | M |   |
| T | E | T | E |   | I | N | N | S |   | T | R | E | S |   |   |
| S | T | A | G | S |   | N | A | E | N | A | E |   | G | T | O |
|   |   |   | Y | A | M | S |   | S | L | U | R | P | E | E | S |
| S | C | I | P | I | O |   |   |   | D | I | S | T | R | O |   |
| C | A | S | T | L | O | T | S |   | R | I | C | H |   |   |   |
| A | P | R |   | S | T | E | E | L | E |   | A | A | R | G | H |
| R | Y | A | N |   | A | R | E | S |   | W | E | R | E |   |   |
|   | B | E | T | A | S |   | R | A | T | I | O |   | S | A | C |
| T | A | L | E | N | T | M | A | N | A | G | E | M | E | N | T |
| C | R | I | S | T | I | A | N | O | R | O | N | A | L | D | O |
| M | A | S | T | E | R | C | O | N | T | R | O | L | L | E | R |

# 131

| A | G | E | D |   | W | A | R | A | C | E |   | B | R | R |
| D | R | A | W |   | B | R | O | T | O | X |   | Y | A | O |
| M | A | T | E |   | O | C | T | A | N | E |   | J | I | B |
| I | N | A | L | L |   | H | E | R | S |   | N | O | S | E |
| R | O | L | L | E | D | R |   | I | T | S | O | V | E | R |
| E | L | I |   | A | R | I | D |   | A | P | T | E | S | T |
|   | A | V | A | D | U | V | E | R | N | A | Y |   |   |   |
|   |   | E | C | I | G | A | R | E | T | T | E | S |   |   |
|   |   |   | U | N | C | L | E | M | I | L | T | I | E |   |
| F | A | J | I | T | A |   | K | A | N | E |   | D | X | C |
| E | D | I | T | O | R | S |   | R | E | S | P | E | C | T |
| L | O | G | Y |   | T | E | A | R |   | E | R | N | I | E |
| O | R | S |   | F | E | L | L | I | N |   | I | O | T | A |
| N | B | A |   | A | L | L | I | E | S |   | S | T | E | M |
| S | S | W |   | A | S | S | T | D | A |   | M | E | D | S |

# 132

| C | L | E | O | P | A | T | R | A |   | E | J | E | C | T |
| A | I | S | L | E | S | E | A | T |   | M | U | N | R | O |
| I | N | T | E | R | L | A | C | E |   | A | S | T | I | N |
| N | O | D |   | E | S | E |   | S | I | T | S | B | Y |   |
|   |   | S | W | E | E | T | T | A | L | K |   |   |   |   |
| I | C | E | C | A | P |   | O | I | L |   | I | S | N | T |
| A | R | I | A | S |   | T | R | E | N | D | I | E | R |   |
| M | E | E | T | I | N | T | H | E | M | I | D | D | L | E |
| S | P | I | T | T | A | K | E |   | K | I | L | L | S |   |
| O | T | O | E |   | N | O | B |   | H | O | N | E | Y | S |
|   |   | R | E | A | S | O | N | I | N | G |   |   |   |   |
| C | H | A | S | M | S |   | T | A | N |   | I | B | M |   |
| L | E | T | H | E |   | S | T | A | T | E | T | R | E | E |
| A | R | M | O | R |   | V | O | C | A | T | I | O | N | S |
| P | A | S | T | Y |   | U | M | P | T | E | E | N | T | H |

## 133

| A | B | L | A | R | E | | | | T | W | I | N | K | L | E |
| B | E | A | T | O | N | | | S | H | A | L | E | O | I | L |
| U | N | F | O | L | D | | | T | A | L | K | T | O | M | E |
| | | J | A | M | E | S | W | A | T | T | | | S | K | I | N |
| M | A | Y | A | S | | | A | Y | S | | | B | U | S | T | A |
| A | M | E | N | | | S | C | I | S | S | O | R | | | |
| L | I | T | T | L | E | K | N | O | W | N | F | A | C | T |
| I | T | T | | | A | L | Y | | | N | I | N | | | P | H | O |
| K | E | E | P | S | I | T | T | O | G | E | T | H | E | R |
| | | | H | E | G | O | A | T | S | | | H | E | A | T |
| A | P | S | E | S | | | B | I | O | | | P | E | R | P | S |
| S | A | W | N | | | D | A | N | K | M | E | M | E | S | |
| I | D | I | O | L | E | C | T | | | A | S | A | S | E | T |
| A | R | M | L | O | C | K | S | | | J | O | S | I | A | H |
| M | E | S | S | B | O | Y | | | | A | S | K | S | T | O |

## 134

| R | A | Z | Z | | | P | I | Z | Z | A | | | | F | I | Z | Z |
| A | L | O | E | | | O | B | E | A | H | | | O | R | E | O |
| G | L | O | B | | | P | I | E | C | E | | | Y | O | R | E |
| N | I | M | R | O | D | S | | | H | A | V | E | N | O | T |
| A | N | S | A | R | I | | | | | D | O | R | M | E | R |
| R | O | O | | | E | V | E | N | N | O | W | | | I | S | O |
| O | N | U | S | | | A | L | O | O | F | | | S | K | I | P |
| K | E | T | C | H | | | E | N | D | | | B | E | E | N | E |
| | | | | H | O | W | G | O | E | S | I | T | | | |
| W | O | R | T | H | Y | | | S | E | N | S | E | D | |
| P | E | L | O | S | I | | | | | X | G | A | M | E | S |
| A | I | D | E | | | Z | Z | T | O | P | | | D | A | L | I |
| G | R | A | D | | | K | E | N | D | O | | | A | J | A | X |
| E | D | G | E | | | I | N | U | I | T | | | T | O | N | E |
| D | O | E | R | | | D | O | T | E | S | | | E | R | O | S |

## 135

| O | R | N | A | T | E | | | | D | I | S | B | A | R |
| H | O | T | R | O | D | S | | | O | N | T | I | M | E |
| B | E | E | R | N | U | T | S | | | T | H | E | G | A | P |
| A | P | S | I | S | | | R | O | M | | | D | E | L | T | A |
| B | E | T | S | | | G | O | F | O | R | | | L | E | O | I |
| Y | R | S | | | C | A | B | A | R | E | T | C | A | R | D |
| | | C | A | M | E | R | A | R | E | A | D | Y |
| | R | A | V | E | L | | | L | O | N | G | S |
| | G | E | N | E | T | I | C | C | O | D | E | |
| S | E | N | D | R | E | G | R | E | T | S | | | O | T | C |
| T | R | O | Y | | | S | H | U | N | S | | | P | A | R | R |
| A | M | U | C | K | | | T | N | T | | | M | O | X | I | E |
| R | A | N | O | U | T | | | K | E | M | O | S | A | B | E |
| E | N | C | A | S | E | | | R | A | T | E | C | A | P |
| S | E | E | T | H | E | | | | P | E | D | A | L | S |

## 136

| B | A | R | B | I | E | D | O | L | L | | | S | P | A | M |
| A | V | E | R | A | G | E | J | O | E | | | T | O | N | E |
| L | I | V | I | N | G | W | A | G | E | | | A | K | I | N |
| M | A | S | T | | | H | A | I | G | | | P | R | E | S | S |
| | | | F | U | R | | | E | R | I | T | R | E | A |
| R | A | I | S | I | N | S | | | D | U | N | S | T | |
| U | P | N | E | X | T | | | W | O | R | K | M | A | T | E |
| B | O | R | A | T | | | H | A | N | | | S | A | B | R | A |
| S | P | A | T | U | L | A | S | | | B | A | L | L | O | T |
| | R | U | R | A | L | | | P | E | L | L | E | T | S |
| T | H | E | R | E | O | F | | | A | R | T | | | |
| H | A | F | T | S | | | D | O | N | A | | | O | G | L | E |
| E | N | O | L | | | N | O | S | E | T | O | T | A | I | L |
| F | O | R | E | | | R | O | L | L | E | R | R | I | N | K |
| T | I | M | S | | | C | R | O | S | S | B | O | N | E | S |

## 137

| S | T | R | I | N | G | O | R | C | H | E | S | T | R | A |
| T | H | E | R | E | S | N | O | I | I | N | T | E | A | M |
| O | R | D | E | R | E | D | A | L | A | C | A | R | T | E |
| G | O | E | S | O | V | E | R | I | T | A | G | A | I | N |
| Y | E | P | | | L | E | S | | | A | U | G | | | B | O | D |
| | O | D | I | N | | | | S | E | X | Y | | | |
| A | L | S | O | | | R | E | D | | | K | T | E | L |
| S | U | I | T | E | D | O | N | E | S | N | E | E | D | S |
| K | I | T | | | L | A | C | O | S | T | E | | | S | O | D |
| | F | O | R | K | | | C | I | G | S | | | |
| | P | G | A | | | L | E | A | R | N | | | H | A | D |
| T | E | L | L | S | I | T | L | I | K | E | I | T | I | S |
| R | E | A | S | O | N | T | O | B | E | L | I | E | V | E |
| O | L | D | E | R | G | E | N | E | R | A | T | I | O | N |
| P | E | E | R | A | S | S | E | S | S | M | E | N | T | S |

## 138

| A | D | S | A | L | E | S | | | | P | A | R | T | I | I |
| B | R | I | N | G | O | U | T | | | E | T | C | E | T | C |
| L | I | L | A | B | N | E | R | | | C | O | A | R | S | E |
| U | N | L | I | T | | | | A | M | O | N | | | M | O | B |
| S | K | I | S | | | T | O | G | A | S | | | R | I | P | E |
| H | U | E | | | K | U | N | I | S | | | G | O | N | E | R |
| | P | R | I | N | C | E | C | H | A | R | M | I | N | G |
| | | D | E | C | O | | | A | L | O | E | | | |
| C | A | P | T | A | I | N | O | B | V | I | O | U | S |
| O | R | E | A | D | | | O | S | L | I | N | | | N | A | M |
| L | A | N | G | | | I | N | P | E | N | | | R | E | N | I |
| U | M | A | | | F | O | E | R | | | | P | E | A | R | L |
| M | A | N | B | U | N | | | E | T | H | E | L | R | E | D |
| N | I | C | E | S | T | | | Y | O | U | G | O | T | M | E |
| S | C | E | N | E | V | | | | P | B | S | S | H | O | W |

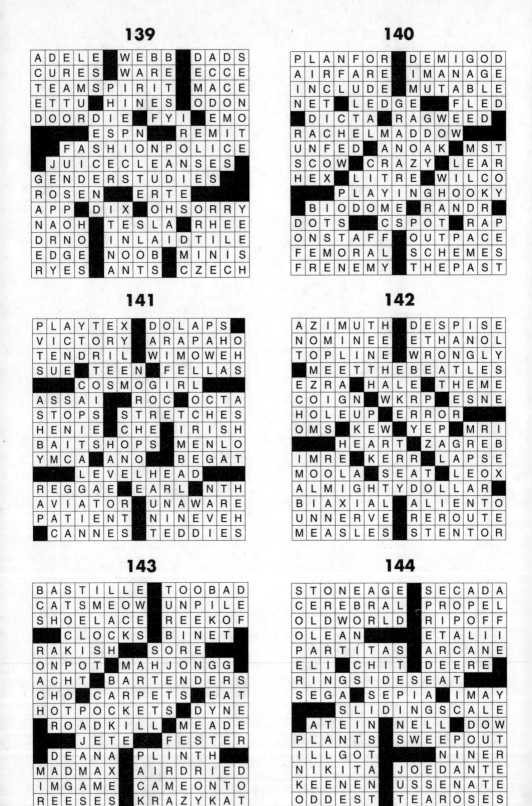

**139**

| A | D | E | L | E | | W | E | B | B | | D | A | D | S |
| C | U | R | E | S | | W | A | R | E | | E | C | C | E |
| T | E | A | M | S | P | I | R | I | T | | M | A | C | E |
| E | T | T | U | | H | I | N | E | S | | O | D | O | N |
| D | O | O | R | D | I | E | | F | Y | I | | E | M | O |
| | | | E | S | P | N | | | R | E | M | I | T | |
| | F | A | S | H | I | O | N | P | O | L | I | C | E | |
| | J | U | I | C | E | C | L | E | A | N | S | E | S | |
| G | E | N | D | E | R | S | T | U | D | I | E | S | | |
| R | O | S | E | N | | | E | R | T | E | | | | |
| A | P | P | | D | I | X | | O | H | S | O | R | R | Y |
| N | A | O | H | | T | E | S | L | A | | R | H | E | E |
| D | R | N | O | | I | N | L | A | I | D | T | I | L | E |
| E | D | G | E | | N | O | O | B | | M | I | N | I | S |
| R | Y | E | S | | A | N | T | S | | C | Z | E | C | H |

**140**

| P | L | A | N | F | O | R | | D | E | M | I | G | O | D |
| A | I | R | F | A | R | E | | I | M | A | N | A | G | E |
| I | N | C | L | U | D | E | | M | U | T | A | B | L | E |
| N | E | T | | L | E | D | G | E | | | F | L | E | D |
| | D | I | C | T | A | | R | A | G | W | E | E | D | |
| R | A | C | H | E | L | M | A | D | D | O | W | | | |
| U | N | F | E | D | | A | N | O | A | K | | M | S | T |
| S | C | O | W | | C | R | A | Z | Y | | L | E | A | R |
| H | E | X | | L | I | T | R | E | | W | I | L | C | O |
| | | | P | L | A | Y | I | N | G | H | O | O | K | Y |
| | B | I | O | D | O | M | E | | R | A | N | D | R | |
| D | O | T | S | | | C | S | P | O | T | | R | A | P |
| O | N | S | T | A | F | F | | O | U | T | P | A | C | E |
| F | E | M | O | R | A | L | | S | C | H | E | M | E | S |
| F | R | E | N | E | M | Y | | T | H | E | P | A | S | T |

**141**

| P | L | A | Y | T | E | X | | D | O | L | A | P | S | |
| V | I | C | T | O | R | Y | | A | R | A | P | A | H | O |
| T | E | N | D | R | I | L | | W | I | M | O | W | E | H |
| S | U | E | | T | E | E | N | | F | E | L | L | A | S |
| | | C | O | S | M | O | G | I | R | L | | | | |
| A | S | S | A | I | | R | O | C | | O | C | T | A | |
| S | T | O | P | S | | S | T | R | E | T | C | H | E | S |
| H | E | N | I | E | | C | H | E | | I | R | I | S | H |
| B | A | I | T | S | H | O | P | S | | M | E | N | L | O |
| Y | M | C | A | | A | N | O | | B | E | G | A | T | |
| | | L | E | V | E | L | H | E | A | D | | | | |
| R | E | G | G | A | E | | E | A | R | L | | N | T | H |
| A | V | I | A | T | O | R | | U | N | A | W | A | R | E |
| P | A | T | I | E | N | T | | N | I | N | E | V | E | H |
| | C | A | N | N | E | S | | T | E | D | D | I | E | S |

**142**

| A | Z | I | M | U | T | H | | D | E | S | P | I | S | E |
| N | O | M | I | N | E | E | | E | T | H | A | N | O | L |
| T | O | P | L | I | N | E | | W | R | O | N | G | L | Y |
| | M | E | E | T | T | H | E | B | E | A | T | L | E | S |
| E | Z | R | A | | H | A | L | E | | T | H | E | M | E |
| C | O | I | G | N | | W | K | R | P | | E | S | N | E |
| H | O | L | E | U | P | | E | R | R | O | R | | | |
| O | M | S | | K | E | W | | Y | E | P | | M | R | I |
| | | | H | E | A | R | T | | Z | A | G | R | E | B |
| I | M | R | E | | K | E | R | R | | L | A | P | S | E |
| M | O | O | L | A | | S | E | A | T | | L | E | O | X |
| A | L | M | I | G | H | T | Y | D | O | L | L | A | R | |
| B | I | A | X | I | A | L | | A | L | I | E | N | T | O |
| U | N | N | E | R | V | E | | R | E | R | O | U | T | E |
| M | E | A | S | L | E | S | | S | T | E | N | T | O | R |

**143**

| B | A | S | T | I | L | L | E | | T | O | O | B | A | D |
| C | A | T | S | M | E | O | W | | U | N | P | I | L | E |
| S | H | O | E | L | A | C | E | | R | E | E | K | O | F |
| | C | L | O | C | K | S | | B | I | N | E | T | | |
| R | A | K | I | S | H | | S | O | R | E | | | | |
| O | N | P | O | T | | M | A | H | J | O | N | G | G | |
| A | C | H | T | | B | A | R | T | E | N | D | E | R | S |
| C | H | O | | C | A | R | P | E | T | S | | E | A | T |
| H | O | T | P | O | C | K | E | T | S | | D | Y | N | E |
| | R | O | A | D | K | I | L | L | | M | E | A | D | E |
| | | J | E | T | E | | F | E | S | T | E | R | | |
| | D | E | A | N | A | | P | L | I | N | T | H | | |
| M | A | D | M | A | X | | A | I | R | D | R | I | E | D |
| I | M | G | A | M | E | | C | A | M | E | O | N | T | O |
| R | E | E | S | E | S | | K | R | A | Z | Y | K | A | T |

**144**

| S | T | O | N | E | A | G | E | | S | E | C | A | D | A |
| C | E | R | E | B | R | A | L | | P | R | O | P | E | L |
| O | L | D | W | O | R | L | D | | R | I | P | O | F | F |
| O | L | E | A | N | | | | E | T | A | L | I | I | |
| P | A | R | T | I | T | A | S | | A | R | C | A | N | E |
| E | L | I | | C | H | I | T | | D | E | E | R | E | |
| R | I | N | G | S | I | D | E | S | E | A | T | | | |
| S | E | G | A | | S | E | P | I | A | | I | M | A | Y |
| | | | S | L | I | D | I | N | G | S | C | A | L | E |
| | A | T | E | I | N | | N | E | L | L | | D | O | W |
| P | L | A | N | T | S | | S | W | E | E | P | O | U | T |
| I | L | L | G | O | T | | | | N | I | N | E | R | |
| N | I | K | I | T | A | | J | O | E | D | A | N | T | E |
| K | E | E | N | E | N | | U | S | S | E | N | A | T | E |
| O | D | D | E | S | T | | T | E | A | R | O | S | E | S |

## 145

FIREFOX MOZILLA
ONARANT CRONIES
EXCITER MENOTTI
SKEETER SENTIN
DOMES SILT
ALFA NEATH TELL
GOOSE GLOOM BOA
HAZARDANOPINION
ADZ GOMAD TERSE
SEIS SEMIS ODES
DEMS SENTA
RUBATO SLEDDOG
APELIKE IPHONES
GOALLIN NOONERS
UNRATED ENCASES

## 146

JOCK DISPOSALS
EZRA JOSHUATREE
SAUL UNLETTERED
SWEETDEAL MTIDA
EAT EYE LAE SSN
ANG CAL
MARSHALLMCLUHAN
ORATORIOSOCIETY
MAJORLEAGUEGAME
STARSANDSTRIPES
SEN EES
IMO PDT ORA BBC
LARGO APRILFOOL
LUKEWILSON AXLE
EVANESCING ZETA
RENERUSSO ERST

## 147

ROADSTERS
SAMUELADAMS
MINNESOTAFATS
LENDER STRATI
ITERS SAP STPAT
TRAY SENET ELKS
TOD SPLITSCREEN
ESO EELLIKE SHO
RECONNOITER COT
EXON TUNED SELF
RUNES TES KINDA
SANSEI WINTER
LOTTERYWINNER
ROASTMASTER
PETEACHER

## 148

CATSCRADLE IGOR
HEATVISION CANE
IRRESOLUTE ENTS
POPE JARS FIGHT
LUANN RINSER
HELEN TABOR TWA
ANORAK LIRE AHI
RASSLES LEBARON
EMS LEND MORALE
MEL INLET AMPED
PLEBES CARTS
AWARD FARO RIFT
NADA DIRTYHARRY
TREF PALACECOUP
SERF STONEHENGE

## 149

OLDGEEZER KAPPA
RARINTOGO ALOAD
CHILDHOOD ZEPPO
ARP TIPS SOCCER
POOL FLO URN
ABLE PADDY BLT
IRONMINER PETIT
DONTMAKEMELAUGH
AWGEE TREASURER
NIL POEMS TERO
OSS CAN OTIS
MULDER DRAT DWI
AGARS POISONOAK
HANNA TRAILBIKE
ARDOR SALADATEA

## 150

BAGGAGE LABCOAT
EQUIFAX ABOLISH
SUNBATH DERALTE
TAN READYTOWEAR
BRIS SLOG SADIE
UINTA EGAD TURN
DAGAMA EGOS PET
BAABAABAA
MSS SALT YIPPED
OOPS SODS LEILA
BRITA GOAT XRAY
BEERGOGGLES AIM
ONLEAVE ANTENNA
STEEPER MOOCHER
SORTERS INPHASE

## 151

```
N I C O L A S C A G E ■ B A H
A D O B E R E A D E R ■ A L E
W A R R E N Z E V O N ■ U T A
■ R A I S A ■ S I S S Y B A R
P E L E ■ Z E A L ■ A L I T
B Y R N E ■ M R P E E P E R S
J O E ■ M A T ■ M A L A ■
S U D S E S ■ V E T O E S ■
■ P R I G ■ Y E N ■ N T H
D A I R Y F A R M ■ A S T R A
A L F A ■ L O A M ■ C H U M
S P I T T O O N ■ O B O E S ■
H E M ■ W O O D F U R N A C E
E R A ■ I N T E R R A C I A L
S T Y ■ G A S L A N T E R N S
```

## 152

```
E G O T I S T ■ O N M E R I T
L O V E M E O R L E A V E M E
A V E R A G E A M E R I C A N
S E R A ■ M A N O R ■ L A G O
T R E ■ H E R D S ■ H O P I N
I N S T A N T S ■ F A M I N E
N O T W I T H ■ M U L E T A S
■ R I O T S ■ P I N E N U T ■
M C M I I ■ G U N K Y ■ L I C
E L A N ■ A R E A S ■ P A V E
N I T ■ B L O B S ■ R A T E L
I N I M I C A L ■ S E R I N E
S T O O D O N O N E S T O E S
C O N N I V E S A G A I N S T
I N S A N E R ■ M A T I S S E
```

## 153

```
S T E P S I T U P ■ T O Q U E
W E L L A W A R E ■ I N U R N
A L M A M A T E R ■ G E I S T
M O S T E S T ■ F R E S C A S
I S T O ■ H E R ■ T R E K ■
■ J A R U L E ■ A B M S
D U C T E D ■ B E S T S U I T
M C R A E ■ A B E ■ B O C C I
A L A N P A G E ■ H A N K E R
J A Z Z ■ P A R L O R ■
■ Y A K S ■ Y U M ■ L A R A
W H I N I E R ■ M E N A C E D
H A D I N ■ E X P L E T I V E
A T E A T ■ C L E A R E D U P
T H A N E ■ D V D B O X S E T
```

## 154

```
C H O O S E O N E S W O R D S
R O C K E T T O T H E M O O N
E M A I L D O M A I N N A M E
V E R N A ■ M I M E D ■ N I E
I D I G ■ V I N E S ■ F O N Z
C I N ■ C A S A S ■ P E K O E
E N A M O R ■ L O C H N E S S
■ O R I G ■ N O I D ■
S P R I N G A T ■ E L I S S A
T H O R S ■ S H E D S ■ O P P
E A S E ■ S O R A S ■ G I L T
R E S ■ C O L O R ■ E L G I N
E D I T O R I A L S T A N C E
O R N A M E N T A L T R E E S
S A I D O N E S P R A Y E R S
```

## 155

```
S E L E N A G O M E Z ■ A B S
E M I L Y B R O N T E ■ U R I
M E S A A R I Z O N A ■ R E S
I R T ■ L A N E ■ A L B E R T
P S I ■ A M C ■ O L A F I
R O N A ■ H O T B U T T O N
O N G O A L ■ D O E S ■ E X E
■ K N O W I T A L L ■
E M S ■ Y E W S ■ M Y O P E S
G O O U T W I T H ■ O R N E
G O N N A ■ E D O ■ E T C
S N O O K I ■ W R I T ■ T E T
A P R ■ E D D I E A R C A R O
C I A ■ R E A L T R O O P E R
S E N ■ S E E D O Y S T E R S
```

## 156

```
M E H ■ T H R O B ■ C L A P S
A X E ■ N I O B E ■ A E R I E
D I M E N S I O N ■ V E T T E
A L A N ■ S L E E P E R C A R
M E N A C E ■ F R I A R ■
■ M A D S C I E N T I S T
A N G E R ■ M A C E ■ T H E
W O R L D D O M I N A T I O N
N B A ■ I K E A ■ P A C E S
S U P E R V I L L A I N ■
■ E T H A N ■ D A N C E R
F I S H I N G R O D ■ I A G O
L O H A N ■ G I V E A N D G O
A N O N O ■ U P E N D ■ G O T
G A T E S ■ N E R D S ■ E N S
```

## 157

```
S C R I P T S ■ T E A M U S A
P I E R R O T ■ S A M O V A R
I N S T O R E ■ P R O V E R B
E C O ■ M I R Y ■ T R E A D S
L O W ■ K E N O S H A ■ ■
■ ■ M I S ■ U T I L I Z E D
S T E I N ■ S N E E ■ N E R O
T H E A G I N G P R O C E S S
L I L T ■ H A G S ■ H A S T E
O N S A F A R I ■ O P S ■
■ E T E R N A L ■ D E M
M A K E M E ■ L A K E ■ E T A
O R I G A M I ■ C L A M B A R
P E D A L E D ■ R E S O R T S
S A D D E N S ■ E Y E W A S H
```

## 158

```
K I C K S O F F ■ A S P E N S
A T O N E F O R ■ R I B L E T
P A K E T T L E ■ E X A C T A
O K I E S ■ D E I S T ■ A W N
W E E L A D ■ T O Y ■ P O L
■ ■ G A I T S ■ D I R E
G O O D C H A R L O T T E
Z I P A D E E D O O D A H
F A M I L Y R E U N I O N
A C M E ■ A U D I T
T E E ■ S C I ■ N E W C A R
B F F ■ N O N E S ■ R H O D E
A R I S E S ■ V W B E E T L E
C O V E R T ■ A A A R A T E D
K N E A D S ■ N B A S T A R S
```

## 159

```
D E P O S I T O N L Y ■ O D D
U T I L I T Y P O L E ■ V I R
B A N A N A C R E A M ■ E L Y
S S E ■ A S H Y ■ N E A R E R
■ A T C O ■ T E N D S T O
I N D I R A ■ M A R I E T T A
C A R L A ■ H E R O S ■ R A S
E P I S ■ T O A D S ■ H U N T
L O L ■ T E S T Y ■ M O N T E
A L L S O R T S ■ W A G G E D
N E P A L I S ■ W E D S ■
D O R S E Y ■ S A I L ■ A L E
E N E ■ D A I L Y M I R R O R
R I S ■ O K S A N A B A I U L
S I S ■ S I L V E R S T A T E
```

## 160

```
C A E S A R S A L A D ■ C B S
A R C H I P E L A G O ■ O R E
M A K I N G A R U N F O R I T
E B E R T ■ F O R E F R O N T
L I R E ■ B A K E S ■ I N G E
S A D ■ J O R E L ■ C E A S E
■ L U G E R ■ C O N D O S
■ M A I L E R ■ B O S T O N
C A R N E Y ■ L A M B S ■
A N T E S ■ H O N E Y ■ A D S
T O F U ■ L A R K S ■ S T E P
S L O P S O V E R ■ F E R M I
P E R S O N A L O P I N I O N
A T M ■ R E N E L A C O S T E
W E S ■ T R A I L M A R K E R
```

## 161

```
P E A R L J A M ■ G A S B A G
A S Q U I E T A S A M O U S E
S T A N D U P S T R A I G H T
D E B T S ■ A H I ■ L E G
E R A ■ C R A M P ■ R E N O
■ M A R ■ U R S A ■
A U T O M O B I L E T I R E S
G R O V E S O F A C A D E M E
U N D E R S T A T E M E N T S
A S S O C I A T E D P R E S S
■ F E N N ■ E S S ■
L A F F ■ G Y R O S ■ A H A
E L L ■ B I B ■ A S S E S
A L E U T I A N I S L A N D S
F O U R W A Y S T O P S I G N
S Y R I A N ■ E S T H E T E S
```

## 162

```
B R A T P A C K E R ■ S I F T
I O N O S P H E R E ■ E V A H
M A K E S S E N S E ■ M E I R
I S L ■ S E E N ■ D A P H N E
N T E S T ■ R E H Y D R A T E
I S T O ■ S I T U ■ R E D I D
■ U P T O H E R E ■ I S A
F R A S E R ■ A P A T H Y
R O T ■ N O T A R I S E ■
A S L I P ■ A V O N ■ R O Y S
B E A N A N G E L ■ M O N E T
J A N G L Y ■ R A C E ■ S S E
O N T O ■ A C T I V E C A S E
U N I T ■ C R E D I T S L I P
S E C S ■ K I D S I S T E R S
```

## 163

| G | A | R | A | G | E | B | A | N | D | | C | N | B | C |
| O | N | E | C | A | L | O | R | I | E | | R | I | A | L |
| I | N | T | E | R | D | I | C | T | S | | A | C | R | O |
| N | E | E | D | L | E | N | O | S | E | | D | K | N | Y |
| | | | A | R | G | | L | I | L | I | E | S | | |
| C | A | J | U | N | S | | F | R | E | N | E | M | Y | |
| A | W | A | R | D | | B | R | I | C | K | | I | F | S |
| A | H | M | E | | P | L | A | I | T | | O | N | I | T |
| N | I | B | | L | I | O | N | S | | C | H | A | F | E |
| | L | A | M | A | R | C | K | | R | A | M | J | E | T |
| T | E | J | A | N | O | | | V | A | L | | | | |
| A | B | U | T | | Z | A | S | I | N | Z | E | B | R | A |
| L | A | I | T | | H | E | A | D | T | O | T | A | I | L |
| E | C | C | E | | K | O | R | E | A | N | A | R | M | Y |
| S | K | E | D | | I | N | D | O | N | E | S | I | A | N |

## 164

| S | T | A | R | J | O | N | E | S | | B | L | A | S | E |
| W | O | R | E | A | W | I | R | E | | M | I | L | K | Y |
| A | N | N | E | M | E | A | R | A | | O | L | L | I | E |
| R | I | E | L | S | | A | S | H | C | A | K | E | S | |
| M | E | S | S | | P | A | T | O | I | S | | I | D | O |
| S | R | S | | T | O | X | I | N | S | | I | N | O | N |
| | | | D | O | R | I | C | | | A | B | D | U | L |
| A | C | T | I | O | N | S | | M | A | J | E | S | T | Y |
| D | B | A | C | K | | | J | A | B | A | T | | | |
| J | A | N | E | | P | F | I | Z | E | R | | C | E | L |
| U | T | Z | | D | A | R | N | E | D | | T | A | L | E |
| S | T | A | T | E | T | A | X | | | S | R | T | A | S |
| T | E | N | O | R | | M | I | L | A | K | U | N | I | S |
| O | R | I | O | N | | E | N | E | M | Y | M | I | N | E |
| R | Y | A | N | S | | S | G | T | P | E | P | P | E | R |

## 165

| S | O | B | E | R | E | D | U | P | | M | O | D | E | L |
| A | L | A | N | A | D | A | L | E | | A | L | E | X | A |
| P | E | N | I | N | S | U | L | A | | J | I | L | T | S |
| S | A | D | D | L | E | B | A | G | | O | V | E | R | T |
| | | | A | L | E | | R | A | R | E | G | A | S | |
| O | N | S | E | T | S | | C | A | P | I | T | A | L | U |
| P | O | E | M | E | | K | E | V | I | N | | T | A | P |
| E | S | A | U | | G | R | E | E | N | | G | O | R | P |
| N | Y | S | | E | M | A | L | L | | D | I | R | G | E |
| I | P | O | D | N | A | N | O | | C | E | N | S | E | R |
| N | A | N | E | T | T | E | | M | I | X | | | | |
| G | R | A | T | E | | P | O | I | N | T | L | E | S | S |
| A | K | B | A | R | | O | R | D | E | R | A | R | M | S |
| C | E | L | I | E | | O | D | D | M | A | N | O | U | T |
| T | R | E | N | D | | L | O | Y | A | L | I | S | T | S |

## 166

| Y | I | D | D | I | S | H | | A | I | R | M | A | I | L |
| A | R | I | A | N | N | A | | C | L | E | A | N | S | E |
| W | I | S | H | F | U | L | D | R | I | N | K | I | N | G |
| E | N | B | L | O | C | | E | Y | E | T | E | S | T | S |
| D | A | E | | K | F | C | | D | A | G | | | | |
| | | | L | A | E | | A | A | H | | O | S | H | A |
| T | W | I | T | T | E | R | F | O | L | L | O | W | E | R |
| O | N | E | T | O | G | O | | P | A | Y | D | I | R | T |
| S | E | V | E | N | O | F | D | I | A | M | O | N | D | S |
| S | T | E | N | | F | E | N | | E | N | G | | | |
| | | | D | E | T | | A | G | O | | | F | U | R |
| T | R | I | A | X | I | A | L | | W | I | N | O | N | A |
| M | I | D | N | I | G | H | T | I | N | P | A | R | I | S |
| E | L | E | C | T | R | A | | D | E | S | P | I | T | E |
| N | E | M | E | S | E | S | | O | R | E | S | T | E | S |

## 167

| T | H | I | S | I | S | T | R | U | E | | A | S | S | T |
| R | A | C | O | N | T | E | U | R | S | | T | K | O | S |
| I | N | A | R | T | I | S | T | I | C | | T | A | L | K |
| C | E | N | T | E | R | S | | R | I | A | T | A | S | |
| E | S | T | E | R | | H | O | O | S | I | E | R | | |
| | | R | I | P | V | A | N | W | I | N | K | L | E | |
| A | N | I | | M | A | U | V | E | | S | T | E | A | L |
| L | A | M | B | | C | L | A | S | H | | S | Y | M | S |
| A | T | P | A | R | | C | R | E | E | D | | S | P | A |
| N | U | R | S | E | R | A | T | C | H | E | D | | | |
| | R | O | S | S | I | N | I | | | S | E | L | M | A |
| C | A | V | I | T | Y | | R | A | I | S | E | U | P | |
| O | L | I | N | | A | N | N | E | B | R | O | N | T | E |
| E | L | S | E | | D | E | A | D | L | E | T | T | E | R |
| N | Y | E | T | | H | O | W | D | Y | D | O | O | D | Y |

## 168

| R | E | S | T | A | I | N | | | C | O | M | E | T | S |
| O | S | C | A | R | N | O | D | S | | O | P | A | Q | U | E |
| S | T | O | R | Y | B | O | O | K | | B | A | K | U | L | A |
| Y | O | W | Z | A | | K | N | O | W | | L | E | A | S | T |
| | | | A | N | S | | T | R | I | B | | A | L | A | S |
| V | O | N | | M | S | T | | N | A | T | S | | | |
| L | I | T | T | L | E | L | E | A | G | U | E | T | E | A | M |
| I | S | T | H | A | T | A | L | L | T | H | E | R | E | I | S |
| B | A | S | E | B | A | L | L | D | I | A | M | O | N | D | S |
| | | | A | S | N | O | | A | P | U | | N | Y | E |
| W | A | S | P | | A | M | F | M | | S | K | G | | |
| A | S | H | E | S | | S | O | A | K | | A | C | O | A | T |
| I | S | O | M | E | R | | A | T | A | G | L | A | N | C | E |
| T | E | J | A | N | O | | M | O | V | I | E | S | E | T | S |
| S | T | I | N | G | Y | | | A | L | L | E | G | E | S |

## 169

| D | R | A | W | E | R | █ | B | A | S | I | L | I | C | A |
|---|---|---|---|---|---|---|---|---|---|---|---|---|---|---|
| R | E | M | O | R | A | █ | A | R | C | H | I | V | A | L |
| E | L | I | J | A | H | █ | H | A | R | A | K | I | R | I |
| W | O | R | T | █ | M | A | I | M | █ | V | E | E | P | S |
| A | S | S | Y | R | █ | S | A | I | L | E | D | █ | █ | █ |
| █ | █ | █ | L | O | T | T | █ | S | A | N | T | A | N | A |
| P | A | R | A | G | U | A | Y | █ | M | O | O | C | O | W |
| O | R | E | █ | U | R | B | A | N | I | I | █ | I | V | A |
| R | I | E | S | E | N | █ | W | I | N | D | Y | D | A | Y |
| T | A | K | E | S | T | O | █ | G | A | E | A | █ | █ | █ |
| █ | █ | █ | A | T | O | N | C | E | █ | A | N | D | E | S |
| S | A | S | H | A | █ | F | O | R | T | █ | G | R | A | M |
| L | O | C | A | T | I | O | N | █ | R | A | T | I | T | E |
| E | N | I | W | E | T | O | K | █ | E | C | Z | E | M | A |
| D | E | S | K | S | E | T | S | █ | F | E | E | D | E | R |

## 170

| C | R | A | Z | I | E | R | █ | A | B | B | O | T | S |
|---|---|---|---|---|---|---|---|---|---|---|---|---|---|
| A | U | G | U | S | T | U | S | █ | B | A | L | B | O | A |
| C | S | I | M | I | A | M | I | █ | C | M | A | J | O | R |
| A | T | L | A | S | █ | B | L | T | S | █ | M | E | L | C |
| O | Y | E | █ | L | A | I | R | █ | M | E | C | C | A |
| █ | M | A | E | █ | C | U | T | E | █ | T | A | S |
| █ | P | O | S | T | M | O | D | E | R | N | I | S | M |
| D | R | S | T | R | A | N | G | E | L | O | V | E | █ |
| D | E | A | T | H | I | N | V | E | N | I | C | E | █ |
| O | M | G | █ | M | P | A | A | █ | I | N | K | █ |
| M | O | M | M | A | █ | G | L | E | E | █ | S | A | C |
| I | T | A | S | █ | F | E | L | L | █ | S | M | I | T | E |
| N | A | T | T | E | R | █ | E | I | T | H | E | R | O | R |
| O | P | I | A | T | E | █ | Y | O | U | O | W | E | M | E |
| S | E | C | R | E | T | █ | T | O | P | L | E | S | S |

## 171

| A | V | A | I | L | A | B | L | E | C | R | E | D | I | T |
|---|---|---|---|---|---|---|---|---|---|---|---|---|---|---|
| P | E | R | C | E | N | T | A | G | E | E | R | R | O | R |
| E | N | T | E | N | T | E | C | O | R | D | I | A | L | E |
| S | T | A | R | S | I | N | O | N | E | S | E | Y | E | S |
| █ | █ | █ | S | E | T | █ | N | S | A | █ | █ | █ | █ | █ |
| J | A | W | █ | S | A | K | I | █ | L | A | C | K | E | Y |
| A | T | A | D | █ | N | A | C | L | █ | M | I | L | N | E |
| M | R | L | U | C | K | Y | █ | O | C | A | N | A | D | A |
| B | I | D | E | S | █ | E | M | I | L | █ | Q | U | I | T |
| S | P | O | T | T | V | █ | O | N | E | D | █ | S | T | S |
| █ | █ | █ | A | T | O | █ | A | E | C | █ | █ | █ | █ | █ |
| A | M | E | R | I | C | A | N | I | N | P | A | R | I | S |
| R | E | G | U | L | A | R | G | A | S | O | L | I | N | E |
| F | E | E | D | I | N | G | O | N | E | S | F | A | C | E |
| S | T | R | E | E | T | A | D | D | R | E | S | S | E | S |

## 172

| A | S | B | I | G | █ | H | S | T | █ | T | O | P | U | P |
|---|---|---|---|---|---|---|---|---|---|---|---|---|---|---|
| S | T | O | R | E | █ | O | O | H | █ | H | Y | E | N | A |
| H | A | S | A | N | I | N | T | E | R | E | S | T | I | N |
| I | R | T | █ | E | L | K | █ | S | O | S | █ | R | O | D |
| P | R | O | C | R | A | S | T | I | N | A | T | I | N | G |
| █ | N | E | A | █ | O | Z | S | █ | H | E | F | █ | █ | █ |
| G | A | S | O | L | I | N | E | S | T | A | T | I | O | N |
| M | A | T | █ | E | K | E | █ | T | A | R | █ | E | R | A |
| C | A | R | E | L | E | S | S | A | B | A | N | D | O | N |
| █ | A | T | E | █ | H | I | T | █ | D | E | F | █ | █ | █ |
| R | A | N | A | C | L | O | S | E | S | E | C | O | N | D |
| E | N | G | █ | T | O | R | █ | M | A | S | █ | R | O | O |
| T | O | L | E | R | A | N | C | E | L | E | V | E | L | S |
| A | L | E | X | I | █ | A | R | N | █ | R | O | S | I | E |
| P | E | R | E | C | █ | T | O | T | █ | T | A | T | E | R |

## 173

| P | U | R | P | L | E | H | A | Z | E | █ | H | S | I | A |
|---|---|---|---|---|---|---|---|---|---|---|---|---|---|---|
| U | N | D | E | C | L | A | R | E | D | █ | A | T | O | P |
| S | T | A | N | D | A | L | O | N | E | █ | B | A | N | S |
| H | O | S | S | █ | T | O | D | █ | H | O | R | S | E |
| █ | I | D | E | E | █ | C | H | A | O | S | █ |
| █ | D | A | V | I | D | S | T | E | I | N | B | E | R | G |
| L | I | N | E | A | █ | W | E | L | D | █ | A | A | R |
| I | N | G | █ | L | A | C | O | S | T | E | █ | R | N | A |
| E | E | L | █ | S | L | I | T | █ | D | E | C | A | F |
| D | R | O | P | O | U | T | O | F | S | I | G | H | T | █ |
| █ | S | H | A | M | E | █ | L | U | N | G | █ |
| S | H | A | R | P | █ | S | I | R | █ | R | B | I | S |
| H | E | X | A | █ | P | O | W | E | R | P | O | I | N | T |
| E | R | O | S | █ | I | M | A | R | E | A | L | B | O | Y |
| D | O | N | E | █ | P | A | T | S | Y | C | L | I | N | E |

## 174

| A | M | I | W | R | O | N | G | █ | J | U | L | I | E |
|---|---|---|---|---|---|---|---|---|---|---|---|---|---|---|
| G | A | M | E | O | V | E | R | █ | S | O | N | A | T | A |
| E | X | H | I | B | I | T | A | █ | O | N | A | P | A | R |
| N | O | U | S | █ | D | I | V | I | N | G | B | E | L | L |
| D | U | R | S | T | █ | Z | I | T | I | █ | A | L | I | G |
| A | T | T | █ | A | C | E | T | E | N | █ | S | P | A | R |
| █ | E | P | O | N | Y | M | █ | T | H | I | N | E |
| A | M | E | X | E | S | █ | T | E | E | N | S | Y |
| D | A | V | I | D | █ | M | E | O | W | E | D | █ |
| A | R | E | S | █ | C | A | N | N | O | N | █ | M | A | T |
| P | I | N | T | █ | O | N | I | T | █ | S | L | U | S | H |
| T | A | K | E | F | L | I | G | H | T | █ | A | R | C | O |
| S | C | E | N | E | I | █ | M | E | R | R | Y | M | E | N |
| T | H | E | C | A | N | █ | A | Q | U | A | L | U | N | G |
| O | I | L | E | R | █ | S | T | E | W | A | R | D | S |

## 175

```
C R E E P S H O W ■ O X B O W
H U R R I C A N E ■ L A R G E
O P E N L A N E S ■ I N A L L
R E C ■ A N D I ■ E V A D E D
D E T E S T E D ■ X E D ■
■ O P T ■ L A S C R U C E S
B U R I E D ■ S T E ■ O L E
U N S C R E W ■ U P R I G H T
R T E ■ M A B ■ T E T R I S
B O T T L E C A P ■ T E A ■
■ V I A ■ N E A R M I S S
P O L L E N ■ D E M O ■ L E I
A R E A S ■ B I K I N I W A X
L E A N T ■ A T A N Y R A T E
M O N D O ■ S O T O M A Y O R
```

## 176

```
S P I T B A L L ■ A B O M B
H A V E I T O U T ■ S U P E R
O R A N G E F R E E S T A T E
T E N T C A T E R P I L L A R
■ A I M S ■ R O S E ■
E J E C T S ■ T A N T R U M S
D O L L Y ■ P E P Y S ■ N A P
I S L E ■ M A X I M ■ C A R E
T I E ■ P A G A N ■ D A R I N
S E N T R I E S ■ T E R M E D
■ R O T A ■ C H E T ■
A F R I C A N E L E P H A N T
L E A V E I T T O B E A V E R
D A V I S ■ S A N A N G E L O
A R E A S ■ T E N D E R L Y
```

## 177

```
T W I T T E R ■ M A A N D P A
R O G A I N E ■ I N D O O R S
Y O U R E A B E T T E R M A N
S L A T ■ C O L T S ■ M I C E
T E N A ■ T O B E Y ■ A N T E
S N A R L ■ T O N ■ B R A I D
■ A N E W ■ S E A N C E
A S S U M E D ■ F A C E T E D
S W A N E E ■ Y U C K ■
S I N E S ■ M O R ■ S A L E M
E T T A ■ P A U L A ■ L E S T
N C A R ■ R U N O N ■ S A K S
T H A N I A M G U N G A D I N
T O N E T T E ■ G I A C O M O
O N A D A T E ■ H E R E N O W
```

## 178

```
■ G A M E C H A N G E R ■
■ B I T E T H E B U L L E T
C A S T I R O N S T O M A C H
O L E ■ N E W N E S S ■ D E I
O L L I E ■ L I N ■ S P I L T
K O L N ■ P I N T A ■ H E L M
S T E T T I N G ■ N E I S S E
■ E I N E ■ B I T S ■
I B A N E Z ■ S A M E H E R E
N I P S ■ A F I L E ■ E T A S
S O R E N ■ E L A ■ C R A S S
I L O ■ A D D E N D A ■ I T E
N A P O L E O N C O M P L E X
■ B O R D E R T E R R I E R ■
■ S A I D A P R A Y E R ■
```

## 179

```
S K I P A G R A D E ■ O R B S
U N D E R L I N E D ■ G O R P
P A L L I A T I V E ■ L A I R
S P E E D D E M O N ■ E D D A
■ T O A T ■ T E Y
T S P ■ S O F T I E ■ B O Z O
I M O U T ■ E O N ■ E R I N
P A S S A G E ■ N O F A U L T
P R I M ■ R A E ■ A V I L A
E T T A ■ R U M P L Y ■ N A N
C P I ■ D A L E ■
A H O Y ■ S E N A T E S E A T
N O N E ■ E V A N S V I L L E
O N A N ■ W I N T E R T I D E
E E L S ■ S E T S E Y E S O N
```

## 180

```
A C T C A S U A L ■ A H A L T
N O O F F E N S E ■ W I N E R
I M S O T I R E D ■ A G G I E
M I T ■ A J A X ■ S C H U S S
A C A B ■ I T U N E S P L U S
L A D E D ■ E A U X ■ R A R E
S L A T E ■ D L I T ■ O R E S
■ A S H ■ S P F ■
R A P T ■ U H O H ■ D I V A S
A C R E ■ M A N Y ■ A L I B I
T H I S S I D E U P ■ E V I L
T I N T E D ■ E N R Y ■ A G E
L E T I N ■ M A D E A P L A N
E V E N S ■ I C A L L E D I T
S E R G E ■ C H I L L P I L L
```

## 181

```
E A S E . L A G E R . A F T A
D U H S . E X A M S . N O O R
I R O C . D O U B T . T R I M
C O W A B U N G A . P I E L S
T R I P U P . U N P E G G E D
S A N E R . W I K I Q U O T E
. . . S L A I N . Q U A N T A
R U B . E R G . D U O . E E L
E N L I S T . F R E T S . . .
C H I S Q U A R E . W I C C A
R E S O U R C E . C A L L O W
E A T M E . T E X A R K A N A
A T E E . I N B E D . H U C K
T E R R . N O I R E . A D U E
E D Y S . Q W E S T . T E R N
```

## 182

```
E P I T A P H . J E W E L E R
T H R I L L A . U N I T I V E
H I A L E A H . S T R O B E S
E L I . R N A . T O E . E L O
L I S P . C H E F . D A R I A
S P E A R . A N O N . R A N K
. . . R A Y . G R A C K L E S
ANTIDISESTABLISHMENTARIANISM
E G G S H E L L . L E S . . .
L A L A . S A I D . D A B L L
B R E N T . T T O P . S L O E
O B I . W V U . R I P . O S A
W A R R I O R . E N R O O T S
E G O I S T E . M O O N P I E
D E N O T E S . I N F E S T S
```

## 183

```
P A P E R B A G . T H E G A P
I T A L I A N O . M O D E L A
P O R T L A N D . A V A T A R
E N R O L . U S O N E . A N I
I C O N . R A G U . L I R A S
N E T . L O L I T A . S O L I
. . . S E S . F D R . S O D A
S T I C K I T T O T H E M A N
O H N O . N A T . I I I . . .
P E N T . S H O R E S . M P H
H O U S E . O W A R . F O R E
I N E . L I E O N . B E R E A
S I N B A D . M C H A M M E R
T O D A T E . E H A R M O N Y
S N O P E S . N O N S E N S E
```

## 184

```
P A S O D O B L E . G R U B
I S T H I S L O V E . A H S O
C H O C O H O L I C . Z E E S
T Y P O . K O A L A B E A R S
. . . M O O D . D R U B . . .
. A M E N S . G O T L O O S E
S W O O S H . R E E L . P E S
H A U N T . C A R . H B E A M
O R R . R O O M . P O O D L E
D E N T I S T S . A R O S E
. . S K I T . S I N G . . .
Q U A K E R O A T S . A P S E
T N U T . I N L A L A L A N D
I D E S . S T E V E D O R E D
P O R K . O K E Y D O K E Y
```

## 185

```
J U I C E B A R . A L L O Y S
A N N E R I C E . L O O K M A
R E D L I G H T . S T A L A G
F A I L E D . U F O . N A S A
U S E S . P R E P S . H U M
L E S . E B O N Y . P R O M O
. . . I S L E T . A L O M A R
Q U A N T U M O F S O L A C E
U S U R E R . R A I S E . . .
E S T E E . B E R T H . C A N
E M O . M C R A E . M E M O
N A B S . A O L . C O U S I N
M I A O W S . I P O D N A N O
U N H O O K . T I R E I R O N
M E N T O S . Y E A R Z E R O
```

## 186

```
P A N D O R A S B O X . S O N
I M O U T O F H E R E . A N E
C R E D I T L I N E S . Y E P
N I X E S . V I M . C O C A
I T I S . A P E T . T O N A L
C A T . U T E R O . O H A R E
. . . O N E A M . O P E R A S
T A L K L I K E A P I R A T E
O N A B E T . T R A C E . . .
A T T Y S . S I L L S . S O C
S E E M S . H M O S . A B B A
T A P E . J A B . S T A R R
E T A . L A K E O N T A R I O
R E S . O V E R A B A R R E L
S R S . G A S S T A T I O N S
```

## 187

| J | I | B | E | D | ■ | ■ | G | L | I | N | D | A |
| E | M | O | T | E | R | ■ | S | P | E | E | D | E | R | S |
| B | E | T | C | H | A | ■ | H | I | M | A | L | A | Y | A |
| B | A | S | H | I | N | ■ | I | N | S | P | I | R | E | S |
| U | N | W | I | S | E | ■ | P | A | T | E | N | T | S |
| S | T | A | N | C | E | ■ | I | F | O | R | G | O | T |
| H | I | N | G | E | ■ | A | N | O | N |
| ■ | T | A | S | S | E | L | ■ | R | E | D | A | N | T |
| ■ | ■ | N | I | C | E | ■ | E | P | E | E | S |
| ■ | S | C | E | P | T | E | R | ■ | I | M | P | U | R | E |
| ■ | T | A | N | L | I | N | E | ■ | S | A | R | T | R | E |
| N | A | R | R | A | T | E | D | ■ | A | N | O | R | A | K |
| A | R | T | I | C | L | E | I | ■ | A | D | V | I | C | E |
| P | R | I | C | I | E | S | T | ■ | K | E | E | N | E | R |
| S | Y | N | O | D | S | ■ | ■ | D | R | O | S | S |

## 188

| A | T | A | V | I | S | M | ■ | I | T | S | O | P | E | N |
| N | O | B | E | L | P | E | A | C | E | P | R | I | Z | E |
| C | I | A | H | E | A | D | Q | U | A | R | T | E | R | S |
| E | L | B | E | ■ | W | I | I | ■ | P | E | E | R | A | T |
| ■ | ■ | M | E | N | A | ■ | H | A | A | G |
| B | A | K | E | R | S | ■ | W | A | R | D | A | N | C | E |
| A | S | O | N | E | ■ | S | E | R | T | ■ | O | H | S |
| S | T | A | T | I | O | N | A | R | Y | O | R | B | I | T |
| T | I | L | ■ | V | A | R | Y | ■ | W | A | I | V | E |
| E | N | A | B | L | E | R | S | ■ | G | E | N | D | E | R |
| ■ | R | A | R | E | ■ | T | A | D | S |
| H | E | R | O | I | C | ■ | S | I | N | ■ | H | E | E | D |
| A | M | A | N | C | A | L | L | E | D | H | O | R | S | E |
| P | I | Z | Z | A | M | A | R | G | H | E | R | I | T | A |
| S | T | E | E | L | E | D | ■ | S | I | X | T | E | E | N |

## 189

| S | P | A | R | T | A | C | U | S | ■ | O | J | A | Y | S |
| H | O | L | E | I | N | O | N | E | ■ | P | O | B | O | Y |
| A | L | O | N | G | S | I | D | E | ■ | T | I | C | K | S |
| N | O | F | E | E | ■ | N | E | S | ■ | I | N | S | E | T |
| E | S | T | E | R | ■ | B | R | O | A | C | H |
| ■ | ■ | C | L | O | G | U | P | ■ | A | C | E | D |
| D | O | N | Q | U | I | X | O | T | E | ■ | N | A | Z | I |
| I | V | T | U | B | E | ■ | M | U | D | P | I | E |
| K | I | W | I | ■ | G | A | R | D | E | N | S | P | O | T |
| E | D | T | V | ■ | E | L | A | I | N | E |
| ■ | E | A | S | E | R | S | ■ | A | S | S | A | M |
| C | H | O | R | D | ■ | K | I | T | ■ | R | A | I | S | A |
| L | O | O | F | A | ■ | S | T | O | U | T | N | E | S | S |
| A | B | Z | U | G | ■ | E | A | R | L | H | I | N | E | S |
| D | O | Y | L | E | ■ | I | N | T | E | S | T | A | T | E |

## 190

| D | I | S | H | F | I | T | F | O | R | A | K | I | N | G |
| I | N | T | E | R | N | A | L | R | E | V | E | N | U | E |
| A | T | O | M | I | C | S | U | B | M | A | R | I | N | E |
| L | I | M | A | ■ | U | S | E | S | ■ | I | N | T |
| E | M | P | T | O | R | ■ | S | L | E | I | G | H |
| R | E | S | I | N | ■ | D | R | O | P | ■ | L | A | R | A |
| ■ | C | O | D | E | I | N | E | ■ | S | L | A | M |
| J | A | R | ■ | R | U | N | A | T | A | B | ■ | S | S | S |
| A | R | E | S | ■ | A | S | T | O | R | I | A |
| W | I | N | K | ■ | N | E | A | P | ■ | B | L | I | S | S |
| S | A | T | I | R | E | ■ | P | I | C | N | I | C |
| ■ | A | P | E | ■ | P | I | N | A | ■ | O | N | M | E |
| I | N | C | O | N | S | I | D | E | R | A | T | I | O | N |
| T | O | A | L | E | S | S | E | R | E | X | T | E | N | T |
| S | T | R | E | E | T | A | D | D | R | E | S | S | E | S |

## 191

| O | H | B | O | Y | ■ | M | F | O | R | ■ | I | P | O | D |
| P | E | R | S | E | ■ | E | I | R | E | ■ | N | A | S | A |
| T | R | E | A | T | ■ | N | A | R | C | I | S | S | U | S |
| I | M | A | G | I | N | A | T | I | O | N | I | S |
| M | A | K | E | S | I | T | ■ | N | U | G | G | E | T | S |
| A | N | S | ■ | S | A | E | ■ | P | E | N | S | E | E |
| ■ | ■ | T | H | E | R | M | S | ■ | S | I | O | U | X |
| ■ | M | O | R | E | I | M | P | O | R | T | A | N | T |
| G | E | N | I | I | ■ | S | T | R | E | S | S |
| R | I | P | E | S | T | ■ | Y | E | N | ■ | R | U | E |
| E | R | A | S | M | U | S | ■ | L | E | C | T | E | R | N |
| ■ | T | H | A | N | K | N | O | W | L | E | D | G | E |
| T | Y | R | A | N | N | I | E | S | ■ | O | T | H | E | R |
| A | M | O | R | ■ | E | N | N | E | ■ | W | R | O | N | G |
| B | A | L | D | ■ | Y | S | E | R | ■ | N | A | T | T | Y |

## 192

| S | P | F | S | ■ | H | A | M | M | ■ | N | I | C | A | D |
| H | E | A | P | ■ | A | L | A | R | ■ | O | S | A | G | E |
| A | R | M | E | ■ | S | T | R | I | P | P | O | K | E | R |
| Q | U | I | C | K | F | I | X | ■ | L | A | N | E | S |
| ■ | L | I | E | U | ■ | I | N | U | I | T |
| L | A | Y | M | E | N | ■ | S | I | R | N | O | S | I | R |
| A | D | R | E | P | ■ | I | M | E | A | N | ■ | A | N | A |
| M | O | O | N | S | E | T | ■ | C | L | O | S | I | N | G |
| P | R | O | ■ | A | G | A | V | E | ■ | G | E | N | I | E |
| S | E | M | I | N | O | L | E | ■ | P | A | R | T | E | D |
| ■ | N | E | I | L | S | ■ | L | I | E | D |
| ■ | T | R | E | Y | S | ■ | S | C | A | N | N | E | R | S |
| J | E | T | S | E | T | T | E | R | S | ■ | A | N | A | T |
| A | R | E | S | O | ■ | A | L | U | M | ■ | D | I | M | E |
| R | I | S | E | N | ■ | U | S | D | A | ■ | E | S | P | N |

## 193

| S | H | T | I | C | K | S | | M | A | E | W | E | S | T |
| T | U | R | N | O | U | T | | A | M | R | A | D | I | O |
| O | L | E | A | N | N | A | | N | A | I | R | O | B | I |
| W | A | Y | N | E | G | R | E | T | Z | K | Y | | | |
| E | S | S | E | S | | D | R | I | E | S | | M | I | R |
| | | | | T | A | O | S | | | W | A | C | O | |
| J | O | A | N | J | E | T | T | | B | R | I | N | E | S |
| E | N | R | I | Q | U | E | I | G | L | E | S | I | A | S |
| L | E | S | T | A | T | | C | O | T | O | P | A | X | I |
| L | A | O | S | | | K | I | D | S | | | | | |
| O | M | N | | A | M | A | S | S | | S | M | E | A | L |
| | | | S | H | R | I | M | P | S | C | A | M | P | I |
| G | A | L | P | A | L | S | | E | A | R | L | I | E | R |
| N | O | S | I | R | E | E | | E | R | I | T | R | E | A |
| P | L | U | N | D | E | R | | D | A | M | A | S | K | S |

## 194

| M | O | R | A | L | E | | | G | A | S | P | E | R | |
| A | R | A | B | I | A | | T | E | S | T | A | T | E | |
| L | A | T | I | N | S | | P | A | S | T | I | C | H | E |
| A | T | T | L | E | E | | A | T | T | A | C | K | E | D |
| B | O | R | E | A | L | | S | T | A | R | K | E | R | S |
| O | R | A | N | G | E | | T | I | L | T | E | R | S | |
| | S | P | E | E | D | O | M | E | T | E | R | S | | |
| | | | | | | P | A | S | | | | | | |
| | S | P | A | R | E | S | T | H | E | R | O | D | | |
| M | O | R | D | A | N | T | | | E | L | O | P | E | S |
| C | A | L | A | M | I | N | E | | R | E | L | A | C | E |
| O | L | D | T | I | M | E | R | | M | A | L | L | O | W |
| W | A | I | T | R | E | S | S | | O | N | S | I | D | E |
| E | Y | E | L | E | N | S | | | S | O | O | N | E | R |
| R | A | R | E | S | T | | | | A | R | N | E | S | S |

## 195

| C | E | R | A | M | I | C | | S | P | E | N | S | E | R |
| O | P | E | N | A | N | D | S | H | U | T | C | A | S | E |
| G | O | T | O | R | A | C | K | A | N | D | R | U | I | N |
| E | X | U | D | E | S | | I | R | K | S | | S | A | T |
| N | I | N | E | S | | T | R | E | Y | | N | A | S | A |
| C | E | E | S | | B | A | T | S | | A | L | G | O | L |
| Y | D | S | | S | I | L | T | | S | I | R | E | N | S |
| | | | B | E | A | C | H | C | O | M | B | | | |
| S | C | R | A | M | S | | E | A | R | S | | C | F | S |
| N | A | O | M | I | | D | I | R | E | | S | O | R | T |
| I | R | M | A | | R | U | S | T | | A | T | S | E | A |
| G | P | A | | S | A | P | S | | I | S | O | M | E | R |
| G | O | N | Z | O | J | O | U | R | N | A | L | I | S | M |
| L | O | C | A | L | A | N | E | S | T | H | E | S | I | A |
| E | L | E | G | I | S | T | | T | R | I | S | T | A | N |

## 196

| J | U | L | I | A | C | H | I | L | D | | S | A | K | S |
| I | R | O | N | M | A | I | D | E | N | | A | M | A | T |
| M | I | C | R | O | N | E | S | I | A | | T | E | R | R |
| A | S | K | O | U | T | | | S | E | A | R | L | E | |
| | | | R | O | B | O | T | | A | N | I | M | A | |
| H | E | S | S | | R | E | M | I | T | S | | C | A | M |
| O | X | L | I | P | | A | N | N | I | E | H | A | L | L |
| T | H | E | B | E | S | T | | Y | O | U | A | N | D | I |
| T | I | E | S | A | K | N | O | T | | P | R | M | E | N |
| A | L | P | | L | A | I | D | O | N | | M | E | N | E |
| M | A | E | V | E | | K | A | T | E | Y | | | | |
| A | R | R | E | S | T | | | W | A | F | E | R | S | |
| L | A | C | S | | O | N | E | C | A | L | O | R | I | E |
| E | T | A | T | | D | E | A | D | R | I | N | G | E | R |
| S | E | R | A | | S | T | R | I | K | E | Z | O | N | E |

## 197

| P | A | T | E | | J | A | B | B | A | | B | A | J | A |
| I | R | E | N | E | A | D | L | E | R | | A | F | A | R |
| C | I | R | C | U | M | V | E | N | T | | S | I | C | K |
| T | A | R | A | R | E | I | D | | S | L | A | C | K | S |
| | | | M | O | S | S | E | S | | I | L | I | A | |
| T | E | R | P | | J | E | L | L | Y | S | T | O | N | E |
| U | A | E | | K | O | S | | R | E | T | I | N | A | S |
| P | R | I | O | R | Y | | | R | E | C | A | P | S | |
| A | T | T | R | A | C | T | | I | B | N | | D | E | I |
| C | H | E | G | U | E | V | A | R | A | | M | O | S | E |
| | S | R | A | S | | A | R | A | B | L | E | | | |
| C | H | A | N | E | L | | S | Q | U | I | R | R | E | L |
| C | I | T | I | | A | R | E | W | E | A | L | O | N | E |
| U | N | E | S | | S | A | N | A | N | T | O | N | I | O |
| P | E | S | T | | S | H | E | R | A | | T | A | D | S |

## 198

| A | D | O | P | T | | | W | H | O | C | A | R | E | S |
| D | A | V | I | E | S | | H | A | N | D | M | A | D | E |
| A | M | E | N | R | A | | A | G | E | L | I | M | I | T |
| M | E | R | E | M | O | R | T | A | L | | | A | T | O |
| W | E | B | S | | I | S | R | | B | A | D | E | N | |
| E | D | O | | I | S | N | T | | S | A | L | A | D | S |
| S | N | O | | N | O | S | H | | A | R | E | | | |
| T | A | K | E | A | D | E | E | P | B | R | E | A | T | H |
| | | | A | B | A | | B | A | R | I | | S | O | U |
| N | O | R | R | I | S | | I | S | A | O | | K | I | N |
| A | C | E | N | T | | S | G | T | | M | A | L | T | |
| C | T | N | | M | O | R | A | L | F | I | B | E | R | |
| H | O | N | O | L | U | L | U | | D | E | N | O | T | E |
| O | P | E | R | A | T | E | S | | S | T | O | U | T | S |
| S | I | S | S | Y | I | S | H | | A | R | T | E | S | |

## 199

```
B L A M E ■ R O D ■ S A H I B
E I R E A ■ E C I ■ T P O D A
A L T E R N A T E R O U T E S
■ ■ I S P E P ■ D E W ■ T A H
C A F E ■ S E P A L ■ T E T E
I L A ■ S T R A W ■ N A R E R
D E C R E E ■ R A F E R ■ ■ ■
■ S T E E R T S Y A W O W T ■
■ ■ ■ A R S O N ■ N E T H E R
F R A C S ■ N I T A L ■ E L O
L E S T ■ D E P O T ■ C A L M
A V E ■ A I D ■ P I L U T ■ ■
R E V E R S E D E C I S I O N
E R E S I ■ A I K ■ T P E D A
S E R T A ■ F D A ■ E S S E N
```

## 200

```
K A W A S A K I ■ A L I G H T
B R A V E M A N ■ M O N R O E
T A X I C A B S ■ I N C I T E
O B I S ■ N U T M E G ■ D I S
Y I N ■ S A K A I ■ I R I S H
S A G A N ■ I N S T ■ O R S O
■ ■ ■ L O S ■ T H A W S O U T
K A R A O K E M A C H I N E S
I C E S K A T E ■ K E N ■ ■ ■
D A N K ■ T A S S ■ L A I K A
S P E A R ■ I S A A K ■ N N W
M E W ■ I M L A T E ■ U V E A
E L A P S E ■ G I R L T A L K
A L L I E D ■ E R I C I D L E
L A S E R S ■ S E E D L E S S
```

# The New York Times
## SMART PUZZLES
### Presented with Style

Available at your local bookstore or online at
us.macmillan.com/author/thenewyorktimes

 ST. MARTIN'S GRIFFIN